EVIDENCE-BASED APPROACHES TO RELATIONSHIP AND MARRIAGE EDUCATION

This is the first book to provide a comprehensive, multidisciplinary overview of evidence-based relationship and marriage education (RME) programs. Readers are introduced to the best practices for designing, implementing, and evaluating effective RME programs to better prepare them to teach clients how to have healthy intimate relationships. Noted contributors from various disciplines examine current programs and best practices, often by the original developers themselves. Readers learn to critically appraise approaches and design and implement effective, evidence-based programs in the future. Examples and discussion questions encourage readers to examine issues and apply what they have learned. The conceptual material in Parts I and II provides critical guidance for practitioners who wish to develop, implement, and evaluate RME programs in various settings.

Chapters in Parts III and IV follow a consistent structure so readers can more easily compare programs—program overview and history, theoretical foundations, needs assessment and target audience, program goals and objectives, curriculum issues, cultural implications, evidence-based research and evaluation, and additional resources. This book reflects what the editor has learned from teaching relationship development and family life education courses over the past decade and includes the key information that students need to become competent professionals.

Highlights of the book's coverage include:

- Comprehensive summary of effective evidence-based RME training programs in one volume
- Prepares readers for professional practice as a Certified Family Life Educator (CFLE) by highlighting the fundamentals of developing RME programs
- Describes the challenges associated with RME program evaluation.

Intended for use in advanced undergraduate or graduate courses in relationship and marriage education, family life education, marriage and relationship counseling/therapy, intimate relationships, relationship development, or home/school/community services taught in human development and family studies, psychology, social work, sociology, religion, and more. This ground-breaking book also serves as a resource for practitioners, therapists, counselors, clergy members, and policy makers interested in evidence-based RME programs and those seeking to become Certified Family Life Educators or preparing for a career in RME.

James J. Ponzetti, Jr. is an Emeritus faculty member of Family Studies at the University of British Columbia, Canada.

Textbooks in Family Studies Series

The *Textbooks in Family Studies Series* is an interdisciplinary series that offers cutting-edge textbooks in family studies and family psychology. Volumes can be complete textbooks and/or supplementary texts for the undergraduate and/or graduate markets. Both authored and edited volumes are welcome. Please contact the series editor, Robert Milardo at *rhd360@maine.edu*, for details in preparing a proposal that should include the goal of the book, table of contents, an overview of competing texts, the intended market including course name(s) and level, and suggested reviewers.

These are the books currently in the series:

Father-Daughter Relationships: Contemporary Research and Issues written by Linda Nielsen (2012)

Stepfamilies: A Global Perspective on Research, Policy and Practice written by Jan Pryor (2014)

Serving Military Families: Theories, Research, and Application, Second Edition written by Karen Rose Blaisure, Tara Saathoff-Wells, Angela Pereira, Shelley MacDermid Wadsworth, and Amy Laura Dombro (2016)

Evidence-based Approaches to Relationship and Marriage Education edited by James J. Ponzetti, Jr. (2016)

Evidence-based Parenting Education: A Global Perspective edited by James J. Ponzetti, Jr. (2016)

Evidence-based Approaches to Sexuality Education: A Global Perspective edited by James J. Ponzetti, Jr. (2016)

EVIDENCE-BASED APPROACHES TO RELATIONSHIP AND MARRIAGE EDUCATION

Edited by James J. Ponzetti, Jr.

Routledge
Taylor & Francis Group

NEW YORK AND LONDON

First published 2016
by Routledge
711 Third Avenue, New York, NY 10017

and by Routledge
27 Church Road, Hove, East Sussex BN3 2FA

Routledge is an imprint of the Taylor & Francis Group, an informa business

Library of Congress Cataloging-in-Publication Data
  Evidence-based approaches to relationship and marriage education / edited by James J. Ponzetti, Jr.
    pages cm. — (Textbooks in family studies)
  Includes bibliographical references and index.
  1. Marriage—Study and teaching. 2. Marriage counseling. 3. Marital quality. 4. Interpersonal relations. I. Ponzetti, James J.
  HQ10.E95 2016
  616.89'1562—dc23
  2015005214

ISBN: 978-1-138-79717-8 (hbk)
ISBN: 978-1-138-79718-5 (pbk)
ISBN: 978-1-315-75735-3 (ebk)

Typeset in Bembo
by Apex CoVantage, LLC

CONTENTS

FOREWORD

The health and well-being of individuals, their relationships, and families has long interested family scholars and for good reason. On the one hand, we are interested in the features of relationships that promote resilience, satisfaction, and a good measure of social capital. We are interested in the features of adult relationships that define effective communication, practices that yield masterful relationships, and similarly the features of parenting that promote optimum child development. On the other hand, our interests are confronted with the challenges of developing effective applications: How do we take the collective knowledge about effective relationship processes so key to individual and relational health, design effective programs, and teach these practices to families? The 21 chapters in this book are arranged to provide a comprehensive accounting of the design and delivery of relationship and marriage education programs. In the first chapters, we are introduced to the requirements of evidenced-based practices. Any effective program should be rooted in the best available research and clinical practice and just as importantly informed by the needs of particular target audiences and their particular experiences. All young couples, for instance, face a selection of similar challenges in developing their relationships, families, and homes, and at the same time a selection of challenges unique to their circumstance. Young couples in an urban setting face different challenges than those living in rural areas, as do straight couples and gay or lesbian couples, as do voluntarily childless couples and expectant parents. The great varieties of evidenced-based programs presented in this book understand these requirements. They are firmly based in research and practice, emphasize specific problem areas and outcomes, and clearly address issues of diversity.

Evidence-based Approaches to Relationship and Marriage Education provides a systematic assessment of the variety of ways in which partners can learn specific skills to improve and maintain their relationships. The programs all aim to improve relationship functioning but vary in their emphasis and intended audiences. All are presented and reviewed by leading experts in their respective fields and share an interest in optimizing core features of relationships such as communication skills, conflict resolution, and financial management, areas where couples often experience the greatest challenges. The contributors offer critical appraisals of evidence-based approaches to relationship and marriage education and a comprehensive treatment of the best practices available when designing and delivering such programs. Students and practitioners will find the book offers a comprehensive resource for understanding the requirements of evidence-based educational programs and their inherent design, delivery, and evaluation. The book is designed to be comprehensive and organized in a way most useful to undergraduate and graduate students as well as practitioners in family studies, marriage and family therapy, social work, family life education, family psychology, pastoral counseling, and other programs all sharing an interest in individual, relationship, and family health and well-being.

Robert M. Milardo, Ph.D.
Professor of Family Relations
University of Maine
Series Editor

PREFACE

Close, long-term, intimate relationships are a source well-being for many people. People in healthy relationships report higher levels of satisfaction, fewer health problems, and longer life spans. Relationship and marriage education (hereafter RME) is aimed at providing information and skills designed to assist partners achieve satisfying and positive relationships. The primary goal of RME is to enrich or enhance close relationships and prevent relationship dissatisfaction or distress. RME realizes this goal by addressing relationship choices and challenges before problems become entrenched and destructive, or relationships move toward dissolution. RME augments couples' maintenance of healthy, committed relationships. Such instruction involves gaining knowledge, exploring attitudes and values, and/or developing skills.

RME has spread in popularity over the past five decades. The growth of RME has generated a concurrent proliferation of descriptors from premarital preparation to marital enrichment, relationship enhancement and couples education. Most of these descriptors are based on the premise that individuals and couples can learn to optimize their relationships. This implies that practitioners know what constitutes a healthy relationship and can transmit this knowledge in the same way that teachers convey knowledge in mathematical or composition skills. There is promising evidence that couples can learn specific skills to improve their relationships. Accordingly, RME programs primarily focus on select relationship dynamics that benefit partners and the relationship they wish to sustain. Yet, evidence in support of such benefits is dispersed in diverse literature and is not easily found or readily accessible.

RME based on substantive evidence offers a more reliable approach. Historically, professional practice has been based on loose, diffuse bodies of knowledge rather than systematic investigation. Much of this knowledge is no more than folklore, custom, or clinical insights, with little, if any, valid scientific evidence on which to justify practice. In response to this circumstance, evidence-based practice (or EBP) was formulated. Evidence-based practice involves complex and conscientious decision making which details best practices supported in empirical studies to inform the improvement of whatever professional task is at hand. EBP is defined on the U.S. government's National Registry of Evidence-based Programs and Practices online database developed by the Substance Abuse and Mental Health Services Administration (see www.samhsa.gov) as approaches to prevention or treatment that are based in theory and have undergone scientific evaluation. EBP stands in contrast to approaches that are based on tradition, convention, belief, or anecdotal evidence. However, this definition must be interpreted broadly so as to not limit EBP only to practices that have supportive random control trials available. EBP, as used in this book, is the integration of preeminent empirical evidence, professional expertise, and client values and preferences in the decision-making process associated with best practice. Thus, EBP is concerned about extant research studies, but considers secondary publications, such as systematic reviews, meta-analyses, and clinical guidelines, too. EBP is a philosophical approach initially applied to medicine but expanded since to a disparate collection of professions that includes nursing and allied health professions, psychology, social work, early intervention, child mental health, and education, among others. The time has come for RME to join these professions in using an evidence-based approach in the design, implementation, and evaluation of RME practice.

A diverse collection of RME programs is currently available in a number of venues. These programs are developed from government, research, or faith-based initiatives or they may operate privately for profit. RME programs are offered in mental health centers, hospitals, public assistance offices, churches, or universities, among other places. Programs vary by curricular focus, learning format, and target audience. Curricula usually deal with various relationship skills or dynamics such as communication, conflict resolution, and financial management. Providers utilize formats that are preventive and group-oriented. Programs operate with different group sizes and treatment dosage amounts (i.e., length of program). In particular, RME targets individuals at risk for relationship problems. However, programs exist for many groups, including individuals (e.g., youth, fathers, mothers), couples (e.g., premarital, married), and families.

Purpose of *Evidence-based Approaches to Relationship and Marriage Education*

The aim of *Evidence-based Approaches to Relationship and Marriage Education* is to provide a critical appraisal of evidence-based approaches to relationship and marriage education. Accordingly, it offers an accessible and comprehensive overview of best practices when designing and implementing couple and relationship educational programs. RME is addressed by numerous professionals representing an array of disciplines (e.g., family studies, psychology, counseling, social work, and other related disciplines). This book aims to bring the diffuse evidence regarding RME together in one volume readily available to students, scholars, and practitioners alike. It offers the foremost resource for those who plan to design, implement, and evaluate preventive RME. In addition, future or current practitioners may find the knowledge presented herein of assistance for their professional practice.

Coverage and Target Audience

The comprehensive coverage of this book is unique and innovative. The chapters are organized in a way that is useful to advanced undergraduate and graduate students in family studies, marriage and family therapy, social work, family life education, psychology, pastoral counseling, mental health and psychiatry programs. An introductory chapter presents a concise historical overview of RME development and expansion. It is followed by 20 chapters divided in six parts and written by notable experts who are eminently qualified to present the latest research on a range of pertinent topics to EBP in RME. The initial four chapters focus on fundamentals of relationship and marriage education; namely, program development, training required of providers, delivery systems, and implementation. Part II, which includes the next three chapters, considers important conceptual and theoretical frameworks used in RME. Best practices in inventory-based programs are reviewed in Part III, comprising chapters 8–10. The chapters in Part IV (chapters 11–16) present the evidence base for six outstanding skills-based programs. These chapters consider program overview and history, theoretical foundations, needs assessment and target audience, program goals and objectives, curriculum and other program issues, cultural implications, evidence-based research and evaluation, and additional resources. This content covers the four categories of effective programs; namely, program design and content, program relevance, program delivery and implementation, and program assessment and quality assurance. Part V (chapters 17–19) presents evidence-based RME with diverse groups. Finally, chapters 20–21 in Part VI review future directions and conclusions. Departments and examples of course titles where Evidence-based approaches to relationship and marriage education may be used:

Departments of Human Development, Family Studies, or Family Science
Interpersonal and Family Relationships
Intimate Relationships

Departments of Psychology
Close Relationships
Interpersonal Relations
Close Relationships
Theory & Research in Dyadic Processes
Topics in Social Psychology

Counseling psychology
Family psychology

Departments of Communication Studies
Seminar in Relational Communication
Interpersonal Communication

Departments of Counseling

Ministry programs

Departments of Sociology, Social Work, and Gender Studies

Acknowledgments

It would be a serious omission not to acknowledge the expertise and willingness of chapter contributors to share their remarkable insight on an array of topics pertinent to readers interested in evidence-based RME. They have made editing this book a privilege and certainly a pleasure. I would also like to thank the series editor, Bob Milardo. Similarly, Debra Riegert and Angela Halliday at Routledge/ Taylor & Francis have been helpful in numerous ways. I also want to thank the reviewers who provided very helpful feedback on the manuscript: Cameron Lee, Fuller Theological Seminary; Alan C. Taylor, East Carolina University; Brian J. Willoughby, Brigham Young University; and two anonymous reviewers. However, the most important people to me have been my family who provided encouragement and support as this book moved forward.

ABOUT THE EDITOR

James J. Ponzetti, Jr., Ph.D., D.Min., C.F.L.E., C.C.F.E., is an Emeritus faculty member of Family Studies at the University of British Columbia. He has served on the faculty at the University of New Mexico, Central Washington University, and Western Illinois University. He founded the Oregon Family Nurturing Center, Inc. before coming to Canada. As a Certified Family Life Educator in both Canada and the United States (C.C.F.E., Family Services Canada, and C.F.L.E., National Council on Family Relations), he is committed to the promotion of family life education. He has been an editor for several reference publications such as *International Encyclopedia of Marriage and Family* (2003), *Encyclopedia of Human Emotions* (1999), and *Encyclopedia of Marriage and the Family* (1995). He currently serves on the editorial board for *Personal Relationships, Journal of Intergenerational Relationships, Journal of Family and Community Ministries*, and *Family Science Review*.

ABOUT THE CONTRIBUTORS

Guy Bodenmann is Professor of Clinical Psychology at the University of Zurich. He is trained in cognitive behavioral therapy and specialized in couple therapy. He developed Couples Coping Enhancement Training (CCET). He is the director of the Clinical Training Program for Psychotherapy in Children and Adolescents, and director of the Clinical Training Program for Couple Therapy at the University of Zurich. He has published extensively on dyadic stress and coping, the prediction of divorce, relationship distress, and prevention of dysfunctional relationships. Dr. Bodenmann is an International Affiliate of the American Psychological Association (APA), the German Association of Psychologists (DGPs), the Swiss Association of Psychologists (FSP), The Swiss Society of Psychology (SGP), and the Swiss Society for Cognitive Behavioral Therapy (SGVT).

Jill Bowers, Ph.D., C.F.L.E., C.F.C.S., is a Researcher and Project Coordinator at the Family Resiliency Center, an academic unit within the Department of Human and Community Development at the University of Illinois at Urbana-Champaign. Dr. Bowers's research focuses on program development and evaluation. Her research has an applied focus, and she has worked on programs for youth and adults, including relationship and divorce education.

Larisa N. Cicila is a graduate student at the University of Miami. One of her primary research interests is sexual satisfaction within the couple relationship. She also is interested in applying stepped-care models of intervention to couple distress.

Morgan Van Epp Cutlip, Ph.D., directs Research and Development at Love-Thinks, LCC where she conducts research on program effectiveness and develops innovative relationship education. Her research on the *How to Avoid Falling for a Jerk* program won the Family and Consumer Science research study of the year. She also is the owner and CEO of STAT Research and Consulting where she provides research and statistical report design services. She has been happily married for six years and is the mother of a rambunctious one-year-old.

Brian D. Doss, Ph.D. is an Associate Professor of Psychology at the University of Miami. Dr. Doss earned his Ph.D. in Psychology at the University of California at Los Angeles. His research seeks to increase the reach of effective couple interventions. Within this broader framework, his research has three specific aims: elucidate couples' help-seeking behaviors, identify mechanisms of couple interventions, and develop and evaluate flexible couple interventions.

Stephen F. Duncan, Ph.D, C.F.L.E. is Professor in the School of Family Life at Brigham Young University. He earned his Ph.D. from Purdue University. His work has been published in several professional journals including *Family Relations, Journal of Couple and Relationship Therapy*, and *Marriage and Family Review*. He serves on the editorial boards of *Family Relations* and *Journal of Couple and Relationship Therapy*.

Joachim Engl, Ph.D. is a psychologist at the Institut für Forschung und Ausbildung in Kommunikationstherapie e.V., which is located in München, Germany. She is also a behavioral therapist, marriage counselor, supervisor and trainer, and author of couple communication trainings (EPL with Kurt Hahlweg) as well as of various books and DVDs on the subject of couple communication.

Sage E. Erickson is a graduate student at Brigham Young University in the Marriage, Family and Human Development Department. Her research focus is on relationship education. Recently, Sage worked for Child Trends, a non-profit research company based in Washington, DC, and the Center for Relationship Education in Denver, Colorado. Sage lived in Sweden from 2010–2012, while she was serving as a missionary for the Church of Jesus Christ of Latter-day Saints.

Ted G. Futris, Ph.D., C.F.L.E. is an Associate Professor in the Department of Human Development and Family Science at the University of Georgia. He earned his Ph.D. at the University of North Carolina at Greensboro. He is also a Certified Family Life Educator and an Extension Specialist who provides statewide support in Georgia focused on developing, disseminating, and evaluating programs that support youth and adults in forming and maintaining healthy couple relationships (www.gamarriages.org). Dr. Futris is co-director of the National Extension Relationship and Marriage Education Network where he has provided leadership in the development of resources to inform best practices in relationship education.

Emily J. Georgia is a graduate student in the Department of Psychology at the University of Miami. Her research focuses on the intersection of sexual trauma and romantic relationships as well as improving the reach of empirically supported treatments for romantic relationships to the underserved.

H. Wallace Goddard, Ph.D., C. F. L. E., has retired from the University of Arkansas Cooperative Extension Service. During his decades in Arkansas and Alabama Extension, he developed many award-winning programs, wrote several books, and created a public television series. He is the recipient of the Margaret E. Arcus Outstanding Family Life Educator Award, Extension Specialists Career Achievement Award, and is a Fellow of National Council on Family Relations (NCFR). He has been married to his wife, Nancy, for 43 years and is father to three children and grandfather of 13.

Sheryl Goodey, M.S., is the Program Coordinator for Utah's federally and state-funded Stepfamily Education courses. She is also pursuing a Ph.D. in the Family, Consumer, and Human Development Department at Utah State University. Her research focuses on the effects of relationship education within diverse populations.

John M. Gottman, Ph.D., is known for his work on marital stability and divorce prediction, involving the study of emotions, physiology, and communication. He has conducted 42 years of research with over 4,000 couples. He is the author of 200 published academic articles and author or co-author of 41 books, including the *New York Times*–bestselling *The Seven Principles for Making Marriage Work, The Relationship Cure, Why Marriages Succeed or Fail*, and *Raising an Emotionally Intelligent Child*, among many others. He presently conducts further research through the Relationship Research Institute, which he founded and is the co-founder of the Gottman Institute, both in Seattle.

Julie Schwartz Gottman, Ph.D., is a licensed clinical psychologist and the President of the Gottman Institute. She specializes in couples therapy, sexual abuse and rape, domestic violence, gay and lesbian adoption, same-sex marriage, cancer patients and their families, and parenting issues. She was recently voted as the Washington State Psychologist of the Year. Dr. Gottman is the author/co-author of three books: *Ten Lessons to Transform Your Marriage, And Baby Makes Three*, and *The Marriage Clinic Casebook*.

Kurt Hahlweg, Ph.D., is Professor at the Technical University Braunschweig, Department of Clinical Psychology, Psychotherapy and Assessment and Niedersachsenprofessor 65+ for Clinical Psychology and Psychotherapy. He is internationally recognized for his work in prevention research, conducting long-term studies in TRIPLE P and in EPL, a program to prevent couple distress. In 2008, he received the German Psychology Prize for outstanding lifetime contributions to Psychology. He has published extensively over several decades (about 310 publications) and has acquired grants over a 30-year period.

Alan J. Hawkins, Ph.D., C.F.L.E. is Professor of Family Life at Brigham Young University in Provo, Utah. He earned a Ph.D. in Human Development and Family Studies at the Pennsylvania State University. His scholarship and outreach focuses on educational and policy interventions to help couples form and sustain healthy relationships and enduring marriages. He directs the BYU Marriage Education and Research Initiative. In 2003–2004, he was a visiting scholar with the Office of Planning, Research, and Evaluation, Administration for Children and Families (U.S. Department of Health and Human Services), working on the federal healthy marriage initiative. He was the Chair of the Utah Healthy Marriage Initiative from 2008–2010. He is a member of the Research Advisory Group of the Oklahoma Healthy Marriage Initiative.

Brian J. Higginbotham, Ph.D., L.M.F.T., is the Associate Vice President for Utah State University Extension. He is also a Professor in the Department of Family, Consumer, and Human Development at Utah State University. Dr. Higginbotham provides statewide leadership and support for programs that strengthen relationships and developmental assets in families, youth, and children. He has implemented and evaluated relationship education for high school students, individuals in dating and cohabiting relationships, married couples, stepfamilies, and incarcerated adults. Currently, Dr. Higginbotham is the Principal Investigator on two multiyear projects that teach relationship skills to ethnically diverse groups of children and adults with step-relationships.

Ann-Katrin Job, M.Sc., is a Research Assistant at the Technical University of Braunschweig, Department of Clinical Psychology, Psychotherapy and Assessment, Braunschweig, Germany. In the context of her Ph.D. studies, she evaluates a new approach to effectively disseminate the couples relationship enhancement program EPL by teaching students to be accredited program trainers. Ann-Katrin is also a licensed Group as well as Stepping Stones Triple P trainer.

Vicki L. Loyer-Carlson, Ph.D., L.M.F.T., is a Clinical Fellow and Approved Supervisor of AAMFT in private practice in Tucson, Arizona. She is the 2015–2017 President of the Arizona Association for Marriage and Family Therapy. Her clinical work is with individuals, couples, and families using a Competency Focused model of Family Therapy. She is also engaged in Equine Assisted Family Therapy shape-shifting experiences with adolescents, adults, couples, and families. She is co-author of *Pathways to Marriage* (2002), *RELATE User's Guide* (2002), and *Youth at Risk: The Research and Practice Interface* (1993), and *RELATE with Your Mate* (2003–2005). Dr. Carlson is an online instructor and subject matter expert in the Psychology and Counseling program at Grand Canyon University in Phoenix, Arizona.

Jacquelyn K. Mallette is a doctoral student in the Department of Human Development and Family Science at the University of Georgia. She studies co-parenting relationship functioning across vulnerable populations and the impact of strengthening co-parenting relationships on family, child, and parental outcomes. She has experience with virtual trainings on healthy marriage and relationship education and has been involved in statewide relationship education trainings and evaluation.

Howard J. Markman, Ph.D., is a Professor and Director of the Center for Marital and Family Studies at the University of Denver in Colorado. He is widely published in academic journals and internationally known for his work on the prediction and prevention of divorce and marital distress. He has often appeared in broadcast and print media, including segments about PREP on *20/20*, *Oprah*, and *48 Hours*. Along with his colleagues, he has co-authored the books *We Can Work It Out: Making Sense of Marital Conflict*, *Fighting for Your Marriage* (with Scott Stanley and Susan Blumberg), *Becoming Parents*, *Empty Nesting*, and *Fighting for Your Jewish Marriage*.

Robert J. Navarra, Psy.D., M.F.T., MAC, is a Senior Certified Gottman Therapist, Speaker, Trainer and Consultant, specializing in treating couples recovering from addiction. He is a Research Associate at Mental Research Institute, Palo Alto, California, where he developed the Couple Recovery Development Approach (CRDA) and a Research Scientist at the Relationship Research Institute in Seattle.

Amy K. Olson, M.A., MFT, is Director of Communications at Life Innovations. She has co-authored several books including the *Couple Checkup*, *Empowering Couples*, *PREPARE-ENRICH-INSPIRE for Youth*, and numerous articles on couple relationships.

David H. Olson, Ph.D., is Professor Emeritus, University of Minnesota where he taught for nearly 30 years. He is Founder and CEO of Life Innovations. He is the developer of PREPARE/ENRICH and the Couple Checkup. He has published over 100 professional articles and 20 books, including the *Couple Checkup*, *Marriage and Family* textbook (8th edition), *Remarriage Checkup*, and *Empowering Couples*. He has appeared on a variety of television shows, including *The Today Show*, *The Early Show*, *Good Morning America*, and the *Oprah Show*.

Marline E. Pearson, M.A., Chair of the Sociology Department at Madison Area Technical College, specializes in criminology and issues surrounding family and youth. She is the author of numerous programs for youth and adults. For instance, *Love Notes* is part of a federal (U.S.) pregnancy prevention study of innovative approaches for older teens. She developed *Relationship Smarts PLUS*, which recently completed an evaluation with over 8,000 diverse teens. She created *Within MY Reach*, a relationship skills and decision-making program for empowering at-risk adults who struggle with economic disadvantage, with Scott Stanley and Galena Rhoades. She also co-authored *Making a Love Connection*, a special report for the National Campaign to Prevent Teen and Unplanned Pregnancy, with Barbara Dafoe Whitehead, and provided material for its website *Stayteen.org*.

Marcie Pregulman is the Project Coordinator at the Center for Marital and Family Studies at the University of Denver. She has worked on multiple grants in the Center since 2006. Working mainly on the intervention side of the research, she has been able to use her PREP training to work with couples and individuals to help them with their relationships. In addition, Marcie is an internationally known PREP trainer and offers relationship help to individuals and couples over the phone.

Kay Reed pioneered the field of youth relationship education by co-founding the Dibble Institute in 1996. She currently serves as President and Executive Director of the Institute. Kay is a national advocate of relationship education for youth. She has consulted with the Brookings Institution, Child Trends, RAND Corporation, and the Administration for Children and Families. Professionally, she has spent over 30 years in the fields of youth development and non-profit management with the March of Dimes, YMCA, and secondary education. Educated in psychology at Lewis and Clark College in Portland, Oregon, she has published on the relationship between children's perceived locus of control and their academic performance.

Evin W. Richardson is a doctoral student in the Department of Human Development and Family Science at the University of Georgia. She studies family systems within high-stress contexts, with a particular focus on the marital and co-parenting relationships of foster and adoptive parents as well as parents of a child with a disability and how family life education can serve these families.

David G. Schramm, Ph.D., C.F.L.E., is a State Extension Specialist and Associate Professor in the Department of Human Development and Family Studies at the University of Missouri. He earned his Ph.D. in Family Studies from Auburn University. He served as the Project Co-Director of a multistate team of Extension Specialists that was awarded $1.2 million by the Administration on Children, Youth and Families, Children's Bureau to fund the *Healthy Relationship and Marriage Education Training Project*. He and his wife Jamie have been married for 16 years and have four children.

Robert F. Scuka, Ph.D., M.S.W., is Executive Director of the National Institute of Relationship Enhancement® (NIRE) in Bethesda, MD, a member of NIRE's

Faculty, and a Master Trainer in Relationship Enhancement® (RE) methods. He received his doctorate in Religious Studies and Philosophy from Southern Methodist University in 1987 and his Master's in Social Work from the University of Maryland, Baltimore in 1994. Dr. Scuka is the author of *Relationship Enhancement Therapy: Healing through Deep Empathy and Intimate Dialogue* (Routledge, 2005). He also is co-author of the *Couples' Relationship Enhancement® Program: Leader's Manual* and has produced three DVD videos, including one on empathy and another on using RE to help couples recover from infidelity.

Franz Thurmaier, Ph.D., is a psychologist and behavioral therapist at the Institut für Forschung und Ausbildung in Kommunikationstherapie e.V., which is located in München, Germany. He also serves as a marriage counselor, supervisor and trainer, and author of couple communication trainings (EPL with Kurt Hahlweg) as well as of various books and DVDs on the subject of couple communication.

Laurie A. Tonelli, Ph.D., is currently a Research Associate for the Center for Marital and Family Studies at the University of Denver where she earned her Ph.D. in Counseling Psychology. She also does family therapy for Shiloh House, an organization that works to better the lives of at-risk youth. She lives in Littleton, Colorado, with her husband and four children.

John Van Epp, Ph.D., President/Founder of LoveThinks, LCC, is the author of *How to Avoid Falling in Love with a Jerk*. His 25 years of clinical experience and extensive research in premarital, marital, and family relations have paved the way for his presentations in diverse settings in all 50 states, 10 countries, and by more than 5,000 military personnel. Van Epp was awarded the Smart Marriage Impact Award (2008). He has been featured in various popular periodicals such as *The Wall Street Journal, Time*, and *Psychology Today*; and he has appeared on the *CBS Early Show* and *Fox News*. He has been happily married for over 35 years and is the father of two daughters.

Sarah W. Whitton, Ph.D., is an Assistant Professor of Psychology at the University of Cincinnati. She earned her Ph.D. at the University of Denver in Colorado. Dr. Whitton's research is focused on links between family and marital relationships and mental health. She conducts basic research exploring how interpersonal relations affect mental health, as well as applied research on relationship education programs for groups who face challenges in sustaining healthy relationships.

Angela Wiley, Ph.D., is an Associate Professor in Human and Community Development at the University of Illinois and an Extension Specialist in Family Life Education. Dr. Wiley's research focuses on individual and family resilience. She is interested in identifying how family strengths such as mealtimes and shared physical activity can improve functioning. Dr. Wiley also is interested in promoting wellness through her outreach work. She has created curricula and materials to help people balance work and personal life and conducted efficacy studies of these materials.

Lee Williams, Ph.D., L.M.F.T., is a Professor in the Marital and Family Therapy program at the University of San Diego. His primary research interests include marriage preparation, couples with religious differences, and family therapy training. Dr. Williams has published multiple articles and book chapters in these areas, and is also is a co-author of *Essential Skills in Family Therapy* (2nd edition), *Essential Assessment Skills for Couple and Family Therapists*, and *Clinician's Guide to Research Methods in Family Therapy: Foundations of Evidence-based Practice*.

PART I

Fundamentals of Relationship and Marriage Education (RME)

1

THE EVOLUTION OF RELATIONSHIP AND MARRIAGE EDUCATION

James J. Ponzetti, Jr.

Introduction

Relationship and marriage education (referred to as RME hereafter) is a form of intervention that encompasses an array of educational services directed at the acquisition of knowledge; exploration of feelings, motivations, and values; and development of interpersonal skills to create and maintain close relationships. The primary goal of RME is not therapeutic in the remedial sense, but educational and preventive. RME typically takes a holistic focus to understand the physical, psychological, social, and spiritual aspects of intimate relationships between persons of varying ages across the life course. Currently, there is a plethora of RME programs and curricula. RME practices and techniques are available in a number of various formats, including classes offered in secondary schools and colleges, individual and couple marriage preparation at churches, online courses and inventories, group sessions, retreats, workshops through community agencies, self-directed curriculum through books, Internet sites, and many others.

RME is directed at the provision of knowledge about sustaining relationships so any distress can be dealt with in a constructive rather than debilitating manner. Three broad groups of RME can be identified, each with distinct perspectives and approaches. These groups are information and awareness, assessment via an inventory and feedback, and behavioral skills training. RME content and curricula is determined in different ways depending on the approach.

The goal of the first group is the provision of information and knowledge to assist individuals become more cognizant of their views and perspectives in addition to clarifying and understanding their partners. Information and awareness of self and relationships is provided through didactic or written materials. Lectures and group discussions of relationship expectations represent a common approach to convey this knowledge and information. Select relationship skills may be demonstrated but only to supplement knowledge. Many programs include content on the benefits of marriage, financial management, sexuality, parenting expectations, religion, and family origins.

The goal of the second group involves offering feedback based on the completion of inventories by participants. Several comprehensive assessment questionnaires have been designed to identify relationship strengths and weaknesses that can then be used to tailor RME to participants (Futris, Barton, Aholou, & Seponski, 2011; Larson, Newell, Topham, & Nichols, 2002). One valuable attribute of this approach is the ability to provide individualized and systematic feedback regarding positive and negative relationship motivations and dynamics. The three most widely used assessments include the Premarital Preparation and Relationship Questionnaire (PREPARE, see chapter 8), the Facilitating Open Couple Communication, Understanding and Study Questionnaire (FOCCUS, see chapter 9); and the RELATionship Evaluation (RELATE, see chapter 10).

The approach taken in the third group includes structured instruction on relationship skills training. Epstein, Warfel, Johnson, Smith, and McKinney (2013) found that skills were taught in seven areas: communication, conflict resolution, knowledge of partner, life skills, self-management, sex and romance, and stress management. Couple communication skills have long been predominant in many RME programs. In fact, many educators consider it the foundation for RME skills programs (Bruhn & Hill, 2004). Curricula typically emphasized communication (e.g., speaker-listener technique), conflict resolution (e.g., anger management), and problem solving (e.g., negotiate disagreements). However, Fowers (2000) has noted that skills acquisition, such as couple communication, is not the panacea for all relationship concerns. Virtues or character strengths are necessary for using communication or conflict resolution skills effectively. Accordingly, a mixed approach is warranted that combines information and awareness on the cultivation of virtues such as commitment, courage, loyalty, kindness, justice, and moderation, with skills development (Fawcett, 2004; Gilliland, Hawkins, Christiaens, Carroll, & Fowers, 2002).

The development of models to direct RME program design and implementation is intensive work, albeit necessary, to ensure that the expansion of the field is accomplished in a systematic manner (see chapter 3). Hawkins, Carroll, Doherty, and Willoughby (2004) offered a framework that emphasized a range of dimensions to consider in the development of RME amenable to broad diverse audiences. The dimensions respond to specific programmatic questions; namely, content (what?), intensity (how much?), methods (delivery?), timing (when?), setting (where?), and target (who?).

Given the utility of RME to health and well-being (see chapter 5), it is surprising that theory advancement on marriage and similar relationships, such as Sound Relationship House Theory (see chapter 6), is not progressing as fast as programmatic efforts. Evidence-based practice must attend to the question: Does RME work? Evidence-based approaches with random control trials are not extensive, but available meta-analytic syntheses appear positive in improving relationship satisfaction and skills albeit with some reservations due to methodological limitations (Fawcett, Hawkins, Blanchard, & Carroll, 2010; Hawkins, Blanchard, Baldwin, & Fawcett, 2008; Ooms, 2005; Stanley, Amato, Johnson, & Markman, 2006). Carroll and Doherty (2003) also concluded that premarital programs achieved significant gains in the short term and these gains are retained. Additional reviews of studies with follow-up data found that relationship satisfaction was sustained over time (Halford & Bodenmann, 2013; Halford, Markman, Kline, & Stanley, 2003).

Another important question is why does RME work? Rauer, Adler-Baeder, Lucier-Greer, Skuban, Ketring, and Smith (2014) astutely used rigorous theory-driven inquiry to explore the processes of change in RME. Three models based on different theoretical premises were investigated. The direct effects model, based on social learning theory, considers the influence of RME on both personal attitudes and motivations, and relational behaviors as directly impacting positive outcomes after RME. The behavioral skills model, which is founded on Gottman's research, considers that RME enhances relational behavior first which motivates personal commitment to a relationship and thus improved relationship quality. Finally, the commitment model, based on interdependence theory and Rushult's investment model, posits that RME enhances personal commitment and a positive mindset toward a relationship that promotes accommodation and adaptation behaviors to enhance relationship continuity. The behavioral model was found to be the most predictive of positive change from RME. This finding raises questions about Fower's (2000) premise to ground marital satisfaction on the cultivation of virtues which are personal attributes; however, virtues may act as mediators between relational dynamics and marital quality.

RME has garnered greater international attention (Halford & Simons, 2005; Markman & Halford, 2005). For example, Couple CARE developed by a team led by Kim Halford (Halford, 2011; Halford, Sanders, & Behrens, 2001) in Australia helps couples to assess their relationship strengths, develop key relationship skills, and identify personal behaviors to strengthen their relationship. Similarly, EPL (see chapter 13) and Couples Coping Enhancement Training (see chapter 14) are renowned in Europe and beyond.

History of Relationship and Marriage Education

Certain social theorists, notably Giddens (1992) and Beck and Beck Gernsheim (1995), have suggested personal relationships are changed by democratization (reordering of relationships between the sexes) and individualism (emphasizing primary of the self). They note the weakening power of social norms and laws as regulating mechanisms for private life is matched by the increasing role of personal choice. This may, at least partially, account for the shift in marriage and personal relationships that ensued in the early decades of the 20th century.

Around the turn of the 20th century, RME developed in response to sociohistorical influences and conditions. Transformations in sexuality, gender roles, and youth culture arose that were in stark contrast to the gender segregation and sexual reticence characteristic of the closing decades of the 19th century. Earlier prescribed forms for marriage were replaced by greater self-determination and more individualistic practices (Coontz, 2005).

As sociocultural, legal, and technological forces altered the internal landscape of marriage, many of the external supports that previously held marriages together were expunged. The blurring of boundaries between men's and women's activities, and the advent of dating as a practice which typically included exploration with alcohol and drugs as well as sexual behaviors led to growing concern about the future of marriage. Ongoing social circumstances, such as urbanization and industrialization, weakened influences that compelled people to marry and abolished economic and political constraints that deterred divorce (Bailey, 1987).

Discussions and advice about close relationships or marriage traditionally transpired in informal networks with family members, friends, and other peers, and as the result of idiosyncratic expectations and folk wisdom. The recognition that such advice often reflected only personal experience prompted the development of formal efforts to bolster relationships and marriage. Informal consultation about unhappy relationships or marital distress was supplanted by a growing network of "experts" (Bailey, 1987). Marriage education had its roots in the Progressive era alongside the growing number of home economists, social workers, and other professionals engaged in sundry social movements oriented toward enhancing marital and family life.

RME developed as a field in response to concerns that marriage as a societal institution was undergoing a significant transformation. Men and women in the 1920s began to view marriage as the center of their emotional lives. The ideal of companionate marriages based on mutual affection was encroaching on notions of "traditional marriage" based on economic necessity, role specialization, and hierarchy. The contradictions and tensions inherent in the emerging expectation that marriage offered personal fulfillment and emotional satisfaction prompted worry that such an ideal could not be prolonged indefinitely. This lofty marriage ideal placed a premium on the quality, rather than stability, of the relationship (Coontz, 2005).

By the end of the 1920s, the expansion of marriage education in colleges and universities across the U.S., measured by the numbers alone, was impressive. Early RME was functional and practical in its approach. However, social science research was to serve as the basis for marriage education. RME was designed to foster rapport between students and instructor so that the instructor could use personal authority to counsel individual students (Bailey, 1987). Sociologist Ernest Groves, an early proponent, moved to the University of North Carolina in 1927 to promote marriage education. In 1928, he wrote *The Marriage Crisis* where he seriously questioned the impracticability of the notion that the traditional burdens of marriage would be offset by individual satisfaction from marriage as espoused in emerging sexual and marital values. Many agreed and thought that putting marriage before friends, parents, and community would not promote stronger relationships.

Marriage education continued to facilitate the transition to marriage through a combination of education and counseling. The Merrill–Palmer Institute in Detroit developed a course in 1932, and the Philadelphia Marriage Council established one nine years later (Mudd, Freeman, & Rose, 1941; Sayers, Kohn, & Heavey, 1998). Yet, several problems were noted in marriage education, particularly in the collegiate setting, as it developed in these early decades. Lantz and Koos (1953) discussed the unrealistic range of topics that educators tried to cover, and whether topics were either already familiar to students, too simplistic for students, or easily covered without the structure of a class. Further, concern about a middle-class bias in content was mentioned.

Religious institutions have historically taken an interest in preparing individuals for marriage. However, the focus of this intervention is different than marriage preparation offered in secular venues. RME in many faith-based communities must extend beyond the interpersonal dynamics that form the focal point of secular programs to include the social and public dimensions of marriage (Nock, 2002). RME must grasp the larger social context through which marriages are sustained and given meaning (Wall, 2002). The Roman Catholic Church was an early force in marriage preparation with the efforts of the Archdiocese of Chicago beginning Pre-Cana conferences (i.e., premarital counseling programs led by priests) in 1946. Marriage preparation was mandatory for Catholic couples to marry in the U.S. by the 1960s (Sayers, Kohn, & Heavey, 1998). These efforts built upon spiritual or scriptural basis for marriage with the creation of Marriage Encounter in Spain by Gabriel Calvo, a Catholic priest, in 1962. The Marriage Encounter movement was brought to the United States in 1966 (Genovese, 1975; Regula, 1975). Despite its popularity, several limitations with the Encounter model were noted (Doherty, McCabe, & Ryder, 1978; Doherty, Lester, & Leigh, 1986). Later, Engaged Encounter for premarital couples and Retrouvaille for distressed marital couples were developed. Despite the popularity of these programs, no evidence other than anecdotal testaments was found to attest to program efficacy.

Clergy and lay leaders from other faith communities were also interested in RME. In 1962, David and Vera Mace offered weekend workshops for married couples at the request of a religious retreat center in Pennsylvania. These retreats marked the beginning of the Marriage Communication Labs, organized by the United Methodist Church in the U.S. (Mace & Mace, 1976) while in Canada both the Anglican Church and the United Church of Canada offered similar RME programs. The Quakers' program, called Marriage Enrichment Retreats, was also started by the Maces (Bader, 1984). H. Norman Wright (1977), a therapist and professor of Christian education, developed a popular premarital program for conservative Christian groups. RME in orthodox Jewish communities has recently received attention (Maybruch, Pirutinsky, & Pelcovita, 2014).

Although clergy continue to provide marriage preparation, little is known about the nature of premarital education they provide. A national survey of Catholic couples conducted by the Center for Marriage and Family (1995) examined marriage preparation in the Catholic Church. Most individuals valued the marriage preparation they experienced despite the mandatory nature of the program. Participants preferred a team of clergy and lay leaders as presenters. They rated communication (74%), commitment (70%), conflict resolution (67%), church (64%), and children (63%) as the most helpful topics. Wilmoth and Smyser (2012) found that clergy left out several practices with demonstrated efficaciousness, including follow-up meetings after the wedding, utilization of mentor couples, and dealing with family-of-origin issues.

The rise in the mental health field and concomitant professionalization of services in the 1970s produced a group of experts. In 1973, the Maces founded the Association for Couples in Marriage Enrichment with the goal of coordinating the efforts of the diverse groups working in the area of marriage enrichment (Mace, 1975). The Practical Application of Relationship Skills (PAIRS) program was developed by social worker Lori Gordon as a graduate course in the counseling program at American University in 1975. She converted this curriculum in 1977 to a course for couples in her practice at Family Relations Institute (DeMaria & Hannah, 2003; Gordon & Durana, 1999). Unfortunately, there has been little evidence-based research other than clinical perceptions of program efficacy for PAIRS.

One of the best-known RME programs was created by Drs. Sherod Miller, Daniel Wackman, and Elam Nunnally at the University of Minnesota Family Study Center in the early 1970s (Miller, Nunnally, & Wackman, 1976; Nunnally, Miller, & Wackman, 1975). The Couple Communication program has been translated and offered around the world. The team subsequently organized Interpersonal Communication Programs, Inc. to train instructors and distribute program materials, and moved operations to Colorado (see http://www.couple communication.com/). The Couple Communication program (Jakubowski, Milne, Brunner, & Miller, 2004) is recognized for its substantive evidence base which includes numerous dissertations, quantitative research, qualitative case studies, and meta-analyses. This program has proven to be one of the most effective showing positive program effects on couple communication (Butler & Wampler, 1999; Russell, Bagarozzi, Atilano, & Morris, 1984; Wampler, 1982a, 1982b; Wampler, 1990).

Bernard Guerney (1977) was the forerunner in the development of psychoeducational relationships skills programs. Significant research has been done on Relationship Enhancement or RE (see chapter 11). Giblin, Sprenkle, and Sheehan (1985) reported RE was the most effective program in a meta-analysis of RME programs. RE has been found to be effective in numerous empirical studies and case reports. It has been found to be effective in improving relationships with a wide variety of clinical and other special populations. Similarly, it has been deemed excellent with respect to gender sensitivity (Accordino & Guerney, 2001).

Although RME flourished in the 1960s, in the mid-1970s a new generation of scholars initiated ambitious research programs on interaction patterns and marital outcomes. For example, John Gottman began his investigation of couple interaction patterns. Using an observational coding system called the Couples' Interaction Scoring System, Gottman noted remarkable regularity in interaction over time. Gottman then focused on marital interaction as predictive of marital distress. Finally, he utilized his research findings in theory development (Gottman & Gottman, 2013). John and Julie Gottman developed the Art and Science of Love workshops based on this research at the Gottman Institute they founded in August 1996. The Gottman Institute focused on the promotion of the Gottman method and training opportunities (Gottman, 2002; http://www.gottman.com/). John also established the Relationship Research Institute as a non-profit organization to continue his research on couples. The Sound Relationship House Theory (see chapter 6), created by John Gottman and Julie Schwartz Gottman, became the basis of interventions with couples in their book *The Marriage Clinic* (Gottman & Gottman, 1999), and Julie's book, *The Marriage Clinic Casebook* (Gottman, 2004).

Around the same time that John Gottman was involved in his research, Howard Markman and his associates at the University of Denver's Center for Marital and Family Studies were investigating the connection between communication and problem solving and effective marital functioning. Markman and Scott Stanley created the Prevention and Relationship Education Program (PREP) from this work (see chapter 12; https://www.prepinc.com). The PREP approach focused on managing stress, investigating the impact of past experiences and commitment, and has a heavy focus on sharing fun. PREP has been delivered and evaluated globally. It has been rated as efficacious in reviews of evidence on relationship education approaches (Jakubowski et al., 2004). Studies on the effectiveness of PREP find that couples that have participated in PREP are less likely to get divorced and have significantly higher levels of marital satisfaction. One long-term study on PREP found that couples who took the program before marriage had less negative interaction, more positive interaction, and higher levels of relationship satisfaction up to five years following the training (Markman, Floyd, Stanley, & Storaasli, 1988; Markman, Renick, Floyd, Stanley, & Clements, 1993).

By the 1980s, there were about two dozen programs evaluated in the literature (Bagarozzi & Rauen, 1981; Sayers et al., 1998). In the late 1990s, some RME programs became commercial ventures; numerous commercially available programs offered materials for use with engaged and already married couples. As a further stimulus to expansion, in 1996 the Coalition for Marriage, Family, and Couples Education was founded by Diane Sollee. This coalition held a national conference in 1997 to serve as both a venue for training and a general, information sharing of RME.

The first decade of the 21st century saw ongoing progress. Halford, Markman, Kline, and Stanley (2003) reviewed best practices in RME, and Larson (2004) edited a special issue of *Family Relations* on innovations in RME. In 2006, the first national Healthy Marriage Resource Center, a web-based clearinghouse of information and research, was funded by a grant from the Administration for Children and Families. The U.S. Department of Health and Human Services through the Administration for Children and Families funded the Healthy Marriage Initiative to expand marriage education nationwide. Three years later a special issue of the *Journal of Couple and Relationship Therapy* on RME best practices was edited by Hawkins (2009).

Prognosis for RME

Improving intimate relationships with preventive, educational interventions has proven to be more difficult than originally conceived (Bradbury & Lavner, 2012). Most programs had research-supported foundations but were lacking in sound theoretical support (Rauer et al., 2014). Qualitative results highlighted strengths and weaknesses among current RME programs. Recommendations are offered for improving RME programs and professional standards in the field (Childs & Duncan, 2012). Because of the complexity of design issues and difficulties inherent in outcome studies, researchers will reasonably continue to debate the effectiveness of premarital education regimens. Furthermore, there is a great deal more to be discovered that will guide prevention efforts in ways that will improve the effectiveness of those efforts in the future (Stanley, 2001). Understanding the dynamics of resilient marriages and enhancing couple competence through prevention programs is viewed as critical to effective couple and parental role performance (Coie, Watt, West, Hawkins, Asarnow, Markman, Ramey, Shure, & Long, 1993; Markman, Floyd, Stanley, & Lewis, 1986).

References and Further Readings

Accordino, M., & Guerney, B., Jr. (2001). The empirical validation of Relationship Enhancement® couple and family therapy. In D.J. Cain & J. Seeman (Eds.), *Humanistic psychotherapies: Handbook of research and practice* (pp. 403–442). Washington, DC: American Psychological Association.

Bader, E. (1984). Marriage enrichment: Friend or foe? *Canadian Family Physician, 30*, 1155–1157. PMCID: PMC2153958

Bagarozzi, D., & Rauen, P. (1981). Premarital counseling: Appraisal and status. *American Journal of Family Therapy, 9*, 13–30.

Bailey, B.L. (1987). Scientific truth . . . and love: The marriage education movement in the United States. *Journal of Social History, 20*, 711–732.

Beck, U., & Beck Gernsheim, E. (1995). *The normal chaos of love.* Cambridge, UK: Polity Press.

Blanchard, V., Hawkins, A., Baldwin, S., & Fawcett, E. (2009). Investigating the effects of marriage and relationship education on couple's communication skills: A meta-analytic study. *Journal of Family Psychology, 23*, 203–214. doi:10.1037/a0015211

Bradbury, T., & Lavner, J. (2012). How can we improve preventive and educational interventions for intimate relationships? *Behavior Therapy, 43*, 113–122.

Bruhn, D., & Hill, R. (2004). Designing a premarital counseling program. *The Family Journal, 12*, 389–391. doi:10.1177/1066480704267233

Butler, M., & Wampler, K. (1999). A meta-analytic update of research on the Couple Communication program. *American Journal of Family Therapy, 27*, 223–237. doi:10.1080/019261899261943

Carroll, J., & Doherty, W. (2003). Evaluating the effectiveness of premarital prevention programs: A meta-analytic review of outcome research. *Family Relations, 52*, 105–118.

Center for Marriage and Family. (1995). *Marriage preparation in the Catholic Church: Getting it right*. Omaha, NE: Center for Marriage and Family, University College, Creighton University.

Childs, G., & Duncan, S. (2012). Marriage preparation education programs: An assessment of their components. *Marriage and Family Review, 48*, 59–81. doi:10.1080/01494929.2011.626893

Coffin, B. (2009). Marriage.gov: A promising public policy. In H. Benson and S. Callan (Eds.), *What works in relationship education: Lessons from academics and service deliverers in the United States and Europe* (pp. 121–136). Doha, Qatar: Doha International Institute for Family Studies and Development.

Coie, J., Watt, N., West, S., Hawkins, J., Asarnow, J., Markman, H., Ramey, S., Shure, M., & Long, B. (1993). The science of prevention: A conceptual framework and some directions for a national research program. *American Psychologist, 48*, 1013–1022.

Coontz, S. (2005). *Marriage, a history: From obedience to intimacy, or how love conquered marriage*. New York, NY: Viking.

Cowan, P., & Cowan, C. (2014, September 8). Controversies in couple relationship education (CRE): Overlooked evidence and implications for research and policy. *Psychology, Public Policy, and Law*. Advance online publication. http://dx.doi.org/10.1037/law0000025

DeMaria, R., & Hannah, M. (2003). *Building intimate relationships: Bridging treatment, education, and enrichment through the PAIRS program*. New York, NY: Routledge.

Doherty, W., Lester, M., & Leigh, G. (1986). Marriage Encounter weekends: Couples who win and couples who lose. *Journal of Marital and Family Therapy, 12*, 49–61.

Doherty, W., McCabe, P., & Ryder, R. (1978). Marriage Encounter: A critical appraisal. *Journal of Marriage and Family Counseling, 4*, 99–108.

Epstein, R., Warfel, R., Johnson, J., Smith, R., & McKinney, P. (2013). Which relationship skills count most? *Journal of Couple and Relationship Therapy, 12*, 297–313. doi:10.1080/15332691.2013.836047

Fagan, P., Paterson, R., & Rector, R. (2002, October 25). *Marriage and welfare reform: The overwhelming evidence that marriage education works*. Backgrounder #1606. Washington, DC: The Heritage Foundation. Retrieved from http://www.heritage.org/research/welfare/bg1606.cfm

Fawcett, E. (2004). *Helping with the transition to parenthood: An evaluation of the Marriage Moments program*. Theses and Dissertations. Paper 1135. Retrieved from http://scholarsarchive.byu.edu/cgi/viewcontent.cgi?article=2134&context=etd

Fawcett, E., Hawkins, A., Blanchard, V., & Carroll, J. (2010). Do premarital education programs really work? A meta-analytic study. *Family Relations, 59*, 232–239.

Fowers, B. (2000). *Beyond the myth of marital happiness*. San Francisco, CA: Jossey-Bass.

Futris, T., Barton, A., Aholou, T., & Seponski, D. (2011). The impact of PREPARE on engaged couples: Variations by delivery format. *Journal of Couple and Relationship Therapy, 10*, 69–86. doi:10.1080/15332691.2011.539175

Genovese, R. (1975). Marriage encounter. *Small Group Behavior, 6*, 45–56. doi:10.1177/104649647500600104

Giblin, P., Sprenkle, D., & Sheehan, R. (1985). Enrichment outcome research: A meta-analysis of premarital, marital, and family interventions. *Journal of Marital and Family Therapy, 11,* 257–271.

Giddens, A. (1992). *The transformation of intimacy: Sexuality, love and eroticism in modern societies.* Cambridge, UK: Polity Press.

Gilliland, T., Hawkins, A., Christiaens, G., Carroll, J., & Fowers, B. (2002). *Marriage moments: Strengthening your marriage as you become parents. An activity guidebook.* Provo, UT: Brigham Young University.

Gordon, L., & Durana, C. (1999). The PAIRS program. In R. Berger & M. Hannah (Eds.), *Preventive approaches in couples therapy* (pp. 346–365). Philadelphia, PA: Brunner/Mazel Inc.

Gottman, J. (2002). *The relationship cure: A 5 step guide to strengthening your marriage, family, and friendships.* New York, NY: Three Rivers Press.

Gottman, J.M., & Gottman, J.S. (1999). *The marriage clinic.* New York, NY: W.W. Norton & Co.

Gottman, J.M., & Gottman, J.S. (2013). *The empirical basis of Gottman Couples Therapy.* Seattle, WA: The Gottman Institute, Inc.

Gottman, J.S. (2004). *The marriage clinic casebook.* New York, NY: W.W. Norton & Co.

Guerney, B. (1977). *Relationship enhancement: Skill-training programs for therapy, problem prevention, and enrichment.* San Francisco, CA: Jossey-Bass.

Halford, W. (2000). *Australian couples in millennium three: A research and development agenda for marriage and relationships education.* Canberra, ACT: Department of Family and Community Services. Retrieved from http://www.dss.gov.au/sites/default/files/documents/australian_couples.pdf

Halford, W. (2004). The future of couple relationship education: Suggestions on how it can make a difference. *Family Relations, 53,* 559–566.

Halford, W. (2011). *Marriage and relationship education: What works and how to provide it.* New York, NY: Guilford Press.

Halford, W., & Bodenmann, G. (2013). Effects of relationship education on maintenance of couple relationship satisfaction. *Clinical Psychology Review, 33,* 512–525.

Halford, W., Markman, H., Kline, G., & Stanley, S. (2003). Best practice in couple relationship education. *Journal of Marital and Family Therapy, 29,* 385–406.

Halford, W., Markman, H., & Stanley, S. (2008). Strengthening couples' relationships with education: Social policy and public health perspectives. *Journal of Family Psychology, 22,* 497–505.

Halford, W., Moore, E., Wilson, K., Farrugia, C., & Dyer, C. (2004). Benefits of flexible delivery relationship education: An evaluation of the Couple CARE. *Family Relations, 53,* 469–476.

Halford, W., Petch, J., & Creedy, D. (2010). Promoting a positive transition to parenthood: A randomised clinical trial of couple relationship education. *Prevention Science, 11,* 89–100.

Halford, W., Sanders, M., & Behrens, B. (2001). Can skills training prevent relationship problems in at-risk couples? Four-year effects of a behavioral relationship education program. *Journal of Family Psychology, 15,* 750–768.

Halford, W., & Simons, M. (2005). Couple relationship education in Australia. *Family Process, 44,* 147–159.

Halford, W., Wilson, K., Watson, B., Verner, T., Larson, J., Busby, D., & Holman, T. (2010). Couple relationship education at home: Does skill training enhance relationship assessment and feedback? *Journal of Family Psychology, 24,* 188–196. doi:10.1037/a0018786

Hawkins, A. (2009). Best-practices innovations in couple and relationship education: Introduction to a special issue. *Journal of Couple and Relationship Therapy, 8,* 91–94. doi:10.1080/15332690902813786

Hawkins, A., Blanchard, V., Baldwin, S., & Fawcett, E. (2008). Does marriage and relationship education work? A meta-analytic study. *Journal of Consulting and Clinical Psychology, 76,* 723–734.

Hawkins, A., Carroll, J., Doherty, W., & Willoughby, B. (2004). A comprehensive framework for marriage education. *Family Relations, 53,* 547–558. doi:10.1111/j.0197-6664.2004.00064.x

Hawkins, A., Wilson, R., Ooms, T., Nock, S., Malone-Colon, L., & Cohen, L. (2009). Recent government reforms related to marital formation, maintenance, and dissolution in the United States: A primer and critical review. *Journal of Couple and Relationship Therapy, 8,* 181–191.

Jakubowski, S., Milne, E., Brunner, H., & Miller, R. (2004). A review of empirically supported marital enrichment programs. *Family Relations, 53,* 528–536.

Lantz, H.R., & Koos, E.L. (1953). Problem areas in marriage education. *Marriage and Family Living, 15,* 116–119.

Larson, J. (2004). Innovations in marriage education: Introduction and challenges. *Family Relations, 53,* 421–424. doi:10.1111/j.0197-6664.2004.00049.x

Larson, J., Newell, K., Topham, G., & Nichols, S. (2002). A review of three comprehensive premarital assessment questionnaires. *Journal of Marital and Family Therapy, 28,* 233–239. doi:10.1111/j.1752–0606.2002.tb00360.x

Mace, D. (1975). We call it ACME. *Small Group Behavior, 6,* 31–44. doi:10.1177/104649647500600103

Mace, D., & Mace, V. (1976). *Marriage enrichment in the church.* Nashville, TN: Broadman Press.

Markman, H., & Floyd, F. (1980). Possibilities for the prevention of marital discord: A behavioral perspective. *American Journal of Family Therapy, 8,* 29–48.

Markman, H., Floyd, F., Stanley, S., & Storaasli, R. (1988). The prevention of marital distress: A longitudinal investigation. *Journal of Consulting and Clinical Psychology, 56,* 210–217.

Markman, H., Floyd, F., Stanley, S., & Lewis, H. (1986). Prevention. In N. Jacobson & A. Gurman (Eds.), *Clinical handbook of marital therapy* (pp. 173–196). New York, NY: Guilford Press.

Markman, H., & Halford, K. (2005). International perspectives on couple relationship education. *Family Process, 44,* 139–146.

Markman, H., Renick, M., Floyd, F., Stanley, S., & Clements, M. (1993). Preventing marital distress through communication and conflict management training: A four- and five-year follow-up. *Journal of Consulting and Clinical Psychology, 61,* 70–77.

Maybruch, C., Pirutinsky, S., & Pelcovita, D. (2014). Religious premarital education and marital quality within the orthodox Jewish community. *Journal of Couple and Relationship Therapy, 13,* 365–381.

Miller, S., Nunnally, E., & Wackman, D. (1976). A communication training program for couples. *Social Casework, 57,* 9–18.

Mudd, E., Freeman, C., & Rose, E. (1941). Premarital counseling in the Philadelphia Marriage Council. *Mental Hygiene, 25,* 98–119.

Nock, S. (2002). The social costs of the de-institutionalization of marriage. In A. Hawkins, L. Wardle, & D. Coolidge (Eds.), *Revitalizing the institution of marriage for the 21st century* (pp. 1–14). Westport, CT: Praeger.

Nunnally, E., Miller, S., & Wackman, D. (1975). The Minnesota Couples Communication program. *Small Group Behavior, 6*, 57–71. doi:10.1177/104649647500600105

Ooms, T. (2005, July). *The new kid on the block: What is marriage education and does it work?* Couples and Marriage series, Brief no. 7. Washington, DC: Center for Law and Social Policy. Retrieved from www.clasp.org

Petch, J., Halford, W., Creedy, D., & Gamble, J. (2012). A randomised controlled trial of a couple relationship and co-parenting program (Couple CARE for Parents) for high- and low-risk new parents. *Journal of Consulting and Clinical Psychology, 80*, 662–673.

Rauer, A., Adler-Baeder, F., Lucier-Greer, M., Skuban, E., Ketring, S., & Smith, T. (2014). Exploring processes of change in couple relationship education: Predictors of change in relationship quality. *Journal of Family Psychology, 28*, 65–76.

Reardon-Anderson, J., Stagner, M., Macomber, J., & Murray, J. (2005). *Systematic review of the impact of marriage and relationship programs.* Washington, DC: Urban Institute. Retrieved from http://www.urban.org/publications/411142.html

Regula, R. (1975). Marriage Encounter: What makes it work? *Family Coordinator, 24*, 153–159.

Rhoades, G., & Stanley, S. (2009). Relationship education for individuals: The benefits and challenges of intervening early. In H. Benson & S. Callan (Eds.), *What works in relationship education: Lessons from academics and service deliverers in the United States and Europe* (pp. 45–54). Doha, Qatar: Doha International Institute for Family Studies and Development.

Rhoades, G., & Stanley, S. (2011). Using individual-oriented relationship education to prevent family violence. *Journal of Couple and Relationship Therapy, 10*, 185–200. doi:10. 1080/15332691.2011.562844

Russell, C., Bagarozzi, D., Atilano, R., & Morris, J. (1984). A comparison of two approaches to marital enrichment and conjugal skills training: Minnesota Couple Communication Program and Structured Behavioral Exchange Contracting. *American Journal of Family Therapy, 12*, 13–15.

Sayers, S., Kohn, C., & Heavey, C. (1998). Prevention of marital dysfunction: Behavioral approaches and beyond. *Clinical Psychology Review, 18*, 713–744.

Silliman, B., Stanley, S., Coffin, W., Markman, H., & Jordan, P. (2001). Preventive interventions for couples. In H. Liddle, D. Santisteban, R. Levant, & J. Bray (Eds.), *Family psychology: Science-based interventions* (pp. 123–146). Washington, DC: APA Publications.

Stanley, S. (2001). Making a case for premarital education. *Family Relations, 50*, 272–280. doi:10.1111/j.1741–3729.2001.00272.x

Stanley, S., Amato, P., Johnson, C., & Markman, H. (2006). Premarital education, marital quality, and marital stability: Findings from a large, random, household survey. *Journal of Family Psychology, 20*, 117–126.

Stanley, S., Markman, H., St. Peters, M., & Leber, B. (1995). Strengthening marriages and preventing divorce: New directions in prevention research. *Family Relations, 44*, 392–401.

Stanley, S. M., Markman, H. J., Prado, L. M., Olmos-Gallo, P. A., Tonelli, L., St. Peters, M., Leber, B. D., Bobulinski, M., Cordova, A., & Whitton, S. (2001). Community-based premarital prevention: Clergy and lay leaders on the front lines. *Family Relations, 50*, 67–76.

Sullivan, K., & Bradbury, T. (1997). Are premarital prevention programs reaching couples at risk for marital dysfunction? *Journal of Consulting and Clinical Psychology, 65*, 24–30.

Wall, J. (2002). The marriage education movement: A theological analysis. *International Journal of Practical Theology, 6*(1), 84–103.

Wampler, K. (1982a). The effectiveness of the Minnesota Couple Communication Program: A review of research. *Journal of Marital and Family Therapy, 8*, 345–356.

Wampler, K. (1982b). Bringing the review of literature into the age of quantification: Meta-analysis as a strategy for integrating research findings in family studies. *Journal of Marriage and the Family, 44*, 1009–1023.

Wampler, K. (1990). An update of research on the Couple Communication program. *Family Science Review, 3*, 21–40.

Wetzler, S., Frame, L., & Litzinger, S. (2011). Marriage education for clinicians. *American Journal of Psychotherapy, 65*, 311–336.

Wilmoth, J., & Smyser, S. (2012). A national survey of marriage preparation provided by clergy. *Journal of Couple and Relationship Therapy, 11*, 69–85. doi:10.1080/15332691.2012.639705

Wright, H. N. (1977). *Before you say "I Do": A marriage preparation manual for couples.* Eugene, OR: Harvest House Publishers.

2

RELATIONSHIP AND MARRIAGE EDUCATION BEST PRACTICES

Conceptual And Methodological Issues

Stephen F. Duncan

LEARNING GOALS

- Learn best practices of relationship and marriage education (RME).
- Learn conceptual and methodological issues raised by these practices.
- Learn how to address the issues in RME practice.

Introduction

Relationship and marriage education (RME) enjoys a long and distinguished history. Some of the earliest formal RME can be traced back to the early 1930s, with the earliest known efforts occurring at the Merrill-Palmer Institute. Early premarital counseling established at the Philadelphia Marriage Council included a strong educational emphasis (Stahmann & Salts, 1993). Churches also played a key role in premarital educational efforts through premarital counseling (Schumm & Denton, 1979).

RME is currently flourishing at an unprecedented level in terms of the number and frequency of offerings, public interest, and especially funding. For example, the federal Healthy Marriage and Responsible Fatherhood Initiative (HMRF), funded by the Administration for Children and Families (ACF), provided over $150,000,000 in five-year grants beginning in 2006. In 2011, ACF awarded 121 grants to community- and faith-based organizations, colleges and universities, and public and private entities in 47 states. These programs were funded for a three-year project period. For fiscal year 2014, ACF made available to the current grantees non-competitive continuation awards for an additional year. The Healthy Marriage Resource Center (http://www.healthymarriageinfo.org/) also continues to serve as a resource to gather, develop, and disseminate information and research related to promoting marriage through a range of activities.

The utilization of RME appears to be increasing compared to earlier eras. Recent research shows that of those married since 1990 approximately 44% had participated in some form of marriage preparation experience (Stanley, Amato, Johnson, & Markman, 2006). Outcome research is generally favorable. Recent decade-long evaluations of RME outcomes (Markman & Rhoades, 2012) and recent **meta-analyses** (Hawkins, Blanchard, & Baldwin, 2008), together with studies from preceding decades, show that RME tends to bring about reliable change, at least in terms of communication and relationship satisfaction.

With increased implementation, a best practices literature has emerged to indicate of what optimal RME looks like (Halford, Markman, Kline, & Stanley, 2003; Markman & Rhoades, 2012; Hawkins et al., 2008; Hawkins, Carroll, Doherty, & Willoughby, 2004), or at least a sense of "group think" (Hawkins, Stanley, Blanchard, & Albright, 2012, p. 85) about how RME should be done. Some of these best practice ideas coincide with quality prevention programming in general (Duncan & Goddard, 2011). However, best practices also raise conceptual and methodological issues pertinent to the way RME programs are conceived, developed, implemented, and evaluated.

The purpose of this chapter is to review seven **RME best practices**, and then discuss some of the conceptual and methodological issues raised by these practices, and how to address the issues in RME practice.

RME Best Practices

Practice #1: Optimal RME programs must be grounded in theory and research. By insisting that RME programs are theory- and research-based, RME program design moves beyond a "service mission" to a "scientific enterprise" (Dumka, Roosa, Michaels, & Suh, 1995, p. 78). While several theoretical perspectives are used, perhaps the most dominant continues to be the **cognitive-behavioral perspective**, found in 8 of the 13 approaches reviewed by Berger and Hannah (1999). This approach assumes that couples can be taught to improve their ways of thinking (i.e., attitudes and expectations) and behaving (i.e., communication and conflict management) to enhance their chances for a positive marriage. Several programs eclectically integrate various other perspectives, including social learning, humanistic, communications, and systems approaches.

All of these theories assume that couples are in a mutually committed, egalitarian-oriented relationship. However, this is a Western ideal that may not be fully embraced by other cultural traditions in the ways assumed by traditional RME programming. Such differences may require modification of RME theory and practice to fit material around the needs of couples. RME programs can assess and refine theories about how couples connect and become stronger, creating a dialectic between theory-driven practice and practice-driven theory.

Quality RME must always be grounded in the best **marital process research** available (Adler-Baeder, Higginbotham, & Lamke, 2004). Current marital process research is threefold, and the best-known RME programs integrate these perspectives (Duncan, Hawkins, & Goddard, 2011). The first perspective places emphasis on marital disruption and understanding the processes that lead to marital breakdown (e.g., Gottman, 1994). This area often focuses on communication processes, how conflict is managed, and how problems are addressed. A second major emphasis addresses the intrapersonal characteristics of spouses and positive interpersonal processes for establishing and maintaining a healthy marriage. According to recent observations (Holman, Carroll, Busby, & Klein, 2007), these positive elements, often referred to as "marital virtues" or "spousal strengths," are considered more frequently. Some of these virtues or strengths include positivity, friendship, generosity (Fowers, 2000; Hawkins, Fowers, Carroll, & Yang, 2007), fairness (Fowers, 2001), fondness, admiration, affection, and respect (Gottman & Gottman, 1999). A third major perspective is attentive to elements some scholars call "transformative processes in marriage" (Fincham, Stanley, & Beach, 2007, p. 277). These elements include forgiveness (Fincham, 2000; McCullough et al., 1998), commitment (Fowers, 2000; Stanley & Markman, 1992), sacrifice (Whitton, Stanley, & Markman, 2002), and sanctification (Mahoney et al., 1999). Programs, based on this research, target the reduction of risk factors and the increase of protective factors at the individual level, couple level, and context of the couple's relational ecology (Halford et al., 2003; Halford, 2004).

Two issues arise when implementing this best practice of basing programs on theory and research. Marital process research, like all social science research, suffers from limitations which ultimately influences practice. The best research is context sensitive, that is, either applicable across audiences or uniquely targeted within audiences. Such research is rare because much of marital process research has been conducted with white, Anglo-Saxon, well-educated audiences. An overreliance upon this somewhat limited research may lead to a one-size-fits-all mentality. With the many and varied ways audiences differ, special application to a particular audience is often needed because the participants' lived experiences as well as the theories and research which guide programming efforts may not offer a precise course.

A second issue involves one of the three emphases in marital process research. There has been a long-standing emphasis on communication and problem-solving skills in the RME literature, with some emerging models. The stronger emphasis on communication as dominant may need to be tempered by other elements that make relationships work. For example, a current practice is to use skill training methods to help couples enhance their communication, but a strong emphasis on a particular set of communication skills may inadvertently sensitize couples to deficits in their relationship (Rogge, Cobb, Lawrence, Johnson, & Bradbury, 2013). Hence, an intended enhancement may create rather than ameliorate problems. Thus, an important modification in RME would be a continuing merger among the three elements of marital process research, as well as adequate attention to the strengths couples already have.

Practice #2: RME programs are evidence-based. It is one thing for a program to be based on defensible theory and research, but quite another for the program to actually work in practice when implemented with real couples. Enter the realm of **evidence-based programs** (EBP) (Small, Cooney, & O'Connor, 2009). In RME, such programs are also called **empirically supported treatments, or ESTs** (Jakubowski, Milne, Brunner, & Miller, 2004). To earn such a label, an RME program needs to have undergone testing in a randomly controlled trial **(RCT)**, showing that participants receiving the intervention fared significantly better than participants in a control group in evaluation studies with two separate teams of researchers. Of the 13 programs reviewed, Jakubowski et al. identified only four which met this high mark: The Prevention and Relationship Enhancement Program (PREP), Relationship Enhancement (RE), Couple Communication Program (CCP), and Strategic Hope-Focused Enrichment. As these authors indicate and as other observers have noted (e.g., Larson, 2004), there are far more programs that have been developed than are ever subjected to this level of empirical scrutiny. "Until most programs are subjected to greater scrutiny, their effectiveness remains uncertain" (Larson, 2004, p. 423).

Programs that are better evaluated are tied to well-established and well-funded research programs. More systematic evaluations of more programs with multiple foci are needed. With some exceptions (e.g., Rogge et al., 2013), only RMEs with a strong skill-based focus have been evaluated in RCTs (Halford et al., 2003). Even some popular programs that claim to have strong evaluation data actually show only small changes on a few of the multitude of measured variables (Jakubowski et al., 2004; Goddard, Marshall, Olson, & Dennis, 2012). Thus proclaiming that a program is an EST needs to be squared against the reality that it may be garnering only some of its intended outcomes.

Only producing a handful of significant effects raises a number of questions. One disturbing possibility is whether RME is substantial enough an intervention to produce measured effects. Another question is whether researchers are measuring the wrong things as outcomes. While communication and problem solving may be important, perhaps other variables pertaining to the deeper inner life of the couple may deserve greater attention. For example, intrapersonal virtues and transformative factors receive less attention, and may be more at the heart of what happens when both partners attend to marital growth processes. Such factors may undergird why couples seek to communicate and handle issues between them respectfully, which may have little to do with interpersonal skills themselves (Carroll, Badger, & Yang, 2006).

While RCT is the gold standard for identifying evidence-based programs, such evaluation is expensive and time-consuming, and may lie outside the interests, abilities, and practicality of community RME. Certainly practitioners should not wait to use a theory and research-based program until it becomes an EST;

non-EST status should not foreclose its usability. Still, in an increasingly rigorous environment, RMEs must ascertain whether programs meet outcomes. A reasonable low-cost alternative may be the **retrospective pretest** (Pratt, McGuigan, & Katzev, 2000). With the demands for evidence-based programs continuing to be high, research suggests that the retrospective pretest is a simple, convenient, and expeditious method of assessing program impact.

In addition, effective **formative evaluation** should not be dismissed as a tool for identifying quality programs. Quality evaluations will combine both formative and **summative** elements. For example, questions addressed to the processes of learning during sessions provide an ongoing feedback loop to program developers as to how to make changes in sessions to better meet participant needs (Long, Angera, & Hakoyama, 2008).

Practice #3: RME programs tailor program development and implementation to the audience. Empirically sound, theory- and research-based programs are tailored to participants' needs in order to reach intended outcomes. Rather than fitting the audience to the curriculum in a one-size-fits-all fashion (Larson & Halford, 2011), practitioners following this best practice seek to fit their program to the audience, from the theory and research that undergirds it, to the methods used to teach it, to the approaches used to promote it. As programs are fit to the needs of the particular audience, it becomes important to not place program fidelity above people fidelity. The participants' needs are the first and foremost concern.

Two methods to assist practitioners in tailoring programs are to (1) use individualized couple assessments to create couple risk profiles (Halford et al., 2003), and (2) conduct audience needs assessments (Duncan & Goddard, 2011; Snyder, Duncan, & Larson, 2010; Smith, Duncan, Ketring, & Abell, 2014).

Couple assessments can help RME professionals adapt education to the risk and resiliency profile of participants. For example, assessments such as RELATE (Busby, Holman, & Taniguchi, 2001), created to help couples assess individual, couple, and contextual assets and liabilities in their relationship, can help guide both couples and relationship educators to a greater understanding of educational needs.

Best practices in prevention science suggest consulting the target audience to learn about their needs prior to attempting to address them (Dumka et al., 1995; Duncan & Goddard, 2011). These assessments help better tailor RME programs to participants. For example, recent needs assessments (Markman & Rhodes, 2012; Snyder et al., 2010; Smith et al., 2014) suggested the importance of making curriculum, teaching method, and marketing approach adjustments according to cultural nuances and background of the audience, including the importance of using incentives and targeting men. For example, male appeal may be enhanced by being specific as to the science-based benefits gained from implementing concepts and skills from the curriculum. Snyder et al. (2010) found with their Latino population that incentives, especially men (if also women), included traditional food and tickets to nearby soccer games. Duncan and Goddard (2011) offer a detailed description of how marketing principles can be used in incentivizing RME populations. Consulting and tailoring efforts to the target audience also assure that content and methods are matched to couples with special needs, such as those heading stepfamilies, those dealing with addictions, and those with other challenges. Studying the demographics of the audience, using needs assessments, and creating risk and resiliency profiles of couples give practitioners a maximum chance of having program materials relevant to the audience.

Fortunately, there is already evidence in contemporary RME that program content is being adapted and tailored to "fit the diverse circumstances of various racial, ethnic, cultural, religious, and special needs populations. This appears to be an emerging 'best practice' in [RME] and we expect that tailored programming will continue to grow over the next decade. However, future research needs to illuminate better the value of tailored content versus the adequacy of more universal content" (Duncan et al., 2011, p. 187). Yet, fitting programs in and around people presents major issues. Since RME practitioners work with groups small and large, there is tremendous challenge inherent in the ideal of targeting programs to needs. This challenge is likely to grow given the growth of RME services and the diversity of clientele served. "Can [RME] practitioners and the scholars who support the field keep up with the demand and provide high-quality preventative services to such a diverse landscape?" (Duncan et al., 2011, p. 188).

One important skill for RME practitioners to develop is **skilled dialogue** (Barrera & Corso, 2003), which includes respect, reciprocity, and responsiveness. "Respect is expressed as a willingness to acknowledge a variety of perspectives as equally valid to achieving a particular goal" (p. 67). Reciprocity "requires entering into interactions ready to learn as well as to teach, ready to receive as well as to give" (p. 69). Responsiveness focuses on communicating both respect and understanding of the others' perspectives. Taken together, these lead to "anchored understanding of diversity"—not generalizations about cultures and peoples but a specific knowledge and appreciation of someone who is different from us.

Monitoring and tailoring dosage is also a method of fitting both the curriculum and method to participants. The modal RME traditional face-to-face program dosage is about 12 hours (Hawkins, Blanchard, Baldwin, & Fawcett, 2009); recent research (Hawkins, Stanley, Blanchard, & Albright, 2012) has shown that dosage is a significant moderator of program outcomes, with longer programs resulting in better outcomes than short- or moderate-dosage programs. Depending on the modality (web-based or traditional RME) and audience need (higher vs. lower risk), wider variation in RME dosage is appropriate. Some couples want communication and conflict management but nothing else; some couples face forgiveness issues and want to know how to implement that transformative process in their relationship. Flexibility in programming will allow participants to get what they need. While longer dosage is associated with better outcomes than moderate-dosage programs, longer-dosage programs may not be able to garner the longer-term commitment from couples.

While the best practices recommendation may be 12 hours of contact or better for reliable behavior change, such an approach may not be needed in every context or even wanted. A stepped approach to RME (Larson & Halford, 2011), beginning with low-level **self-directed interventions** to greater-intensity interventions like PREP, may be what is indicated to meet couple needs.

Practice #4: Encourage involvement of higher-risk couples. Long-standing research verifies that while all couples potentially benefit from RME, those with either lower preprogram marital satisfaction or higher risks benefit the most (Giblin, Sprenkle, & Sheehan, 1985; Halford et al., 2001). The task has been how to attract those at higher risk to RME. The past few years, however, have seen a dramatic increase in RME targeted to lower-income and more diverse couples and individuals. This trend is due in large part to increased public funding and initiatives to help more disadvantaged populations (Hawkins et al., 2009).

While there has not been systematic evaluation of strategies that would encourage attendance by high-risk couples (Halford et al., 2003), several ideas seem to be moving the field in the correct direction. For example, Karney, Davila, Cohan, Sullivan, Johnson, and Bradbury (1995) suggest recruiting couples through media advertisements as an effective way to garner a wider diversity of participants. Both Halford et al. (2001) and Duncan, Steed, and Needham (2009) applied this strategy to RME, using a variety of mass media outreach. Halford et al. used newspaper articles that described risk factors then pointed the audience to programs that would address these factors. Duncan et al. (2009) used announcements on radio stations and articles in newspapers with an invitation to participate in a study assessing the effectiveness of RME.

Recent trends show RME is catching up with the need to reach out to higher-risk couples, as more effort and funding is being made in this direction. For example, one RME program, *Within Our Reach* (Ragan, Einhorn, Rhoades, Markman, & Stanley, 2009), has been developed with attention to the needs of higher-risk couples such as cohabiting couples and couples with less formal education. One of the notable adjustments attending to educational differences is in the method of instruction, which is more hands-on, less didactic approaches. Such programs, adapted to the cultural nuances of an area, and fit with individual couple situations (Larson & Halford, 2011), may be successful both in expanding the reach of RME to all interested couples, regardless of official marital status and educational background, and reducing the risks inherent in such unions. More research is needed on ways to reach this audience and understand unique relationship processes in these couples so we can lead them to the most favorable outcomes.

While RME began and continues to be emphasized in religious organizations, unaffiliated couples face additional risks that can be addressed in tailored programs. RME would be wise to deemphasize a connection to only conservative and religious views, and instead emphasize the relevance of RME to couples of all sorts (Halford, 2004). Making RME a part of an overall community health package would go a long way in this regard. For example, community marriage initiatives such as in the state of Oklahoma and in Australia could convey a strong marriage-strengthening message at the population level with direct marketing campaigns.

Practice #5: Offer RME at change points. Historically, the modal time for couples to receive RME was during engagement before marriage. Recently, however, RME is accessible during any time a couple is seeking to form and sustain a committed relationship, including during cohabitation. These times of transition from singlehood to long-term couple formation will continue to be an important time for intervention and support. Once in the relationship, other transitions couples face may place the relationship at risk, such as the transition to parenthood, when the couple must learn how to continue prioritizing their marriage when baby makes three.

There is wisdom in providing RME at these change points. However, it may be too little, too late to promote the kind of relationship outcomes envisioned. Several realities need to be acknowledged before couples ever receive such intervention. First, attitude-forming schema which influence beliefs about intimate relationships such as marriage and mate selection are already taking shape well before formative coupling time (Kerpelman, Pittman, Adler-Baeder, Stringer, Eryigit, Cadely, & Harrell-Levy, 2010). Hawkins (2012, p. 271) offers this sobering assessment:

> The period of the life course between adolescence and first marriage has increased substantially, such that for most young adults there will be nearly a decade between high school graduation and a wedding (Arnett, 2000). In the meantime, there is a prolonged period of sexual and relationship exploration relatively unconnected to the ultimate goal of marriage shared by most youth (Carroll, Willoughby, Badger, Nelson, Barry, & Madsen, 2007). In addition, high divorce rates—and high rates of non-marital family formation and dissolution—among parents mean that many contemporary youth cannot rely on the social modeling of their parents to find a pathway to their own healthy marriages. Indeed, in some disadvantaged communities, healthy marriages are nearly extinct and youth may not even have a clear concept of what a healthy marriage or relationship is (Hymowitz, 2006). And through the media, youth are exposed to a dizzying array of models of romantic relationships. (Kunkel, Eyal, Finnerty, Biely, & Donnerstein, 2005)

This assessment suggests RME must do something earlier in the life course to help individuals and couples establish and sustain a marriage. Thus, in addition to transition points, wise RMEs would also focus on helping young people become "relationship literate" (Hawkins) during their adolescent years. Evidence with samples of youth, including those from more disadvantaged social strata, suggests these programs can have positive effects, such as modifying young peoples' faulty beliefs about relationships and marriage (Kerpelman et al., 2010).

Practice #6: Promote early presentation of relationship problems. In his best practices article, Halford and colleagues (2003) promoted RME and clinical interventions when marital challenges are mild enough that the tide could be turned, perhaps averting severe relationship decline. There is wisdom in this approach. Wisdom would recommend addressing problems before they become too severe. Secondary prevention is usually more cost-effective, and problems easier to resolve than remedial intervention. The essence of RME is, metaphorically, "working upstream" referring to "working with couples before problems become too serious and entrenched and focuses on an educational and preventive rather than a remedial approach to helping couples" (Larson, 2004, p. 421).

While this approach is great on paper as a recommended best practice, at issue here is how to encourage couples to make regular marital care an ongoing and proactive activity. Couples often wait until problems are too severe for either educational or clinical interventions. However, much can be done to encourage healthy marriage awareness norms through a variety of approaches. One useful idea is a regular marriage tune-up. Well-known RME scholar Jeffry Larson (2002) has written a trade book, *The Great Marriage Tune-up Book*, based on over 50 years of research. This book provides couples with helpful, and easy-to-use self-tests and assessments that help them comprehend and use their strengths and weaknesses to strengthen their relationship.

Practice #7: Enhance accessibility of evidence-based RME programs. Notwithstanding evidence of their benefits to couples, traditional RME programs are notoriously underattended, with research suggesting that from 31% to 37% of couples participate in any form of premarital education (Stanley, Amato, Johnson, & Markman, 2006; Stanley & Markman, 1992). Use goes up with increased availability (Schumm & Silliman, 1997). Hence, it is critical to continue to increase the reach of evidence-based RME programs (Halford et al., 2003; Larson & Halford, 2011) and expand the range and flexibility of available formats (Halford, 2004; Larson & Halford, 2011). While research to date may support the idea that the best practice in RME is a traditional face-to-face approach with a significant number of contact hours, having a varied and flexible approach may be the best approach to reaching the largest number of couples.

What is being done to increase accessibility of evidence-based programs? While faith settings continue to be important settings for traditional RME (Duncan et al., 2011), in recent years settings where RME is offered is being expanded. For example, there has recently been a dramatic increase in RME for military couples. Deployments increase the stresses military couples face, so *PREP for Strong Bonds* has been developed specifically for this audience. A large, randomized controlled trial of this program found participating couples had one third the divorce rate of the control group (Stanley, Allen, Markman, Rhoades, & Prentice, 2010).

In addition to efficacious traditional programs and their adaptations for specialized audiences, non-traditional, **flexible delivery programs** have been emerging. One such program, *CoupleCare* (Halford, 2011), shares similar conceptual and theoretical underpinnings with *PREP* but is also based strongly on quality adult education principles. The program is offered in a flexible delivery format, which couples largely complete on their own at their own pace at home, with some involvement by telephone with a relationship educator. The Jakubowski et al. (2004) review categorized *CoupleCare* as "possibly efficacious" but it is likely moving toward EST status after a decade of continued research. Self-directed approaches, such as websites (e.g., Duncan et al., 2009), are also showing they can be effective RME options. A recent meta analysis (McAllister, Duncan, & Hawkins, 2012) showed that the programs with the strongest effect sizes were those which combined traditional and self-directed elements, or blended programs.

Methodologies that fit the privatized needs of the user have just begun to be implemented. For example, marriage-strengthening apps are now in the RME marketplace and appearing on handheld devices. The Gottman Institute now features the *Gottman Love Jungle*, a free app which helps committed couples use research to strengthen the intimacy and friendship they experience in their relationship. Many more of these digitized means of relationship strengthening are likely to be generated and their effectiveness has yet to be evaluated. If full access to RME is to be realized, the future of RME may lie in various handheld device applications. However, the evaluation of such technological interventions presents a challenge that has yet to be studied.

At issue, especially to RME traditionalists, may be that a variety of self-directed or flexible delivery approaches such as the web, mobile app, or a variety of digital venues yet to be conceived would weaken or even overrun the delivery of face-to-face RME. This digital innovation may be the very doorway to help others gain access to marriage-strengthening information they need but would not otherwise seek. Participants may benefit when these modern innovations are combined with traditional programs recognized as effective. Given the emerging findings on blended learning, it is likely that RME practitioners could profitably supplement and reinforce face-to-face learning with online learning. Some audiences, especially those in outlying remote areas, may not have face-to-face resources available to them, and evidence suggests that participating in some form of RME is better than doing nothing at all (Duncan et al., 2009).

Higher-risk populations may also benefit from a self-directed approach. McAllister, Duncan, and Busby (2013) found that healthier couples, from healthy family backgrounds, were more likely to turn to traditional RME programs, while couples with more risk factors tended to turn to self-directed RME. These results for self-directed RME participation were similar to research by Doss, Rhoades, Stanley, and Markman (2009), which found that couples who reported higher negative communication, more physical violence, and lower marital satisfaction were more likely to turn to self-help books.

Population-based RME interventions created to reach millions of potential couples have not been systematically developed nor specifically evaluated, but may be one innovation needed for future RME programming. For example, mass media plays an important role in health promotion (e.g., Egger, Donovan, & Spark, 1993) and television is a primary medium through which such promotion occurs in contemporary society. Television has been shown to influence awareness of healthy ideals, leading to changes in attitudes, beliefs, and behaviors, "making it potentially one of the most powerful educational resources available at the present time" (Sanders, Montgomery, & Brechman-Toussaint, 2000, p. 939). One Australian study presented a 12-episode program called "Families" in an experimental design study and explored its impact on disruptive child behavior and family adjustment (Sanders et al., 2000). Results showed that following the parenting episodes participating parents reported higher levels of parenting competence and lower levels of child behavior problems when compared to a wait-list control group. A more recent study (Sanders, Calam, Durand, Liversidge, & Carmont, 2008) found similar positive outcomes among those viewing the episodes alone, and even better results when the viewing experience was combined with additional support materials. It is not known how such an approach would work with RME couples, but this idea deserves exploration.

A modest version of a population-based approach may be the website Stronger Marriage (http://strongermarriage.org/), developed by Utah State University Extension Service. Several 30-second video public service announcements have been produced to promote the website on television, but they also teach simple marriage-strengthening concepts largely visually. The difficult next step is to assess whether audiences benefit with low-dosage, population-based interventions.

Conclusion

This is an exciting time to be in the field of RME. Recent years have seen a proliferation of scholarship and practice in RME, increased public interest and involvement, and unprecedented government support. While issues in development, implementation, and evaluation present challenges, several tentative best practices and conceptual frameworks exist to guide these efforts. Succeeding well at RME requires practitioners' best efforts at combining best practices, addressing the issues that may arise with these practices, and being open to learning even better best practices moving into the future.

Key Points

- RME enjoys a long and distinguished history, and recent years have seen a proliferation of scholarship and practice in RME, increased public interest and involvement, and unprecedented government support.

- Tentative best practices have emerged to guide the development, implementation, and evaluation of RME. These include RME programs having a theory, research, and evidence base, tailored to the needs of an audience, involving higher-risk couples, being offered at change points, promoting early presentation of relationship problems, and widely accessible via a variety of venues and methods.
- Each best practice presents some dilemmas for the RME practitioner that need to be considered and addressed.

Discussion Questions

1. What are the three foci of current marital process research forming the basis of most of today's RME programming?
2. What is the dominant theoretical perspective driving RME?
3. Identify and describe in a single sentence each of the seven best practices of RME noted by Duncan. Are any of these practices more important than others? Defend your answer.
4. What is the difference between the best practice that a program be theory- and research-based and the best practice that a program be evidence-based?
5. What is EST and how does an RME program earn that distinction? How does that compare with a RCT and how are these designations related?
6. List and describe several ideas for enhancing the accessibility of RME. Can you think of additional ways to extend availability of RME?

References and Further Readings

Adler-Baeder, F., Higginbotham, B., & Lamke, L. (2004). Putting empirical knowledge to work: Linking research and programming on marital quality. *Family Relations, 53,* 537–546.

Arnett, J. (2000). Emerging adulthood: A theory of development from the late teens through the twenties. *American Psychologist, 55,* 469–480.

Barrera, I., & Corso, R. (2003). *Skilled dialogue: Strategies for responding to cultural diversity in early childhood.* Baltimore, MD: Brookes Publishing.

Berger, R., & Hannah, M. (1999). Introduction. In R. Berger & M. Hannah (Eds.), *Preventive approaches in couples therapy* (pp. 1–27). Philadelphia, PA: Brunner/Mazel.

Busby, D., Holman, T., & Taniguchi, N. (2001). RELATE: Relationship evaluation of the individual, family, cultural, and couple contexts. *Family Relations, 50,* 308–316.

Carroll, J., Badger, S., & Yang, C. (2006). The ability to negotiate or the ability to love? Evaluating the developmental domains of marital competence. *Journal of Family Issues, 27,* 1001–1032.

Carroll, J., Willoughby, B., Badger, S., Nelson, L., Barry, C., & Madsen, S. (2007). So close, yet so far away: The impact of varying marital horizons on emerging adulthood. *Journal of Adolescent Research, 22,* 219–247.

Childs, G., & Duncan, S. (2012). Marriage preparation education programs: An assessment of their components. *Marriage and Family Review, 48,* 59–81.

Doss, B., Rhoades, G., Stanley, S., & Markman, H. (2009). Marital therapy, retreats, and books: The who, what, when, and why of relationship help-seeking. *Journal of Marital and Family Therapy, 34,* 527–538.

Dumka, L., Roosa, M., Michaels, M., & Suh, K. (1995). Using research and theory to develop prevention programs for high-risk families. *Family Relations, 44,* 78–86.

Duncan, S., & Goddard, H. (2011). *Family life education: Principles and practices for effective outreach* (2nd ed.). Thousand Oaks, CA: Sage.

Duncan, S., Hawkins, A., & Goddard, H. (2011). Marriage and relationship education. In S. Duncan & H. Goddard (Eds.), *Family life education: Principles and practices for effective outreach* (2nd ed., pp. 164–190). Thousand Oaks, CA: Sage.

Duncan, S., Steed, A., & Needham, C. (2009). A comparison evaluation study of web-based and traditional marriage and relationship education. *Journal of Couple and Relationship Therapy, 8,* 162–180.

Egger, G., Donovan, R., & Spark, R. (1993). *Health and the media.* Sydney: McGraw-Hill Book Company.

Fincham, F. (2000). The kiss of the porcupines: From attributing responsibility to forgiving. *Personal Relationships, 7,* 1–23.

Fincham, F., Stanley, S., & Beach, S. (2007). Transformative processes in marriage: An analysis of emerging trends. *Journal of Marriage and Family, 69,* 275–292.

Fowers, B. (2000). *Beyond the myth of marital happiness: How embracing the virtues of loyalty, generosity, justice, and courage can strengthen your relationship.* New York, NY: John Wiley.

Fowers, B. (2001). The limits of a technical concept of a good marriage: Exploring the role of virtue in communication skills. *Journal of Marital and Family Therapy, 27,* 327–340.

Giblin, P., Sprenkle, D., & Sheehan, R. (1985). Enrichment outcome research: A meta-analysis of premarital, marital, and family interventions. *Journal of Marital and Family Therapy, 11,* 257–271.

Goddard, H., Marshall, J., Olson, J., & Dennis, S. (2012). Steps toward creating and validating an evidence-based couples curriculum. *Journal of Extension, 50*(6). Retrieved from http://www.joe.org/joe/2012december/a6.php

Gottman, J. (1994). *Why marriages succeed or fail: And how you can make yours last.* New York, NY: Simon & Schuster.

Gottman, J., & Gottman, J. (1999). The marriage survival kit: A research-based marital therapy. In R. Berger & M.T. Hannah (Eds.), *Preventive approaches in couples therapy* (pp. 304–330). Philadelphia, PA: Brunner/Mazel.

Halford, W. (2004). The future of couple relationship education: Suggestions on how it can make a difference. *Family Relations, 53,* 559–566. doi:10.1111/j.0197-6664.2004.00065.x

Halford, W. (2011). *Marriage and relationship education.* New York, NY: Guilford Press.

Halford, W., Markman, H., Kline, G., & Stanley, S. (2003). Best practice in couple relationship education. *Journal of Marital and Family Therapy, 29,* 385–406.

Halford, W., O'Donnell, C., Lizzio, A., & Wilson, K. (2006). Do couples at high risk of relationship problems attend premarriage education? *Journal of Family Psychology, 20,* 160–163.

Halford, W., Sanders, M., & Behrens, B. (2001). Can skills training prevent relationship problems in at-risk couples? Four-year effects of a behavioral relationship education program. *Journal of Family Psychology, 14,* 750–768.

Halford, W.K., Markman, H.J., Kline, G.H., & Stanley, S. (2003). Best practice in couple relationship education. *Journal of Marital and Family Therapy, 29,* 385–406.

Hawkins, A. (2012). A public policy agenda to help couples form and sustain healthy, stable marriages. In A. Hawkins, D. Dollahite, & T. Draper (Eds.), *Successful marriages and families* (pp. 269–278). Provo, UT: Brigham Young University.

Hawkins, A., Blanchard, V., & Baldwin, S. (2008). Does marriage and relationship education work? A meta-analytic study. *Journal of Consulting and Clinical Psychology, 76*, 723–734.

Hawkins, A., Blanchard, V., Baldwin, S., & Fawcett, E. (2009). Investigating the effects of marriage and relationship education on couples' communication skills: A meta-analytic study. *Journal of Family Psychology, 23*, 203–214. doi:10.1037/a0015211

Hawkins, A., Carroll, J., Doherty, W., & Willoughby, B. (2004). A comprehensive framework for marriage education. *Family Relations, 53*, 547–558.

Hawkins, A., Fowers, B., Carroll, J., & Yang, C. (2007). Conceptualizing and measuring marital virtues. In S.L. Hofferth & L.M. Casper (Eds.), *Handbook of measurement issues in family research* (pp. 67–83). Mahwah, NJ: Lawrence Erlbaum.

Hawkins, A., Stanley, S., Blanchard, V., & Albright, M. (2012). Exploring programmatic moderators of the effectiveness of marriage and relationship education programs: A meta-analytic study. *Behavior Therapy, 43*, 77–87.

Holman, T., Carroll, J., Busby, D., & Klein, D. (2007, November). *Preparing, coupling, and marrying: Toward a unified theory of marriage development.* Paper presented at the Theory Construction and Research Methodology Conference of the National Council on Family Relations, Pittsburgh, PA.

Hymowitz, K.S. (2006). *Marriage and caste in America.* Chicago: Ivan R. Dee.

Jakubowski, S., Milne, E., Brunner, H., & Miller, R. (2004). A review of empirically supported marital enrichment programs. *Family Relations, 53*, 528–536.

Karney, B., Davila, J., Cohan, C., Sullivan, K., Johnson, M., & Bradbury, T. (1995). An empirical investigation of sampling strategies in marital research. *Journal of Marriage and the Family, 57*, 909–920.

Kerpelman, J., Pittman, J., Adler-Baeder, F., Stringer, K., Eryigit, S., Cadely, H., & Harrell-Levy, M. (2010). What adolescents bring to and learn from relationship education classes: Does social address matter? *Journal of Couple and Relationship Education, 9*, 95–112.

Kunkel, D., Eyal, K., Finnerty, K., Biely, E., & Donnerstein, E. (2005). Sex on TV 4. Menlo Park, CA: Kaiser Family Foundation. Retrieved from http://www.kff.org/entmedia/upload/Sex-on-TV-4-Full-Report.pdf

Larson, J. (2002). *The great marriage tune-up book.* San Francisco, CA: Jossey-Bass.

Larson, J. (2004). Innovations in marriage education: Introduction and challenges. *Family Relations, 53*, 421–424.

Larson, J., & Halford, W. (2011). One size does not fit all: Customizing couple relationship education for unique couple needs. In J.L. Wetchler (Ed.), *Handbook of clinical issues in couple therapy* (pp. 293–309). New York, NY: Routledge.

Long, E., Angera, J., & Hakoyama, M. (2008). Transferable principles from a formative evaluation of a couples' empathy program. *Journal of Couple and Relationship Therapy, 7*, 88–112.

Mahoney, A., Pargament, K., Jewell, T., Swank, A., Scott, E., Emery, E., & Rye, M. (1999). Marriage and the spiritual realm: The role of proximal and distal religious constructs in marital functioning. *Journal of Family Psychology, 13*, 321–338.

Markman, H., & Rhoades, G. (2012). Relationship education research: Current status and future directions. *Journal of Marital and Family Therapy, 38*, 169–200.

McAllister, S., *Duncan*, S., & Busby, D. (2013). Exploratory analysis of factors associated with participation in self directed and traditional marriage and relationship education. *Marriage and Family Review, 49*, 563–584.

McAllister, S., Duncan, S., & Hawkins, A. (2012). Examining the early evidence for self-directed marriage and relationship education: A meta-analytic study. *Family Relations, 61*, 742–755. doi:10.1111/j.1741-3729.2012.00736.x

McCullough, M., Rachal, K., Sandage, S., Worthington, E., Brown, S., & Hight, T. (1998). Interpersonal forgiving in close relationships: II. Theoretical elaboration and measurement. *Journal of Personality and Social Psychology, 75*, 1586–1603.

National Fatherhood Initiative. (2005). Germantown, MD. Retrieved from http://www. fatherhood.org/

Pratt, C., McGuigan, W., & Katzev, A. (2000). Measuring program outcomes: Using retrospective pretest methodology. *American Journal of Evaluation, 21*, 341–349.

Ragan, E., Einhorn, L., Rhoades, G.., Markman, H.., & Stanley, S.. (2009). Relationship education programs: Current trends and future directions. In J. Bray and M. Stanton (Eds.), *The Wiley-Blackwell handbook of family psychology* (pp. 450–462). Malden, MA: Wiley-Blackwell.

Rogge, R., Cobb, R., Lawrence, E., Johnson, M., & Bradbury, T. (2013). Is skills training necessary for the primary prevention of marital distress and dissolution? A 3-year experimental study of three interventions. *Journal of Consulting and Clinical Psychology, 81*, 949–961.

Sanders, M., Calam, R., Durand, M., Liversidge, T., & Carmont, S. (2008). Does self-directed and web-based support for parents enhance the effects of viewing a reality television series based on the Triple P—Positive Parenting Programme? *Journal of Child Psychology and Psychiatry, 49*, 924–932.

Sanders, M., Montgomery, D., & Brechman-Toussaint, M. (2000). The mass media and the prevention of child behavior problems: The evaluation of a television series to promote positive outcomes for parents and their children. *Journal of Child Psychology and Psychiatry, 41*, 939–948.

Schumm, W., & Denton, W. (1979). Trends in premarital counseling. *Journal of Marital and Family Therapy, 5*, 23–32. doi:10.1111/j.1752-0606

Schumm, W., & Silliman, B. (1997). Changes in premarital counseling as related to older cohorts of married couples. *Journal of Sex and Marital Therapy, 23*, 98–102.

Small, S., Cooney, S., & O'Connor, C. (2009). Evidence-informed program improvement: Using principles of effectiveness to enhance the quality and impact of family-based prevention programs. *Family Relations, 58*, 1–13.

Smith, C., Duncan, S., Ketring, S., & Abell, E. (2014). Assessing marriage and relationship education needs in Aruba. *Journal of Couple and Relationship Therapy, 13*, 133–152.

Snyder, I., Duncan, S., & Larson, J. (2010). Assessing perceived marriage education needs and interests among Latinos in a select western community. *Journal of Comparative Family Studies, 41*, 347–367.

Stahmann, R., & Salts, C. (1993). Educating for marriage and intimate relationships. In M. Arcus, J. Schvaneveldt, & J. Moss (Eds.), *Handbook of family life education* (Vol. 2, pp. 33–61). Newbury Park, CA: Sage.

Stanley, S., Allen, E., Markman, H., Rhoades, G., & Prentice, D. (2010). Decreasing divorce in U.S. army couples: Results from a randomized controlled trial using PREP for strong bonds. *Journal of Couple and Relationship Therapy, 9*, 149–160.

Stanley, S., Amato, P., Johnson, C., & Markman, H. (2006). Premarital education, marital quality, and marital stability: Findings from a large, random, household survey. *Journal of Family Psychology, 20*, 117–126.

Stanley, S., & Markman, H. (1992). Assessing commitment in personal relationships. *Journal of Marriage and the Family, 54*, 595–608.

Whitton, S., Stanley, S., & Markman, H. (2002). Sacrifice in romantic relationships: An exploration of relevant research and theory. In A. Vangelisti, H. Reis, & M. Fitzpatrick (Eds.), *Stability and change in relationships* (pp. 156–182). New York, NY: Cambridge University Press.

3

RELATIONSHIP AND MARRIAGE EDUCATION PROGRAM DESIGN AND IMPLEMENTATION

Ted G. Futris, Jacquelyn K. Mallette, and Evin W. Richardson

LEARNING GOALS

- Identify key elements of relationship and marriage education program design based on a logic model framework.
- Understand the application of research in informing program design and implementation.
- Make programmatic decisions that are data-informed (e.g., needs assessment, empirical research) and grounded in family life education best practices.
- Develop SMART objectives that reflect the program's relevance (situation), activities (outputs), and intended impact (outcomes).

Introduction

Developing and implementing relationship and marriage education (RME) that offers participants a meaningful and impactful learning experience is an involved and thoughtful process. It requires more than simply purchasing a curriculum and offering classes. Duncan and Goddard (2011; see chapter 2 this volume) offer best practices in designing a family life education program. This chapter builds and expands on these practices by structuring RME **program design and implementation** within a logic model framework (Taylor-Powell, Jones, & Henert, 2003). As summarized in Figure 3.1 and outlined below, a **logic model** illustrates the *theory of change* guiding a program. During the development process, educators

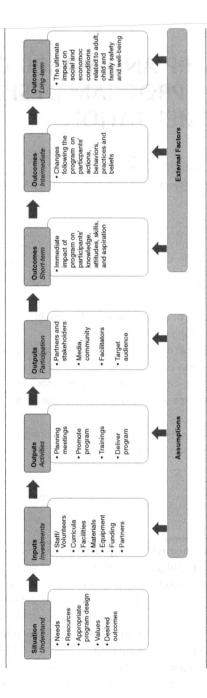

FIGURE 3.1 Program Development Logic Model

Note: Based on Taylor-Powell, Jones, & Henert (2003).

establish why their program is relevant (the *situation*), what is necessary to launch and sustain the program (*inputs*), what is done and who is reached during implementation (*outputs*), and how their program impacts participants and the community (*outcomes*). After describing each step in the process, the value in using this process to clearly establish explicit *assumptions* driving your program as well as *external factors* that may facilitate and/or impede a program's capacity to achieve the desired outcomes is emphasized.

Define the Situation

It is necessary to first clarify and become familiar with the situation that is driving the need for RME when designing an RME program. Doing so requires understanding the needs and desired outcomes of the community and target audience. In the logic model, this is referred to as defining the situation. The situation statement communicates the need for the program and establishes a baseline for program evaluation (McCawley, 2001). Below are steps to take and consider when defining the situation.

Use Theory and Research to Guide Program Development. A primary step in the development of an RME program that can provide the most effective learning and yield the greatest impact begins with reviewing existing research and theory. A comprehensive review of the existing research helps educators understand the originating problem set within a context of sociopolitical, environmental, and economic circumstances, and ensure that the proposed program can meet the needs of the target audience. The research review can also assist with determining appropriate programmatic design and outcomes based on evidence from existing programs. Identifying the current and relevant research can be an overwhelming task—here are a few steps to help make the process more manageable (Adler-Baeder, Higginbotham, & Lamke, 2004):

* *Start broadly and then narrow your focus.* Search for key words that are most closely related to your RME goals (e.g., marital, relationship, satisfaction, quality). Because this will garner a large amount of literature from which to begin, you can then narrow your search by focusing on target audience (e.g., youth, engaged, remarried) and applied research (e.g., education, counseling, evaluation). A quick read of an article's abstract will help decipher the fit of the research with your interests and needs. Also, consult with university and community partners for their insight into successful strategies, recommended readings, or summaries they compiled.
* *Summarize and categorize.* Compile the research identified into a table or spreadsheet that allows for easy accessibility and categorization. Focus on summarizing information that will be pertinent to your proposed program, such as program content, goals and objectives, methods, and outcomes.

- *Identify relevant themes and patterns.* Once the literature is summarized, what themes emerged? Focus on principles and skills that are relevant to fostering healthy couple relationships and that can be taught. These themes will inform the logic model for the program by clarifying the need that the program intends to address, establishing teachable concepts, determining appropriate implementation methods, and establishing clear short-term, intermediate, and long-term program outcomes.

> For an example of a research-based RME resource that outlines key patterns of thinking and behaviors associated with healthy, stable couple relationships taught in an educational setting, visit http://www.nermen.org/NERMEM.php

In addition to existing research, an RME program based on one or more relevant theories helps to clarify the program's "values" and delineate how the program's activities are related to desired outcomes (Hughes, 1994). Examine theories that have been applied in research and the development of similar programs. Specification of the theory and its connection to program components from the outset provides a program with a solid starting point and clearer vision of how the program is intended to proceed. These connections should be outlined clearly in the logic model in order to provide all those involved in planning and implementation a working knowledge of the chosen theory and how it is informing the program. Table 3.1 provides a sample of theories that may be helpful in informing RME programs (Futris & Adler-Baeder, 2013).

Conduct Needs Assessments to Inform Program Design. In addition to grounding an RME program in research and theory, the unique and specific needs of the target audience should also be understood. A **needs assessment** is a helpful strategy for identifying what the target community needs and wants in a program. While the research can inform what content may be useful and relevant, community input helps establish "buy-in" to the program which can facilitate participant attendance and satisfaction in the program and lead to more achievable learning outcomes (Ballard & Morris, 2005). Below are the "Five Ws" to consider when conducting a needs assessment:

- *Who is most affected by the problem?* Empirical evidence has shown that RME can benefit married and unmarried couples of various racial/ethnic and socioeconomic backgrounds (Blanchard, Hawkins, Baldwin, & Fawcett, 2009; Fawcett, Hawkins, Blanchard, & Carroll, 2010; Hawkins, Blanchard, Baldwin, & Fawcett, 2008; Hawkins, & Fackrell, 2010; Markman & Rhoades, 2012). Still, in designing an RME program, direct attention to those who may benefit the most from the program (Hawkins, Carroll, Doherty, & Willoughby, 2004). Engage potential program participants, staff, and

TABLE 3.1 Common Theoretical Perspectives that Ground Research on Relationships and Marriages

Theory and Key Principles	Application to RME
Ecological (e.g., Bronfenbrenner, 1979) and systems (e.g., Whitchurch & Constantine, 1993) theories focus on the interaction between multiple levels of influence. From an ecological systems approach, intimate partner relationship attitudes and behaviors are shaped by sociocultural (e.g., expectations about relationships and marriage), community (e.g., resources to support healthy relationships and marriages), and familial norms and practices (e.g., models of healthy relationships and marriages). A systems approach to understanding couple relationships focuses more on the interaction between "sub-system" relationships embedded within the family (e.g., couple, parent–child, sibling, in-laws, etc.) and how those relationships influence the development and maintenance of healthy couple relationships.	Through RME, couples can develop a better awareness of these influences, process how these influences have shaped their current relationship, and explore ways to negotiate and manage the impact of these influences on their relationship as well as the impact of their relationship on others.
Spillover theories (e.g., Saxbe, Rodriguez, & Margolin, 2013), derived from a broader systems view, emphasize how experiences (both positive and negative) in one domain (e.g., work) or relationship (e.g., couple) affect experiences in another domain (e.g., home) or relationship (e.g., parent–child).	RME can help couples understand these spillover effects and develop skills to manage negative spillover from one domain to another. Conversely, when improvements are made in one area, it can be expected that other areas may benefit as well.
A life course approach (e.g., Bengtson & Allen, 1993) to RME programming implies the value placed on linking past experiences (e.g., parental divorce, sexual onset, intimate partner violence) and relationships (e.g., prior marital and parenting experiences) to understanding how and why individuals transition into new relationships and the continuity and change that occurs in these relationships.	RME can offer individuals opportunities to identify and understand these influences and explore ways to make conscious and informed decisions as they develop new relationships and move forward in current relationships.
Social exchange theories (e.g., Thibaut & Kelley, 1959) suggest that individuals choose to remain in or exit relationships by weighing the rewards (e.g., connectedness, quality time) and costs (e.g., re-occurring disagreements, unmet needs) experienced in a relationship as well as alternative possibilities (e.g., prospect of finding someone else; ability to have needs met by others).	RME can support couples in developing skills that, when practiced, would lead to more satisfying exchanges within their relationship.

(Continued)

TABLE 3.1 Continued

Theory and Key Principles	Application to RME
From a social learning perspective (e.g., Bandura, 1977), models of healthy versus unhealthy relationships serve as a source for learning what to expect and how to think, feel, and act in intimate partner relationships.	Although relationship attitudes and behaviors are learned during childhood from one's family of origin and experiences shared in intimate partner relationships, knowledge acquired through RME can reinforce healthy practices or facilitate change in practices that do not support healthy stable relationships by providing new models. This theory also assumes an intergenerational influence in that children of RME participants may benefit from observing healthier couple dynamics between parents.
Attribution theory (e.g., Bradbury & Fincham, 1990) contends that individuals make affective and cognitive assessments of their partner's behavior that influence how they react in future interactions with their partner. Attributions often reflect one's judgment of whether the behavior is stable versus unstable (e.g., "He forgot our anniversary because he doesn't care" versus "he has been under a lot of pressure at work lately."), an internal or external quality (e.g., "She yelled because she is an angry person" versus "there was a lot of noise in the room and she had to raise her voice."), and within their partner's control (e.g., "The car accident happened because you were texting" versus "the other driver ran a red light.").	RME can help couples tune in to their attitudes and attributions and learn skills to reframe and process (individually and together) disagreements and challenges that arise within relationships in order to foster positivity.
A feminist perspective (e.g., Fox & Murry, 2000) encourages the understanding of how gender attitudes and practices are developed through socialization and interpersonal experiences and how these attitudes may influence couple dynamics in positive or negative ways. The perspective calls attention to the importance of valuing and supporting roles and experiences in couple relationships that make each individual feel valued and empowered.	RME can facilitate feelings of safety and respect in intimate partner relationships and help couples develop skills to negotiate clear and equitable roles and expectations that support and fulfill each partner's needs in the relationship.

Note: Adapted from Futris & Adler-Baeder (2013).

community partners to serve on an advisory committee who will participate in data collection, decision making, and planning based on the needs assessment (Altschuld & Kumar, 2010).

- *What is the issue?* Identify the issue the program addresses, what is currently known about its cause, and what is currently being done to address the problem. This information helps prioritize goals (*outcomes*), inform decision making regarding the resources (*inputs*), and establish implementation plans (*outputs*) to support desired changes.
- *What is the desired outcome?* After determining the current condition, establish what change the community desires. Assess the following questions: What is the ideal situation? What would be an acceptable situation? What change is feasible?
- *Why?* A need is the measureable gap between what currently exists and what is desired. When there is a gap between the current and the ideal situation, consider the following questions: Why does the situation need to be changed? What are the consequences for not changing the situation? What is causing the gap? What strategies could be used to decrease the gap?
- *When?* A needs assessment is an ongoing effort that continues throughout program development and implementation. In addition to establishing the *who* and *what* during pre-program assessment, gauging participants' needs during and after the program can help ensure their needs are being met and whether new needs are emerging. This continuous needs assessment process can identify gaps in the program and help to refocus the program as needed.

Developing Program Goals and Objectives. At the conclusion of the pre-program needs assessment, sufficient information should be available to establish the goals and outcome objectives of the program. What change is expected in the participants who complete the RME program (short-term and intermediate outcomes) and what impact on the community is anticipated (long-term outcomes)? During the early stages of the needs assessment, it is acceptable to think more broadly about the objectives, however, toward the end of the process, the goals should be more clearly defined and measureable. The goals and objectives indicate what and how much will be accomplished and by when it is expected, in both the short and long term (Futris, 2007). Further, goals and objectives must be realistic, representative of the research and theory guiding the program, and clearly specify the changes to be achieved. One effective way to accomplish this is to write *SMART* objectives:

- *Specific.* Use action words to state specifically and concretely who is the target audience and what is expected to be achieved or changed in the target audience.
- *Measurable.* Describe the achievement, action, or behavior in quantitative terms that states both the current and the desired situation.

- *Attainable/Achievable.* Verify that the objective can reasonably be accomplished during the program and is within the program's influence.
- *Realistic/Relevant/Results Oriented.* Establish measurable outputs and achievements which are related to the program's focus and content.
- *Time Bound.* Identify the target date by which the objective will be met and include interim steps and a plan to monitor the progress of the objective.

Examples of *SMART* objectives:

- Compared to the start of the program, the proportion of youth reporting usage of positive communication and conflict management techniques in their own peer, romantic, and familial relationships will increase by 25% at 3-months post-program completion.
- By the conclusion of the program, 80% of single parents will be able to identify healthy strategies related to "deciding not sliding" into future romantic relationships.
- At the conclusion of the program, 90% of couples will be able to correctly identify and describe at least three listener techniques to maintaining positive communication with their romantic partner.
- Three months after program completion, at least 75% of program participants will report their partners are positively responding to their bids for connection.
- Six months after completing the program, at least 60% of participants will report that they and their partners utilize soft start-ups to initiate conflict.
- One year after completing 75% of the program, 90% of couples will report being strongly committed to and satisfied with their marriage compared to couples who did not attend the program or only completed less than 50% of the program.

Program Inputs

The successful launch and sustainability of an RME program depends on the availability and selection of certain resources. In a logic model these resources are referred to as *inputs*—what your organization invests in the process of designing and implementing a program. Below is a description of some of the resources essential to successful programming.

- *Staff.* One of the most important resources needed is a caring, knowledgeable, and trained staff. Staff could include community volunteers (e.g., couple mentors or participants who have completed the program in the past) as well as paid staff. Importantly, consider the costs of staff training and ongoing professional development to facilitate program integrity.

- *Curricula.* Careful consideration must be given to selecting a curriculum that best matches with the needs of your intended audience and overall program goals. While there are free and low-cost RME curricula available, some curricula require additional costs associated with training and the purchase of supplemental materials.

For more information regarding low- to no-cost curricula, review the following resources:

- National Extension Relationship and Marriage Education Network (NERMEN): www.nermen.org
- National Resource Center for Healthy Marriage and Families: www. healthymarriageandfamilies.org
- National Healthy Marriage Resource Center: www.healthymarriage info.org

---

- *Location.* When selecting an appropriate learning environment consider a learning space conducive to active learning (e.g., open space that facilitates interaction), is easily accessible to the intended audience, and is comfortable for the participants. For example, while certain locations may be accessible and convenient to some (e.g., religious institutions, schools, neighborhood/ community agencies, healthcare settings), they may not appeal to others not affiliated or comfortable with that location. Be open to offering repeated sessions of the program in multiple locations. The advisory board, identified during the needs assessment process, can be helpful in identifying the best location. Other things to consider include possible rental fees, furniture, teaching equipment, and transportation costs.
- *Room setup.* The setup of the room can have an impact on the attentiveness and comfort of the participants. For example, some participants may have an aversion to learning in a group of strangers and feel more willing to share personal information in smaller groups consisting of friends and/or family (Wiley & Ebata, 2004). In this instance, it may be beneficial to plan the room in such a way that would keep couples or family members grouped together.
- *Recruitment materials.* Recruiting the intended audience requires the utilization of a variety of marketing resources including, but not limited to, radio, newspaper, television advertisements, printed flyers and brochures, social media, billboards, and word-of mouth. The needs assessment can be helpful in identify strategies that would be most effective in engaging your audience.
- *Retention materials.* A variety of incentives may facilitate program participation and retention, including gift cards, meals, transportation, and child care.
- *Funding.* Funding to cover the costs for these resources come from a variety of sources, including grants from federal, state, and local agencies, private foundations, as well as community and business donations. Be creative in

identifying funding sources and do not "put all your eggs in one basket"—when funding from one source ends, have funding available from another source to continue the program while additional funding is secured.

While these resources can be costly, community collaborations and partnerships can be very helpful in securing resources as well as supporting other key aspects for a successful program.

Building community collaborations *to support* RME. The community, developmentally and ecologically, plays a major role in the well-being of individuals, couples, and families (Bogenschneider, 1996), so it would be logical that the community also plays an important role in the health of couple and marital relationships (Futris, 2007). In fact, the most successful RME programs are not generally supported by one agency or organization alone, but include partnerships and collaborations with community members and other organizations. Through collaborations, communities can create a culture of healthy couple and marital relationships by creating support mechanisms that make resources more available to couples and individuals seeking out information and opportunities to strengthen their relationships.

Social organization and community collaboration includes building assets for the community and maximizing opportunities for individuals, families, and the community as a whole (Mancini, Bowen, & Martin, 2005). Below are a few recommendations to consider when establishing your community collaborations (for more information, see Futris, 2007):

- *Engage the intended audience.* By involving the people of the community at every level of planning and implementation, you are sending a message that this program is for the community and that the needs of the community are important. They can help identify the needs of the community and the resources and barriers present that may influence success. As well, they understand cultural norms (e.g., etiquette, acceptable greetings, rules about how to address others, taboo topics, rules of emotional expression, nonverbal communication, and public touching) that may turn participants toward or away from the program, and can serve as sounding boards by sharing their opinion about how the program is being received and ways to improve the program.
- *Identify the "right" partners.* When selecting partners from agencies that serve couples and families and/or want to support your program, identify members who are diverse and understand your community. Do members represent a variety of different constituent groups or cultural perspectives? What members of the community can help bring credibility to our cause? What skills, information, and resources does the program need and which partners fulfill those needs? What expertise and services can they contribute? Will certain

organizations or individuals need incentives to join? What will they gain by joining the effort?

- *Establish a shared vision and action plan.* Collaboration entails working toward a common vision, jointly taking action, and sharing the decision-making process. Therefore, it is important that a clear and shared mission be established by the members of the collaboration and everyone is committed to allocating time and resources toward achieving that mission. Providing a written agreement to each partner that clarifies the mission of the program and each partner's role(s) can be beneficial to all parties.
- *Regularly evaluate and evolve as needed.* Competing demands, limited time and resources, and shifting priorities should be anticipated when working with others. Checking in with partners on a regular basis can help ascertain whether the collaboration is still meeting their need and whether they are meeting the needs of the program. Be prepared to make adjustments in membership and the responsibilities shared by partners.

Creating a team of leadership, staff, facilitators, and advisors that consists of community members who will support relationship education efforts sends the message that the program is community-based and there to benefit the community.

Selecting appropriate RME curricula. Finding an appropriate curriculum for an RME program is essential to reaching the program's goals and objectives. While there are many research- and evidence-based programs available, there is not a one-size-fits-all curriculum. Here are a few things to consider when selecting an appropriate RME curriculum (for more information, see Hughes, 1994):

- *Supporting materials.* The availability of clear and appropriate teaching aids (e.g., videos, handouts, presentation slides) that reinforce learning concepts can facilitate the successful implementation of the program.
- *Literacy of the participants.* Be sure to determine whether any written materials given to the audience match their literacy levels. Be considerate of the design and layout of printed materials to ensure they are suitable for the RME program and audience. As a general rule, materials should be similar to popular media materials.
- *Developmentally appropriate.* Select curricula that include developmentally relevant content and engage your audience in developmentally appropriate activities and discussions. For example, RME programs for teens versus young adults would require a different curriculum, much like a program for first-married versus remarried couples.
- *Program design fit.* Curricula are often developed with a specific service delivery strategy (e.g., weekend retreat, weekly sessions) and dosage in mind. For example, if an RME program will be offered as a one-day weekend (7-hour)

workshop but the curriculum is designed for six weekly sessions (each class lasting 90 minutes) consider the following: Can the audience (e.g., teens vs. adults) remain focused for a full day? Is there enough time to engage in and process activities? If assignments between sessions are intended to reinforce teaching principles, how will changing the delivery design impact learning outcomes? Choose a curriculum that fits with program needs, or has been found to be successfully adapted to do so. Consult with the authors of the curriculum for their input and recommendations.

- *Cultural sensitivity*. Culture influences sex roles and expectations in relationships. As such, choose a curriculum that is sensitive to the cultural needs and diversity of program participants. If you are unable to identify a curriculum that is culturally specific to the audience, or to ensure that the selected curriculum is culturally appropriate, consult with potential participants to develop an awareness of how their culture influences relationship views and practices. Share materials from the curriculum with them for their input as to whether the curriculum is culturally appropriate.

- *Activity-driven*. Learning is done best when participants are given the opportunity to put into immediate practice the knowledge and skills they are learning. Activities in which participants are able to interactively discuss and practice their new skills have been shown to boost knowledge, self-awareness, skill-building, and values (Murrell, Webb, Harrison, & Rubio, 2013).

It can be difficult to find a curriculum that fits a program perfectly. Adaptations may be needed in order to best meet the needs of the intended audience. Strategies to successfully adapt curricula will be reviewed later in the chapter.

Identifying and training effective RME facilitators. In addition to identifying the right curriculum, the potential impact of your RME program will be influenced by the ability of the program facilitator(s) to teach the skills in an appropriate and influential way (Hughes, 1994). Facilitators are the face of the program and establish with the audience what the purpose of the program is and how it impacts participants. Therefore, take the time to identify effective facilitators who will engage and connect with the participants. Effective program facilitators must exhibit good interpersonal skills (e.g., ability to emotionally stimulate participants, engage participants one-on-one and in groups) and written and oral communication skills. They must be effective problem solvers and possess intrapersonal qualities (e.g., genuine caring attitude, professionalism, emotion stability, maturity, empathy, self-confidence, flexibility, respect, a sense of humor) that will enable them to work well with diverse individuals (Powell & Cassidy, 2007; Hawkins et al., 2004).

Similarity in the characteristics between the facilitator and audience is important. Below are some facilitator characteristics to consider:

- *Race/ethnicity.* When a program targets a specific racial or ethnic group, it may be wise for the facilitator(s) to be of the same racial or ethnic group of the audience. For more diverse groups, the race or ethnicity of the facilitator may not matter as much. However, it is important for the facilitator to be aware of the cultural values of all participants (Ooms & Wilson, 2004).
- *Sex.* Although lacking empirical support, family life scholars have suggested that having male–female facilitator dyads are ideal (Ooms & Wilson, 2004; Hawkins et al., 2004). However, in a study evaluating an RME program with stepfamilies, Higginbotham and Myler (2010) found that both male and female participants preferred a female facilitator over a male facilitator. Sex-match between facilitator and participants has been found to result in higher perceived facilitator quality, which predicts couple and individual functioning (Bradford, Adler-Baeder, Ketring, & Smith, 2012).
- *Life experiences.* It seems logical to believe that facilitators with similar life experiences to that of participants (e.g., age, cultural values, marital and/or parenting status) would be a better choice for programs geared toward a specific group (Ooms & Wilson, 2004). In fact, facilitators who have had similar life experiences to those of the audience members may also have increased credibility and may be seen as more empathetic, caring, and supportive (Adler-Baeder, Higginbotham, & Lamke, 2004; Bradford et al., 2012; Hawkins et al., 2004; Higginbotham & Myler, 2010). While sharing of experiences among program members is an important aspect of effective family life education, no program should be based on life experiences alone (Ballard & Taylor, 2012).

Although it may be useful for recruitment and retention purposes to match facilitators with participants based on demographic and life experiences, it may not always be possible to do so because of staff availability, scheduling issues, or hiring policies which forbid discrimination based on race, sex, age, and marital status (Higginbotham & Myler, 2010). While the above characteristics should be considered when identifying facilitators, it is more important that the quality of the facilitation, as opposed to physical or personal traits of the facilitator, be prioritized (Higginbotham & Myler, 2010). In fact, research has shown that facilitation and interpersonal skills are more strongly associated with participant satisfaction than facilitator traits (Ballard & Taylor, 2012; Cooney, Huser, Small, & O'Connor, 2007; Higginbotham & Myler, 2010).

While some individuals are naturally better facilitators, training is always important for the successful implementation of the program (Small, Cooney, & O'Connor, 2009). One of the key components of training is ensuring that facilitators understand the mission of the program and are able to consistently and accurately teach the curriculum. As well, training should also reinforce and/or enhance facilitators' teaching skills (e.g., classroom management, balancing lecture with discussion and activities, engaging participants in the learning process), interpersonal skills (e.g., speaking clearly, listening and paraphrasing, building rapport), and capacity to adapt (e.g., examples, scenarios, activities) in order to connect with the audience (Borkowski, Akai, & Smith, 2006; Small et al., 2009). While the physical or life characteristics of facilitators cannot be changed, facilitation skills can be taught and enhanced.

In summary, program inputs are the resources needed to launch and sustain a program. These resources may require funding or may be acquired through community partnerships. Additional inputs include establishing community collaborations, choosing an appropriate curriculum, and identifying and training facilitators. These inputs are essential to the success of RME programming and thoughtful attention should be given to identify inputs that best fulfill your program's goals and objectives.

Program Outputs

Outputs are defined as *what we do* or *what we offer* (Goldman & Schmalz, 2006; McCawley, 2001) and include activities, services, events, goods, and products for participants. Outputs also include workshops or classes, meetings, curricula, resources, training, and the people reached. In describing outputs specific to RME programs, Hawkins et al. (2004) outlined a comprehensive framework for RME that describes key elements of effective educational interventions that are relevant to our discussion of output here. As well, we also address issues related to recruitment and retention of program participants as an output.

Program content—What will be taught? It is important to clarify and delineate the program's outputs and how they link with the intended outcomes of the program (McCawley, 2001). As part of the process of defining the situation, a comprehensive review of the literature and thorough needs assessment aid in directing the content focus of the RME program and its match with program goals and objectives. Furthermore, this will ensure that the program is suitable to the targeted population by taking their unique developmental, social, and cultural needs and differences into account (Small et al., 2009). Also, as reinforced earlier, a curriculum should be grounded in research and teach principles and skills that have been proven to influence relationship quality and stability. Hawkins et al. (2004) described three essential sub-dimensions of RME program content:

- *Relational skills.* The quality of communication patterns, interaction processes, and conflict management behaviors is strongly related to the health of the relationship over time (Halford & Snyder, 2012; Markman & Rhoades, 2012).
- *Awareness, knowledge, and attitudes.* Even in the presence of healthy relational skills, it is important that partners have an understanding of how their knowledge and attitudes about each other as well as their context affect their relationship (Markman & Rhoades, 2012; Wadsworth & Markman, 2012).

- *Motivation/virtues.* Commitment, sacrifice, and forgiveness are individual qualities that increase motivation to remain in the relationship (Fincham, Stanley, & Beach, 2007).

Consistent with these three sub-dimensions, the National Extension Relationship and Marriage Education Network (www.nermen.org) outlines similar core principles and skills essential to healthy couple and marital relationships, and how they can be infused in RME programming (see Futris & Adler-Baeder, 2013).

PROGRAM FIDELITY AND ADAPTATION

Deviating from the original content and design of a curriculum may consequently yield a different (or no) impact on couples (O'Connor, Small, & Cooney, 2007). Still, while there is a need to maintain fidelity in a program, there may be times when adaptations are necessary in order to meet the needs of the target audience. In "finding the balance" between program fidelity and adaptation, Backer (2001) suggested the following steps:

- First the balance between fidelity and adaptation must be defined and then community issues assessed.
- Examine similar programs and determine any fidelity/adaptation issues along with their theoretical base, logic model, and program components.
- Consider available trainings for staff and how adaptation will be documented.
- Consult with other deciding members of the program and others in the community.

Effective program modification strategies should be empirically and theoretically informed and sensitive to the characteristics and needs of the targeted audience (Castro, Barrera, & Martinez, 2004). Conduct ongoing evaluations of fidelity and adaptation issues to determine what works best while helping you achieve program goals and objectives.

Intensity—What is the dosage? Adequate dosage is influential to achieving the goals and objectives of your RME program. The program must be long enough to teach enough material to create lasting change in the intended audience. However, if the program is too long, it can become too costly for the developer and too time-consuming for the participants (Hawkins, Stanley, Blanchard, & Albright, 2012).

- *Low-dosage* programs (e.g., media messages; 1–8 contact hours) require less time and cost, and may also attract participants who may be less inclined to participate in RME. They may not be sufficient to address more substantial issues, however, there is evidence that such programs can yield positive, yet modest, impacts (Futris, Barton, Aholou, & Seponski, 2011). For example, college students who completed a 1-hour computerized RME program displayed better outcomes in their dating relationships (Braithwaite & Fincham, 2009).

- *Moderate-dosage* programs (e.g., half-day seminars; 2-day weekend retreats; 9–20 contact hours) allow for the coverage of more content, albeit not comprehensive and intense in focus, while encouraging attendance due to reduced participant time commitment. Hawkins et al. (2012) report that this level of dosage may be associated with the strongest outcomes. For example, parents who attended a 12-hour program over 3 days reported less conflict and higher relationship functioning (Owen & Rhoades, 2012).

- *High-dosage* programs (e.g., 21+ contact hours; multisession series) may not yield outcomes that differ significantly from moderate-dosage programs. However, these programs have the potential to cover a broader array of content, provide more in-depth coverage of topics, and fully explore issues faced by the participants in the program, which may be ideal for at-risk couples (Hawkins et al., 2012). For instance, couples who completed an 8-session program reported more positive co-parenting, less maternal depression, and fewer problematic interactions with their children as compared with couples who did not complete the program (Feinberg & Kan, 2008).

Hawkins et al. (2004) recommend that RME programs vary dosage based on the intensity of the problems being addressed. If possible, offer programs that vary in dosage, and evaluate which dosage is cost-effective, produces greater participant attendance, and yields the greatest influence on achieving program goals and objectives.

Methods—How is it learned? Teaching process is as essential to achieving program goals and objectives as is the content. While considering program design, address the following two questions: (1) how will learning take place? and (2) how will learning be sustained? As previously noted, it is recommended that the facilitator(s) be well trained, flexible in their teaching approach, familiar with the topic and issues, and able to adapt the curriculum content to participants' needs and experiences. Ballard and Taylor (2012) describe three approaches, first introduced by Myers-Walls (2000), to effective facilitation:

- *Expert approach.* The educator functions as a vessel that contains knowledge and information to be imparted to the participants.
- *Collaborator approach.* The educator and the participants function as both teacher and learner by sharing information and personal perspectives.
- *Facilitator approach.* The needs and interests of the participants are what matter. The educator functions as a guide, directing participants through their desired learning.

Because facilitation is a fluid process, educators may apply different strategies at different times during the program to accommodate the various cognitive and experiential learning styles of the participants. Most curricula incorporate several different teaching methods in order to accommodate the diverse learning styles of the participants, but the degree to which they do so will vary. Integrating active learning strategies (e.g., interactive discussions, role-playing, videos, activities, games) will provide participants with the opportunity to practice what they have learned and yield more positive outcomes for participants (Antle et al., 2013; Ooms & Wilson, 2004). For example, an activity such as Think–Pair–Share promotes engagement and understanding by providing participants the opportunity to think about a problem on their own, work with their partner to solve it together, and then share their ideas with the whole group.

> Self-directed RME programs have been utilized as an alternative to in-class programming. In this method of training, the couple participates in the program from home, by working either from a book or an Internet website (see McAllister, Duncan, & Hawkins, 2012). These techniques have also been combined with more traditional classroom settings, with participants both attending classes and working together at home. *See chapter 20 for more information about web-based RME.*

In addition to creating an active learning environment that fosters immediate and positive outcomes, consideration should be given to outputs that may be required to maintain long-term program effects. Will completing the program be enough, or will more learning need to happen outside of the program or after program completion? For instance, some programs expect participants to complete and process assignments at home, either in a workbook or on the Internet (Halford, Petch, & Creedy, 2010). Some programs are also providing follow-up booster sessions which may promote higher program satisfaction and sustain the learning received during the program (Braukhaus, Hahlweg, Kroeger, Groth, & Fehm-Wolfsdorf, 2003; Vaterlaus, Allgood, & Higginbotham, 2012).

Timing—When to offer RME? According to Hawkins et al. (2004), "the more tailored educational offerings are to the temporal and life circumstances of their participants, the more likely they are to meet perceived needs. By extension, they also might attract more participants" (p. 47). As such, when establishing an RME program, consider the life course situation and needs of the targeted audience. See Table 3.2 for examples of life course changes and developmental needs to consider.

Recruitment and retention. A critical output related to program implementation is recruitment and retention efforts—even the most well thought out and executed program will fail if there are no participants. In addition to reaching the target audience at a time when they are most in need of, and thus receptive to,

TABLE 3.2 Examples of Life Course Changes and Developmental Needs and Their Application to RME

Life Course/Stage and Developmental Need	Application to RME
Youth. Young people begin learning about romantic relationships during adolescence as a part of identity development. At this point in time, they often have idealized beliefs about romance and love and often model relationship behaviors based on family members, peers, and social media influences (Kerpelman et al., 2010). Thus, adolescents need to learn how to identify positive and negative relationship behaviors.	RME for youth is aimed at influencing their beliefs and developing skills and understanding about relationships, including making smart relationship choices and differentiating between healthy and unhealthy relationships (Kerpelman et al., 2010). When engaging youth, hands-on engaging activities, multimedia, and social networking will help to make the content interesting and relevant. (*See chapter 16 for more suggestions for engaging youth.*)
Emerging adulthood. Emerging adults are especially teachable and open to learning about relationships. They have already begun or will shortly begin forming committed romantic relationships that can result in marriage, and may also be forming sexual or co-parenting relationships, with or without marriage. However, emerging adult relationships often exhibit harmful characteristics such as intimate partner violence and risky sexual situations, such as "hooking up" or "friends with benefits" (Fincham, Stanley, & Rhoades, 2011).	Programs for emerging adults have been successfully implemented in college environments (Fincham, Stanley, & Rhoades, 2011). RME for emerging adults would benefit from focusing on mindfulness in relationships, making conscious relationship choices (vs. "sliding"), and physical and emotional safety.
Premarital and early marital. Engaged and recently married couples tend to experience a "ceiling effect" or "honeymoon effect" in which they report very high levels of satisfaction in their relationship (Fawcett, Hawkins, Blanchard, & Carroll, 2010) which can make it difficult to see improvement during the course of a program. Thus, the need for these couples is to learn skills that will help them to maintain their relationship satisfaction over time.	Programs for couples who are engaged or newlyweds focus on the little issues that are common in newly formed marital relationships that can become big issues that damage the relationship later on. Programs should focus on fostering foundational relationship skills that will continue to serve the couple throughout their marriage and reinforcing the value of seeking out RME later in their marriage as a means to sustain their efforts and marital quality. (*See chapters 8–10 for assessing relationship topics for premarital couples to consider.*)

Life Course/Stage and Developmental Need	Application to RME
Parenting years. Research has shown that marital quality shifts at critical family transitions (e.g., birth of child, adolescents, empty nesting) due to the stress of demands and time constraints associated with parenting (Halford et al., 2010; Umberson, Pudrovska, & Reczek, 2010).	Tailor the RME program to the life stage of the parents. For instance, new parents will need specific information about caring for their young child while simultaneously caring for themselves and maintaining a focus on their relationship, whereas couples who have older children may need information on how to work together to attending to the needs of a busy family as well as extended family caregiving responsibilities.
Stepfamilies/remarried. Couples who come into a marriage having already been married or having had children from a previous relationship have unique challenges (e.g., competing family histories and traditions, ex-partner relations and co-parenting responsibilities, stepparenting concerns).	Couples with varying marital histories have been found to benefit from RME programs (Lucier-Greer, Adler-Baeder, Ketring, Harcourt, & Smith, 2012). Effective RME programs for these couples will combine typical relationship education content with content that addresses the distinct challenges associated with the repartnering status of the participants. (*See chapter 19 for more suggestions for engaging remarried couples and stepfamilies.*)
Cohabiting. Research has consistently demonstrated unique challenges that cohabitation poses on the health and stability of couple relationships (Jose, O'Leary, & Moyer, 2010), with recent research showing that the intention behind the couple's decision to cohabit as being influential to their relationship success or failure (Stanley, Rhoades, & Markman, 2006).	In order to best meet the needs of these couples, RME should focus on helping them process their choices (e.g., sliding versus deciding; Stanley et al., 2006) while also sharing information on marriage preparation (Hawkins et al., 2004).
Divorced/divorcing. Individuals who are going through divorce or have already divorced face many stressors, such as the experience of loss, navigation of changing roles and responsibilities, co-parenting challenges, and a multitude of emotions surrounding the divorce (Cohen & Finzi-Dottan, 2013).	Couples who have made the decision to separate or divorce may benefit from learning healthy relationship skills. These couples may have shared children and will need assistance with learning how to deal with each other in a positive way for the sake of their children, or they may desire to learn about healthy habits for use in future relationships (Hawkins et al., 2004).

(*Continued*)

TABLE 3.2 Continued

Life Course/Stage and Developmental Need	Application to RME
Same-sex couples. Research shows that same-sex relationships are influenced by the same set of factors as heterosexual relationships (Kurdek, 2005), but may face more stressful circumstances outside of their relationship (societal, legal, personal) that can affect relationship stability (Whitton & Buzzella, 2012).	The core relationship skills that are typically taught in RME are appropriate for use with same-sex couples, but the terminology (e.g., *husbands, wives,* or *marriage* need to be changed to *partners* or *relationships*) and supplemental teaching resources (e.g., video or pictorial examples) need to be adapted in order to engage this audience effectively (Whitton & Buzzella, 2012). (*See chapter 17 for more suggestions for engaging same-sex couples.*)

the information, below are a few strategies to help demonstrate to participants the value and usefulness of the program (Cooney, Small, & O'Connor, 2007; Small et al., 2009):

- *Engage the community.* Potential participants may be more likely to be involved if recruited by someone familiar to them or that they trust. Invite members of the targeted population as well as local agencies, businesses, and institutions (e.g., hospitals, schools) to help with recruiting.
- *Make it a family affair.* Involve extended family members or other support networks when possible, and make adjustments to the program to meet basic needs (e.g., child care, food, transportation). Be flexible in scheduling to accommodate competing family demands. Also, as noted above, ensure that program activities and content reflect the characteristics and developmental needs of the participants.
- *Active staff makes a difference.* Establishing trust and rapport with the target audience takes time. As such, maintain continuity in facilitators and other staff for the duration of the program as well as regular contact (e.g., in person, by phone, text, e-mail) with participants.

Program Outcomes

In contrast to outputs which focus on what was done (*activities*) and who was reached (*participants*), outcomes focus on the direct results or benefits for participants and the community and answer "What happened as a result of the program?" (McCawley, 2001). These include short-term (e.g., an increase in awareness, skills, or knowledge; change in attitudes, opinions, aspirations, and motivations), intermediate (e.g., changes in behavior, practice, action, decision making, or policies), and long-term (e.g., change in community and environmental conditions) results. Outcomes should be measurable, and an evaluation plan should identify appropriate desired outcomes at all three time points (McCawley, 2001). Examples are provided in Table 3.3, and additional information is shared in chapter 5 regarding prior RME program evaluation efforts and findings.

TABLE 3.3 Examples of RME Program Outcomes and Indicators

Example Goals and Outcomes	Sample Indicators
Couples manage conflict effectively	
Short-term: Couples are aware of soft, start-up strategies.	List three examples of soft, start-ups.
Intermediate: Couples apply soft, start-ups when conflicts arise.	During the past week, how often did your partner share concerns in a calm, respectful tone? (1) never, (2) rarely, (3) sometimes, (4) often, (5) always.
Long-term: Reduce risk of intimate partner violence.	In the last month, how often were you afraid that your partner would hit you? (1) never, (2) sometimes, (3) often.
Demonstrate stronger marital commitment	
Short-term: Couples commit to making the relationship a priority.	I will not let other things get in the way of me spending time with my partner. (1) strongly disagree, (2) disagree, (3) agree, (4) strongly agree.
Intermediate: Couples protect their time from outside influences.	During the past week, how often did distractions—like work, friends, children, or hobbies—interfere with your time together? (1) never, (2) rarely, (3) sometimes, (4) often.
Long-term: Increase marital stability.	I want this marriage to last. (1) strongly disagree, (2) disagree, (3) neither agree nor disagree, (4) agree, (5) strongly agree.
Maintain greater intimate knowledge	
Short-term: Couples feel more comfortable with self-disclosure.	I feel comfortable opening up to my partner about my personal needs, feelings, desires, and life events. (1) strongly disagree, (2) disagree, (3) neither agree nor disagree, (4) agree, (5) strongly agree.
Intermediate: Couples report greater self-disclosure.	During the past month, how often did your partner share with you his/her personal needs, feelings, desires, and life events? (1) never, (2) rarely, (3) sometimes, (4) often.
Intermediate: Couples feel supportive of each other.	My partner understands and supports me. (1) never, (2) rarely, (3) sometimes, (4) often, (5) always.

Note: Outcomes are based on the *Choose, Know,* and *Manage* principles of healthy relationships described in the National Extension Relationship and Marriage Education Model (Futris & Adler-Baeder, 2013).

When defining the situation and during program development, establish ways to measure and document whether the program achieved the desired goals and objectives. Demonstrating the difference your program makes on participants, and sharing that information with the community, participants, and supporters (e.g., collaborators, funders) can help with sustaining both public and financial support of RME efforts (Small et al., 2009). It is important that leadership, staff, volunteers, and facilitators understand the importance of evaluation and that they are committed to the evaluation process (Nation et al., 2003; Weissberg, Kumpfer, & Seligman, 2003). The evaluation process involves documenting not just participant information and attendance (*outputs*) but also reflecting on the inputs invested in the program (e.g., partners, curriculum, setting, staff) to determine what is working and what may require change (*formative* **evaluation**) as well as collecting feedback from participants to assess the worth of the program (*summative* **evaluation**). Program evaluation is an ongoing process that is initiated during the planning stages of the program and continues throughout and following implementation (Jacobs, 1988).

FORMATIVE VERSUS SUMMATIVE EVALUATION

A *formative* evaluation is an evaluation of the program process, and asks: *How did it go? How did the classes go? Why did the participants choose to participate? How did the facilitators do? If adaptations were made, how well were they received?* The information received in a formative evaluation can be used for future programs to determine what worked and what did not work. In contrast, a *summative* evaluation focuses on the impact of the program on the participants. Various indicators reflecting program goals and objectives are documented to determine whether or not the program really did make the difference you intended.

Importantly, establishing the worth of a program involves more than merely assessing participant satisfaction with the program—it requires measuring the direct impact the program had on participants' relationship and family health. Thorough documentation is vital to understanding not only how the program was carried out, but the impact of the program on the participants and the community (Small et al., 2009). A logic model is useful in determining what to evaluate, outcome indicators, and how and when to collect the necessary information, or data (McCawley, 2001).

Evaluation by design. There are various types of evaluation strategies that can be employed to document changes in desired outcomes. Here are a few examples:

- A *true pre-post design* measures indicators before the participant joins in the program or class and re-measures the indicators after the participant has finished the program. This is generally used to measure the impact of the program on the individual. This evaluation design does take some pre-planning and preparation on the part of the leadership and staff to find a way to measure indicators prior to the participant coming to the program.

- In a *retrospective pre-post design*, the participants complete a pre- and post-survey at once, after the program is complete. In other words, the participants are asked to reflect on indicators at the conclusion of the program and then compare what they know, think, or feel to how they did so before the start of the program. Although many would believe that this does not capture true pre-program indicators, for a low-dosage program (e.g., one class), this approach may be more practical in terms of cost and participants' time. Additionally, participants are more aware of their true knowledge and skills prior to the program after developing the knowledge and skills during the program (Nielsen, 2011).

- *Pre-, retrospective pre-, and post- design.* In this design, participants take a true pre-survey before the beginning of the program measuring indicators, a retrospective pre-survey, and a post-survey. This type of design may control for participants' perspectives prior to the program (Rockwell & Kohn, 1989). For example, a husband may believe before the program that he has the skills to communicate well with his wife, but after participating in the program and learning proper communication skills may realize that he really did not have the skills that he thought he did prior to participation. This approach may capture a more accurate change in knowledge, skills, attitudes, and behaviors.

Choosing or creating the right evaluation design for an RME program is an often-overlooked aspect of program development. Some curricula include evaluation tools; if not available, consult with the authors to inquire what they (or others) have used to document impact. Also, consider whether information should be collected in print or online, and at home or on-site; the number of and type of questions necessary to accurately capture outcome indicators; whether observational data may help confirm participants' ability to exhibit the skills learned; and, how soon after the program should data be collected in order to observe changes over time. Thus, give attention to an evaluation plan when designing an RME program that yields data demonstrative of program achievements and worth.

Clarifying Assumptions and External Factors

Program design would not be complete without acknowledging the internal and external factors that can influence program implementation and success. This involves clarifying the assumptions, or beliefs, about the program, targeted audience, and how the program will work. Illustrated separately in the logic model (see Figure 3.1), assumptions take into account the educators' personal and professional experiences and preconceived notions about what may work and not work as well as the research conducted to define the situation, identify important inputs, and establish relevant outputs. Thus, this is an opportunity for developers and educators to confront personal biases and beliefs that may compromise the program's success. *Faulty assumptions are often the reason for poor results* (Taylor-Powell et al., 2003).

Participants typically come into the RME program with previously formed opinions, beliefs, worldviews, and expectations. For a program to meet the needs of the targeted audience, take into account the external factors that affect how the program is experienced by the participants and whether or not they practice what they learn. Failing to take into consideration barriers to attendance as well as participant and community characteristics that influence relationship outcomes and proceeding with a program in a "one-size-fits-all" manner could lead to reduced program participation and impact. When economically feasible and practical, collect information on these external factors in order to assess if and how they actually did influence differences in program outcomes.

Conclusion

Much thought and planning needs to go into the development of an RME program. A logic model is a useful tool that can systematically outline the linkages between the purpose of the program, what the program entails, who the program reaches, and what the program is expected to achieve. Existing research, theory, and input from the community and potential participants are essential resources used to inform program content and methods. Importantly, the program design should always have the ultimate goal and objective in mind. In other words, "How does each aspect of the program logic model relate to the situation the program is trying to change—the long-term outcome?" As such, after defining the situation, consider developing the logic model from right-to-left, focusing on the short-term and intermediate outcomes necessary to achieve the long-term outcomes, followed by "what you do" and "who you reach" (the *outputs*) to meet the short-term outcomes, and concluding with "what you need" (the *inputs*) in order to implement the program outputs.

Key Points

- A critical first step in program design involves understanding the *situation* that is driving the need for RME programming.
- The successful launch and sustainability of an RME program depends on the availability, selection, and utilization of relevant and influential resources, or *inputs*.
- The activities, services, products, and audience of an RME program, also referred to as *outputs*, should be clearly linked to the need and intended outcomes of the program.
- Outcomes should be measurable and clearly reflect the RME program's direct short-term and intermediate impact on participants as well as long-term results that demonstrate change in the situation.

- Clearly identify assumptions and external factors that could influence the successful implementation of the RME program and the program's capacity to demonstrate impact.

Discussion Questions

1. How would using a right-to-left approach to logic model development be beneficial for program design?
2. What is the purpose of establishing a situation statement during the program development process?
3. How can a needs assessment inform program development? Whose needs should be considered when conducting a needs assessment?
4. What is a *SMART* objective? Give an example.
5. How are program outputs different from program outcomes?
6. What is the difference between a short-term, intermediate, and long-term outcome? Give an example of each.
7. What are program inputs and how do they contribute to program success?
8. Identify and describe three things to consider when establishing community collaborations.
9. What are important qualities and characteristics to look for in a successful program facilitator?
10. Explain the three approaches to effective facilitation and describe pros and cons for each.
11. Why is it important to spend time on strategies for recruitment and retention of participants?
12. How do internal and external factors influence program implementation and success? Give examples of each and how they may influence the implementation of relationship and marriage education.

References and Further Readings

Adler-Baeder, F., Higginbotham, B., & Lamke, L. (2004). Putting empirical knowledge to work: Linking research and programming on marital quality. *Family Relations, 53,* 537–546. doi:10.1111/j.0197-6664.2004.00063.x

Altschuld, J., & Kumar, D. (2010). *Needs assessment: An overview.* Thousand Oaks, CA: Sage Publications.

Antle, B., Sar, B., Christensen, D., Ellers, F., Barbee, A., & van Zyl, M. (2013). The impact of the Within My Reach relationship training on relationship skills and outcomes for low-income individuals. *Journal of Marital and Family Therapy, 39,* 346–357.

Backer, T. (2001). *Finding the balance—Program fidelity and adaptation in substance abuse prevention: A state-of-the-art review.* Rockville, MD: Center for Substance Abuse Prevention.

Ballard, S., & Morris, M. (2005). Factors influencing midlife and older adults' attendance in family life education programs. *Family Relations, 54,* 461–472. doi:10.1111/j.1741-3729.2005.00331.x

Ballard, S., & Taylor, A. (2012). *Family life education with diverse populations.* Thousand Oaks, CA: Sage Publications.

Bandura, A. (1977). *Social learning theory.* Englewood Cliffs, NJ: Prentice Hall.

Bengtson, V., & Allen, K. (1993). The life course perspective applied to families over time. In P. Boss, W. Doherty, R. LaRossa, W. Schumm, & S. Steinmetz (Eds.), *Sourcebook of family theories and methods: A contextual approach* (pp. 469–499). New York, NY: Plenum Press.

Blanchard, V., Hawkins, A., Baldwin, S., & Fawcett, E. (2009). Investigating the effects of marriage and relationship education on couples' communication skills: A meta-analytic study. *Journal of Family Psychology, 23*, 203–214.

Bogenschneider, K. (1996). An ecological risk/protective theory for building prevention programs, policies, and community capacity to support youth. *Family Relations, 45*, 127–138.

Borkowski, J., Akai, C., & Smith, E. (2006). The art and science of prevention research: Principles of effective programs. In J. Borkowski & C. Weaver (Eds.), *Prevention: The science and art of promoting healthy child and adolescent development* (pp. 1–16). Baltimore, MD: Brookes Publishing.

Bradbury, T., & Fincham, F. (1990). Attributions in marriage: Review and critique. *Psychological Bulletin, 107*, 3–33.

Bradford, A., Adler-Baeder, F., Ketring, S., & Smith, T. (2012). The role of participant facilitator demographic match in couple and relationship education. *Family Relations, 61*, 51–64.

Braithwaite, S., & Fincham, F. (2009). A randomized clinical trial of a computer based preventive intervention: Replication and extension of ePREP. *Journal of Family Psychology, 23*, 32–38.

Braukhaus, C., Hahlweg, K., Kroeger, C., Groth, T., & Fehm-Wolfsdorf, G. (2003). The effects of adding booster sessions to a prevention training program for committed couples. *Behavioral and Cognitive Psychotherapy, 31*, 325–336.

Bronfenbrenner, U. (1979). *The ecology of human development: Experiments by nature and design.* Cambridge, MA: Harvard University Press.

Castro, F., Barrera, M., & Martinez, C. (2004). The cultural adaptation of prevention interventions: Resolving tension between fidelity and fit. *Prevention Science, 5*, 41–45.

Cohen, O., & Finzi-Dottan, R. (2013). Defense mechanisms and negotiation as predictors of co-parenting among divorcing couples: A dyadic perspective. *Journal of Social and Personal Relationships, 30*, 430–456.

Cooney, S., Huser, M., Small, S., & O'Connor, C. (2007). Evidence-based programs: An overview. *What Works, Wisconsin Research to Practice Series*, Issue #6. Madison: University of Wisconsin-Madison Extension. Retrieved from http://whatworks.uwex.edu/Pages/1researchbriefs.html

Cooney, S., Small, S., & O'Connor, C. (2007). Strategies for recruiting and retaining participants in prevention programs. *What Works, Wisconsin Research to Practice Series*, Issue #2. Madison, WI: University of Wisconsin-Madison Extension. Retrieved from http://whatworks.uwex.edu/Pages/1researchbriefs.html

Duncan, S., & Goddard, H. (2011). *Family life education: Principles and practices for effective outreach* (2nd ed.). Thousand Oaks, CA: Sage Publications.

Fawcett, E., Hawkins, A., Blanchard, V., & Carroll, J. (2010). Do premarital education programs really work? A meta-analytic study. *Family Relations, 59*, 232–239.

Feinberg, M., & Kan, M. (2008). Establishing family foundations: Intervention effects on coparenting, parent/infant well-being, and parent-child relations. *Journal of Family Psychology, 22*, 253–263.

Fincham, F., Stanley, S., & Beach, S. (2007). Transformative processes in marriage: An analysis of emerging trends. *Journal of Marriage and Family, 69*, 275–292.

Fincham, F.D., Stanley, S.M., & Rhoades, G.K. (2011). Relationship education in emerging adulthood: Problems and prospects. In F. Fincham & M. Cui (Eds.), *Romantic relationships in emerging adulthood* (pp. 293–316). New York, NY: Cambridge University Press.

Fox, G., & Murry, V. (2000). Gender and families: Feminist perspectives and family research. *Journal of Marriage and Family, 62,* 1160–1172. doi:10.1111/j.1741-3737.2000.01160.x

Futris, T. (2007). Building community collaborations to support healthy and stable marriages. In T. Futris (Ed.), *Cultivating healthy couple and marital relationships: A guide to effective programming* (pp. 65–74). Athens, GA: The University of Georgia Cooperative Extension. Retrieved from www.nermen.org/programresources.php

Futris, T., & Adler-Baeder, F. (Eds.). (2013). *The National Extension Relationship and Marriage Education Model: Core teaching concepts for relationship and marriage enrichment Programming.* (Publication No. HDFS-E-157). Athens, GA: The University of Georgia Cooperative Extension. Retrieved from www.nermen.org/NERMEM.php

Futris, T., Barton, A., Aholou, T., & Seponski, D. (2011). The impact of PREPARE on engaged couples: Variations by delivery format. *Journal of Couple and Relationship Therapy, 10,* 69–86.

Goldman, K., & Schmalz, K. (2006). Logic models: The picture worth ten thousand words. *Health Promotion Practice, 7,* 8–12.

Halford, W., Petch, J., & Creedy, D. (2010). Promoting a positive transition to parenthood. A randomized clinical trial of couple relationship education. *Prevention Science, 11,* 89–100.

Halford, W., & Snyder, D. (2012). Universal processes and common factors in couple therapy and relationship education. *Behavior Therapy, 43,* 1–12.

Hawkins, A., Blanchard, V., Baldwin, S., & Fawcett, E. (2008). Does marriage and relationship education work? A meta-analytic study. *Journal of Consulting and Clinical Psychology, 76,* 723–734.

Hawkins, A., Carroll, J., Doherty, W., & Willoughby, B. (2004). A comprehensive framework for marriage education. *Family Relations, 53,* 547–558.

Hawkins, A., & Fackrell, T. (2010). Does couple education for low-income couples work? A meta-analytic study of emerging research. *Journal of Couple and Relationship Therapy, 9,* 181–191.

Hawkins, A., Stanley, S., Blanchard, V., & Albright, M. (2012). Exploring programmatic moderators of the effectiveness of marriage and relationship education programs: A meta-analytic study. *Behavior Therapy, 43,* 77–87.

Higginbotham, B., & Myler, C. (2010). The influence of facilitator and facilitation characteristics on participants' ratings of stepfamily education. *Family Relations, 59,* 74–86. doi:10.1111/j.1741-3729.2009.00587.x

Hughes, R. (1994). A framework for developing family life education programs. *Family Relations, 43,* 74–80.

Jacobs, F. (1988). The five-tiered approach to evaluation: Context and implementation. In H. Weiss & F. Jacobs (Eds.), *Evaluating family programs* (pp. 37–68). New York, NY: Aldine deGruyter.

Jose, A., O'Leary, K., & Moyer, A. (2010). Does premarital cohabitation predict subsequent marital stability and marital quality? A meta-analysis. *Journal of Marriage and Family, 72,* 105–116. doi:10.1111/j.1741-3737.2009.00686.x

Kerpelman, J., Pittman, J., Adler-Baeder, F., Stringer, K., Eryigit, S., Cadely, H., & Harrell-Levy, M. (2010). What adolescents bring to and learn from relationship education classes: Does social address matter? *Journal of Couple and Relationship Therapy, 9,* 95–112.

Kurdek, L. (2005). What do we know about gay and lesbian couples? *Current Directions in Psychological Science, 14,* 251–254.

Lucier-Greer, M., Adler-Baeder, F., Ketring, S., Harcourt, K., & Smith, T. (2012). Comparing the experiences of couples in first marriages and remarriages in couple and relationship education. *Journal of Divorce and Remarriage, 53,* 55–75.

Mancini, J., Bowen, G., & Martin, J. (2005). Community social organization: A conceptual linchpin in examining families in the context of communities. *Family Relations, 54,* 570–582.

Markman, H., & Rhoades, G. (2012). Relationship education research: Current status and future directions. *Journal of Marital and Family Therapy, 38,* 169–200.

McAllister, S., Duncan, S., & Hawkins, A. (2012). Examining the early evidence for self-directed Marriage and Relationship Education: A meta-analytic study. *Family Relations, 61,* 742–755.

McCawley, P. (2001). *The logic model for program planning and evaluation.* Moscow, ID: University of Idaho Extension. Retrieved from http://www.uidaho.edu/extension/LogicModel.pdf

Murrell, S., Webb, J., Harrison, C., & Rubio, L. (2013). *Marriage and Relationship Education (MRE) program development and management manual.* National Healthy Marriage Resource Center. Washington, DC: U.S. Department of Health and Human Services, Administration for Children and Families, Office of Family Assistance.

Myers-Walls, J. (2000). Family diversity and family life education. In D. Demo, K. Allen, & M. Fine (Eds.), *Handbook of family diversity* (pp. 359–379). New York, NY: Oxford University Press.

Nation, M., Crusto, C., Wandersman, A., Kumpfer, K., Seybolt, D., & Morrissey-Kane, E. (2003). What works in prevention: Principles of effective prevention programs. *American Psychologist, 58,* 449–456.

National Council on Family Relations. (2011). *Certified family life education employer work experience assessment and validation form.* Retrieved from http://www.ncfr.org/sites/default/files/downloads/news/Employer_Assessment_and_Verification_Form_2011.pdf

Nielsen, R. (2011). A retrospective pretest-posttest evaluation of a one-time personal finance training. *Journal of Extension, 49*(1), Article 1FEA4. Retrieved from http://www.joe.org/joe/2011february/a4.php

O'Connor, C., Small, S., & Cooney, S. (2007). Program fidelity and adaptation: Meeting local needs without compromising program effectiveness. *What Works, Wisconsin Research to Practice Series,* Issue #4. Madison: University of Wisconsin-Madison Extension. Retrieved from http://whatworks.uwex.edu/Pages/1researchbriefs.html

Ooms, T., & Wilson, P. (2004). The challenges of offering relationship and marriage education to low-income populations. *Family Relations, 53,* 440–447.

Owen, J., & Rhoades, G. (2012). Reducing interparental conflict among parents in contentious child custody disputes: An initial investigation of the Working Together Program. *Journal of Marital and Family Therapy, 38,* 542–555.

Powell, L., & Cassidy, D. (2007). *Family life education: Working with families across the life span* (2nd ed.). Long Grove, IL: Waveland Press.

Rockwell, S., & Kohn, H. (1989). Post-then-pre evaluation. *Journal of Extension, 27*(2), Article 2FEA5. Retrieved from http://www.joe.org/joe/1989summer/a5.php

Saxbe, D., Rodriguez, A., & Margolin, G. (2013). Understanding family conflict: Theoretical frameworks and directions for future research. In M. Fine & F. Fincham (Eds.), *Handbook of family theories: A content-based approach* (pp. 169–189). New York, NY: Routledge Press.

Small, S., Cooney, S., & O'Connor, C. (2009). Evidence-informed program improvement: Using principles of effectiveness to enhance the quality and impact of family-based prevention programs. *Family Relations, 58,* 1–13. doi:10.1111/j.1741-3729.2008.00530.x

Stanley, S., & Markman, H. (1992). Assessing commitment in personal relationships. *Journal of Marriage and the Family, 54,* 595–608.

Stanley, S., Rhoades, G., & Markman, H. (2006). Sliding versus deciding: Inertia and the premarital cohabitation effect. *Family Relations, 55,* 499–509.

Taylor-Powell, E., Jones, L., & Henert, E. (2003). *Enhancing program performance with logic models.* Retrieved from http://www.uwex.edu/ces/lmcourse/

Thibaut, N., & Kelley, H. (1959). *The social psychology of groups.* New York, NY: Wiley.

Umberson, D., Pudrovska, T., & Reczek, C. (2010). Parenthood, childlessness, and well-being: A life course perspective. *Journal of Marriage and Family, 72,* 612–629. doi:10.1111/j.1741-3737.2010.00721.x

Vaterlaus, J., Allgood, S., & Higginbotham, B. (2012). Stepfamily education booster sessions. *Social Work with Groups, 35,* 150–163.

Wadsworth, M., & Markman, H. (2012). Where's the action: Understanding what works and why in relationship education. *Behavior Therapy, 43,* 99–112.

Weissberg, R., Kumpfer, K., & Seligman, M. (2003). Prevention that works for children and youth. *American Psychologist, 58,* 425–432.

Whitchurch, G., & Constantino, L. (1993). Systems theory. In P. Boss, W. Doherty, R. LaRossa, W. Schumm, & S. Steinmetz (Eds.), *Sourcebook of family theories and methods: A contextual approach* (pp. 325–352). New York, NY: Plenum Press.

Whitton, S., & Buzzella, B. (2012). Using relationship education programs with same-sex couples: A preliminary evaluation of program utility and needed modifications. *Marriage and Family Review, 48,* 667–688. doi:10.1080/01494929.2012.700908

Wiley, A., & Ebata, A. (2004). Reaching American families: Making diversity real in family life education. *Family Relations, 53,* 273–281. doi:10.1111/j.0022-2445.2004.0003.x

4

DOES IT WORK? EFFECTIVENESS RESEARCH ON RELATIONSHIP AND MARRIAGE EDUCATION

Alan J. Hawkins

LEARNING GOALS

- Learn about the diversity of RME programs available to help individuals and couples at different points in the life span, different circumstances, and targeted to different demographic groups.
- Learn about the substantial evaluation work documenting the effectiveness of RME programs.
- Learn about the need for more research:
  - the effectiveness of programs targeted to less educated and lower-income couples
  - the mechanisms of change in RME programs that create positive change
- Learn about the need for more efficient delivery of RME services:
  - naturalistic micro-interventions
  - narrowcast interventions
  - regular relationship check-ups

Introduction

It is challenging in contemporary societies to form and sustain healthy relationships and enduring marriages, especially for more disadvantaged populations (Cherlin, 2009; Kennedy & Ruggles, 2014). Yet a large body of research has identified knowledge, attitudes, motivations, behaviors, and circumstances that support the formation and maintenance of healthy, enduring relationships (Bradbury & Karney, 2012). Translating this knowledge into helpful educational interventions is the goal of **relationship and marriage education**, or **RME** (Halford, 2011). Documenting the effectiveness of RME is crucial to beneficial programming efforts.

RME evaluation research is needed for at least two reasons. First, public and private institutions that support RME services with scarce funding are demanding accountability. In order to compete with other service demands for these scarce funds, RME programs must provide evidence of effectiveness. This is especially the case now that government agencies are investing public funds to assess whether RME services can strengthen relationships and reduce relationship instability (Hawkins & VanDenBerghe, 2014). Just as important, however, RME evaluation is needed by practitioners to identify who benefits most from interventions and what aspects of programs produce positive change (active ingredients), so that interventions can be targeted, modified, and fine-tuned to be more effective (Markman & Rhoades, 2012). Of course, valuable effectiveness research is not easy; it requires complex decision making, attention to detail, and is a long-term process, not a one-shot project. Accordingly, sound evaluation research takes significant training, experience, and of course, time and resources.

The Evidence Base for Relationship and Marriage Education

Fortunately, there is an impressive body of evaluation research assessing the effectiveness of RME, including specific RME programs (now approaching 300 studies) as well as about a dozen meta-analytic studies and other reports that assess the general (non–program-specific) effectiveness of RME. In this review, general effectiveness studies are highlighted; other chapters in this volume highlight research on specific programs. However, specific program evaluation studies are discussed where appropriate and illuminating. While some RME programs are promoted as universal interventions to strengthen relationships regardless of circumstances, often programs target specific populations, including age and family life course groups (e.g., youth, engaged couples, new parents, remarried couples), diverse families (e.g., racial/ethnic groups, same-sex couples), and families in challenging circumstances (e.g., low-income families, incarcerated spouses). RME effectiveness research has advanced over the past decade to match some of the diversity of family and relationship circumstances. The research in these different categories is briefly reviewed, and finally, some brief thoughts about the challenges facing RME and effectiveness research over the next decade are offered.

RME Effectiveness Research for Age and Family Life Course Groups

Relationship literacy education for youth and young adults. Youth **relationship literacy education (RLE)** targets youth and young adults to help them gain basic relationship literacy, relationship skills, and make sound decisions (and avoid unhealthy ones) about close relationships. The goal is to help them establish healthy relationships and avoid harmful relationships. RLE is directed to individuals rather than couples, although participants often are in relationships. It is the least developed and least researched area in the RME field. This is unfortunate, because long before young people are thinking seriously about marriage, they are making important close relationship decisions and transitions, many of them without forethought (Rhoades & Stanley, 2014). Nearly half of young adults ages 18–25 are cohabiting or seriously dating (Scott, Steward-Streng, Manlove, Schelar, & Cui, 2011). And more than 40% of young adult romantic relationships involve some kind of physical relationship violence (Berger, Wildsmith, Manlove, & Steward-Streng, 2012).

The most rigorous youth RLE outcome research to date has been conducted by Kerpelman and her colleagues (Kerpelman, Pittman, Adler-Baeder, Eryigit, & Paulk, 2009; Kerpelman et al., 2010). They analyzed data collected from more than 1,400 economically and racially diverse high school students in 39 public schools across Alabama. Health classes were randomly assigned to either receive the *Relationship Smarts Plus* (*RS+*) curriculum (treatment group) or not (treatment-as-usual control group). Results at 1 year after the program showed that students in the *RS+* health classes decreased more in their faulty belief that "love is enough" and increased more in their conflict-management skills compared to students in the **control-group** classes. Moreover, improvements in faulty beliefs were found regardless of race/ethnicity, family income, and family structure. Improvements for conflict-management skills were found for students in less advantaged groups, but not the more advantaged groups. In another report using this same sample of youth, researchers found that students who took the *RS+* program increased their disapproval of using aggression in dating relationships and, more important, that these attitudes were related to less use of physical aggression in their dating relationships 2 years later (Kerpelman, 2012). This is an encouraging finding.

Of course, how these initial lessons translate into adult relationship choices and behaviors is still unknown. Much more research—including more rigorous research and studies that can illuminate the mechanisms and processes that produce positive program effects—is needed. Also, there is little solid research yet on RLE programs targeting young adults (e.g., *How to Avoid Falling for a Jerk or Jerkette*). Nevertheless, early studies suggest that youth RLE programs may be able to help some adolescents gain valuable skills and knowledge that would help them stay on a better path to healthy and safe relationships in young adulthood.

Relationship development education for cohabiting couples. **Relationship development education (RDE)** for young, unmarried couples (usually parents) is an emerging, important area of the RME field, due to increasing rates of nonmarital cohabitation and childbearing (Rhoades, Stanley, & Markman, 2009). Many of these couples are in fragile relationships that have formed quickly due to an unintended pregnancy. Yet most of them have hopes for building a stable and satisfying relationship for the benefit of their children (McLanahan & Beck, 2010). Like youth RLE, RDE involves some basic relationship literacy education to help individuals make wise decisions about the potential and future of the current relationship; it does not assume that there is a strong commitment to each other or to an ongoing relationship, even when there is hope for that. Relationship violence is an important topic in RDE. For those who desire to strengthen the relationship, RDE provides knowledge and skills to help them do so, usually with a strong emphasis on positive communication and effective problem solving. Often the programs include infant care and parenting skills, as well as effective **coparenting** strategies.

The volume of studies in this latest area of the field is small and inconsistent. But there is one large and rigorous (**randomized controlled trial**) study of RDE that deserves attention here. The *Building Strong Families (BSF)* study evaluated the short- and long-term outcomes of 30–40 hours of education (and support services) for lower-income, unmarried parents in eight sites across the United States using diverse curricula (Wood, Moore, Clarkwest, & Killewald, 2014). At three years after enrolling in the program, researchers found few positive outcomes of the interventions and a few negative outcomes. But participation (as opposed to enrollment) in the programs was low; only 60% of couples attended one session and only 10% received a strong dosage. The site with the highest level of participant engagement showed a positive effect on couple relationship stability. Also, a re-analysis of the short-term effects for *BSF* found a range of small but positive effects for the most disadvantaged couples in the study (Amato, 2014).

Like RLE for youth, much more work is needed to develop RDE programs, evaluate their effectiveness, and identify underlying mechanisms and moderators of change. Particularly because these programs are being used experimentally as social policy to increase family stability and reduce poverty, we need stronger evidence of their potential.

Marriage preparation education for engaged couples. There is great deal of **marriage preparation education (MPE)** for engaged couples, often provided by religious organizations, and a commensurate body of evaluation research. In the context of a couple committed to marriage, the goals of MPE are to help individuals asses their readiness for marriage, evaluate the quality of the match, align expectations and plans, and strengthen relationship skills for a stronger foundation on which to build a healthy, enduring marriage. While many think of engaged couples as having stars in their eyes, confidence in forever, and no significant problems, research paints a more complex portrait. Many couples enter into marriage with significant relationship problems, doubts, and ambiguous commitment, and these couples face greater risk for divorce (Lavner, Bradbury, & Karney, 2012; Lavner, Karney, & Bradbury, 2012).

Surveys using correlational methods have pointed at the potential positive effects of MPE (Stanley, Amato, Johnson, & Markman, 2006), especially for those at greater risk for divorce (Nock, Sanchez, & Wright, 2008). A recent study followed a large national sample of unmarried young adults over five years (Rhoades & Stanley, 2014). About 40% of those who married during that period reported that they invested in some kind of marriage preparation education (or MPE). Fifty-seven percent of those who invested in MPE had marital quality in the top 40% of the sample distribution, while only a third of those who did not participate in MPE scored in the top 40% of the marital quality distribution. A **meta-analytic study** that identified nearly 50 MPE evaluation studies with well-educated, middle-class samples (Fawcett, Hawkins, Blanchard, & Carroll, 2010) found positive effects for improving communication skills, effects that were stronger when researchers invested in observational measures of communication rather than relying on self-reports. The effect of MPE on overall relationship satisfaction is questionable, however, perhaps because improving relationship quality may bump up against a ceiling effect with happy engaged couples.

Despite a substantial body of research on MPE there are holes and weaknesses in this work. More research is needed on whether MPE can help couples at high risk for divorce change their trajectory of marital success (or change their plans for marriage altogether). Also, few studies to date have evaluated MPE programs targeted to lower-income and less-educated engaged couples, who are at higher risk for relationship problems. Moreover, these couples appear less likely to participate in marriage preparation education. In the Rhoades and Stanley (2014) study cited earlier, the researchers found that those with more demographic risk factors for lower marital quality were the least likely to participate in MPE. In addition, more research is needed to establish the long-term effects of MPE. One classic study (Markman, Renick, Floyd, Stanley, & Clements, 1993) found positive communication effects five years after participating in MPE for treatment-group couples. But more research is needed.

Marriage maintenance education for married couples. High divorce rates for first marriages (and even higher rates for second marriages) suggest the need for ongoing maintenance of marital relationships, or what may be called **marriage maintenance education (MME)**. Some marriages begin on a foundation with cracks already showing, while serious problems emerge over time for others. Marriages are complex systems subject to the same forces of entropy as physical and biological systems. Without ongoing inputs of energy into the relationship, marital systems will naturally tend towards chaos and disintegration. MME is designed to support couples' efforts to maintain and strengthen their relationships. There is a great deal of MME offered by religious and educational institutions, as well as the military, workplaces, healthcare systems, and human service agencies.

Most RME evaluation research has been done on programs targeted primarily to married couples. A handful of recent meta-analytic studies document that MME can produce modest gains in relationship skills and self-reports of marital quality that are maintained at least over the short periods of time covered by typical studies (Blanchard, Hawkins, Baldwin, & Fawcett, 2009; Hawkins, Blanchard, Baldwin, & Fawcett, 2008; Hawkins, Stanley, Blanchard, & Albright, 2012; Pinquart & Teubert, 2010). Also, research is beginning to document MME's potential to reduce divorce rates. A rigorous study of U.S. Army couples found reduced divorce rates 2 years after participating in an MME program (Stanley et al., 2014). A study with a German sample found reduced divorce and separation rates for MME participants a decade later (Hahlweg & Richter, 2010). A large, rigorous, multisite study with lower-income married couples did not find an effect for marital stability 2 years after participating in MME, but did find small but significant effects on a wide range of marital quality and relationship skills outcomes (Lundquist et al., 2014).

New parent education. Educational intervention for new parents going through the transition to parenthood is a subset of relationship development education and marriage maintenance education. The transition to parenthood, with its new demands to care for small children and other life adjustments, can take a toll on relationships (Cowan & Cowan, 2000). A number of programs have been developed and evaluated that target this special stress point for (primarily married) couples. A recent meta-analysis of these programs found small but significant positive effects on couple communication skills, relationship satisfaction, and psychological well-being (Pinquart & Teubert, 2010). Effects were somewhat stronger for higher-dosage programs and for programs with both antenatal and postnatal components, as well as when observational measures were used. Nevertheless, the effectiveness of these kinds of programs for unmarried lower-income new parents remains in question (Wood et al., 2014).

Remarriage education. Programs targeting remarried couples are a special instance of MME. One third to one half of all marriages in the United States now are remarriages for one or both spouses (Kreider & Ellis, 2011). But remarriages face additional challenges that make them harder to sustain (Adler-Baeder & Higginbotham, 2004). Not surprisingly, the divorce rate for remarriages is even higher than for first marriages (Bramlett & Mosher, 2001). Accordingly, program developers have developed educational interventions targeted specifically to remarrying and remarried couples to help strengthen these relationships, deal with unique stresses of remarriage and blended families, and improve family functioning. While the research in this area is still limited, a meta-analytic study of 14 evaluation studies (about half with control-group designs) found small-to-modest positive effects overall (Lucier-Greer & Adler-Baeder, 2012). Much more work is needed in this important area.

RME Effectiveness for Diverse and Distressed Couples

Low-income couples. Most research on the effectiveness of RME, including most of the research cited thus far, has been done with samples of White, well-educated individuals (Hawkins et al., 2008). But the last decade has seen a needed and timely flourishing of RME research with diverse, lower-income couples and individuals. This research has paralleled the significant growth of RME programs targeted to lower-income populations. This growth, in turn, was spurred by social policy experiments supported by state and federal dollars to help couples form and sustain healthy relationships and marriages (Hawkins & VanDenBerghe, 2014).

A recent meta-analytic study synthesized the research to date in this area. Hawkins and Erickson (2015) identified 22 control-group studies and 25 one-group/pre-post studies of RME programs targeted to lower-income individuals and couples (defined as income less than twice the poverty rate). They found couple and relationship education for diverse, lower-income couples has small, positive relationship effects on self-reports of relationship quality, communication, and aggression. There were somewhat stronger effects for married couples, "near-poor" (versus poor) participants, those experiencing more relationship distress at program entry, and participants who received a strong dosage of the program. In addition, a few studies of individuals involved in publicly supported RME programs have found greater positive change for lower-income participants (e.g., Rauer et al., 2014).

There is a lively debate about the merits of public policy support for RME to increase relationship stability (Hawkins, 2014; Hawkins et al., 2013; Johnson, 2012; Johnson, 2014). If government funds are to continue to support RME, probably all sides of the debate agree that the small effects identified in research to date imply that practitioners will need to continue to find ways to increase participant engagement, innovate curriculum design and pedagogy, and improve other programmatic elements to achieve greater success with the precious public funds.

Racial/ethnic minority couples. Research with lower-income couples has produced more racial and ethnic diversity in RME samples over the past decade. A number of studies have examined whether race/ethnicity moderates effects of RME programs. Overall, these studies suggest that, at a minimum, racial/ethnic participants benefit similarly from RME as Whites (e.g., Cowan et al., 2009; Cowan, Cowan, Pruett, Pruett, & Gillette, 2014), and some research suggests they may benefit more (Stanley et al., 2014).

Distressed couples. Similarly, research on RME programs for lower-income couples has documented that many couples experiencing significant relationship distress and ambiguous commitment to the future are participating in RME (Bradford, Hawkins, & Acker, 2015). RME is generally considered preventative intervention, "an attempt to steer couples away from the cliff of relationship distress, whereas couple therapy is the ambulance at the bottom of the cliff available to treat those couples who have fallen" (Halford, 2011, p. ix). But the on-the-street reality is that distressed couples are attending RME programs in substantial numbers, often more than half (Bradford, Hawkins, & Acker, 2015). The Hawkins and Erickson (2015) meta-analysis of RME for lower-income couples found that more-distressed couples benefitted more from RME than non-distressed couples. Similarly, a meta-analytic study of RME with well-educated, White samples found stronger effects on communication skills for more-distressed couples (Blanchard et al., 2009). Also, in a study of participants in RME programs in Alabama, Rauer and her colleagues (2014) found that individuals who began programs with greater relationship distress and lower commitment levels benefitted more from participation in the intervention.

Other diverse groups. This review hardly exhausts potential diverse family circumstances. RME work with other diverse populations, such as incarcerated/reentry spouses (Shamblen, Arnold, McKiernan, Collins, & Strader, 2013) or same-sex couples (Whitton & Buzzella, 2012), is still rare, but will likely grow over the next decade.

The Next Generation of RME and Effectiveness Research

This review of the effectiveness research on RME documents that it can help many who avail themselves of it and stick with it. Nevertheless, the most significant challenge for the future of RME is to engage more people in it, especially those at greater risk for relationship problems and dissolution. There is a lack of reliable research that documents what proportion of couples participate in RME. Some research suggests that maybe about a third of Americans participate in some kind of formal marriage preparation education (Hawkins, 2013; Stanley et al., 2006), although the quality of many of those programs is unknown. But how many individuals and couples participate in other forms of RME is not known. Government support of RME over the past decade has dramatically increased the number of lower-income and higher-risk individuals participating in various kinds of RME. But these programs reach only a fraction of tens of millions of lower-income families in the United States. And efforts so far have proven quite expensive. In addition, how long public policy will continue to support these efforts is uncertain.

Accordingly, the biggest challenge facing relationship educators is to develop cost-effective interventions that can reach much larger proportions of individuals and be effective. To do this, interventions need to be less intensive, more focused, and more regular. The current traditional model is to recruit participants and get them to commit to multiple sessions of face-to-face instruction of 10 to 40 hours. While there will always be a role for this kind of traditional, time-intensive, programmatic education, there is also a need to develop other, less-intensive approaches to make a difference for many more people than is now the case. The challenge for the next generation of relationship educators is to develop these more streamlined, efficient, and appealing interventions.

Practitioners and researchers are beginning to move in this direction by developing **naturalistic micro-interventions**, and also providing narrowcast interventions. Interventionists who can capture natural, regular, recurring events and help couples make use of them to strengthen their relationships may reach more people with RME and intervene more often. To illustrate, the eminent social psychologist, Frank Fincham, and his colleagues, developed a micro-intervention that taught and encouraged religious couples how to make use of daily prayers to strengthen their relationship. A series of studies suggested that this approach may help individuals increase gratitude for their partner and the capacity to forgive (Lambert, Fincham, Stillman, Graham, & Beach, 2010; Lambert, Fincham, Braithwaite, Graham, & Beach, 2009).

In addition, some interventionists have wondered whether the typical date night could be enhanced to strengthen relationships. Individuals who report having fun couple time at least once a week are three times more likely to report that they are happy in their marriage (Wilcox & Dew, 2012). One intervention study showed that couples assigned to engage in enhanced date nights for 10 weeks with mutually agreed-on, fun, and expanding activities (e.g., hiking, dancing) significantly improved their marital quality compared to couples who were assigned to engage in movie dates or no regular dates (Reissman, Aron, & Bergen, 1993). These kinds of interventions take advantage of naturally occurring, regular behaviors and then enhance them to strengthen relationships. In contrast to traditional RME, which requires large investments in recruitment and retention, intensive programmatic instruction, and substantial time and resources, naturalistic micro-interventions are low-intensity, inexpensive, and enhance naturally occurring behaviors. As creative interventionists develop new micro-intervention approaches, RME researchers will need to adapt their methods to test the effectiveness of these interventions over time.

Traditional RME usually includes a wide range of topics that are known to affect relationship quality and stability. They are broadcast interventions, in that the wide range of topics covered is not tailored to the specific needs of participants, but most participants find some topics useful if they invest in the full program. In contrast, some RME educators now are trying to assess couple needs and then tailor brief interventions to meet those needs (e.g., *Couple C.A.R.E.*; Halford, 2011). Similarly, some RME programs are narrowcast interventions in that they focus on a specific topic or challenge. The logic of narrowcast interventions is that people learn best when the intervention is focused on a specific challenge that they are facing right now or anticipating facing soon. And a brief intervention focused on a current known need will likely attract more participants. Some examples might be brief interventions to help couples communicate more effectively about financial issues and plan together; money differences are particularly potent at harming marriages (Dew, Britt, & Huston, 2012). Busy dual-earner couples struggle to effectively share domestic labor, but a time-intensive program with a broad range of topics will struggle to recruit these couples. Instead, a brief intervention focused on sharing domestic labor may be more appealing and more efficient. Rather than stuff a single intervention with content to deal with many of the potential problems couples face, narrowcast interventions focus on specific issues of current salience. Over time, couples may avail themselves of more narrowcast interventions to help them with specific issues as they arise.

The previous discussion on new approaches to RME implies that practitioners and programs need to move away from an inoculation model—a one-time event that prevents relationship deterioration for a lifetime—to something more akin to dental checkups or annual flu shots. The skills that make relationships work change over time, and stable relationships are always under the threat of entropy. As a result, a model of multiple, regular, brief exposures to RLE across the life span and at key times and circumstances should be promoted. Some interventionists have been experimenting with the notion of regular relationship checkups that provide the time and space to inspect and recalibrate relationships (Córdova, 2009; Olson, Larson, & Olson-Sigg, 2009). For instance, Córdova (2009) has developed and tested the effectiveness of a micro-intervention called the *Marriage Checkup*, intended to help couples regularly assess the health of their relationship, highlight strengths, identify some specific areas for improvement, and receive suggestions for how to work on areas for improvement.

Conclusion

Relationship and marriage education programs need strong evaluation research to continue to receive support, especially because many of these programs are funded by government grants to reach lower-income individuals. Evaluation research also is needed to improve the quality and effectiveness of RME curricula, services, and policies. This chapter has summarized and synthesized a large body of RME evaluation research on the diversity of programs available, including relationship literacy education for youth and young adults, relationship development education for cohabiting couples, marriage preparation education for engaged couples, marriage maintenance education for married couples (including new-parent couples), and remarried couples. The large body of research evaluating marriage preparation education and marriage maintenance education documents their potential to help individuals form and sustain healthy relationships and marriages. But much more work is needed in emerging areas of the field. The early evidence is that RME has only small effects on lower-income couples, suggesting the need for substantial improvement. However, this same body of research suggests that programs can be effective for diverse racial/ethnic populations and for distressed couples who invest fully in RME. Perhaps the biggest challenge for the future of RME is to expand its reach, but this probably won't be achieved with traditional, intensive, programmatic interventions. Instead, we will need to develop and test different, more efficient approaches, including naturalistic micro-interventions, narrowcast interventions, and regular relationship checkups.

Key Points

- RME programs have been developed for diverse target audiences and for different periods of the life span and different family circumstances.
- Couples in relationship distress are participating in RME in significant numbers.

- Research on RME programs show they have promise, but some kinds of programs need much more rigorous evaluation research.
- Studies on programs targeted to more disadvantaged individuals and couples generally show only small effects, so these programs will need to improve.
- One of the biggest challenges for the future of RME is to expand its reach. This will require developing and testing more efficient approaches, including naturalistic micro-interventions, less intense narrowcast interventions, and regular relationship checkups.

Discussion Questions

1. How has the body of evaluation research of the effectiveness of RME advanced over the past decade?
2. What two areas of work in the field of relationship education over the early life course are the least developed and need much more evaluation research?
3. In general, what has early evaluation research on the effectiveness of RME for lower-income couples found?
4. What is perhaps the greatest challenge for the future for RME?
5. What are two strategies the author recommends for meeting this future challenge for RME?

Additional Resources

The *National Association for Relationship and Marriage Education (NARME)* is the professional umbrella organization specifically for RME practitioners: www.narme.org

The *National Healthy Marriage Resource Center* is a web-based resource center for RME practitioners funded by the Administration for Children and Families and developed by Public Strategies, Inc.: www.healthymarriageinfo.org

The *National Resource Center for Healthy Marriages and Relationships*, also funded by the Administration for Children and Families, offers a variety of tools and resources designed to educate interested stakeholders in the benefits of integrating healthy relationship and marriage education into existing social service systems. It also provides a range of training, services, and support to interested state, local, and tribal government agencies as they work to integrate these skills into their existing services in order to best support the families served in their communities: healthymarriageandfamilies.org

References and Further Readings

Adler-Baeder, F., & Higginbotham, B. (2004). Implications of remarriage and stepfamily formation for marriage education. *Family Relations, 53*, 448–458.

Amato, P. (2014). Does social and economic disadvantage moderate the effects of relationship education on unwed couples? An analysis of data from the 15-month Building Strong Families evaluation. *Family Relations, 63*, 343–355.

Berger, A., Wildsmith, E., Manlove, J., & Steward-Streng, N. (2012). Relationship violence among young adult couples. *Child Trends Research Brief*, #2012–14. Retrieved from http://www.childtrends.org/Files//Child_Trends-2012_06_01_RB_CoupleViolence.pdf

Blanchard, V., Hawkins, A., Baldwin, S., & Fawcett, E. (2009). Investigating the effects of marriage and relationship education on couples' communication skills: A meta-analytic study. *Journal of Family Psychology, 23*, 203–214.

Bradbury, T., & Karney, B. (2012). *Intimate relationships.* New York, NY: W.W. Norton.

Bradford, A., Hawkins, A., & Acker, J. (2015). If we build it, they will come: Exploring policy and practice implications of public support for couple and relationship education for lower income and relationally distressed couples. *Family Process.* doi: 10.1111/famp.12151

Bramlett, M., & Mosher, W. (2001). *First marriage dissolution, divorce and remarriage: United States.* Advance Data from Vital and Health Statistics, No. 323. Hyattsville, MD: National Center for Health Statistics.

Cherlin, A. (2009). *The marriage go round: The state of marriage and the family in America today.* New York, NY: Alfred A. Knopf.

Córdova, J. (2009). *The Marriage Checkup: A scientific program for sustaining and strengthening marital health.* Lanham, MD: Jason Aronson.

Cowan, C., & Cowan, P. (2000). *When partners become parents: The big life change for couples.* Mahwah, NJ: Lawrence Erlbaum Associates.

Cowan, P., Cowan, C., Pruett, M., Pruett, K., & Gillette, P. (2014). Evaluating a couples group to enhance father involvement in low-income families using a benchmark comparison. *Family Relations, 63*, 356–370.

Cowan, P., Cowan, C., Pruett, M., Pruett, K., & Wong, J. (2009). Promoting fathers' engagement with children: Preventive interventions for low-income families. *Journal of Marriage and Family, 71*, 663–679.

Dew, J., Britt, S., & Huston, S. (2012). Examining the relationship between financial issues and divorce. *Family Relations, 61*, 615–628.

Fawcett, E., Hawkins, A., Blanchard, V., & Carroll, J. (2010). Do premarital education programs really work? A meta-analytic study. *Family Relations, 59*, 232–239.

Hahlweg, K., & Richter, D. (2010). Prevention and marital instability and distress: Results of an 11-year longitudinal follow-up study. *Behaviour Research and Therapy, 48*, 377–383.

Halford, W. (2011). *Marriage and relationship education: What works and how to provide it.* New York, NY: Guilford Press.

Hawkins, A. (2013). *The forever initiative: A feasible public policy agenda to help couples form and sustain healthy marriages and relationships.* North Charleston, SC: CreateSpace Independent Publishing Platform.

Hawkins, A. (2014). Continuing the important debate on government-supported healthy marriages and relationships initiatives: A brief response to Johnson's comment. *Family Relations, 63*, 305–308.

Hawkins, A., Amato, P., & Kinghorn, A. (2013). Are government-supported healthy marriage initiatives affecting family demographics? A state-level analysis. *Family Relations, 62*, 501–513.

Hawkins, A., Blanchard, V., Baldwin, S., & Fawcett, E. (2008). Does marriage and relationship education work? A meta-analytic study. *Journal of Consulting and Clinical Psychology, 76*, 723–734.

Hawkins, A., & Erickson, S. (2015). Is couple and relationship education effective for lower income participants? A meta-analytic study. *Journal of Family Psychology, 29*, 59–68. doi: 10.1037/fam0000045.

Hawkins, A., Stanley, S., Blanchard, V., & Albright, M. (2012). Exploring programmatic moderators of the effectiveness of marriage and relationship education: A meta-analytic study. *Behavior Therapy, 43*, 77–87.

Hawkins, A., Stanley, S., Cowan, P., Fincham, F., Beach, S., Cowan, C., Rhoades, G., Markman, H., & Daire, A. (2013). A more optimistic perspective on government-supported marriage and relationship education programs for lower income couples. *American Psychologist, 68*, 110–111.

Hawkins, A., & VanDenBerghe, B. (2014). *Facilitating forever: A feasible public policy agenda to help couples form and sustain healthy relationships and enduring marriages.* Charlottesville, VA: National Marriage Project.

Johnson, M. (2012). Healthy marriage initiatives: On the need for empiricism in policy implementation. *American Psychologist, 67*, 296–308.

Johnson, M. (2014). Government-supported healthy marriage initiatives are not associated with changes in family demographics: A comment on Hawkins, Amato, and Kinghorn (2013). *Family Relations, 63*, 300–304.

Johnson, M., & Anderson, J. (2013). The longitudinal association of marital confidence, time spent together, and marital satisfaction. *Family Process, 52*, 244–256.

Kennedy, S., & Ruggles, S. (2014). Breaking up is hard to count: The rise of divorce in the United States, 1980–2010. *Demography, 51*, 587–598.

Kerpelman, J. (2012, October). "Relationship Smart" youth: A statewide study of relationship education for high school students. Paper presented at the National Council on Family Relations Annual Conference, Phoenix, AZ.

Kerpelman, J., Pittman, J., Adler-Baeder, F., Eryigit, S., & Paulk, A. (2009). Evaluation of a statewide youth-focused relationships education curriculum. *Journal of Adolescence, 32*, 1359–1370.

Kerpelman, J., Pittman, J., Adler-Baeder, F., Stringer, K., Eryigit, S., Cadely, H., & Harrell-Levy, M. (2010). What adolescents bring to and learn from relationship education classes: Does social address matter? *Journal of Couple and Relationship Therapy, 9*, 95–112.

Kreider, R., & Ellis, R. (2011). *Number, timing, and duration of marriages and divorces: 2009.* Current Population Reports, P70–125. Retrieved from http://www.census.gov/prod/2011pubs/p70-125.pdf

Lambert, N., Fincham, F., Braithwaite, S., Graham, S., & Beach, S. (2009). Can prayer increase gratitude? *Psychology of Religion and Spirituality, 1*, 139–149.

Lambert, N., Fincham, F., Stillman, T., Graham, S., & Beach, S. (2010). Motivating change in relationships: Can prayer increase forgiveness? *Psychological Science, 21*, 126–132.

Lavner, J., Bradbury, T., & Karney, B. (2012). Incremental change or initial differences? Testing two models of marital deterioration. *Journal of Family Psychology, 26*, 606–616.

Lavner, J., Karney, B., & Bradbury, T. (2012). Do cold feet warn of trouble ahead? Premarital uncertainty and four-year marital outcomes. *Journal of Family Psychology, 26*, 1012–1017.

Lucier-Greer, M., & Adler-Baeder, F. (2012). Does couple and relationship education work for individuals in stepfamilies? A meta-analytic study. *Family Relations, 61*, 756–769.

Lundquist, E., Hsueh, J., Lowenstein, A., Faucetta, K., Gubits, D., Michalopoulos, C., & Knox, V. (2014). A family-strengthening program for low-income families: Final impacts from the Supporting Healthy Marriage evaluation. OPRE Report 2013–49A. Washington, DC: Office of Planning, Research and Evaluation, Administration for Children and Families, U.S. Department of Health and Human Services.

Markman, H., Renick, M., Floyd, F., Stanley, S., & Clements, M. (1993). Preventing marital distress through communication and conflict management training: A four- and five-year follow-up. *Journal of Consulting and Clinical Psychology, 61*, 70–77.

Markman, H., & Rhoades, G. (2012). Relationship education research: Current status and future directions. *Journal of Marital and Family Therapy, 38*, 169–200.

McLanahan, S., & Beck, A. (2010). Parental relationship in fragile families. *Future of Children, 20*(2), 17–37.

Nock, S., Sanchez, L., & Wright, J. (2008). *Covenant marriage: The movement to reclaim tradition in America.* New Brunswick, NJ: Rutgers University Press.

Olson, D., Larson, P., & Olson-Sigg, A. (2009). Couple checkup: Tuning up relationships. *Journal of Couple and Relationship Therapy, 8,* 129–142.

Orr, L. (1999). *Social experiments: Evaluating public programs with experimental methods.* Thousand Oaks, CA: Sage.

Pinquart, M., & Teubert, D. (2010). A meta-analytic study of couple interventions during the transition to parenthood. *Family Relations, 59,* 221–231.

Rauer, A., Adler-Baeder, F., Lucier-Greer, M., Skuban, E., Ketring, S., & Smith, T. (2014). Exploring processes of change in couple relationship education: Predictors of change in relationship quality. *Journal of Family Psychology, 28,* 65–76.

Reissman, C., Aron, A., & Bergen, M. (1993). Shared activities and marital satisfaction: Causal direction and self-expansion versus boredom. *Journal of Social and Personal Relationships, 10,* 243–254.

Rhoades, G., & Stanley, S. (2014). *Before "I do": What do premarital experiences have to do with marital quality among today's young adults?* Charlottesville, VA: The National Marriage Project at the University of Virginia.

Rhoades, G., Stanley, S., & Markman, H. (2009). Working with cohabitation in relationship education and therapy. *Journal of Couple and Relationship Therapy, 8,* 95–112.

Rossi, P., Lipsey, M., & Freeman, H. (2004). *Evaluation: A systematic approach.* Thousand Oaks, CA: Sage.

Scott, M., Schelar, E., Manlove, J., & Cui, C. (2009). Young adult attitudes about relationships and marriage: Time may have changed, but expectations remain high. *Child Trends Research Brief,* Publication #2009–30. Retrieved from http://www.childtrends.org/_docdisp_page.cfm?LID=248A8BBE-0415-48D2-BDC9A5731DBDFB93

Scott, M., Steward-Streng, N., Manlove, J., Schelar, E., & Cui, C. (2011). Characteristics of young adult sexual relationships: Diverse, sometimes violent, often loving. *Child Trends Research Brief,* Publication #2011–01. Retrieved from http://www.childtrends.org/_listAllPubs.cfm?LID=9B37B55C-75A1-4061-8856FFA5123A43A7

Shamblen, S., Arnold, B., McKiernan, P., Collins, D., & Strader, T. (2013). Applying the Creating Lasting Family Connections marriage enhancement program to marriages affected by prison reentry. *Family Process, 52,* 477–498.

Stanley, S., Amato, P., Johnson, C., & Markman, H. (2006). Premarital education, marital quality, and marital stability: Findings from a large, random household survey. *Journal of Family Psychology, 20,* 117–126.

Stanley, S., Rhoades, G., Loew, B., Allen, E., Carter, S., Osborne, L., Prentice, D., & Markman, H. (2014). A randomized controlled trial of relationship education in the U.S. Army: 2-year outcomes. *Family Relations, 63,* 482–495. doi:10.1111/fare.12083

Whitton, S., & Buzzella, B. (2012). Using relationship education programs with same-sex couples: A preliminary evaluation of program utility and needed modifications. *Marriage and Family Review, 48,* 667–688.

Wilcox, W., & Dew, J. (2012). *The date night opportunity: What does couple time tell us about the potential value of date nights?* Charlottesville, VA: The National Marriage Project at the University of Virginia.

Wood, R., Moore, Q., Clarkwest, A., & Killewald, A. (2014). The long-term effects of Building Strong Families: A program for unmarried parents. *Journal of Marriage and Family, 76,* 446–463.

PART II

Conceptual and Theoretical Frameworks

5

A HEALTH MODEL FOR RELATIONSHIP AND MARRIAGE EDUCATION

Angela Wiley and Jill Bowers

LEARNING GOALS

- Explore how health is multidimensional and intimately connected to the wellbeing of couple relationships.
- Consider a new model for health promotion that can enhance couples and relationship education efforts.
- Learn how couple wellbeing can be enhanced by addressing health in four important domains: physical, mental, social, and spiritual.

Introduction

Health, a critical indicator of individual and societal wellbeing (Carr & Springer, 2010), is often an overlooked component of relationship and marriage education (RME). Health is "complete physical, mental, and social wellbeing and not merely the absence of disease or infirmity" (World Health Organization, 1946). This multidimensional definition, like RME, focuses on positive development and prevention. RME has educated couples about modifiable protective and risky behaviors to improve the quality or wellbeing of their relationships (Adler-Baeder, Higgenbotham, & Lamke, 2004) although the scope has been modest. However, multiple dimensions of health (each with protective and risky factors) are intimately intertwined with relationship wellbeing and consideration of these areas would improve RME. Drawing on the health and relationship literatures, a model of health for relationship and marriage education (HRME) is proposed to enhance existing RME effort by focusing on four dimensions of health (Figure 5.1). It is beyond the scope of this chapter to provide exhaustive reviews of the relationship

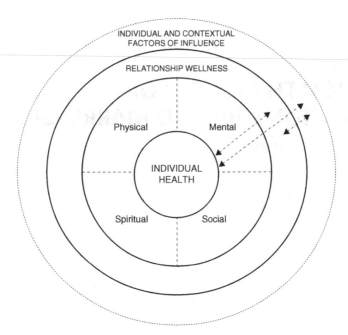

FIGURE 5.1 Health for Relationship and Marriage Education Model

science or health literature; rather, select examples are presented to provide a foundation for the model.

Health in Relationship and Marriage Education (HRME)

HRME emerged from a synthesis of relationship science and health literature, informed by human development theories and wellness paradigms. Ecological (Bronfenbrenner, 1994) and transactional models (Sameroff, 2010) have advanced the understanding of the interconnectedness of individuals and their environments, as well as the bidirectional relationships between behaviors and emotions of individuals and their partners. **Wellness paradigms** (i.e., Roscoe, 2009) have inspired focus on strengths and challenges across dimensions (Adams, Bezner, & Steinhardt, 1997) and describe individuals' health status as a resource or burden to the relationships in which they are involved (Christakis & Allison, 2008). Synthesizing these views, HRME encourages consideration of health behaviors across physical, mental, social, and spiritual domains. Because research has shown that many health behaviors are amenable to change (Freijy & Kothe, 2013), RMEs can use the model to help couples optimize relationship quality across dimensions and over time.

HRME is applicable to various relationship stages and across cultures, yet for brevity, this chapter focuses on adults in married or committed, longer-term relationships and largely draws on research conducted with couples from the United

States. Literature at the intersection of individual health and couple relationship wellbeing (including functioning such as communication and conflicts and outcomes such as satisfaction) is considered focusing on the HRME domains.

Physical Health Domain

Most **physical health** (PH) research has addressed individual outcomes (illnesses or diseases), subjective health reports, and health behaviors. Illness, pain, and chronic conditions (e.g., obesity) have been associated with poor quality of life for individuals (Fontaine & Barofsky, 2001; Schoormans et al., 2014). PH is relevant for RME, given the intertwined nature of relationship wellbeing and PH outcomes. Research has indicated that PH influences relationship wellbeing, the PH of one partner influences that of the other, and relationship wellbeing influences the PH of individual partners (Wiley, Adler-Baeder, & Warnick, 2013).

Physical health influences relationship wellbeing. Poor PH can stress couple relationships, sometimes challenging the resilience of families (Patterson, 1988). For example, research has shown that marital communication and satisfaction decline after heart surgery (Van Der Poel & Greeff, 2003), and diabetes symptoms have been linked to lower enjoyment of couple interactions (Iida, Stephens, Franks, & Rook, 2013). Declines in partner health have been found to impact perceptions of relationship quality (Yorgason, Booth, & Johnson, 2008). Some investigations have indicated that mediators between PH and relationship quality may include psychological stress (Hagedoorn et al., 2000), caregiver burden (Langer, Abrams, & Syrjala, 2003), or unwanted changes in sexual activity quality (Galinsky & Waite, 2014).

Mutual influence of partner physical health. Individual PH status and behaviors are remarkably congruent within couples over time, with one partner's health behavior before marriage influencing the other partner's health behavior later (Homish & Leonard, 2008). There have been associations between relationship quality and dietary and exercise patterns (Macken, Yates, & Blancher, 2000), diseases (Hippisley-Cox, Coupland, Pringle, Crown, & Hammersley, 2002), and obesity and adiposity (Katzmarzyk, Pérusse, Rao, & Bouchard, 1999). Moreover, a caregiving partner's own health has been found to deteriorate with that of the ill spouse (Nijboer et al., 1998).

Relationship wellbeing influences physical health. Relationships also influence PH. Many studies have documented better PH for individuals in relationships (Dupre & Meadows, 2007) although gender and other factors may influence the effects (Berge, Bauer, MacLehose, Eisenberg, & Neumark-Sztainer, 2014). Overall, relationship wellbeing has predicted higher perceived PH over time (Proulx & Snyder-Rivas, 2013) and lower risk of mortality (Robles, Slatcher, Trobello, & McGinn, 2014). Further, declines in marital quality with age have been associated with poor PH (Miller, Hollist, Olsen, & Law, 2013).

The PH domain is relevant for RME although the bidirectional influence of individuals' PH and relationship wellbeing and the mechanisms involved warrant more attention. Intimate relationships and PH may be related in a cyclical fashion with multiple entry points (Schmaling & Sher, 1997); such a cycle could describe the complicated linkages between relationship wellbeing and all four health domains.

Mental Health Domain

Like PH, **mental health** (MH) is not merely the absence of illness; it is a state of psychological and emotional wellbeing which has been characterized by individuals experiencing self-acceptance, purpose in life, positive relationships with others, autonomy, positive coping with life stressors, environmental mastery, and ability to work productively (Keyes, 2002). This section addresses MH and relationship wellbeing and explores how MH (positive and negative) and relationship wellbeing mutually impact each other.

Mental health impacts relationship wellbeing. Individuals who are mentally healthy tend to report better relationship quality (Blum & Mehrabian, 1999) while those experiencing negative affect and maladaptive attributions have reported lower marital satisfaction (Karney, Bradbury, Fincham, & Sullivan, 1994). Individuals who are more mindful (mentally engaged and well-adjusted) report high marital satisfaction (Burpee & Langer, 2005). Further, poor MH has been linked to marital struggles and divorce, even when accounting for a variety of individual and contextual factors (Breslau et al., 2011). As examples, depressive symptoms (Walker, Isherwood, Burton, Kitwe-Magambo, & Luszcz, 2013), anxious tendencies (Caughlin, Huston, & Houts, 2000), and hostile/angry temperament (Renshaw, Blais, & Smith, 2010) have predicted lower relationship satisfaction.

MH may influence relationship wellbeing in several ways. For example, mentally healthy individuals are more optimistic and able to manage stress (Scheier & Carver, 1992), which can improve marital satisfaction, in contrast to the marital conflict that has been predicted by psychological distress (Papp, Goeke-Morey, & Cummings, 2007). Many MH problems are characterized by difficulty in regulating emotions in ways that may increase marital discord (South, Kreuger, & Iacono, 2011). Future research should include longitudinal examinations of healthy and unhealthy relationships and consider factors that are risky for some and protective for others (e.g., see McNulty & Fincham, 2012).

Relationship wellbeing impacts mental health. Relationship difficulties may threaten MH. For example, marital dissatisfaction has been associated with depressed mood (Whisman, Weinstock, & Uebelacker, 2002), and poorer marital quality has predicted higher anxiety and depressive symptoms (Figueiredo, Field, Diego, Hernandez-Reif, Osvelia, & Ascencio, 2008). Higher marital satisfaction has been linked to lower depression and higher life satisfaction (Holt-Lunstad, Birmingham, & Jones, 2008). At the same time, the direction of effects is inconclusive (Be, Whisman, & Uebelacker, 2013; Bulloch, Williams, Lavorato, & Patten, 2009), and careful consideration of mechanisms is needed. Nonetheless, the domain of MH is clearly relevant for relationship wellbeing and warrants greater attention in RME.

Social Health Domain

RME traditionally has emphasized the social interactions between partners, so **social health** (SoH) is explored with respect to the interactions of individual partners and the couple with others, including extended kin, friends, and community members. Social networks connect couples to their families, communities and others with whom they share similarities (Wrzus, Hänel, Wagner, & Neyer, 2013). The social web surrounding romantic relationships interacts over time with couple characteristics and dynamics, contributing to relationship satisfaction and longevity (Niehuis, Huston, & Rosenband, 2006). SoH influences relationship wellbeing and conversely, relationship wellbeing impacts SoH.

Social health impacts relationship wellbeing. As couples face challenges over time, SoH can help sustain them; SoH problems can also further contribute to their demise. For example, the use of social networks (e.g., spending time with mutual friends) for relationship maintenance has been associated with marital quality across studies (Ogolsky & Bowers, 2013; Stafford & Canary, 1991) while disclosures about relationship difficulties to intimate friends (and not to partner) have been linked to relationship problems (Helms, Crouter, & McHale, 2003). Moreover, relationships that are endorsed by friends and relatives are less likely to terminate, compared to those subjected to disapproval (e.g., Lehmiller & Agnew, 2007; Sprecher et al., 2006).

Relationship wellbeing impacts social health. Relationship status, stage, and quality influence individuals' SoH patterns. For example, individuals' networks decrease with age and life events (Wrzus et al., 2013), yet couples tend to share more friendships over time (Kalmijn, 2003). Individuals in distressed relationships have been found to be more likely to socialize with friends without their partner (Smith, Snyder, Trull, & Monsma, 1988). Said couples may experience relationship uncertainty and unease about partner's friendships or family relationships (e.g., see Knobloch, 2008 for research surrounding relationship uncertainty). It is possible that relationship uncertainty influences SoH when partners isolate themselves from each other or from friends or kin who are in their partners' social networks. Moreover, abusive relationships have been found to present special challenges to SoH (i.e., when a controlling partner constrains the social connections of the victim, restricting the victim's contact with family and friends and other sources of social support; Murphy & Hoover, 1999).

Spiritual Health Domain

Spiritual health (SpH) refers to the belief systems and accompanying behaviors (secular or religious) that are central in resilient relationships (Walsh, 2006). Belief systems include "values, convictions, attitudes, biases, and assumptions which coalesce to form a set of basic premises that trigger emotional responses, inform decisions, and guide actions" (Walsh, 2006, p. 50). Drawing on Coyle's (2002) framework of spirituality and health, SpH is assessed as hope, beliefs, values, and behaviors that support health or resiliency, especially as it relates to couple wellbeing. Because belief systems can help couples make meaning of **adversity** or develop coherence, optimism, and a shared sense of transcendence, SpH is relevant for RME.

Often used interchangeably, religion and spirituality are distinct (e.g., Koenig, King, & Carson, 2012). Spirituality encompasses finding and realizing an essential self and connecting with a transcendent secular or sacred purpose (Pargament, 2007) while religion has been defined as "the search for significance that occurs within the context of established institutions" (Pargament, Mahoney, Exline, Jones, & Shafranske, 2013, p. 15). With the HMRE model, the broader term, spiritual, is used to refer to this health domain.

Spiritual health impacts relationship wellbeing. SpH has been found to impact individual health (Coyle, 2002), and likewise, the influence of SpH on relationship wellbeing has been documented (Fincham & Beach, 2013; Mahoney, 2010). More religious newlywed couples have been found to be more well-adjusted in their relationships than those who are less religious (Schramm, Marshall, Harris, & Lee, 2011). Additionally, partners who employ spiritual rituals or routines may be better equipped to manage conflict. Couple conflicts often manifest in a predictable cycle of negativity and escalation (Gottman & Levenson, 2002) that are rooted in the neurobiological hardware of our species (e.g., Robles & Kiecolt-Glaser, 2003). Spiritual techniques may help partners disengage from the other's negative emotions to de-escalate and soothe (Saxbe & Repetti, 2010). In one study with romantic couples, mindfulness strategies assisted individuals in regulating their stress responses (Laurent, Laurent, Hertz, Egan-Wright, & Granger, 2013).

Greater religiosity may be associated with more negative outcomes in some circumstances (Mahoney, Pargament, Tarakeshwar, & Swank, 2008). Negative forms of religious coping can be deleterious (Ano & Vasconcelles, 2005). Ideologies, such as *religious familism*, may exert influence on aspects of family life, sometimes idealize and support hetero-normative and patriarchal views on family life (Edgell, 2005). Moreover, religiosity has, in general, been associated with lower levels of couple violence (Ellison & Anderson, 2001), yet there may be increased conflict and risk of interpersonal violence when more ideologically conservative men are partnered with relatively liberal women (Ellison, Bartkowski, & Anderson, 1999). And finally, increased homophobia has been documented among some conservative religious individuals (Balkin, Schlosser, & Levitt, 2009), adding to the potential challenges of same-sex couples in affected families and communities.

Relationship wellbeing impacts spiritual health. Scant research has examined the influence of couple relationship factors on SpH. Researchers have begun to explore spiritual change and reconciliation among individuals who are LGBT

(Levy, 2012). Religious identity is malleable for many people (Sherkat, 2014), and some individuals have reported love as a reason for leaving their own religious communities and marrying into the faith of their partners (Racin & Dein, 2010). Further, interfaith coupling can involve significant negotiation and blending of rituals and practices (Horowirz, 1999).

More research is needed to better understand the links between SpH and relationship wellbeing (Booth, Johnson, Branaman, & Sica, 1995). Past studies have extensively relied on unidimensional single-item measures, such as attendance, as well as cross-sectional designs (Mahoney, 2010). The bulk of work on couples and religion has also neglected non-traditional relationships such as same-sex couples (Mahoney, 2010), and studies have often not considered the differences in first and subsequent marriages (Schramm et al., 2012). Nevertheless, because SpH has both positive and negative implications for family life (Burr, Marks, & Day, 2011), RME practitioners should address spiritual health competencies, such as those proposed for psychologists (Vieten et al., 2013).

Utility of the HRME Model and RME Considerations

This chapter provides evidence of the ways in which the four domains of health (physical, mental, social, and spiritual) in the HRME model are relevant for couple wellbeing. RMEs could use this model to assess couples' strengths and potential areas for improvement.

The HRME model depicts health domains as distinct for illustration, but in fact, there are a variety of ways that each of the domains of individual health may interact. In the stress–social support hypothesis (Burman & Margolin, 1992), poorer-quality relationships may contribute to poorer mental health (i.e., stress and anxiety), which negatively impacts physical health. On the other hand, better relationships may provide social support to bolster physical health (McEwen, 1998). Aspects of social health (i.e., social integration) have been found to be a stress buffer for mental and physical health outcomes (Thoits, 2011). Further, spirituality can work to improve mental, physical, and social health (e.g., through community networks that can provide social support; Dollahite & Marks, 2009 or spiritual techniques, such as meditation that can reduce stress; Varvogli & Darviri, 2011). There are, in fact, a number of links between each of the facets of health included here that have been documented throughout the literature, and these are important to consider in future research.

HRME advances relationship and marriage education programming by encouraging systematic attention to relevant health domains for the purpose of addressing modifiable protective and risky behaviors to improve relationship wellbeing. For example, couples often engage in relationship role negotiations following significant physical health diagnoses or events. Several roles have been described with the best outcomes associated when partners create a cohesive system, characterized by mutual participation in implementing changes with negotiation and flexibility (Kärner, Dahlgren, & Bergdahl, 2004). RMEs could help couples communicate and negotiate their roles following health diagnoses. Likewise, RMEs may want to pay particular attention to educating couples about how mental health concerns may trigger relationship problems (e.g., alcohol abuse and depression; Breslau et al, 2011). Because mental issues may impact effective navigation of relationship difficulties (Papp et al., 2007), RMEs may need to help partners identify and address these issues and find mental health professionals that can adequately address these concerns.

In the social health domain, RMEs provides more focus to the importance of social interactions and networks beyond the dyad. This attention could mean encouraging couples to develop shared networks that support their couple relationship when inevitable difficulties arise to discourage marginalization (Lehmiller & Agnew, 2007). RME educators working with couples desiring denser shared social networks may want to encourage joint hobbies or involvements that are likely to involve meeting others with like interests.

Regarding spiritual health, RMEs working with individuals who are religious may help couples to communicate about religion, their relative levels of religiosity, or discrepancies in their beliefs as research has shown these aspects of spiritual health have been linked to relationship wellbeing (Schramm et al., 2012). More generally, there have been a number of evaluations that have illustrated the effectiveness of secular mindfulness-based stress reduction techniques (Grossman, Niemann, Schmidt, & Walach, 2004). This approach has been used with couples (Carson, Carson, Gill, & Baucom, 2004), and RMEs may promote such tools as an option in their programming.

Finally, HRME recognizes individual and contextual influences on health and relationship wellbeing, including age, life stage, gender, SES, and public and social policies. These factors are vital in RME programming that addresses health domains. For example, there are age-associated normative challenges to health in most couple relationships (Booth & Johnson, 1994), and some evidence point toward health concerns being particularly potent during certain life stages (e.g., MH during the transition to parenthood; Figueiredo, Field, Diego, Hernandez-Reif, Osvelia, & Ascencio, 2008). Individual and contextual factors are relevant for health and relationships and merit further attention.

Conclusion

Health promotion empowers individuals to control and improve their lives (World Health Organization, 1986). As an example of this, RME has traditionally addressed modifiable **protective** and **risk factors** to improve the wellbeing of couple relationships (Adler-Baeder, Higgenbotham, & Lamke, 2004). Topics have included communication and emotional expressivity, conflict management, and maintenance strategies. RME could better support relationship wellbeing by addressing modifiable protective and risk factors present in multiple health dimensions. The HRME model provides a framework and starting point for such an effort. In a time of increasing life spans and interest on health, integration of this framework can only enhance the relevance and expand the impact of RME endeavors.

Key Points

- Past RME efforts have focused on a limited range of modifiable protective and risky behaviors to improve couple relationships.
- The field needs an expanded framework for addressing the interrelated nature of individual health and couple wellbeing.
- The HRME model provides a framework for considering modifiable protective and risky behaviors in four important and interrelated domains: physical, mental, social, and spiritual.
- RMEs could use this model to assess couples' strengths and potential areas for improvement.
- The HRME model provides a template for comprehensive program development that addresses an expanded range of modifiable protective and risky behaviors in each health domain.

Discussion Questions

1. The HRME is comprehensive including four domains of health that are critical to RME. It was created to help educators think about relationships and health outcomes holistically and to encourage educators to think about the bidirectional nature of health and romantic relationships. How might you use the HRME model in program development and evaluation?
2. What are implications of an increased average life span for the links between individual physical health and couple wellbeing? How might couple relationships change (for better and for worse) when one partner must provide care for the other?
3. Create a list of several mental health issues (depression, anxiety). Then, design a list of common relationship issues (e.g., the division of household tasks, balancing work and the partner relationship, infidelity, finances, disagreements about raising children). Drawing from this list, create a scenario map (could be based on someone you know or something you have read). You could start with the outcomes for an individual who was/is in a romantic partnership and work your back through the underlying antecedents (what you believe may have caused the issues), OR you could begin by thinking about the relationship issues and look at mental health issues that may have caused the relationship issues. Write two hypothesis or theories about what caused the mental health outcomes and why mental health is linked to relationships. In what ways might the links between individual health and relationships be bidirectional?

4. If you had an RME program on a given topic, what mental health outcomes would you look at? How would you propose to support couples' mental health in the program?

5. In what ways does social health impact relationship wellbeing? In RME many educators focus on the social health with respect to the couples' communication and how they handle conflict. What are examples of other ways social health may impact relationship outcomes? How could you address these issues in an RME program? What topics would you cover?

6. Spiritual health can be a sensitive topic, especially if "spiritual" is conflated with "religious."

   • Think of as many examples as you can of how your future clients or program participants might care for their spiritual health. Think of non-religious as well as religious examples.

   • How important is it for a professional who works with couples to understand different religious traditions and how those may intersect with couple relationships? How might professionals prepare themselves to encourage health in this area?

Additional Resources

A Marriage to Remember by filmmaker Banker White. This short documentary (approximately 8.5 minutes) explores how Alzheimer's disease revealed the strength in a couple's relationship. http://www.nytimes.com/2014/08/26/opinion/a-marriage-to-remember.html?_r=0

Hidden Heart. Documentary by Zara Afzal that explore the experiences of Muslim women who marry outside their faith. http://hiddenheartfilm.com/

References and Further Readings

Adams, T., Bezner, J., & Steinhardt, M. (1997). The conceptualization and measurement of perceived wellness: Integrating balance across and within dimensions. *American Journal of Health Promotion, 11*, 208–218. doi:10.4278/0890-1171-11.3.208

Adler-Baeder, F., Higginbotham, B., & Lamke, L. (2004). Putting empirical knowledge to work: Linking research and programming on marital quality. *Family Relations, 53*, 537–546. doi:10.1111/j.0197-6664.2004.00063.x

Ano, G., & Vasconcelles, E. (2005). Religious coping and psychological adjustment to stress: A meta-analysis. *Journal of Clinical Psychology, 6*, 461–480. doi:10.1002/jclp.20049

Balkin, R., Schlosser, L., & Levitt, D. (2009). Religious identity and cultural diversity: Exploring the relationships between religious identity, sexism, homophobia, and multicultural competence. *Journal of Counseling and Development, 87*, 420–427. doi:10.1002/j.1556-6678.2009.tb00126.x

Be, D., Whisman, M., & Uebelacker, L. (2013). Prospective associations between marital adjustment and life satisfaction. *Personal Relationships, 20*, 728–739. doi:10.1111/pere.12011

Berge, J., Bauer, K., MacLehose, R., Eisenberg, M., & Neumark-Sztainer, D. (2014). Associations between relationship status and day-to-day health behaviors and weight among diverse young adults. *Families, Systems, and Health, 32*, 67–77. doi:10.1037/fsh0000002

Blum, J., & Mehrabian, A. (1999). Personality and temperament correlates of marital satisfaction. *Journal of Personality, 67*, 93–125. doi:10.1111/1467-6494.00049

Booth, A., & Johnson, D. (1994). Declining health and marital quality. *Journal of Marriage and Family, 56*, 218–223.

Booth, A., Johnson, D., Branaman, A., & Sica, A. (1995). Belief and behavior: Does religion matter in today's marriage? *Journal of Marriage and Family, 57*, 661–671.

Bradbury, T., & Karney, B. (2014). *Love me slender: How smart couples team up to lose weight, exercise more, and stay healthy together*. New York, NY: Simon and Schuster.

Breslau, J., Miller, E., Jin, R., Sampson, N., Alonso, J., Andrade, L., . . . Kessler, R. (2011). A multinational study of mental disorders, marriage, and divorce. *Acta Psychiatria Scandinavica, 124*, 474–486. doi:10.1111/j.1600-0447.2011.01712.x

Bronfenbrenner, U. (1994). Ecological models of human development. In *International encyclopedia of education* (Vol. 3, 2nd ed.). Oxford, UK: Elsevier.

Bulloch, A., Williams, J., Lavorato, D., & Patten, S. (2009). The relationship between major depression and marital disruption is bidirectional. *Depression and Anxiety, 26*, 1172–1177. doi:10.1002/da.20618

Burman, B., & Margolin, G. (1992). Analysis of the association between marital relationships and health problems: An interactional perspective. *Psychological Bulletin, 112*, 39–63. doi:10.1037/0033-2909.112.1.39

Burpee, L., & Langer, E. (2005). Mindfulness and marital satisfaction. *Journal of Adult Development, 12*, 43–51. doi:10.1007/s10804-005-1281-6

Burr, W., Marks, L., & Day, R. (2011). *Sacred matters: Religion and spirituality in families*. New York, NY: Taylor and Francis Group.

Carr, D., & Springer, K. (2010). Advances in families and health research in the 21st century. *Journal of Marriage and Family, 72*, 743–761. doi:10.111/j.1741-3737.2010.00728.x

Carson, J., Carson, K., Gil, K., & Baucom, D. (2004). Mindfulness-based relationship enhancement. *Behavior Therapy, 35*, 471–494. doi:10.1016/S0005-7894(04)80028-5

Caughlin, J., Huston, T., & Houts, R. (2000). How does personality matter in marriage? An examination of trait anxiety, interpersonal negativity, and marital satisfaction. *Journal of Personality and Social Psychology, 78*, 326–336. doi:10.1037/0022-3514.78.2.326

Christakis, N., & Allison, P. (2008). Inter-spousal mortality effects: Caregiver burden across the spectrum of disabling diseases. In D. Cutler, D. Wise, & R. Woodbury (Eds.), *Health at older ages: The causes and consequences of declining disability among the elderly* (pp. 455–478). Chicago, IL: University of Chicago Press.

Coyle, J. (2002). Spirituality and health: Towards a framework for exploring the relationship between spirituality and health. *Journal of Advanced Nursing, 37*, 589–597. doi:10.1046/j.1365-2648.2002.02133.x

Dollahite, D., & Marks, L. (2009). A conceptual model of family and religious processes in highly religious families. *Review of Religious Research*, 373–391.

Dupre, M., & Meadows, S. (2007). Disaggregating the effects of marital trajectories on health. *Journal of Family Issues, 28*, 623–652. doi:10.1177/0192513X06296296

Edgell, P. (2005). *Religion and family in a changing society*. Princeton, NJ: Princeton University Press.

Ellison, C., & Anderson, K. (2001). Religious involvement and domestic violence among US couples. *Journal for the Scientific Study of Religion, 40*, 269–286. doi:10.1111/0021-8294.00055

Ellison, C., Bartkowski, J., & Anderson, K. (1999). Are there religious variations in domestic violence? *Journal of Family Issues, 20*, 87–113. doi:10.1177/019251399020001005

Figueiredo, B., Field, T., Diego, M., Hernandez-Reif, M., Osvelia, D., & Ascencio, A. (2008). Partner relationships during the transition to parenthood. *Journal of Reproductive and Infant Psychology, 26*, 99–107. doi:10.1080/02646830701873057

Fincham, F., & Beach, S. (2013). Can religion and spirituality enhance prevention programs for couples? In K. Pargament, A. Mahoney, & E. Shafranske (Eds.), *APA handbook of psychology, religion, and spirituality* (Vol. 2, pp. 461–479). Washington, DC: American Psychological Association.

Fontaine, K., & Barofsky, I. (2001). Obesity and health-related quality of life. *Obesity Reviews, 2*, 173–182. doi:10.1046/j.1467-789x.2001.00032.x

Freijy, T., & Kothe, E. (2013). Dissonance-based interventions for health behaviour change: A systematic review. *British Journal of Health Psychology, 18*, 310–337. doi:10.1111/bjhp.12035

Galinsky, A., & Waite, L. (2014). Sexual activity and psychological health as mediators of the relationship between physical health and marital quality. *The Journals of Gerontology Series B: Psychological Sciences and Social Sciences, 69*, 482–492. doi:10.1093/geronb/gbt165

Gottman, J., & Levenson, R. (2002). A two-factor model for predicting when a couple will divorce: Exploratory analyses using 14-year longitudinal data. *Family Process, 41*, 83–96. doi:10.1111/j.1545-5300.2002.401020000

Grossman, P., Niemann, L., Schmidt, S., & Walach, H. (2004). Mindfulness-based stress reduction and health benefits: A meta-analysis. *Journal of Psychosomatic Research, 57*, 35–43. doi:10.1016/S0022-3999(03)00573-7

Hagedoorn, M., Kuijer, R., Buunk, B., DeJong, G., Wobbes, T., & Sanderman, R. (2000). Marital satisfaction in patients with cancer: Does support from intimate partners benefit those who need it most? *Health Psychology, 19*, 274–282. doi:10.1037/0278-6133.19.3.274

Helms, H., Crouter, C., & McHale, S. (2003). Marital quality and spouses' marriage work with close friends and each other. *Journal of Marriage and Family, 65*, 963–977. doi:10.1111/j.1741-3737.2003.00963.x

Hippisley-Cox, J., Coupland, C., Pringle, M., Crown, N., & Hammersley, V. (2002). Married couples' risk of same disease: Cross sectional study. *British Medical Journal, 325*, 636–640. doi:10.1136/bmj.325.7365.636

Holt-Lunstad, J., Birmingham, W., & Jones, B. (2008). Is there something unique about marriage? The relative impact of marital status, relationship quality, and network social support on ambulatory blood pressure and mental health. *Annals of Behavioral Medicine, 35*, 239–244.

Homish, G., & Leonard, K. (2008). Spousal influence on general health behaviors in a community sample. *American Journal of Health Behavior, 32*, 754–763. doi:10.5993/AJHB.32.6.19

Horowirz, J. (1999). Negotiating couplehood: The process of resolving the December dilemma among interfaith couples. *Family Process, 38*, 303–323. doi:10.1111/j.1545-5300.1999.00303.x

Iida, M., Stephens, M., Franks, M., & Rook, K. (2013). Daily symptoms, distress and interaction quality among couples coping with type 2 diabetes. *Journal of Social and Personal Relationships, 30*, 293–300. doi:10.1177/0265407512455308

Kalmijn, M. (2003). Shared friendship networks and the life course: An analysis of survey data on married and cohabiting couples. *Social Networks, 25*, 231–249. doi:10.1016/S0378-8733(03)00010-8

Kärner, A., Dahlgren, M., & Bergdahl, B. (2004). Rehabilitation after coronary heart disease: Spouses' views of support. *Journal of Advanced Nursing, 46,* 204–211. doi:10.1111/j.1365-2648.2003.02980.x

Karney, B., Bradbury, T., Fincham, F., & Sullivan, K. (1994). The role of negative affectivity in the association between attributions and marital satisfaction. *Journal of Personality and Social Psychology, 66,* 413–424. doi:10.1037/0022-3514.66.2.413

Katzmarzyk, P., Pérusse, L., Rao, D., & Bouchard, C. (1999). Spousal resemblance and risk of 7-year increases in obesity and central adiposity in the Canadian population. *Obesity, 7,* 545–551. doi:10.1002/j.1550-8528.1999.tb00712.x

Keyes, C. (2002). The mental health continuum: From languishing to flourishing in life. *Journal of Health and Social Behavior, ?, 207–222.* doi:10.2307/3090197

Knobloch, L.K. (2008). The content of relational uncertainty within marriage. *Journal of Social and Personal Relationships, 25,* 467–495. doi:10.1177/0265407508090869

Koenig, H., King, D., & Carson, V. (2012). *Handbook of religion and health.* New York, NY: Oxford University Press.

Langer, S., Abrams, J., & Syrjala, K. (2003). Caregiver and patient marital satisfaction and affect following hematopoietic stem cell transplantation: A prospective, longitudinal investigation. *Psycho-Oncology, 12,* 239–253. doi:10.1002/pon.633

Laurent, H., Laurent, S., Hertz, R., Egan-Wright, D., & Granger, D. (2013). Sex-specific effects of mindfulness on romantic partners' cortisol responses to conflict and relations with psychological adjustment. *Psychoneuroendocrinology, 38,* 2905–2913. doi:10.1016/j.psyneuen.2013.07.018

Lehmiller, J., & Agnew, C. (2007). Perceived marginalization and the prediction of romantic relationship stability. *Journal of Marriage and Family, 69,* 1036–1049. doi:10.1111/j.1741-3737.2007.00429.x

Levy, D. (2012). The importance of personal and contextual factors in resolving conflict between sexual identity and Christian upbringing. *Journal of Social Service Research, 38,* 56–73. doi:10.1080/01488376.2011.586308

Macken, L., Yates, B., & Blancher, S. (2000). Concordance of risk factors in female spouses of male patients with coronary heart disease. *Journal of Cardiopulmonary Rehabilitation and Prevention, 20,* 361–368. doi:10.1097/00008483-200011000-00005

Mahoney, A. (2010). Religion in families, 1999–2009: A relational spirituality framework. *Journal of Marriage and Family, 72,* 805–827. doi:10.1111/j.1741-3737.2010.00732.x

Mahoney, A., Pargament, K., Tarakeshwar, N., & Swank, A. (2008). Religion in the home in the 1980s and 90s: A meta-analytic review and conceptual analysis of religion, marriage, and parenting. *Journal of Family Psychology, 15,* 559–596. doi:10.1037/1941-1022.S.1.63

McEwen, B. (1998). Protective and damaging effects of stress mediators. *New England Journal of Medicine, 338,* 171–179. doi:10.1056/NEJM199801153380307

McNulty, J., & Fincham, F. (2012). Beyond positive psychology? Toward a contextual view of psychological processes and well-being. *American Psychologist, 67,* 101–110. doi:10.1037/a0024572

Miller, R., Hollist, C., Olsen, J., & Law, D. (2013). Marital quality and health over 20 years: A growth curve analysis. *Journal of Marriage and Family, 75,* 667–680. doi:10.1111/jomf.12025

Murphy, C., & Hoover, S. (1999). Measuring emotional abuse in relationships as a multifactorial construct. *Violence and Victims, 14,* 39–53.

Newman, M., & Roberts, N. (2013). *Health and social relationships: The good, the bad, and the complicated.* Washington, DC: American Psychological Association.

Niehuis, S., Huston, T., & Rosenband, R. (2006). From courtship into marriage: A new developmental model and methodological critique. *Journal of Family Communication, 6,* 23–47. doi:10.1207/s15327698jfc0601_3

Nijboer, C., Tempelaar, R., Sanderman, R., Triemstra, M., Spruijt, R., & Van Den Bos, G. (1998). Cancer and caregiving: The impact on the caregiver's health. *Psycho-Oncology, 7,* 3–13.

Ogolsky, B., & Bowers, J. (2013). A meta-analytic review of relationship maintenance and its correlates. *Journal of Social and Personal Relationships, 30,* 343–367. doi:10.1177/0265407512463338

Ogolsky, B., Lloyd, S., & Cate, R. (2013). *The developmental course of romantic relationships.* New York, NY: Routledge.

Papp, L., Goeke-Morey, M., & Cummings, E. (2007). Linkages between spouses' psychological distress and marital conflict in the home. *Journal of Family Psychology, 21,* 533–537. doi:10.1037/0893-3200.21.3.533

Pargament, K. (2007). *Spiritually integrated psychotherapy: Understanding and addressing the sacred.* New York, NY: Guilford Press.

Pargament, K., Mahoney, A., Exline, J., Jones, J., & Shafranske, E. (2013). *Envisioning an integrative paradigm for the psychology of religion and spirituality* (pp. 3–19). Washington, DC: American Psychological Association. doi:10.1037/14045-001

Patterson, J. (1988). Families experiencing stress: I. The Family Adjustment and Adaptation Response Model: II. Applying the FAAR Model to health-related issues for intervention and research. *Family Systems Medicine, 6,* 202–237. doi: 10.1037/h0089739.

Proulx, C., & Snyder-Rivas, L. (2013). The longitudinal associations between marital happiness, problems, and self-rated health. *Journal of Family Psychology, 27,* 194–202. doi:10.1037/a0031877.

Racin, L., & Dein, S. (2010). Jewish-Arab couple relationships in Israel: Underlying motives for entering and engaging in intermarriage. *Journal of Muslim Mental Health, 5,* 278–300. doi:10.1080/15564908.2010.551276

Renshaw, K., Blais, R., & Smith, T. (2010). Components of negative affectivity and marital satisfaction: The importance of actor and partner anger. *Journal of Research in Personality, 44,* 328–334. doi:10.1016/j.jrp.2010.03.005

Robles, T., & Kiecolt-Glaser, J. (2003). The physiology of marriage: Pathways to health. *Physiology and Behavior, 79,* 409–416. doi:10.1016/S0031-9384(03)00160-4

Robles, T., Slatcher, R., Trombello, J., & McGinn, M. (2014). Marital quality and health: A meta-analytic review. *Psychological Bulletin, 140,* 140–187. doi:10.1037/a0031859

Roscoe, L. (2009). Wellness: A review of theory and measurement for counselors. *Journal of Counseling and Development, 87,* 216–226. doi:10.1002/j.1556-6678.2009.tb00570.x

Sameroff, A. (2010). A unified theory of development: A dialectic integration of nature and nurture. *Child Development, 81,* 6–22. doi:10.111/j.1467-8624.2009.01378

Saxbe, D., & Repetti, R. (2010). For better or worse? Coregulation of couples' cortisol levels and mood states. *Journal of Personality and Social Psychology, 98,* 92–103. doi:10.1037/a0016959

Scheier, M., & Carver, C. (1992). Effects of optimism on psychological and physical well-being: Theoretical overview and empirical update. *Cognitive Therapy and Research, 16,* 201–228. doi:10.1007/BF01173489

Schmaling, K., & Sher, T. (1997). Physical health and relationships. In W. Halford & H. Markman (Eds.), *Clinical handbook of marriage and couples interventions* (pp. 323–345). Hoboken, NJ: John Wiley & Sons.

Schoormans, D., Mulder, B., van Melle, J., Pieper, P., van Dijk, A., Sieswerda, G., Hulsbergen-Zwarts, M., Plokker, T., Brunninkhuis, L., Vliegen, H., & Sprangers, M. (2014). Illness perceptions of adults with congenital heart disease and their predictive value for quality of life two years later. *European Journal of Cardiovascular Nursing, 13*, 86–94. doi:10.1177/1474515113481908

Schramm, D., Marshall, J., Harris, V., & Lee, T. (2012). Religiosity, homogamy, and marital adjustment: An examination of newlyweds in first marriages and remarriages. *Journal of Family Issues, 33*, 246–268. doi:10.1177/0192513X11420370

Shecket, D. (2014). *Changing faith: The dynamics and consequences of Americans' shifting religious identities.* New York, NY: New York University Press.

Smith, G., Snyder, D., Trull, T., & Monsma, B. (1988). Predicting relationship satisfaction from couples' use of leisure time. *American Journal of Family Therapy, 16*, 3–13. doi:10.1080/01926188808250702

South, S., Krueger, R., & Iacono, W. (2011). Understanding general and specific connections between psychopathology and marital distress: A model based approach. *Journal of Abnormal Psychology, 120*, 935–947. doi:10.1037/a0025417

Sprecher, S., Felmlee, D., Schmeeckle, M., Shu, X., Fine, M., & Harvey, J. (2006). No breakup occurs on an island: Social networks and relationship dissolution. In M.A. Fine & J.H. Harvey (Eds.), *Handbook of divorce and relationship dissolution* (pp. 457–478). New York, NY: Taylor and Frances.

Stafford, L., & Canary, D. (1991). Maintenance strategies and romantic relationship type, gender and relational characteristics. *Journal of Social and Personal Relationships, 8*, 217–242. doi:10.1177/0265407591082004

Thoits, P. (2011). Mechanisms linking social ties and support to physical and mental health. *Journal of Health and Social Behavior, 52*, 145–161. doi:10.1177/0022146510395592

Van Der Poel, A., & Greeff, A. (2003). The influence of coronary bypass graft surgery on the marital relationship and family functioning of the patient. *Journal of Sex and Marital Therapy, 29*, 61–77. doi:10.1080/713847098

Varvogli, L., & Darviri, C. (2011). Stress management techniques: Evidence-based procedures that reduce stress and promote health. *Health Science Journal, 5*, 74–89.

Vieten, C., Scammell, S., Pilato, R., Ammondson, I., Pargament, K., & Lukoff, D. (2013). Spiritual and religious competencies for psychologists. *Psychology of Religion and Spirituality, 5*, 129–144. doi:10.1037/a0032699

Walker, R., Isherwood, L., Burton, C., Kitwe-Magambo, K., & Luszcz, M. (2013). Marital satisfaction among older couples: The role of satisfaction with social networks and psychological well-being. *The International Journal of Aging and Human Development, 76*, 123–139. doi:10.2190/AG.76.2.b

Walsh, F. (2006). *Strengthening family resilience.* New York, NY: Guilford Press.

Whisman, M., Weinstock, L., & Uebelacker, L. (2002). Mood reactivity to marital conflict: The influence of marital dissatisfaction and depression. *Behavior Therapy, 33*, 299–314. doi:10.1016/S0005-7894(02)80030-2

Wiley, A., Adler-Baeder, F., & Warzinik, K. (2013). Care for self: Maintaining physical, sexual, emotional, and spiritual wellness. In T. G. Futris & F. Adler-Baeder (Eds.), *The*

National Extension Relationship and Marriage Education Model (pp. 17–24). Athens: The University of Georgia Cooperative Extension.

World Health Organization. (1946). Constitution of the World Health Organization. Retrieved from http://www.who.int/about/definition/en/print.html

World Health Organization. (1986). The Ottawa Charter for Health Promotion. Retrieved from http://www.who.int/healthpromotion/conferences/previous/ottawa/en/

Wrzus, C., Hänel, M., Wagner, J., & Neyer, F. (2013). Social network changes and life events across the life span: A meta-analysis. *Psychological Bulletin, 139*, 53–80. doi:10.1037/a0028601

Yorgason, J., Booth, A., & Johnson, D. (2008). Health, disability, and marital quality: Is the association different for younger versus older cohorts? *Research on Aging, 30*, 623–648. doi:10.1177/0164027508322570

6

SOUND RELATIONSHIP HOUSE THEORY AND RELATIONSHIP AND MARRIAGE EDUCATION

Robert J. Navarra, John M. Gottman, and Julie Schwartz Gottman

---

LEARNING GOALS

- Learn about the research background and development of Dr. John Gottman's divorce prediction studies.
- Learn about the effectiveness of Gottman's relationship prediction research and its relevance for RME programs.
- Learn about the Sound Relationship House Theory, the relationship model used to explain what we have learned from Dr. Gottman's research.
- Learn about current intervention studies and pending research from Gottman's Relationship Research Institute.

Introduction

Gottman Couples Therapy (GCT) is a research-based therapy developed over four decades of observational research to determine if it was possible to discover reliable patterns of interaction that discriminate between happy couples that are on a stable path from couples that were unhappy and either eventually divorce or stay together but remain unhappy. The result of Dr. Gottman's research and collaboration with his friend and colleague Dr. Robert Levenson is that we can now reliably predict with over 90% accuracy which relationships would succeed and which relationships would fail if untreated, six years later.

This 40-year research journey has included 12 studies with over 3,000 couples, including seven studies on what predicts divorce. Six of these studies are predictive, longitudinal studies with some couples having been followed for as long as 20 years, including a 12-year study on gay and lesbian couples (Gottman,

Levenson, Gross, Frederickson, McCoy, Rosenthal, Ruef, & Yoshimoto, 2003), and a 10-year study with couples suffering from domestic violence (Jacobson & Gottman, 1998). Treatment and intervention research have involved over 4,000 couples.

More recently, Dr. John Gottman has studied and developed theories on trust and betrayal based on new applications of game theory. This research-based understanding of how couples build trust versus the steps that lead to betrayal and eroding trust has led to a model of prevention and treatment described in two books, *The Science of Trust* (Gottman, 2011), and *What Makes Love Last?* (Gottman, and Silver, 2012).

From research to theory to practice. John Gottman and Robert Levenson had been studying relationships for over 20 years when John began working with his wife, clinical psychologist Dr. Julie Schwartz Gottman, in 1994, developing the Sound Relationship House (SRH) Theory and interventions based on John's research. Learning from successful couples what was needed for lasting and thriving romantic relationships, the Gottmans identified seven building blocks for relationships and interventions to deepen friendship and intimacy, strengthen conflict management, and create shared meaning and purpose. The SRH theory became the basis of the design of clinical interventions for couples described in *The Marriage Clinic* (Gottman, 1999b) and in Dr. Julie Gottman's book *The Marriage Clinic Casebook* (Gottman, 2004).

It is important to note that the Gottman Method is not a school of therapy, rather, it is a research-based theory to practice model that provides a definable explanation of why some relationships are successful, and why others are not and either end up in divorce or in distress. Through continuing research and by incorporating other research-based methods created by others that have been proven to be effective, GCT will continue to evolve and develop. There is always more to learn as new findings also raise more questions.

The implications of Gottman research for educators. Unfortunately, family life educators, counselors and therapists, clergy, and others in the helping professions are often trained to help couples based on untested ideas and theories about what healthy relationships should look like. For example, one of the most popular and enduring hypotheses in determining relationship and communication health is the "active listening model," using I-statements, as a basis for developing empathy and creating effective relationship communication and stability. The active listening model, inspired largely by Carl Rogers, was further developed and adapted by Bernard Guerney (Guerney, 1977; Guerney & Guerney, 1985) and subsequently has been advocated by countless educators, communication workshop facilitators, and therapists.

While initially Dr. John Gottman recommended this intervention (Gottman, 1994; Gottman, Markman, & Notarius, 1977), it turns out that after researching active listening as a predictive variable in relationship satisfaction, active listening exchanges, as commonly taught to couples in workshops and in the therapy room, occurred only 4.4% of the time for all couples; furthermore, these exchanges didn't predict anything. After qualitative analysis with another research cohort of couples with happy and stable relationships, Gottman found again that couples were not paraphrasing what their partners were saying, nor were they summarizing their partner's feelings. Rather, partner response to negativity was more about processing their own reactions rather than their partner's emotions.

While there was no evidence to support the active listening hypothesis, Gottman did discover in subsequent research that how couples managed negativity was highly predictive of relationship health. He found that negativity was met with negativity in stable relationships, but in distressed relationships the negativity escalated and presented as a very different trajectory (Gottman, 1999a). While active listening undoubtedly is a core therapeutic skill in the therapy room that facilitates empathy and connection between client and counselor, it turns out it is a lot easier to respond empathically when the listener is not the one being talked about.

The importance of familiarity with relationship research for marriage and relationship educators, in this case, highlights the importance of normalizing the dynamic that negative interactions tend to lead to more negative responses in all relationships. However, escalating anger with physiological arousal, determined by changes in heart rate, skin conductance, gross motor activity, and blood velocity, leads to pervasive patterns of negative communication which is predictive of relationship dissatisfaction and divorce. Rather than emphasizing active listening in managing conflict, this research suggests the importance of teaching couples ways to manage physiological arousal and escalating anger.

Differentiating evidence-based theories about relationship health from the myths, the assumptions, and the untested hypotheses provides relationship and marriage educators empirically based principles, methods, and practices for helping couples strengthen, maintain, and repair relationships.

Empirical Basis for Gottman Couples Therapy

The Sound Relation House Theory emerged out of the systematic analyses of patterns and dynamic processes in couple interactions. Furthermore, the SRH theory outlines steps to help couples get on a healthier path. Gottman Couples Therapy has been tested and shown to greatly improve relationships, including help for very distressed couples, for couples transitioning into parenthood, and for couples experiencing minor domestic violence. A version of Gottman Couples Therapy has proven to be effective for couples suffering from the traumatic effects of poverty. Gottman Couples Therapy has been taught worldwide, including Europe, Asia, Australia, and the Americas. To date there have been over 30,000 therapists and educators who have received training in the Gottman Method.

The Discovery of Reliable Patterns of Interaction

In 1938 Louis Terman researched the question of what makes some couple relationships work, while other couples are unhappy? His research methodology included the use of questionnaires and interviews. Systematic observation only started in the 1970s, in Gottman's lab and a few others. At the time efforts to establish reliable patterns in personality theory were not met with success, so there was very little support for research aimed at finding reliable patterns in relationships, seemingly exponentially more difficult. Additionally, marriage and relationships had been the area of study for sociologists, not psychologists. A new era was starting in understanding relationships because it turns out that while individual behavior is hard to predict, the research would reveal the fact that there is tremendous regularity in relationship behavior.

By definition, observational research is atheoretical, at least initially, in that the researcher draws conclusions only after comparing subjects, in this case, determining differences between happy and unhappy couples. Observing and analyzing interactions requires a system of psychometrics and mathematical modeling to determine empirically what is actually being measured so that patterns can be identified (Gottman, Murray, Swanson, Tyson, & Swanson, 2005). Additionally, as with other methods of research, reliability of the measuring instruments needs to be well established (Bakeman & Gottman, 1997).

John Gottman teamed with Roger Bakeman to develop a mathematical model and methodology for sequential analysis to differentiate satisfied from dissatisfied couples based on Jim Sackett's ideas (Gottman, 1979). This new system of cataloging codes to measure interaction and relationship behavior led to a remarkable discovery. Gottman and Bakeman began to find consistent sequences of interactions that differentiated happy marriages from unhappy marriages.

The Gottman lab used different observational coding systems in various studies examining the following: problem solving, affect, physiology, power, non-problem-solving conversations, positive and negative reciprocity, and distance and isolation (Gottman, 1994). Gottman developed with his students Cliff Notarius and Howard Markman the Couples' Interaction Scoring System (CISS), designed to separate dimensions of behavior from affect and to differentiate satisfied from dissatisfied couples. The lab continued to apply new methods for studying sequences of interaction and continued to modify and improve those systems.

Gottman also applied, for the first time, an application of game theory to couples' interactions. Influenced by Thibaut and Kelley's book *The Social Psychology of Groups* (1959), he devised the "talk table," a system for individuals to rate how positive or negative their intentions were, and how positive or negative were the effects of the messages they received.

The Gottman lab used these methods to define reliable patterns of interaction and thought during conflict. Following a series of peer-reviewed journal articles, in 1979 Gottman published these results in a series of scientific papers and a book called *Marital Interaction: Experimental Investigations* (Gottman, 1979).

Divorce Prediction Research

The research on the longitudinal course of relationships began in 1975 when John Gottman first teamed with Robert Levenson to research on divorce prediction, involving measures for perception, interaction, and physiology. At the time there were only six longitudinal prospective studies, and those studies were very poor at prediction with correlations around 0.25 or so (Gottman, 1999a, 1999b).

Gottman and Levenson conducted their first study in 1980 using their multi-method approach by combining the study of emotion with psycho-physiological measurement and video-recall method (Levenson & Gottman, 1983). Thirty couples came to their lab and were instructed to have two conversations: a low-conflict discussion involving a neutral "reunion conversation" talking about the events of the day, and a high-conflict discussion of an issue in their relationship that was creating a major source of disagreement.

While Gottman and Levenson did not make any predictions in this first study, they were very interested in the linkage between physiology, emotions, and relationship distress. In a previous study simple physiologic measurements suggested a relationship between relatedness and physiology (Kaplan et al., 1964). Gottman and Levenson thought this might be linked to negative affect in couples, and they were right.

Couples were videotaped during discussions as the research team took physiologic measurements: heart rate, skin conductance, gross motor activity, and blood velocity, all synced to video time code. The couples separately returned later to the lab and watched a video of their reunion and conflict conversations. They were asked questions about what they were thinking and feeling and to make guesses as to what they thought their partner was thinking and feeling, while using a rating dial to measure what emotions and how strongly the participant felt the emotion during the interaction.

Gottman also began applying time-series analysis to the analysis of interaction data. Gottman and Levenson then got their first grant together and began attempting to replicate their observations from the first study. In 1983 they completed the longitudinal study, computing first the amount and direction of changes to the initial marital satisfaction scores. Then they determined which of the affective and physiological variables measured three years earlier were predictive of change in marital satisfaction. After controlling for the initial levels of marital satisfaction the results indicated that the more physiologic arousal there was in couples three years earlier, the more relationship satisfaction declined during the three years (Levenson & Gottman, 1985).

The researchers were amazed that in their first study with 30 couples they were able to predict the change in marital satisfaction almost perfectly with the physiological measures. The results were that the more physiologically aroused couples were in all channels (heart rate, skin conductance, gross motor activity, and blood velocity) the more their marriages deteriorated in happiness over a three-year period, even controlling for the initial level of marital satisfaction. The rating dial and their observational coding of the interaction also correlated with differences in relationship satisfaction. Gottman and Levenson had never seen such large correlations in their data. They also found that a harsh, critical beginning by women in the conflict discussion was associated by the male partner's disinterest or irritability in the events of the day discussion. In a reciprocal dynamic, they also found that the quality of the couple's friendship and closeness, especially as maintained by men, was critical in understanding conflict and most likely related to the harsh start. This finding supported the "attack-defend" pattern characteristic of ailing marriages. The ability to rebound from conflict to the positive conversation became a marker of emotion-regulation ability of couples.

Both Robert Levenson and John Gottman had discovered Paul Ekman and Wallace Friesen's **Facial Affect Coding System (FACS)**, and Gottman subsequently developed the **Specific Affect Coding System (SPAFF)**, which was an integration of FACS and earlier systems in the Gottman lab. The SPAFF became the main system that Gottman used to code couples' interaction giving greater precision in describing the positive-negative affective interactions (Gottman & Krokoff, 1989) by adding other channels to facial coding such as language, voice inflection, body movement, and the context of the interaction (Gottman, 1994). SPAFF codes classify at each turn of speech as affectively negative, neutral, or positive. Gottman's works in the lab, coined by the press as the "Love Lab," gained attention and interest as the divorce prediction outcome studies were publicized. The **two trajectories of marriage**, characterized as the **"Masters and the Disasters,"** defined the differences between couples on a stable path, who wanted to be together, verses couples that either divorced or if they stayed together were unhappy.

The core findings identify four negative and **corrosive patterns of interaction** highly correlated with divorce called the "Four Horsemen of the Apocalypse."

- **Criticism**. Patterns of blame expressed in attacks of the partner's character or personality. Criticism is often expressed with "you always" or "you never."
- **Defensiveness**. Refusing to accept responsibility or acknowledging fault. Characterized by either counterattacks or defending innocence.
- **Contempt**. The most destructive of the four negative interactions is defined as adding contempt, superiority, or disgust to the criticism.
- **Stonewalling**. Occurs when the person feels overwhelmed and unable to respond. The person shuts down and doesn't offer verbal or nonverbal responses because of a high arousal state. In the research 85 percent of the stonewallers were men.

The subsequent research on divorce prediction, including collaborative work in other labs, eventually spanned the entire life course from a study following newlyweds through the transition to parenthood (Gottman, 1994; Gottman, Katz, & Hooven, 1996; Gottman, Coan, Carrére, & Swanson, 1998), a study in the Levenson Berkeley lab on the transition through retirement, following couples for as long as 20 years (Levenson, Carstensen & Gottman, 1994), and one study with violent couples (Jacobson & Gottman, 1998).

The predictions replicated, Gottman could predict whether a couple would divorce with an average of over 90% accuracy, across studies using the ratio of positive to negative SPAFF codes, the Four Horsemen of the Apocalypse (Criticism, Defensiveness, Contempt, and Stonewalling), physiology, the rating dial, and an Oral History Interview (asking how the couple met), as coded by Buehlman's coding system assessing in particular the husbands' responses to six different dimensions related to positivity or negativity (Gottman, 1994). They could predict whether or not the stable couples would be happy or unhappy using measures of positive affect during conflict, which Coan and Gottman discovered would physiologically soothe the partner. How couples manage conflict is highly predictive of relationship trajectory.

The research indicates during conflict discussions happy, stable couples are able to maintain a 5:1 ratio of positivity to negativity. They also discovered that men accepting influence from women were predictive of happy and stable marriages. Levenson, along with Ruef, also found humor was physiologically soothing, and empathy had a physiological substrate with using the rating dial.

Gottman and Levenson discovered that couples interaction had enormous stability over time (about 80% stability in conflict discussions separated by 3 years). They also discovered that most relationship problems (69%) never get resolved but are "perpetual" problems based on personality differences between partners. This finding was discovered by follow-up and seeing couples in the lab every 3 years.

In 1986, Gottman built an apartment laboratory in a park-like setting at the University of Washington. Volunteer couples from every major ethnic and racial group in the U.S. were observed in the apartment lab for a 24-hour period. Couples were encouraged to act as naturally as possible and to relax and to do whatever they might do on a typical weekend. They could bring groceries to cook, games to play, movies to watch, read the newspaper, basically just to be together.

Gottman discovered how couples create and maintain friendship and intimacy and how it was related to conflict. For example, newlyweds who divorced 6 years after the wedding had turned towards bids (the partner's attempt to connect) 33% of the time, while newlyweds who stayed married 6 years after the wedding had turned towards bids 86% of the time. The idea of the friendship "**emotional bank account**" was verified. It was related to repair of negativity, and, amazingly to the quality of sexual intimacy.

When 14-year longitudinal data became available Levenson and Gottman discovered a second dysfunctional pattern, emotional disengagement. It was marked by the absence of positive affect during conflict (no interest, affection, humor, or empathy). Now they could predict not only *if* a couple would divorce, but *when*. Couples who had the Four Horsemen divorced an average of 5.6 years after the wedding, while emotionally disengaged couples divorced an average of 16.2 years after the wedding.

Intervention Research

Bringing Baby Home. The Gottmans first began testing their interventions by exploring what happened to a couple when the first baby arrived. In this longitudinal study they began studying young couples in first marriages a few months after their wedding, following couples into pregnancy and studying parent-infant interactions. They discovered that 67% of couples experienced a precipitous decline in relationship satisfaction in the first 3 years of the baby's life. Gottman's student Alyson Shapiro compared the 33% of couples who did not experience the downturn in satisfaction with the 67% who did.

A randomized clinical trial study with long-term follow-up indicates that the preventative psychoeducational intervention of the two-day Bringing Baby Home (BBH) workshop, designed by the Gottmans (Gottman & Gottman, 2007), was effective in achieving positive results. Based on comparisons with the couples who declined and did not decline in relationship satisfaction after baby, workshop participants showed improvement in the domains of marital quality, wife and husband postpartum depression, and wife and husband hostile affect observed during conflict (Shapiro & Gottman, 2005). The BBH workshop has now been taught to 1,000 birth educators from 24 countries. The effects have been replicated in Australia and Iceland.

The emotion-coaching intervention. This intervention is described in *Raising an Emotionally Intelligent Child* (Gottman & DeClaire, 1998). The intervention has been evaluated in 3 randomized clinical trials by Australian psychologist Sophie Havighurst (Havighurst, Wilson, Harley, & Prior, 2009; Havighurst, Wilson, Harley, Prior, & Kehoe, 2010; Wilson, Havighurst, & Harley, 2012) and has also been found effective in a study in South Korea, led by certified Gottman therapist Christina Choi both in orphanages in Seoul and in Busan. Emotion coaching is now being taught to teachers throughout South Korea. Research and training is also taking place in the UK on emotion coaching.

The couples workshop. Exit studies surveys from couples attending the Gottman Art and Science of Love Workshops indicate that 86% of people completing the 2-day workshop report making significant progress on conflicts. A 1-year follow-up study was done to see if the results would stand the test of time. This was a randomized clinical trial of a couples' group psychoeducational intervention, the Art and Science of Love, with 80 distressed married couples randomly assigned to one of four conditions: (1) friendship enhancement alone—day 1 of the workshop, (2) conflict management alone—day 2 of the workshop, (3) both friendship enhancement and conflict management—both days of the workshop, and (4) bibliotherapy only.

Outcome assessment included three dimensions: (1) relationship satisfaction, (2) friendship quality, and (3) destructive conflict at pre-, post-, and 1 year following the intervention. While all conditions were found to increase relationship satisfaction with couples demonstrating fewer problems with friendship and destructive conflict at the 1-year follow-up, the combined condition suggests the greatest changes in marital satisfaction and in decreases in problems in friendship and conflict (Babcock, Gottman, Ryan, & Gottman, 2013).

Plans for current intervention studies. Plans for collaborative research studies are in process for the following projects:

- Effectiveness of a relational approach to addiction recovery, integrating Navarra's research-based theory the **Couple Recovery Development Approach** (CRDA) (Navarra, 2007, 2009) with interventions when we adapted from the SRH model (Navarra & Gottman, 2011).
- Replicate a study with Warford on situational domestic violence differentiating it from characterological domestic violence (Bradley, Drummey, Gottman & Gottman, 2014; Bradley, Friend, & Gottman, 2011; Friend, Bradley, Thatcher, & Gottman, 2010).
- A randomized clinical trial for couples healing after an extramarital affair with Peluso.

Sound Relationship House (SRH) Theory

John Gottman began working with his wife, Julie Schwartz Gottman, in 1994, co-creating the Gottman Institute, moving the science from predicting divorce to preventing divorce. Experimenting with research-based interventions, the Gottmans began working with couples, developed the Art and Science of Love Workshop, and developed training programs for therapists, and more recently for educators, on the research-based findings and tools to help couples (Gottman & Gottman, 2006) (see Figure 6.1). Combining John's research with Julie's years of clinical experience was the perfect blend of the scientist–practitioner model.

The **Sound Relationship House Model** (SRH) serves as a blueprint to help couples deepen their closeness, manage conflict, and share in what is meaningful to both of them, individually, and as a couple. The findings from the research supported in the SRH model leads to two essential conclusions about what makes for happy relationships:

1. Partners treat each other like good friends, with the relationship characterized by respect, empathy, affection, and positivity.
2. Partners manage conflict in gentle and positive ways, literally maintaining a 5:1 ratio of positive to negative comments during the conflict discussion.

There are seven levels to the SRH described in three components: the Friendship System, The Conflict System, and the Meaning System. As opposed to a hierarchical model starting at the bottom before moving to the next level, the SRH is an interactional model, with each level impacting other levels. There is a

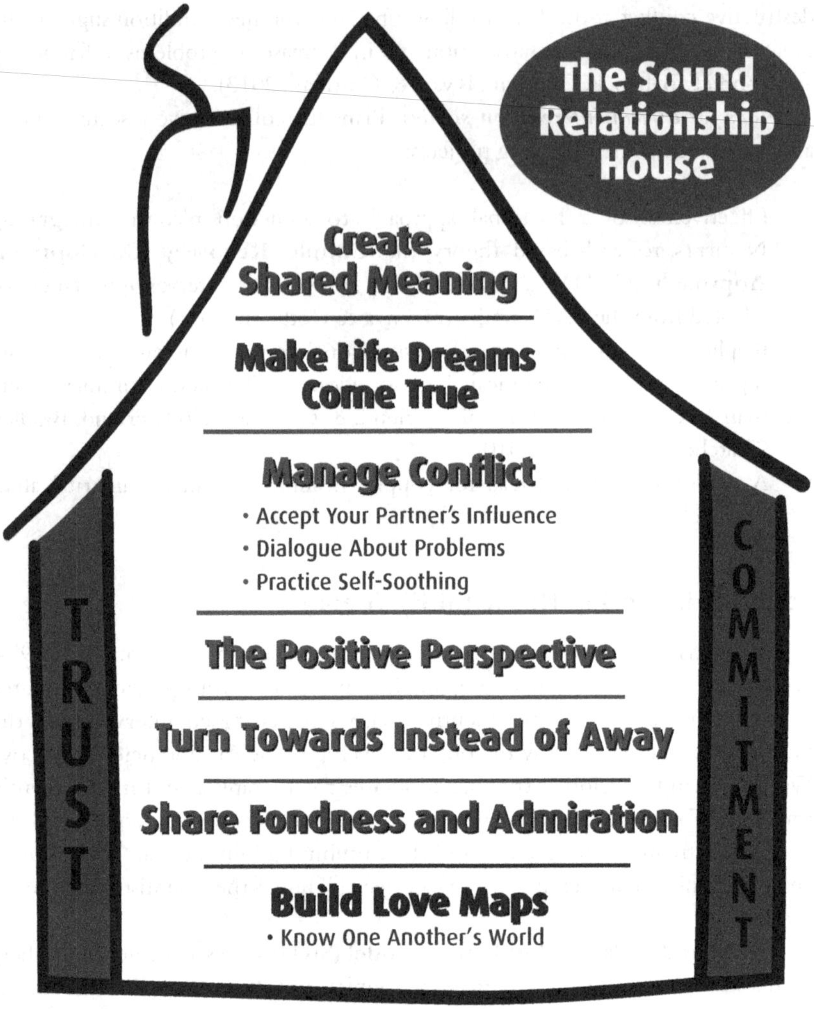

FIGURE 6.1 The Sound Relationship House Model

Copyright © 2000–2011 by Dr.John Gottman. Distributed under license by the Gottman Institute, Inc.

bidirectional influence between the three levels. The first three levels of the SRH describe the Friendship System.

Trust and Commitment. Subsequent to John Gottman's research on trust and betrayal, Trust and Commitment were added to the SRH Model, supporting the seven levels, or building blocks, of the components needed for a happy relationship.

Trust is a state that occurs when a person knows that the partner puts his or her own interests and benefits secondary to the partner's own interests and benefits. This translates to the couple feeling "My partner has my back and is there for me." Commitment is cherishing one's partner, the belief that "This is the relationship I want to be in. This is the person I want to be with."

Levels of the Sound Relationship House

1. *Build Love Maps.* **Love maps** refer to how well each partner knows each other. It refers to the partners' knowledge and interest in each other's internal world of thoughts, hopes, ideas, and feelings. Knowing the partner's likes and dislikes, aspirations, hopes, and dreams creates a sense of connection and of being known. Having this map is the most basic level of friendship, but when this level is not working well, partners feel distant, uncared for, and the emotional distance creates feelings of alienation.

2. *Share fondness and admiration.* This level describes partners' ability to notice and express what they appreciate about each other, building affection and respect for one another. Noticing and expressing the things partners admire and appreciate in each other creates a feeling of being cared for and valued. Contempt is the antithesis of respect, and when partners feel attacked or criticized, they are not likely to feel loved.

3. *Turn towards instead of away.* This is the smallest measureable unit of intimacy reflected in how partners attempt to reach out or connect with each other. These attempts, referred to as bids, are opportunities for connection when the other partner turns towards the bid, thus building the emotional bank account. When bids are made and either not responded to, or responded to negatively, it takes money out of the emotional bank account. In the latter case, after a while partners are likely to stop making bids.

4. *The Positive Perspective.* When the first three levels of the SRH are working well, couples will be in Positive Perspective. Partners are able to let things go more easily and not take things personally. There is more humor, affection, and less reactivity. When one or more levels of the Friendship System are not healthy, the couple will most likely be in Negative Perspective where perceptions are colored by negative thoughts and feelings; neutral and even positive interactions will still be perceived as negative and partners will be hypervigilant for negativity. Negative Perspective can be reversed by strengthening the first three levels of the SRH.

5. *Manage conflict.* The term "**manage conflict**" versus "resolve conflict" is used to normalize conflict as a natural and positive aspect of healthy relationships. The research indicates that 69% of couples' problems were perpetual relating to differences in individual personalities, preferences in life style, and differences in needs. Only 31% of couples' problems fall in the category of solvable. The Masters of relationships manage conflict with the 5:1 ratio of positive to negative interactions. They are gentle towards one another, they avoid blame,

they accept influence, they are more calm, they repair and de-escalate, and they are able to offer compromise.

6. *Make life dreams come true.* A level of building Love Maps, partners inquire and are able to talk honestly about their dreams, values, hopes, convictions, and aspirations. They feel that the relationship supports those life dreams. Often times when perpetual problems become gridlocked, at the root are hidden stories and core needs at the deepest levels of meaning that need to be expressed and understood.

7. *Create shared meaning.* This level refers to another existential perspective, one that involves shared meaning and purpose. Couples define roles, goals, and values that are meaningful. We return once again to building Love Maps, at that deeper level. It is about building a life together, creating formal and informal rituals that bring integration and connection.

Conclusion

SRH theory emerged out of the systematic analyses of patterns and dynamic processes in couple interactions. Furthermore, the SRH theory outlines steps to help couples get on a healthier path. Gottman Couples Therapy has been tested and shown to greatly improve relationships, including help for very distressed couples, for couples transitioning into parenthood, and for couples experiencing minor domestic violence. A version of Gottman couples Gottman Couples Therapy has been taught worldwide, including Europe, Asia, Australia, and the Americas to over 30,000 counselors, therapists, and educators.

The Gottman Institute provides educator training for three different community-based programs. Gottman **Seven Principles Educator Training** provides tools for educators to facilitate community-based classes for couples, based on Dr. Gottman's book *The Seven Principles for Making Marriage Work* (2000). A second program, *Bringing Baby Home*, offers educators a 2-day training to provide workshops designed to help pregnant couples prepare for the transition to parenthood. Lastly, the *Emotion Coaching Program* provides a resource for parents and parent groups on how to equip children to understand and regulate their emotional world. To date, about 2,000 Educators worldwide have been trained in the Bringing Baby Home Program and The Gottman Seven Principles Program.

Key Points

- John Gottman has been studying relationships for over 40 years and based on his research has been able to predict divorce with over 90% accuracy.
- The Gottman research methodology is a multimethod approach, analyzing perception, interaction, and physiology.
- Gottman prediction research has included over 3,000 couples and intervention studies with over 4,000 couples.

- The seven building blocks of relationships predictive of relationship stability are described in Sound Relationship House Theory.
- Predictors of divorce include the "Four Horsemen of the Apocalypse," physiology arousal during conflict, negative affect when describing relationship history, and less than a 5:1 ratio of positive to negative interactions during conflict.

Discussion Questions

1. How does physiology impact relationship satisfaction?
2. What are the advantages of observational research over interviewing and questionnaires?
3. What are the most important discoveries in the Gottman research in divorce prediction?
4. Sound Relationship House Theory proposes that there are three components of relationship functioning that collectively predict relationship happiness. How do you describe the relationships between these levels? For example, how might the strength of the Friendship System impact the couple's ability to manage conflict and vice versa?
5. How might marriage and relationship educators integrate what we have learned about relationship satisfaction in prevention programs for parents, school age children, college students, and community-based programs?
6. The four big predictors of divorce and relationship dissatisfaction are the "Four Horsemen of the Apocalypse." How might educators orient communication workshops to include a presentation and discussion on these destructive patterns of communication?
7. What adaptations from the Gottman research might be applied to the work environment, i.e., organizational development, human resources, team building?
8. How might staff development programs benefit from what we have learned from the Gottman research?
9. What cultural considerations might educators consider in presenting concepts from the Gottman research?
10. What should educators be aware of and address when differentiating psycho-educational workshops from therapy?

References and Further Readings

Babcock, J., Gottman, J.M., Ryan, K., & Gottman, J.S. (2013). A component analysis of a brief psycho-educational couples' workshop: One-year follow-up results. *Journal of Family Therapy*, 35, 252–280.

Bakeman, R., & Gottman, J.M. (1997). *Observing interaction: An introduction to sequential analysis*. New York, NY: Cambridge University Press.

Bradley, R., Drummey, K., Gottman, J.M., & Gottman, J.S. (2014). Treating couples who mutually exhibit violence or aggression: Reducing behaviors that show a susceptibility for violence. *Journal of Family Violence, 29,* 549–558.

Bradley, R., Friend, D., & Gottman, J.M. (2011). Supporting healthy relationships in low-income, violent couples: Reducing conflict and strengthening relationship skills and satisfaction. *Journal of Couple and Relationship Therapy, 10,* 97–116.

Friend, D., Bradley, R., Thatcher, R., & Gottman, J.M. (2010). Typologies of intimate partner violence: Evaluation of a screening instrument for differentiation. *Journal of Family Violence, 25,* 357–448.

Gottman, J.M. (1979). *Marital interaction: Experimental investigations.* New York, NY: Academic Press.

Gottman, J.M. (1994). *What predicts divorce? The relationship between marital processes and marital outcomes.* Hillsdale, NJ: Lawrence Erlbaum Associates.

Gottman, J.M. (1999a). *The seven principles for making marriage work.* New York, NY: Three Rivers Press.

Gottman, J.M. (1999b). *The marriage clinic: A scientifically based marital therapy.* New York, NY: W.W. Norton & Company.

Gottman, J.M. (2011). *The science of trust: Emotional attunement for couples.* New York, NY: W. W. Norton & Company.

Gottman, J.M., Coan, J., Carrére, S., & Swanson, C. (1998). Predicting marital happiness and stability from newlywed interactions, *Journal of Marriage and Family, 60,* 5–22.

Gottman, J.M., & DeClaire, J. (1998). *Raising an emotionally intelligent child.* New York, NY: Simon & Schuster.

Gottman, J.M., & Gottman, J.S. (2006). *10 lessons to transform your marriage.* New York, NY: Crown Publishers.

Gottman, J.M., & Gottman, J.S. (2007). *And baby makes three.* New York, NY: Crown Publishers.

Gottman, J.M., & Katz, L. (1989). The effects of marital discord on young children's peer interaction and health. *Developmental Psychology, 25,* 373–381.

Gottman, J.M., Katz, L., & Hooven, C., (1996). Parental meta-emotion philosophy and the emotional life of families: Theoretical models and preliminary data. *Journal of Family Psychology, 10,* 243–268.

Gottman, J.M., & Krokoff, L. (1989). The relationship between marital interaction and marital satisfaction: A longitudinal view. *Journal of Consulting and Clinical Psychology, 57,* 47–52.

Gottman, J.M., & Silver, N. (2000). *The seven principles for making marriage work.* New York, NY: Three Rivers Press.

Gottman, J.M. & Silver, N. (2012). *What makes love last. How to build trust and avoid betrayal.* New York, NY: Simon & Schuster Paperbacks.

Gottman, J.M., Levenson, R., Gross, J., Frederickson, B., McCoy, K., Rosenthal, L., Ruef, A., & Yoshimoto, D. (2003). Correlates of gay and lesbian couples' relationship satisfaction and relationship dissolution. *Journal of Homosexuality, 45,* 23–43.

Gottman, J.M., Markman, H., & Notarius, C. (1977). The topography of marital conflict: A study of verbal and non-verbal behavior. *Journal of Marriage and Family, 39,* 461–477.

Gottman, J.M., Murray, J., Swanson, C., Tyson, R., & Swanson, K. (2005). *The mathematics of marriage.* Cambridge, MA: MIT Press.

Gottman, J.S. (Ed.). (2004). *The marriage clinic casebook.* New York, NY: W.W. Norton & Company.

Guerney, B. (1977). *Relationship enhancement.* San Francisco, CA: Jossey-Bass.

Guerney, B., & Guerney, L. (1985). Marital and family problem prevention and enrichment programs. In L. L'Abate (Ed.), *Handbook of family psychology and therapy* (pp. 1179–1217). Homewood, IL: Dorsey Press.

Havighurst, S., Wilson, K., Harley, A., & Prior, M. (2009). Tuning in to kids: An emotion-focused parenting program—initial findings from a community trial. *Journal of Community Psychology, 37*, 1008–1023.

Havighurst, S., Wilson, K., Harley, A., Prior, M., & Kehoe, C. (2010). Tuning in to Kids: Improving emotion socialization practices in parents of preschool children—findings from a community trial. *Journal of Child Psychology and Psychiatry, 51*, 1342–1350.

Jacobson, R., & Gottman, J.M. (1998). *When men batter women: New insights into ending abusive relationships*. New York, NY: Simon & Schuster.

Kaplan, H., Burch, N., & Bloom, S.W. (1964). Physiologic covariation in small peer groups. In P. Leiderman & D. Shapiro (Eds.), *Psychobiological approaches to social behavior* (pp. 92–109). Stanford, CA: Stanford University Press.

Katz, L., & Gottman, J.M. (1991a). Marital discord and child outcomes: A social and psychophysiological approach. In K. Dodge & J. Garber (Eds.), *The development of emotion regulation and deregulation* (pp. 129–158). New York, NY: Cambridge University Press.

Katz, L., & Gottman, J.M. (1991b, April). Marital interaction processes and preschool children's peer interactions and emotional development. Paper presented at the meeting of the Society for Research in Child Development, Seattle, WA.

Levenson, R., Carstensen, L., & Gottman, J.M. (1994). Influence of age and gender on affect, physiology and their interrelations: A study of long-term marriages. *Journal of Personality and Social Psychology, 67*, 56–68.

Levenson, R., & Gottman, J.M. (1983). Martial interaction: Physiological linkage and affective exchange. *Journal of Psychology, 45*, 587–597.

Levenson, R., & Gottman, J.M. (1985). Physiological and affective predictors of change in relationship satisfaction. *Journal of Personality and Social Psychology, 49*, 85–94.

Navarra, R. (2007). Family response to adults and alcohol. In J. Fischer, M. Mulsow, & A. Korinek (Eds.), *Familial responses to alcohol problems* (pp. 85–103). Binghamton, NY: Haworth Press.

Navarra, R. (2009). Alcoholism and drug addiction co-morbidity. *Level II: Assessment, intervention and co-morbidities*. Seattle, WA: The Gottman Institute, Inc.

Navarra, R., & Gottman, J.M. (2011). Gottman method couple therapy: From theory to practice. In D. Carson & M. Casado-Kehoe (Eds.), *Case studies in couples therapy: Theory-based approaches* (pp. 331–343). New York, NY: Routledge.

Shapiro, A., & Gottman, J.M. (2005). Effects on marriage of a psycho-communicative-educational intervention with couples undergoing a transition to parenthood, evaluation at the 1-year post intervention. *Journal of Family Communication, 5*, 1–2.

Shapiro, A.F., Gottman, J.M., & Carrère, S. (2000). The baby and the marriage: Identifying factors that buffer against decline in marital satisfaction after the first baby arrives. *Journal of Family Psychology, 14*, 59–70.

Thibaut, J., & Kelley, H. (1959). *The social psychology of groups*. New York, NY: Wiley.

Wilson, K., Havighurst, S., & Harley, A. (2012). Tuning in to Kids: An effectiveness trial of a parenting program targeting emotion socialization of pre-schoolers. *Journal of Family Psychology, 26*, 56–65.

7

DEVELOPING A MODEL FOR RELATIONSHIP AND MARRIAGE EDUCATION

Efforts and Lessons from the U.S. Cooperative Extension

H. Wallace Goddard and David G. Schramm

LEARNING GOALS

- Be aware of Extension efforts to create research summaries or models in parenting and couple relationships.
- Understand some ways models are developed and tested.
- Be prepared to use Extension models in the creation of presentations, programs, and curricula.

Introduction

Cooperative Extension Service (CES) is a network of specialists and agents in most states and counties of the United States. The central mandate of CES is to deliver research-based knowledge to the citizens of the states. The assumption is that the taxpayers who fund research should benefit from its findings (see http://www.csrees.usda.gov/Extension/).

While Extension has been best known for agricultural programs, it has also provided research-based programs for family life education. The university faculty who create curricula and train agents in Extension are commonly called specialists. Most of them have Ph.D.s in relevant fields. Those who work in a county or multicounty area delivering programs to citizens are called agents or regional specialists. They commonly have a college degree, many with graduate education.

Two fundamental values have driven CES family programming. Programs are to be research-based and customized to the needs of the communities. Like all program developers, Extension specialists typically have their own preconceptions or preferences, which may inadvertently lead them to craft biased programs. Further, the value of local customization can lead to programs that reflect the unique experience and biases of the communities in which they are offered. That is to say, a program may fit the personal life experience of the developer, community, or both better than it fits extant research. Yet, with its emphasis on evidence-based programs, Extension emphasizes a regard for universal principles applicable to healthy relationships articulated in research, without ignoring local applications. For example, families in stressful situations may benefit from instruction about these general principles, yet need special consideration for the stresses they experience as well. An evidence-based model can minimize the effect of biases and idiosyncratic preferences.

As programs proliferate and diverge, CES national leaders saw the need to create models that summarized the common principles that should be acknowledged in all programs. What core processes apply across communities? While allowing for cultural adaptation, what principles are universal?

Early Extension Efforts at Creating a Model

The CES first efforts at building a model began in the area of parent education. About 1991, Ron Daly, the national program leader for Extension family programs, gathered four specialists from around the U.S. who had scholarly interest in parenting. They met in Manhattan, Kansas, under the leadership of Charles Smith with the challenge of creating a model or summary of research on parenting.

The first, and possibly most daunting, task was to decide what a model might look like. Should it be dynamic—connecting parenting processes with outcomes? Or should it be a summary of research findings?

The team worked for about three years to create a model, summarize the related research, and to recommend programs that supported principles in the model. The full report was 96 pages long but the heart of the report was a one-page summary that identified six principles and listed related practices. The finished report (Smith, Cudaback, Goddard, & Myers-Walls, 1994) was titled The **National Extension Parent Education Model** (NEPEM; for the model and an additional model for professional development (DeBord et al., 2006), see http://www1.cyfernet.org/ncsu_fcs/nepef/index.htm). See Figure 7.1.

In an effort to establish the face validity of the finished model, a survey of CES professionals nationwide was conducted. The study (Goddard, Smith, Myers-Walls, & Cudaback, 1994) found strong support for the model. For example, 94% of respondents agreed that the six sets of critical practices are appropriate goals for extension parent education.

Another application of the model was the development of a parent self-assessment (Edgmon, Goddard, Solheim, & White, 1996) that could give parents feedback on their strengths and guide their development as parents.

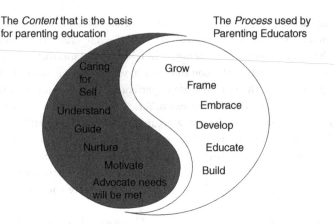

The *Content* that is the basis for parenting education

The *Process* used by Parenting Educators

Caring for Self
Understand
Guide
Nurture
Motivate
Advocate needs will be met

Grow
Frame
Embrace
Develop
Educate
Build

FIGURE 7.1 National Extension Parenting Educators' Model

Source: DeBord, K., Bower, D., Goddard, H., Wilkins, J., Kobbe, A., Myers-Walls, J., Mulroy, M., & Ozretich, R. (2006). A professional guide for parenting educators: The National Extension Parenting Educators' Framework. *Journal of Extension, 44*(3), Article Number 3FEA8. See http://www.joe.org/joe/2006june/a8.php Reprinted with permission of the Cooperative Extension System, U.S. Department of Agriculture.

Copyright 2000-2011 by Dr. John Gottman. Distributed under license by the Gottman Institute, Inc.

A Model of Couple Relationships

Following the creation of NEPEM, many in Extension saw a need to produce a model of couple relationships. In 2002, a session at a national specialists' conference was convened to discuss a model of couple relationships (Goddard, 2002). In contrast to the small group that met to create a model of parenting, this group included more than 20 self-selected people. The discussion focused on critical practices for effective couple relationships. The group listed dozens of practices that might be incorporated into a model. If one lesson was learned from the meeting, it was that 20 people are too many to effectively converge on a model. The smaller working group for NEPEM (four people) with a strong leader was far more effective.

A smaller group of about 10 people met in Washington, DC, in the summer of 2003 under the direction of the new national program leader, Anna Mae Kobbe. Rather than start with a blank slate and nominate dimensions and practices that are critical to healthy relationships, the group began with existing models. NEPEM, though focused on parenting, was thought to have important counterparts in couple relationships (see column 1 in Table 7.1).

Research on family strengths (DeFrain & Stinnett, 2003) was considered (column 2). In addition, David and Vera Mace's early model of marriage enrichment (Roth, 1991, column 3), and Adler-Baeder and Higginbotham (2002) summary of empirical findings (column 4) were considered. Goddard (Goddard & Olsen, 2004) had developed a model of couple relationships called the Marriage and Couples Education Model (M/CEM, column 5) that was also included.

TABLE 7.1 Different Models Related to Couple Relationships

NEPEM	Family Strengths	Maces' Model	Empirical Summary	M/CEM
Care for Self	Spiritual well-being			Grow
(Advocate)	Commitment	Commitment	Reasonable expectations and standards	Commit
Understand		Communication	Knowledge and awareness of partner's world	Understand
(Guide)	Ability to cope with stress and crisis	Creative use of conflict	Expressions of negativity	Solve
Nurture	Appreciation and affection		Expressions of positivity, friendship building	Nurture
Motivate			Shared meaning	Serve

Note: NEPEM dimensions in parentheses may not be closely related to dimensions in other models.

These established models and research summaries sparked a lively and focused discussion. Thus, beginning with respected models or summaries appears to smooth the progress of efforts to build new models. There was another important caveat that came out of this meeting. The people involved in the model building should be knowledgeable about the relevant literature. It may be less important in building a model that every region of the country is represented in the discussions than that the participants are familiar with the research. While it is commendable to have geographic diversity, it may be more important for adaptation of programs than for building of models.

Although some progress was made on forming a model, the task of writing descriptions for various dimensions of the model was challenging. The National Extension Relationship and Marriage Education Network (or NERMEN) was formalized in 2004 to further the development of a relationship and marriage education (RME) model. Francesca Adler-Baeder and Ted Futris agreed to serve as co-directors. Further progress was made in e-mail discussions, but significant progress came through face-to-face meetings.

The conceptualization of the core concepts of the **National Extension Relationship and Marriage Education Model** (or NERMEM) continued in September 2005 when the NERMEN met at the University of Illinois. The group now involved Francesca Adler-Baeder (Alabama), Karen Shirer (Michigan), Angela Wiley (Illinois), Ted Futris (Ohio), H. Wallace Goddard (Arkansas), Brian Higginbotham (Utah), Charlotte Olsen (Kansas), and Sean Brotherson (North Dakota). These capable scholars made substantial progress in honing and augmenting the model. However, it became clear that sundry deliberations in the field made it challenging to converge on an organized model. For example, exchange theory suggests that people make rational decisions that optimize their benefits. Yet, some research suggests that people who make sacrifices for their relationships enjoy better relationships (Clements, Stanley, & Markman, 2004; Fincham, Stanley, & Beach, 2007). How can basic precepts of exchange theory be reconciled with concepts like sacrifice? Model building can get bogged down in efforts to resolve such disagreements. In the end, the development of the model was guided by the best empirical work available. Despite such challenges, NER-MEN team members drafted a preliminary framework for the National Extension Relationship and Marriage Education model.

NERMEM was initially presented in 2006 as part of a Family Life E-Seminar sponsored by the Ohio State University Extension (see http://www.nermen.org/cultivatinghrm.php). These papers were later published in a 2007 special issue of *The Forum for Family and Consumer Issues* (see http://ncsu.edu/ffci/publications/2007/v12-n1–2007-spring/index-v12-n1-may-2007.php), and included in *Cultivating Healthy Couple and Marital Relationships: A Guide to Effective Programming* (Futris, 2007).

Work on the model continued in a subcommittee meeting at the National Extension Specialists' meeting, in the summer of 2007 in Atlanta, GA. The refining—and the challenges—continued. Discussions regarding content and chapter outlines, timelines, and the peer review process took time to reach consensus. A simple disagreement about terminology provides an example of this necessary although tedious work: Some group members objected to the use of "commitment" because it has some unpleasant clinical meanings and has been used to hold women hostage in unhealthy relationships. The group discussion led to replacing the word "commit" with the word "choose," which emphasizes both agency and investment.

As the model was finalized, members of the NERMEN volunteered to write chapters on each of the dimensions of the NERMEM. Chapter authors were equipped with the model and a summary of research (Adler-Baeder, Higginbotham, & Lamke, 2004). Francesca Adler-Baeder and Ted Futris served to coordinate and edit the development of the NERMEM with its summary of research. Key variables for the completion of the project were in place—including capable scholars and strong leaders. Yet, when a project is advanced through volunteered time, it may languish. In 2007, chapters were drafted and peer-reviewed in 2008, but the model was not completed and published until 2013.

Testing Early Models

As the efforts to create a national model of couple relationships proceeded, Goddard (2002) created the **Marriage and Couples Education Model** (M/CEM) which is shown in the fifth column of Table 7.1 and first column of Table 7.2. While the model was intended to be a distillation of research, it was considered sensible to test the constructs in the model as predictors of relationship satisfaction (Goddard, Marshall, Olson, & Dennis, 2012). A self-report questionnaire was developed to operationalize the six dimensions of M/CEM. Data were collected from 1,204 married people in Arkansas to assess the psychometric properties of the questionnaire and the usefulness of the M/CEM model in predicting relationship satisfaction.

An exploratory factor analysis found four rather than six factors. The commitment and service constructs emerged as independent factors as expected. However, growth and understanding items loaded on a single factor. It is possible that the measures were inadequate. It is also possible that those who are growing and feeling good about their lives are better able to show compassion and understanding. The nurturance and problem-solving items also loaded on a single factor. It seems likely that positive sentiment override (Hawkins, Carrère, & Gottman, 2002) may be the common element. In other words, when partners have a strong positivity bias from a nurturing relationship, they may be better able to engage in problem solving.

Each of the factors correlated significantly with relationship satisfaction. Further research is needed to disentangle measurement issues from distinct factor issues. It is important that models be drawn from research, operationalized, and tested. In addition, curricula based on models must be evaluated in rigorous designs.

Translating the Model into a Curriculum

The extensive work of Cooperative Extension educators and program specialists in developing NERMEM is commendable. This model provides an evidence-based guide that advances the knowledge and best practices in relationship and marriage education. Throughout the development of the model, team members expressed a hope that the model could be developed into an actual curriculum. The challenge was finding funding for the investment of time necessary to create a full curriculum.

In the fall of 2008, a team of extension specialists, led by David Schramm along with Kim Allen and Ted Futris (see http://www.nermen.org/HRMET/projectpartners.php), was awarded a five-year $1.2 million cooperative agreement from the Children, Youth and Families Children's Bureau to fund the **Healthy Relationship and Marriage Education Training** (HRMET) project (see http://www.HRMET.org for more information). The primary purpose of the project was to develop, deliver, and evaluate a relationship and marriage education (RME) curriculum based on NERMEM that provides tools for child welfare professionals (CWPs). Historically, the educational training child welfare and social workers receive focuses on intervening in situations related to child abuse and neglect (i.e., helping when things go wrong). The HRMET curriculum was developed to give CWPs information to help things go right, by promoting and strengthening healthy couple and family relationships.

In the first year of the project, Futris led efforts to conduct statewide needs assessment of over 1,000 CWPs in North Carolina and Missouri to identify and explore their initial attitudes and experience with RME, to see if it is something they need, and uncover possible barriers and concerns. It was important to know whether CWPs felt like RME was appropriate and relevant to the work they do with families. Formative evaluation results revealed they were largely open to the idea of RME and recognized the link between healthy couple relationships and healthy parent–child relationships (Schramm, Futris, Galovan, & Allen, 2013).

The project subsequently focused on the use of a logic model in program development and implementation (see chapter 3 in this book). Focus groups revealed that traditional methods of delivering RME to lay audiences, including the typical 1-hour delivery of information and materials per module, in a specific order, to individuals and couples, would not work for families in the child welfare system. Child welfare professionals indicated they had minimal time with families so the materials and principles needed to be short, easy to explain, and easy to understand. The information also needed to be adaptable, so the team designed the curriculum so information could be taught in any order at any time, based on the needs of the families. Using the seven principles of the NERMEM, the team examined decades of research and developed the 6.5 hour training. The curriculum also includes more than 60 tools and fact sheets aimed at giving CWPs concise information to help the clients they serve (Schramm, Futris, Warzinik, & Allen, 2013).

During years 3–5 of the project, the 1-day HRMET curriculum was delivered to CWPs by Extension specialists in Missouri, Iowa, Arkansas, North Carolina, and Georgia. Over the course of the 3 years, 52 trainings took place, reaching 1,375 professionals. Led by Futris, a rigorous evaluation of the trainings was conducted, involving a pre-test, post-test, 1-week follow-up, and 2- and 6-month follow-ups with the CWPs. Overall, the results indicated that CWPs benefited from the training, felt comfortable about delivering the material, and felt like the tools were a great way to help families who desired healthy relationships (Futris, Schramm, Lee, Thurston, & Barton, 2014). The HRMET curriculum and results, including a 2.5-hour online version of the training, is available for free at www. HRMET.org.

National Extension Relationship and Marriage Education Model

Creating the HRMET curriculum helped further refine the National Extension Relationship and Marriage Education Model (NERMEM). The creation of summaries, worksheets, and teaching materials helped to focus and refine the model. NERMEM with its supporting research is available in a 76-page publication or online (Futris & Adler-Baeder, 2013; see http://www.nermen.org/NERMEM_Chapters.php). The Model is summarized in Figure 7. 2.

Table 7.2 compares NERMEM and M/CEM.

Several differences between NERMEM (Futris & Adler-Baeder, 2013) and the earlier M/CEM (Goddard & Olsen, 2004) are evident. Some dimensions changed

FIGURE 7.2 The National Extension Relationship and Marriage Education Model: Core Teaching Concepts for Relationship and Marriage Enrichment Programming

From Futris, T., & Adler-Baeder, F. (Eds.). (2013). *The National Extension Relationship and Marriage Education Model: Core Teaching Concepts for Relationship and Marriage Enrichment Programming.* (Publication No. HDFS-E-157). Athens, GA: The University of Georgia Cooperative Extension. Retrieved from www.nermen.org/NERMEM.php

names. For example, as described earlier, *Commit* was replaced with *Choose* with its emphasis on wise choices. Some changes involved significant conceptual changes. For example, *Nurture* was divided into two dimensions: *Care* and *Share*. *Care* suggests that a person can invest in a relationship even when the partner does not reciprocate. In contrast, *Share* emphasizes the reciprocal elements of nurturing relationships. *Serve* was broadened into *Connect* suggesting a network of social relationships.

TABLE 7.2 Comparison of M/CEM and NERMEM Dimensions

M/CEM	NERMEM Dimension	NERMEM Description
Commit	Choose	Deliberate and conscious decisions demonstrate commitment and effort in a relationship. It is important to be intentional when establishing and nurturing healthy relationships.
Grow	Care for Self	Individual health impacts the health of couple relationships. Taking care of oneself can help improve the wellness of the relationship.
Understand	Know	Sharing and developing an understanding with one's partner increases awareness about the partner and the relationship. In turn, this promotes stability in the relationship.
Nurture	Care	Keeping a relationship healthy is the responsibility of each person in that relationship. Showing support, affection, and respect for one's partner can result in greater relationship satisfaction and quality.
	Share	Developing and maintaining a friendship with one's partner helps build couple identity. Learning and growing together as a couple further establishes this friendship.
Solve	Manage	Dealing with differences in healthy ways can minimize friction among couples. Problems in healthy couple relationships may never be resolved, but they can be managed in effective ways.
Serve	Connect	Engaging in a supportive, positive social network can be beneficial to any couple. Maintaining these relationships can act as safety nets that provide security to couples during good and challenging times.

Each section in the NERMEM final report summarizes the research on the dimension and includes resources such as applications to parenting and child well-being, cultural considerations, working with youth, and implications for practice.

The NERMEN model is useful in many ways. For instance, it can introduce a person to a summary of the research on couple relationships. It can act as a guide in the development or evaluation of curricula in RME.

Curricula Resulting from Extension Marriage Models

Specialists in Arkansas Cooperative Extension developed a couples curriculum based on M/CEM. The curriculum, titled "The Marriage Garden," includes a folder and six lesson guides that can be used in self-study, couple mentoring, or group learning. All lesson guides are available free online at http://www.uaex.edu/health-living/personal-family-well-being/couples/marriage-garden.aspx

Another RME curriculum was developed jointly by Adler-Baeder at Auburn University and Futris at the University of Georgia called ELEVATE. ELEVATE: Taking Your Relationship to the Next Level (see //www.nermen.org/ELEVATE.php) is based on the NERMEM model. Adapted from HRMET, it combines practical skills with applications of the physiology of human interaction, and targets a broader population of individuals and couples, as opposed to HRMET, which was developed specifically for CWPs to use in their work with families.

Conclusion

It is not easy to reduce a body of research to a simple, practical model. It requires commitment by a reasonable number of well-informed professionals as well as persistence. The best teams include competent thinkers who are also excellent negotiators. The small team with a strong leader and project funding that created NEPEM was ideal.

The development of an extension couples model was delayed by large and shifting membership of the creation team, a lack of funding for the effort, and changes in leadership. While the NEPEM model was completed and published within two to three years, NERMEM took much longer for many reasons, not least of which was reviewing the evidence base for each component.

Yet, the result can make important contributions to education as well as program development and evaluation. Just as NEPEM has been used as a guide and template for the creation of parenting programs even when professionals find important concepts missing, it serves as the springboard for discussion. NERMEM has been useful in developing curriculum. It may prove useful to professionals for many years as they attempt to organize and summarize the findings of research and translate those findings into practical and helpful programs.

In the years ahead, these models will be refined by new discoveries. Additional models may be developed. For example, a model of personal well-being may emerge from the growing research on personal development (see Lopez & Snyder, 2002). Further, additional models may be developed in other areas of personal and relationship functioning.

Key Points

- Cooperative Extension has experience developing research-based models such as the National Extension Parent Education Model.
- Creating a model is a complex process that requires the efforts of committed scholars.
- A couples education model, NERMEM, was developed and tested by Extension.
- The model has been used to develop curricula and can be useful as research and education are developed.

Discussion Questions

1. What is the utility of a model?
2. What are some of the keys to creating a model?
3. What are the core elements of the National Extension Relationship and Marriage Education Model?
4. Based on your experience, how would you modify NERMEM?

Additional Resources

The National Extension Parent Education Model is available online and can be instructive in exploring the nature and uses of models. http://www1.cyfernet.org/ncsu_fcs/nepef/index.htm

The National Extension Relationship and Marriage Education Model can be used to gain an introduction into the vast area of couples research and can be helpful in creating presentations, programs, and curricula. www.nermen.org

References and Further Readings

Adler-Baeder, F., & Higginbotham, B. (2002, November). Putting empirical knowledge to work: How does current marriage education program content measure up? Symposium presentation at Annual Conference of the National Council on Family Relations, Houston, TX.

Adler-Baeder, F., Higginbotham, B., & Lamke, L. (2004). Putting empirical knowledge to work: Linking research and programming on marital quality. *Family Relations, 53*, 537–546.

Clements, M., Stanley, S., & Markman, H. (2004). Before they said "I do": Discriminating among marital outcomes over 13 years. *Journal of Marriage and Family, 66*, 613–626.

DeBord, K., Bower, D., Goddard, H., Wilkins, J., Kobbe, A., Myers-Walls, J., Mulroy, M., & Ozretich, R. (2006). A professional guide for parenting educators: The National Extension Parenting Educators' Framework. *Journal of Extension, 44*(3), Article Number 3FEA8. Retrieved from http://www.joe.org/joe/2006june/a8p.shtml

DeFrain, J., & Stinnett, N. (2003). Family strengths. In J. Ponzetti (Ed.), *International encyclopedia of marriage and family* (Vol. 2, pp. 637–642). New York, NY: Macmillan Reference.

Edgmon, K., Goddard, H., Solheim, C., & White, M. (1996). Development of the Parent Self-Evaluation instrument. *Psychological Reports, 79*, 643–646.

Fincham, F., Stanley, S., & Beach, S. (2007). Transformative processes in marriage: An analysis of emerging trends. *Journal of Marriage and Family, 69*, 275–292.

Futris, T. (Ed.) (2007). *Cultivating healthy couple and marital relationships: A guide to effective programming* (Publication No. CHFD-E-82). Athens, GA: The University of Georgia Cooperative Extension. Available at http://www.fcs.uga.edu/nermen/program-guide

Futris, T., & Adler-Baeder, F. (Eds.). (2014). *The National Extension Relationship and Marriage Education Model: Core teaching concepts for relationship and marriage enrichment programming.* Athens, GA: The University of Georgia Cooperative Extension.

Futris, T., Schramm, D., Lee, T., Thurston, W., & Barton, A. (2014). Training child welfare professionals to support healthy couple relationships: Examining the link to training transfer. *Journal of Public Child Welfare, 8*, 560–583. doi:10.1080/15548732.2014.953719

Goddard, H. (2002, March). A National Extension Marriage Education Model? Networking sessions at the National Extension Family Life Specialists' Conference, Kansas City, MO.

Goddard, H., Marshall, J., Olson, J., & Dennis, S. (2012). Steps toward creating and validating an evidence-based couples curriculum. *Journal of Extension, 50*(6), Article Number 6FEA6. Retrieved from http://www.joe.org/joe/2012december/a6.php

Goddard, H., & Olsen, C. (2004). Cooperative Extension initiatives in marriage and couples education. *Family Relations, 53*, 433–439.

Goddard, H., Smith, C., Myers-Walls, J., & Cudaback, D. (1994). A national model for parent education: Practices and empirical bases. *Family Science Review, 7*, 79–92.

Hawkins, M., Carrère, S., & Gottman, J. (2002). Marital sentiment override: Does it influence couples' perceptions? *Journal of Marriage and Family, 64*(1), 193–201.

Lopez, S., & Snyder, C. (Eds.). (2002). *Oxford handbook of positive psychology* (2nd ed.). New York, NY: Oxford University Press.

Roth, L. (Ed.). (1991). *Marriage enrichment: The life and work of Drs. David and Vera Mace.* Winston-Salem, NC: The Association for Couples in Marriage Enrichment.

Schramm, D., Futris, T., Galovan, A., & Allen, K. (2013). Is relationship and marriage education relevant and appropriate to child welfare? *Children and Youth Services Review, 35*, 429–438. doi:10.1016/j.childyouth.2012.12.013

Schramm, D., Futris, T., Warzinik, K., & Allen, K. (Eds.). (2013). *Healthy Relationship and Marriage Education Training curriculum.* Retrieved from http://www.nermen.org/HRMET/curriculum/index.php

Smith, C., Cudaback, D., Goddard, H., & Myers-Walls, J. (1994). *National Extension Parent Education Model of critical parenting practices.* Manhattan, KS: Kansas State University.

PART III

Evidence-based Practices in Inventory-based Programs

8

DISCOVERIES ABOUT COUPLES FROM PREPARE/ENRICH

Amy K. Olson and David H. Olson

LEARNING GOALS

- Learn the six goals for the PREPARE/ENRICH Program and matching couple exercises.
- Gain an understanding of the major concepts/scales in the couple assessment.
- Understand how the PREPARE/ENRICH assessment is used online and is tailor made to each couple based on relevant background information.
- Learn the four premarital and five marital couple types and their similarities and differences.
- Understand the Couple and Family Map based on the Circumplex Model.
- Learn the Resources that a professional receives when the couple completes an assessment: *Facilitator's Report, Couple's Report, Couple Discussion Guide.*
- Know the similarities and differences between the two couple assessments: PREPARE/ENRICH and the Couple Checkup.

Introduction

This chapter provides an overview of the PREPARE/ENRICH Program and its effectiveness with couples. PREPARE/ENRICH is called a program because it contains both a couple assessment and a series of couple feedback exercises that teach relationship skills. Although most professionals know the value of **PREPARE** as a comprehensive premarital couple assessment, they typically are less aware of the relevance of the assessment for married couples (**ENRICH**).

PREPARE/ENRICH can be delivered in several different formats: individual couple with a Facilitator, by a mentor couple, or in a small group.

The Customized Version of PREPARE/ENRICH is the sixth version and it is called Customized because the couple assessment is tailored to each couple based on the stage of their relationship (e.g., dating, engaged, married) and other characteristics (whether there are children, previous marriage, etc.). The total system is online which means the couple takes the assessment online using their computer, tablet, or smartphone. The Facilitator Report is provided online as well as materials for the couple—the Couple Report and Discussion Guide. The Customized Version also contains a variety of new scales in the areas of personality, cohabitation, stress, commitment, forgiveness, and stepfamilies.

Over 3.5 million couples (3 million nationally; half million internationally) have participated in the PREPARE/ENRICH program since it was developed 35 years ago. Data collected from participating couples have resulted in a large national and international database that provides unique research opportunities to make discoveries about premarital and married couples. Over 15 studies have been done with PREPARE/ENRICH, and they are located on the website under "Research." Some of the studies have used a sample size of over 50,000 couples. More than 150,000 professionals (100,000 nationally; 50,000 internationally in 13 countries) have been trained as Facilitators in the PREPARE/ENRICH Program. Facilitators include marital and family therapists, psychologists, social workers, and other counseling professionals. Clergy from all denominations, including military chaplains, have used and endorse the program as being highly relevant and user-friendly to learn and use with couples.

Theoretical Foundations and History

Theoretically, the couple assessment is based on system theory and integrates concepts from the field of marital and family therapy. The assessment is also grounded in a Strengths model that helps to identify couple and family strengths. Further, the **Circumplex Model** of Marital and Family Systems (Olson, 2000; Olson, Sprenkle, & Russell, 1979) is integrated into the assessment as a simplified version called the **Couple and Family Map**. The Circumplex Model is based on cohesion/closeness and flexibility/adaptability which are assessed for the couple relationship and for their family of origin.

PREPARE/ENRICH scales have been scientifically developed and the scales have high alpha and test-retest reliability, high validity (content, construct, discriminant, and predictive validity), and large national norms with couples from various ethnic groups. Numerous studies demonstrate the rigor of the assessment and its relevance to couples from a variety of ethnic groups (Olson, 1998; Asai & Olson, 2004; Allen & Olson, 2001; Li, 2014).

The systemic components of the PREPARE/ENRICH scales illustrated in Figure 8.1 include the 10 Core Scales, the SCOPE Personality assessment,

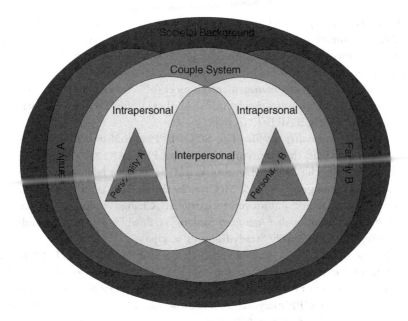

FIGURE 8.1 Systemic Framework of PREPARE/ENRICH Program

Relationship Dynamics scales, the Couple Map and the Family Map (Family of Origin for each person), the cultural context.

The core scales in PREPARE/ENRICH cover the topics of communication, conflict resolution, partner style and habits, financial management, leisure activities, affection and sexuality, family and friends, relationship roles, and spiritual beliefs. Customized scales are added if they are relevant to the couple such as cohabitation issues, cultural/ethnic issues, interfaith/interchurch, dating issues, forgiveness, and a variety of scales for parenting based on the age of the child and parenting situations (parenting expectations, stepparenting, intergenerational issues, etc.).

PREPARE/ENRICH assesses a couple's closeness and flexibility, family-of-origin for each person, personal stress, four areas of relationship dynamics, and five factors of personality. Finally, facilitators can select customized spiritual belief scales from a variety of faith traditions (Protestant, Catholic, Jewish, etc.).

An assessment and program which attempts to improve a couple's relationship should obtain information on the most critical factors in premarital relationship development that are predictive of later marital satisfaction. In a comprehensive review of eight marriage preparation educational programs, Childs (2008) found the PREPARE/ENRICH program ranked first in terms of content with a score of 92%. This overall content score was based on four criteria: theory and research (97%), context (82%), practice (96%), and premarital predictors (88%). In addition, Stahmann and Hiebert (1997) identified factors which relate to marital success. A diverse group of 238 clergy who provided premarital counseling were asked to estimate the percentage of premarital couples experiencing problems or complaints in 29 possible areas. The five problem areas ranked as occurring most frequently were communication (63%), unrealistic expectations of marriage or spouse (62%), money management/finances (60%), decision making/problem solving (55%), and power struggles (51%). All these topic have been systematically integrated into PREPARE/ENRICH.

SCOPE personality profile. The **SCOPE Personality Scale** was created and integrated into the Customized Version of PREPARE/ENRICH. SCOPE is based on the "Big Five" personality assessment that has been validated worldwide by psychologists (Costa & McCrae, 2003). SCOPE is an acronym for the five areas assessed: Social (introvert vs. extrovert), Change (openness to change vs. closed and conventional), Organized (orderly vs. flexible), Pleasing (agreeable vs. assertive), and Emotionally Steady (calm vs. reactive).

In a study of 10,000 married couples who took the PREPARE/ENRICH assessment, a cross-tabulation was done on each of the scales to examine whether people tend to marry those with similar or dissimilar personalities (Kaufman & Larson, 2011). SCOPE categorizes individuals into a high, average, or low score on each personality factor. In 60% of the cases, couples married someone with a different personality—one person scored in a higher range while the other was in a lower range. In about 20% of the cases, both persons had moderate scores; in 10% both had low scores, and the remaining 10% were both high.

Further analysis was conducted to investigate whether similarities or differences in personality were related to couple satisfaction. For 80% of the couples, marital satisfaction was not related to similarity or differences in personality. However, the 10% of couples who were both high on the Emotionally Steady, Pleasing, or Organized scales were the happiest couples, and the 10% who were both low on these scales were the least happy.

Stress in Premarital and Married Couples

The **Personal Stress Profile** is a new scale that has been integrated into the Customized Version. This scale contains 25 of the most frequently cited stressful issues based on research by David Olson and colleagues. Each person indicates how often each item is a stressor for him or her in the past year. An analysis was done by Larson and Olson (2010a) with about 10,000 premarital couples and 10,000 married couples who took PREPARE/ENRICH in 2009.

Significant differences were found in the top five stressors for premarital couples and married couples (see Table 8.1). The top issue for premarital couples was "my job" and the top issue for married couples (and individually for both husbands and wives) was "my partner." Premarital couples also had stress about finances, cost of the wedding, lack of exercise, and sleep. Married couples were stressed about their job, feeling emotionally upset, inadequate income, and too

TABLE 8.1 Top Stressors Reported from Personal Stress Profile

Premarital Couples	Married Couples
My job	My spouse
Financial concerns	My job
Cost of wedding	Feeling emotionally upset
Lack of exercise	Inadequate income
Lack of sleep	Too much to do around the home

much to do around the house. Males and females had similar top five issues, although they were in a slightly different order.

Commitment and forgiveness. Commitment and forgiveness are two new scales added to the Customized Version of PREPARE/ENRICH. Commitment is assessed by four questions related to commitment to their partner. Forgiveness is a new 10-item scale that assesses whether a partner has requested and was granted forgiveness. This scale was validated in a dissertation by Mouttet (2009), who found that it correlated well with other established scales of forgiveness.

A very positive relationship was found between commitment and couple satisfaction. In a study of over 1,200 married couples that were "Vitalized," it was found that 95% of them had scores high on the commitment scale. Conversely, in a sample of over 2,000 "Devitalized" married couples, only 23% of them scored high on commitment and 26% were in the low range (Larson & Olson, 2010b). It is, of course, unclear whether high commitment leads to higher marital satisfaction or higher satisfaction leads to higher commitment.

Forgiveness was found to be a very significant component in the relationship of happy couples. In a study of over 7,000 married couples, 87% of the Vitalized couples had high scores in forgiveness indicating it as a strength in their relationship. Conversely, Devitalized couples had low scores in forgiveness indicating this was a growth area in their relationship (Larson & Olson, 2010c). An important part of feedback with PREPARE/ENRICH in working with Devitalized and Conflicted couples is to teach effective ways to seek and grant forgiveness.

Circumplex Model and Couple and Family Maps. The Circumplex Model of Marital and Family Systems was developed in 1979 as an attempt to bridge the gap that typically exists between research, theory, and practice (Olson, 2000). This widely researched theory integrates three important dimensions: cohesion, flexibility, and communication. Marital and family cohesion is defined as the emotional bonding that family members have toward one another and can range from the extremes of *disengaged* (very low) to *enmeshed* (very high). Marital and family flexibility refers to the amount of change in leadership, role relationships, and relationship rules and can range from the extremes of *rigid* (very low) to *chaotic* (very high). Communication is the third dimension and is considered a facilitating dimension, meaning it facilitates movement on the other two dimensions.

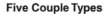

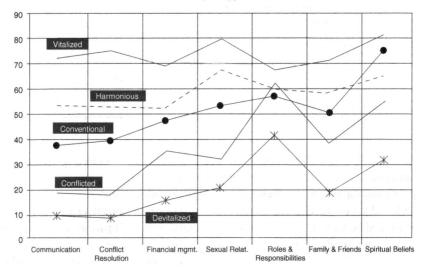

FIGURE 8.2 Five Types of Married Couples Based on PREPARE/ENRICH

The most basic hypothesis derived from the Circumplex Model is that couples and families who find balance on these dimensions will typically be healthier than those in the unbalanced range.

The Family Adaptability and Cohesion Scales (FACES) is a brief self-report measure that allows couple and family systems to be assessed on the dimensions of the Circumplex Model (Olson, 2000). The PREPARE/ENRICH Inventories contain the Circumplex Model, but it is presented with less clinical terminology as the *Couple and Family Map*. The Couple and Family Map is composed of 5 levels of closeness and 5 levels of flexibility on a grid creating 25 possible types of couple and family relationships. See Figure 8.2.

Each partner taking the PREPARE/ENRICH inventory answers questions about the flexibility and closeness of their family-of-origin as well as their perceptions of the flexibility and closeness of their couple relationship. This allows two scores to be plotted on the Couple and Family Map for each partner; family-of-origin score and a couple relationship score. The Couple and Family Maps provide a highly researched, simple, and powerful tool for measuring couple and family-of-origin systems. In clinical settings, the map becomes an effective springboard for dialogue, education, and interventions involving couple and family systems.

Needs Assessment and Target Audience

PREPARE/ENRICH was developed in the late 1970s in response to the growing divorce rate. The original assessment was designed only for premarital couples but a married couple version soon followed. Today PREPARE/ENRICH can be used with any couple, as there are customized scales for couples in any relationship stage (dating, engaged, married) and structure (cohabiting, presence of children, etc.). The need for PREPARE/ENRICH continues as strong couple relationships are the foundation for healthy families and societies. Several independent studies have found that an assessment taken at the beginning of a program can improve the impact of a relationship education program by 30% (Stanley et al., 2006). PREPARE/ENRICH outcome research found that couples who participate in a premarital program using PREPARE/ENRICH significantly increased their relationship satisfaction and improved their relationship pre-post on 10 out of 13 categories (Knutson & Olson, 2003).

Program Goals and Objectives

There are six major goals of the PREPARE/ENRICH program and matching couple exercises to help couples achieve these goals. The six goals are:

- Explore strength and growth areas
- Improve communication by teaching assertiveness and active listening
- Identify and manage stressors using the Stress Profile
- Resolve conflict by using the 10 Step Model for Conflict Resolution
- Explore family-of-origin and develop a more balanced relationship using the Couple and Family Map (based on the Circumplex Model)
- Explore personalities of each person using the SCOPE Personality Profile and how to work better as a team

Curriculum and Other Program Issues

A person would probably not wait a lifetime to have his or her car tuned up, get a dental checkup, or have a physical exam. Yet married couples rarely, if ever, do a checkup or tune-up on their marriage. When they do seek help for their marriage, they often wait too long and are already considering separation or divorce. Couples in this distressed state have often lost sight of their relationship strengths and focus mainly on their conflicts and issues.

Helping a couple prepare for marriage is a positive and effective experience for couples. Good premarital counseling helps the couple get their marriage off to a more positive start and has been shown to reduce their chance of divorce by 30% (Stanley, 2001). Premarital counseling stimulates meaningful dialogue for the couple and teaches them communication and conflict resolution skills they can use to resolve current and future issues. Couples also learn the value of proactively working on their relationship and how they can maintain a healthy relationship.

The first step in working with a couple is that the couple is asked to take the online PREPARE/ENRICH assessment. While the PREPARE couple assessment was originally designed for premarital counseling, ENRICH was created to be used with married couples. Now with the online Customized Version, the assessment is tailored for each couple based on relationship status (dating, engaged, or married) and other background and family factors (age, first marriage, children, etc.) (Olson & Larson, 2008).

Once the couple has completed the PREPARE or ENRICH assessment, their Facilitator (counselor, therapist, pastor) receives an email notifying them that the couple has completed their assessment and the results are ready to review, save, and/or print. There are three documents available to use with each couple: *Facilitator's Report, Couple's Report*, and *Couple's Workbook*. Before meeting with a couple, the Facilitator reviews the *Facilitator's Report* (about 25 pages) on the couple and may choose to give the couple a *Couple's Report* (10 pages) and a *Couple's Workbook* (about 25 pages) which contains over 20 couple exercises used for teaching the relationship skills. The Facilitator typically meets with the couple over 3–6 sessions and shares the results from the *Facilitator's Report* while teaching relationship skills from the *Couple's Workbook*. Feedback and skill building is driven by the results from the couple assessment.

PREPARE/ENRICH Group Program. Most counselors and clergy use PREPARE/ENRICH with an individual couple; however, there is also a Group Program that builds off of the main program. The PREPARE/ENRICH Group Program can be used with couples at the same stage of the family life cycle (dating, engaged, or married) and couples from different stages of life. Bringing couples from various relationship stages can lead to a dynamic experience for all couples. The program is easily adaptable to faith-based settings and can be incorporated in various types of weekly small groups.

An *Instructor's Guide* outlines discussion questions, teaching points, and exercises for all 10 lessons. It also describes the various formats (several weeks or weekends) and the various options for topics. The Group Program is very similar to the approach used with an individual couple where the couple completes exercises with their partner to resolve issues and learn relationship skills. The advantage of the group is that they are able to share their experiences with other couples and potentially build a new network of friends.

The Couple Checkup is an online couple assessment based on PREPARE/ENRICH. The Checkup assessment and Checkup Report are designed to go directly to couples at any stage of their relationship (dating, engaged, or married). The online system allows for dynamic customization of the assessment to each couple based on how the couple answers background questions. The goal is for the Couple Checkup to reach a more diverse group of couples, to empower couples to deal with issues on their own, and to emphasize prevention.

The Couple Checkup is an online assessment process specifically designed to help couples stay connected with each other and find ways to keep their relationship growing. Individuals change and so do their preferences, needs, and desires for their relationships. Without a way to check-in with each other, couples often tend to drift apart. One way to prevent relationship problems is to identify issues early on and resolve them. Also, couples need to be reminded of their strengths and build on them by overcoming current issues.

A major goal of the Couple Checkup is to encourage couples to explore and discuss their relationship with each other. The Couple Checkup helps to identify a couple's strengths as well as issues they need to resolve. With the direction provided by the Couple Checkup Report and online Discussion Guide, the couple can begin to resolve ongoing issues and create a stronger relationship.

The Couple Checkup was designed in response to a changing market of couples and a changing social context in the fields of marriage and family education and therapy. There has been increasing recognition that the field is moving toward competency-based, preventative approaches, and couple empowerment rather than only remedial treatments. Also, the online marketplace appears to be the arena of the future and an efficient and effective way to reach a more diverse population of couples.

The *Couple Checkup* book (Olson, Olson-Sigg, & Larson, 2008) is often used in conjunction with the use of the Checkup assessment whether the couple does it on their own or in a group setting. The book is based on a study of 50,000 married couples and the goal was to identify what are the strengths of happy compared to unhappy couples. Using discriminant analysis, five scales were found to be able to predict with over 90% accuracy if the couples were in the happy or unhappy group. The five predictors, in rank order, were communication, closeness, flexibility, personality compatibility, and conflict resolution.

The Couple Checkup Group Program has become popular for a variety of reasons. First, there is a Leader's Guide that makes it easy to run a couples group. Second, couples take the assessment on their own and print their own Checkup Report. Third, there is *The Couple Checkup* book or a Couple Discussion Guide (couple can print) with couple exercises designed to help build relationship skills. Lastly, there is a complimentary Group Summary Report which summarizes the strength and growth areas for the couples in the group. This provides an overview of the group and it is useful feedback for couples to learn that they have similar issues to other couples.

Meier (2010) assessed the benefits of the online Couple Checkup for couples using it on their own ("Self-Directed") and in a "Small Group" setting. Compared to a Control (wait-list) group, couples in the two treatment groups improved significantly on 8 out of 10 categories, including marital satisfaction while the Control group made no significant change.

Open-ended questions revealed the couples liked the ease of taking the Couple Checkup online, the objective feedback provided by their personal report, and the practical help found in the Discussion Guide. The Self-Directed group appreciated the flexibility of completing sessions on their own schedule. Couples in the Small Group reported that group dynamics were helpful and supportive of their marriage. Over 87% of the couples (108 out of 124) would recommend the Couple Checkup to their friends. This study demonstrates the power of the Couple Checkup in both Self-Directed and Small Group formats.

Cultural Implications

PREPARE/ENRICH has been translated and adapted to eight other languages, including Chinese (Simplified and Traditional), French, German (Deutsch and Swiss), Japanese, Korean, Romanian, Portuguese, and Spanish. In addition to translating the specific items, the relevance of the item is evaluated and items are revised to make them more appropriate for each culture. Once data are collected from couples in each country, norms are updated and alpha reliability is used to ensure that the scales are reliable.

Five distinct types (or patterns) of couples were identified when cluster analysis was used with a sample of 6,267 couples across the 10 core categories of PRE-PARE/ENRICH (Fowers & Olson, 1993). The five types of married couples range from those very high in marital satisfaction to very low: Vitalized, Harmonious, Conventional, Conflicted, and Devitalized. About 15–20% of the couples fell into each of these types. These types are very useful descriptive terms for groups of couples. Another useful aspect of the types is that other findings can be linked to these types. For example, research shows that with the most happily married type (Vitalized), there is very little spouse abuse, but abuse is very high in the Conflicted and Devitalized types (Asai & Olson, 2003). See Figure 8.3.

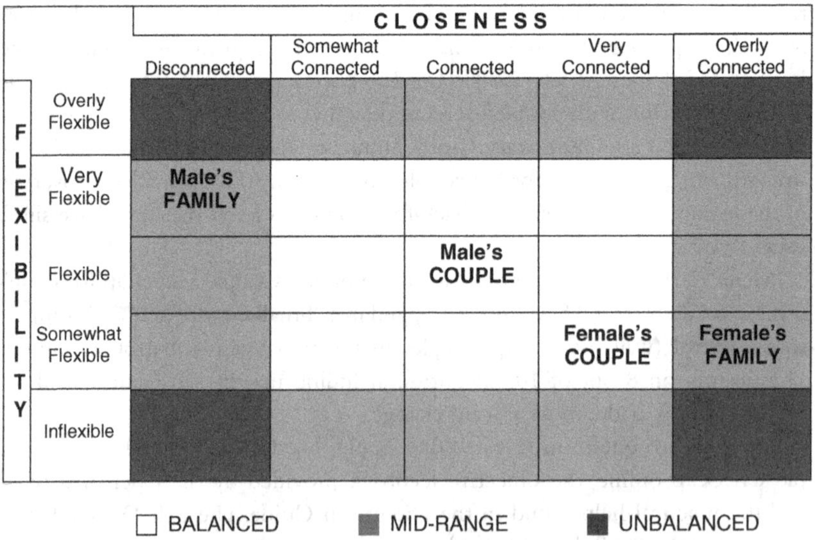

		CLOSENESS				
		Disconnected	Somewhat Connected	Connected	Very Connected	Overly Connected
F L E X I B I L I T Y	Overly Flexible					
	Very Flexible	**Male's FAMILY**				
	Flexible			**Male's COUPLE**		
	Somewhat Flexible				**Female's COUPLE**	**Female's FAMILY**
	Inflexible					

☐ BALANCED ■ MID-RANGE ■ UNBALANCED

FIGURE 8.3 Couple and Family Map Based on Circumplex Model

The five-couple typology has been replicated with African American couples (Allen & Olson, 2001), Hispanic couples (Garrett & Olson, 2006), and Chinese couples (Li, 2014). While the types replicate across ethnic groups, what varies across groups is the percentage of couples in the various couple types. For example, a higher percentage of married couples in Asian countries are classified as "Harmonious" and "Conventional" when compared with the United States and other Western cultures. Also, on the Couple and Family Map, couples and their families of origin in Asian cultures will tend to be closer (higher levels of cohesion) and less flexible (more structured) than American couples and families.

Evidence-based Research on PREPARE/ENRICH

An important study compared the PREPARE/ENRICH Program delivered in both an individual and group format. Both approaches were found to be equally effective. Couples in both approaches had significant gains in knowledge, felt more confident in their relationship, engaged in more positive conflict management behaviors, and were more satisfied with their relationship. In terms of the goals of the PE Program, the couples significantly gained in assertiveness, active listening, conflict resolution, developing financial budget, and setting personal, couple, and family goals (Futris, Barton, Aholou, & Seponski, 2011).

Another study (Knutson & Olson, 2003) compared three levels of premarital programming; one group took the PREPARE/ENRICH assessment and had four feedback sessions (PE and Feedback), the second group only took the assessment (PE only), and the third group received neither (they did receive PE and feedback after the study). The PE Feedback group changed the most, with 8 of 10 areas significantly improving. The PE-only group improved in 3 of 10 areas, and the control group made no changes. The PE and Feedback group had a 52% increase in the number of Vitalized couples (most happy couples) and an 83% decrease in the number of Conflicted couples (who are at high risk for divorce). Mentor couples have also been shown to be effective in working with both premarital and married couples (VOW, 2011). The PREPARE/ENRICH Program was offered by marriage mentors to 1,070 low-income married couples over a four-year period and 62% were married and 38% were premarital couples. The mentors worked with each couple for one hour per week for 8 weeks using the Computer Report and Couple Exercises. One part of the analysis used the couple typology, which summarizes the couple's scores across 10 major content areas including communication, conflict resolution, role relationship, sexual relationship, and the like. At post-test, the Vitalized couples (most happy group) increased from 20% to 47% and the Devitalized (least happy group) decreased from 20% to 5%. The other unhappy group, the Conflicted type, also decreased from 15% to 3%. The study clearly demonstrated the couples significantly improved their relationships across a variety of areas.

Professional Preparation and Training Issues

There are two training options for PREPARE/ENRICH—a day workshop or "Self-Training" using the Online, On-Demand System. Both of these options include the opportunity to obtain 7 CEU credits. The advantage of the day workshop is that participants can learn from a person very experienced in the program. About 1,000 workshops are offered nationally each year and a workshop can be found by searching the website (www.prepare-enrich.com) and clicking on "Become a Facilitator." There is also a Self-Training approach available as an option for mental health professionals. For more information about all aspects of PREPARE/ENRICH go to the website: www.prepare-enrich.com.

Conclusion

The PREPARE/ENRICH (PE) Program has two components: a couple assessment and couple exercises designed to teach relationship skills (i.e., communication, conflict resolution, stress management). The online Customized Version tailor makes the assessment to each couple (dating, engaged, or married), and the Facilitator (counselor, therapist, clergy, mentor couple) receives a Facilitator's Report (25 pages) which identifies the strength and growth areas for the couple. The couple receives a Couple Report (10 pages) and a Discussion Guide (25 pages) which contains over 20 couple exercises to help build relationship skills. The couple assessment has high reliability, validity, and educational utility. The Program has high relevance and value in other cultures and is translated and used in 10 other countries. Outcome studies have demonstrated the value of the program whether used with one couple or in a group setting, whether offered by a professional therapist, clergy, or mentor couple.

Key Points

- PREPARE/ENRICH is a Program because it contains a comprehensive couple assessment and over 20 couple skill-building exercises.
- This couple assessment is systemic and includes scales at the following domains: intrapersonal, personality, interpersonal, and couple and family system.
- There are four types of premarital couples from most happy to least happy (Vitalized, Harmonious, Conventional, and Conflicted). There are five types of married couples (same four as premarital) and a fifth one called Devitalized.
- The Couple and Family Map is based on the Circumplex Model of Marital and Family Systems and assesses closeness/cohesion and flexibility.
- SCOPE Personality Profile is based on the "Big Five" personality assessment and the dimensions are Social, Change, Organization, Pleasing, and Emotionally Stable.

- Several outcome studies have demonstrated significant positive change in relationship skills and couple satisfaction using the PREPARE/ENRICH Program, whether used with one couple or in a group setting.
- Professionals can get trained using the On-Demand Online system or by attending a day workshop, both of which provide 7 CEU credits.
- The Couple Checkup is considered PE Lite since it is built on PREPARE/ ENRICH and contains many of the same scales. A major difference is that PE is more clinical and the counselor receives the Report, while the Couple Checkup Report goes directly back to the couple,

Discussion Questions

1. What are the six goals of the PREPARE/ENRICH Program and matching couple exercises?
2. What are the two major components in PREPARE/ENRICH?
3. What are four of the major areas assessed in PREPARE/ENRICH?
4. What are the four types of premarital couples and the fifth type of married couples?
5. What are the two major dimensions in the Couple and Family Map?
6. What are two major ways that the Couple Checkup and PREPARE/ ENRICH are different?

Additional Resources

For more information about the PREPARE/ENRICH Program, go to www. prepare-enrich.com and for the Couple Checkup, go to www.couplecheckup.com

For more information on studies cited in this chapter, go to www.prepare-enrich.com/ research

Send correspondence to aolson@prepare-enrich.com or dolson@prepare-enrich.com

References and Further Readings

Allen, W., & Olson, D. (2001). Five types of African-American couples. *Journal of Marital and Family Therapy, 27,* 301–314.

Asai, S., & Olson, D. (2003). *Spouse abuse and marital system based on ENRICH.* Unpublished manuscript. Retrieved from http://www.prepare-enrich.com/research

Asai, S., & Olson, D. (2004). Culturally sensitive adaptation of PREPARE with Japanese premarital couples. *Journal of Marital and Family Therapy, 30,* 411–426.

Childs, G. (2008). *Marriage preparation marriage education programs: An evaluation of essential elements of quality.* Unpublished master's thesis. Brigham Young University, Provo, UT.

Costa, P., & McCrae, R. (2003). *Five factor model of personality.* Lutz, FL: Psychological Assessment Resources, Inc.

Fowers, B., & Olson, D. (1993). Four types of premarital couples: An empirical typology based on PREPARE. *Journal of Family Psychology, 6,* 10–21.

Futris, T., Barton, A., Aholou, T., & Seponski, D. (2011). The impact of PREPARE on engaged couples: Variations by delivery. *Journal of Couple and Relationship Therapy, 10,* 69–86.

Garrett, J., & Olson, D. (2006). *ENRICH couple typology and Hispanic and Caucasian married couples*. Unpublished manuscript. Minneapolis, MN: Life Innovations.

Kaufman, A., & Larson, P. (2011). *Personality and marital satisfaction*. Unpublished manuscript. Retrieved from http://www.prepare-enrich.com/research

Knutson, L., & Olson, D. (2003). Effectiveness of PREPARE program with premarital couples in a community setting. *Marriage and Family Journal, 6,* 529–546.

Larson, P., & Olson, D. (2010a). *Stress in premarital and married couples*. Unpublished manuscript. Retrieved from http://www.prepare-enrich.com/research

Larson, P., & Olson, D. (2010b). *Commitment in marriage*. Unpublished manuscript. Retrieved from http://www.prepare-enrich.com/research

Larson P., & Olson, D. (2010c). *Forgiveness in marriage*. Unpublished manuscript. Retrieved from www.prepare-enrich.com/research

Li, X. (2014). *Empirical typology of Chinese versus American premarital couples*. Unpublished doctoral dissertation. University of Minnesota, Minneapolis, MN.

Meier, B. (2010). *The Couple Checkup: Evaluating a new marriage intervention*. Unpublished D.Min. dissertation. Denver Seminary, Littleton, CO. OCLC #827944640. See Theological Research Exchange Network (TREN) database: http://www.tren.com/search.cfm.

Mouttet, K. (2009). *A comparative analysis of three scales intended to measure forgiveness*. Unpublished doctoral dissertation. Regent University, Virginia Beach, VA.

Olson, D. (1998; 2000). *PREPARE/ENRICH counselor's manual: Version 2000*. Minneapolis, MN: Life Innovations, Inc.

Olson, D. (2000). Circumplex Model of Marital and Family Systems. *Journal of Family Therapy, 22,* 144–167.

Olson, D., & Garrett, J. (2006). *Hispanic and Caucasian couples have similar couple types*. See https://www.prepare-enrich.com/pe/pdf/research/hispanic_study.pdf.

Olson, D., & Larson, P. (2008). *The customized version of PREPARE/ENRICH*. Minneapolis, MN: Life Innovations, Inc.

Olson, D., Olson-Sigg, A., & Larson, P. (2008). *The couple checkup*. Nashville, TN: Thomas Nelson.

Olson, D., Sprenkle, D., & Russell, C. (1979). Circumplex Model of Marital and Family Systems: I. Cohesion and adaptability dimensions, family types, and clinical applications. *Family Process, 18,* 3–28.

Stahmann, R., & Hiebert, W. (1997). *Premarital and remarital counseling: The professional's handbook* (2nd ed.). San Francisco, CA: Jossey-Bass.

Stanley, S. (2001). Making a case for premarital education. *Family Relations, 50,* 272–280.

Stanley, S., Amato, P., Johnson, C., & Markman, H. (2006). Premarital education, marital quality, and marital stability: Findings from a large, random household survey. *Journal of Family Psychology, 20,* 117–126.

VOW Program. (2011). *Impact of PREPARE-ENRICH Program using mentor couples*. Unpublished manuscript. Retrieved from http://www.prepare-enrich.com/research

9

FOCCUS AND REFOCCUS

Preparing and Sustaining
Couples for Marriage

Lee Williams

LEARNING GOALS

- Be able to articulate how FOCCUS and REFOCCUS can be used to help engaged and married couples strengthen their relationship.
- Understand the key considerations for administering, interpreting, and providing feedback to couples using the FOCCUS and REFOCCUS inventories.
- Be aware of the empirical evidence that supports FOCCUS as a tool for marriage preparation.
- Know the ways that FOCCUS has been adapted to work with couples from diverse backgrounds.

Introduction

The **FOCCUS** (Facilitating Open Couple Communication, Understanding, & Study) **Pre-marriage Inventory** was created in 1986 by three therapists (B. Markey, M. Micheletto, and A. Becker) who wanted to design an affordable instrument that couples could use to prepare for marriage (FOCCUS, Inc. USA, n.d.). The developers of FOCCUS wanted a tool that would facilitate the couple discussing their relationship. Therefore, they designed FOCCUS to address important topics that couples should discuss prior to getting married. FOCCUS was evaluated to ensure that it had strong **psychometric properties**. In their review of premarital assessment questionnaires, Larson and his colleagues concluded that FOCCUS was one of three instruments that "may be confidently used in premarital assessment and counseling" (Larson, Newell, Topham, & Nichols, 2002, p. 238).

Theoretical Foundations and History

FOCCUS requires the use of a **facilitator**, who both administers the inventory and reviews the results with the couple. However, FOCCUS was developed so that both lay individuals and professionals with proper training could become facilitators.

History

Since its creation in 1986, over a half million couples have taken the FOCCUS inventory (FOCCUS, Inc. USA, n.d.). One reason that so many couples have taken FOCCUS is that it has been widely adopted in the Catholic Church for marriage preparation. However, there are variations of FOCCUS (e.g., general, Christian) that can be used with non-Catholic populations.

FOCCUS, Inc. USA has continued to revise the inventory to improve it and address emerging issues (e.g., cohabitation). FOCCUS is currently in its 4th edition, which was released in early 2014. The new edition includes a special section for couples with children. New items related to technology, pornography, pets, and prayer were also added.

In 1988, the developers of FOCCUS also created an inventory that married couples could use called the **REFOCCUS Marriage Enrichment Inventory** (FOCCUS, Inc. USA, n.d.). Like FOCCUS, REFOCCUS has been updated and revised since its first creation.

Target Audience

FOCCUS was designed to assist couples preparing for marriage. Therefore, engaged couples typically take FOCCUS as part of their marriage preparation. However, couples seriously contemplating marriage may potentially benefit from taking FOCCUS.

REFOCCUS was developed specifically for married couples that want to identify possible strengths and areas of growth within their relationship (FOC-CUS, Inc. USA, n.d.). However, REFOCCUS should not be used for couples that are in seriously distressed marriages. Rather, it is intended for couples seeking to enrich or enhance their relationship. Although REFOCCUS is suitable for couples at any stage of their marriage, newly married couples may benefit more from taking FOCCUS (Markey & Micheletto, 1997).

Program Goals and Objectives

FOCCUS was designed to provide couples individualized feedback on their relationship so they can learn more about it, including the expectations that they each have for one another. The feedback is intended to facilitate couple discussion, which should help the couple deepen their understanding of the relationship.

FOCCUS was not designed to be a test for evaluating whether a couple should marry or not (FOCCUS, Inc. USA, 2013).

REFOCCUS was developed for couples that are already married and want to work on enriching their relationship. Similar to FOCCUS, the REFOCCUS questions are intended to facilitate couple discussion by providing couples feedback on their marriage.

Curriculum and Other Program Issues

Inventory description. The FOCCUS inventory addresses a number of topics that are important for couples to explore prior to marriage. FOCCUS is the least expensive of the three major premarital inventories (FOCCUS, PREPARE, and RELATE), and costs $15 per couple to be scored. FOCCUS provides couples individualized feedback about their relationship in the following 13 content categories (FOCCUS, Inc. USA, 2013):

- *Lifestyle expectations* explores whether the couple shares similar expectations around roles and responsibilities, as well as career and life goals.
- *Friends and couple interests* examines if the couple experiences conflict over friends, and if the couple has found a good balance between having separate and shared interests/friends.
- *Personality match* explores the extent to which partners can accept and respect differences in personality
- *Personal issues* addresses concerns that individuals may have regarding their partner's behavior (e.g., substance use, pornography, jealousy).
- *Communication* examines the extent to which the couple believes that they can share with one another, be good listeners, and deal with hurts.
- *Problem-solving* assesses whether the couple believes they have effective or ineffective ways of handling problems when they arise.
- *Religion, spirituality, and values* helps couples explore the role that religion, spirituality, and values will have in their relationship, including the potential to create conflict or enhance the relationship. It also addresses the couple's expectations regarding the religious socialization of children.
- *Parenting issues* assesses if the couple have similar expectations about having children and how they should be raised.
- *Extended family issues* focuses on how extended family may impact the couple through conflict over family, issues of acceptance, or having significantly different backgrounds.
- *Sexuality issues* examines the couple's attitudes and expectations regarding their sexual relationship.
- *Financial issues* explores the extent to which the couple is in agreement on how to manage their finances, and if there are any concerns about how individuals handle finances.

- *Readiness issues* assesses if the couple is experiencing ambivalence or pressure to marry, or if there are unrealistic expectations regarding marriage.
- *Covenant/commitment* examines the extent to which the couple views their marriage as a lifelong, sacred commitment, including how their religious/ spiritual values will support this.

Selected items from the content categories are also used to construct four summary categories that provide couples additional insight about their relationship. For example, the *Key Problem Indicators* category combines items from the other content areas that deserve special attention. Items highlighted as *Key Problem Indicators* may point to serious problems that need to be addressed (e.g., concerns about substance use, concerns about marrying the right person, partner's behavior is sometimes frightening). The *Family of Origin* summary category combines items from other categories that reflect how family-of-origin messages may impact the future marriage. The *Dual Careers* summary category combines items that relate to how couples anticipate balancing work responsibilities with their relationship as a couple and family. Finally, various items from the inventory are used to construct the *Commitment* summary category, which examines whether the couple has the necessary elements to maintain a long-term commitment to their marriage. Unlike the other summary categories, results for the *Commitment* summary category are not presented on the FOCCUS Couple Report. The items that relate to the three elements of commitment (process, priorities, and attitudes) are only described in the facilitator manual so that facilitators have a better understanding of couples.

All couples complete the 151 items that are used to compose the 13 content categories and the four summary categories described above. FOCCUS also includes additional items for interfaith couples, cohabiting couples, couples with children, or couples where one or both partners are remarrying. These additional items, along with a select number of other items from the other categories, are used to construct the special issues categories described below.

- *Interfaith couples* examines religious differences, including whether it creates conflict for the couple. This category also addresses if the couple can successfully bond over religion, as well as the religious socialization of children.
- *Cohabitating couples* touches on a number of different topics that may be salient to cohabitating couples, including reasons and the expectations surrounding the transition from cohabitation to marriage.
- *Couples with children* assesses the couple's roles and expectations around parenting, including potential areas of conflict regarding discipline.
- *Remarriage couples* examines concerns with previous marriages and potential areas of conflict in creating a new, shared household (e.g., agreement on what possessions each will bring, where to live).

Administering and scoring of FOCCUS. Prior to taking the inventory, the couple meets with the facilitator, who gives the couple instructions on how to complete the inventory. Couples are assured that FOCCUS is not a pass/fail test, and are encouraged to answer the questions as honestly as possible. Each partner independently completes FOCCUS, which can either be taken online or with a paper version of the instrument. Most couples can complete FOCCUS within 45–60 minutes (FOCCUS, Inc. USA, 2013). For each inventory item, individuals indicate whether they agree or disagree with the statement, or if they are uncertain. For couples that complete a paper copy of FOCCUS, the results from the answer sheet are entered online by the facilitator. The inventory answers are scored by the FOCCUS organization, which provides the facilitator the FOCCUS Couple Report that contains individualized feedback for each couple.

For each item on FOCCUS, there is a preferred response. The preferred response is either agreeing that a positive attribute exists in the relationship (e.g., my future spouse listens to me) or disagreeing that a problem exists (e.g., my future spouse sometimes puts me down). If both individuals' answers match the preferred response, then the item is scored as an agreement item. If one or both answers are different from the preferred response, then it is scored as a disagreement item. If one or both mark undecided, then it is marked as a disagreement item because it differs from the preferred response.

The first page of the FOCCUS Couple Report summarizes information about the couple, including each person's age, level of education, income, religious affiliation, current marital status, and race/ethnicity. The first page also graphs the number of agreement items for each category, which gives an indication as to whether the topic is a potential strength or area of improvement for the couple. Categories with 75% agreement or above are considered relationship strengths, while agreement scores below 40% deserve special attention (FOCCUS, Inc. USA, 2013). The remainder of the FOCCUS Couple Report lists the answers to each statement by category for both partners, along with the preferred response.

Providing feedback. Once the facilitator has downloaded and printed the FOCCUS Couple Report, he or she will arrange to meet with the couple to discuss the results. Typically the feedback is given to the couple over two to six sessions, each session being approximately an hour in length (FOCCUS, Inc. USA, 2013).

During the first feedback meeting, it may be helpful to begin by asking the couple if they had any reactions or discussions after taking the inventory. Indeed, it is hoped that the couple would have begun that process shortly after completing the inventory, even before meeting with the facilitator. If the couple expresses concerns that the results will be negative, then the facilitator can reassure them that all couples have areas of growth and remind them that the inventory is not used to determine whether or not a couple should marry.

The overall goal of the feedback sessions is to help the couple have an open and honest discussion about their relationship, using the results as a catalyst. Therefore, the facilitator's role is to encourage the couple to talk with one another, rather than the conversation being directed primarily through the facilitator. The facilitator also encourages the individuals to communicate their thoughts, feelings, or desires in a respectful, non-blaming manner.

Some facilitators like to review the percent agreement scores for each category, which can help couples identify potential areas of strengths and growth within the relationship. However, the richest discussions usually arise by having the couple share why they responded to specific items in certain ways. So, the majority of time is spent having the couple discuss expectations or concerns that relate to specific items. The FOCCUS manual contains examples of questions that the facilitator can ask couples to open up the conversation around each item.

It is not necessary (and can be time-consuming) to review the responses to each and every item in the inventory. Rather, the facilitator selects items that may be most important for the couple to discuss. Typically these will be items in which the couple is in disagreement or expressed being undecided. Often themes emerge when exploring results, allowing one to consolidate the discussion of multiple items under a particular theme. Although areas of concern deserve the most attention, it is important that the facilitator not overlook positive aspects of the relationship. The couple needs to be encouraged by noting their strengths.

In addition to the FOCCUS *Couple Report*, the facilitator can use other resources available through the FOCCUS organization (FOCCUS, Inc. USA, 2013). After the initial feedback session, *b'tween* resources are provided to participants by the facilitator. These resources reinforce the communication that takes place during facilitation and encourage it to continue throughout marriage. Available as free downloads in the FOCCUS facilitator's account, the *b'tween reflection and discussion guide* encourages the couple to continue to reflect upon and discuss the topics explored in each feedback session. The couple is also given the *b'tween FOCCUS for the future* to complete prior to the last session, which helps them integrate what they have learned, as well as develop an action plan for enhancing their relationship in the future.

In some cases, FOCCUS may uncover issues that the couple will have difficulty resolving unless they receive professional help. If the facilitator is a trained mental health professional, then he or she could offer to re-contract with the couple to explore these issues using more traditional psychotherapy approaches. Otherwise, the facilitator will need to refer the couple for additional help to resolve the issue. In addition, many couples can benefit from **psychoeducational programs** that offer knowledge and skills (e.g., communication, conflict resolution) for building a successful marriage. Therefore, the facilitator may also consider this as a possible referral for some couples. Several examples of these programs are described in other chapters in this book.

REFOCCUS Description

As stated earlier, REFOCCUS is intended to help married couples enhance their relationship. REFOCCUS includes six topic areas (FOCCUS, Inc. USA, n.d.), which include:

- *Marriage as process*—Items in this category primarily focus on how each perceives that changes have impacted the marriage, including the couple's ability to adjust to changes.
- *Intimacy*—Items in this area explore how various factors (e.g., careers, sex, religion/spirituality, and parenting) have detracted or enhanced the couple's connection.
- *Compatibility*—These items explore the extent to which the couple experiences problems related to differences in personality, values, backgrounds, and expectations regarding roles.
- *Communication*—These items examine how well the couple feels that they can share and listen to one another's concerns, as well as their ability to effectively solve problems or handle conflict when it arises.
- *Commitment*—These items examine the couple's level of commitment to their marriage, including factors that might impact commitment.
- *Ministry marriages*—These questions were recently added to REFOCCUS, and encourage couples with an active faith to examine what impact a call to serve may have on their marriage.

Unlike FOCCUS, couples can purchase and take the REFOCCUS inventory without a facilitator. Each partner independently completes the REFOCCUS inventory, either online or by completing a pencil-and-paper questionnaire. Similar to FOCCUS, the couple indicates their level of agreement, disagreement, or indecision with each statement in the inventory. Couples who complete REFOCCUS online receive a report with their results. Otherwise, the couple self-scores their questionnaires by comparing their answers to those on the preferred response sheet. REFOCCUS contains information in each topic area that the couple can read as part of the self-study. The inventory also includes questions for each statement, which couples can use as a springboard for discussing their results. REFOCCUS currently costs $15 per couple.

REFOCCUS can also be used in a group setting. The *REFOCCUS Guide for Couple or Group Discussion* is available to therapists, clergy, or family life ministers who want to use the inventory in a group setting, and offers activities and suggestions for leading discussions when using REFOCCUS.

Cultural Implications

One of the key strengths of FOCCUS is that it has been translated into multiple languages. FOCCUS is available in English, Spanish, Chinese Traditional, Chinese Simplified, Portuguese (Brazilian), Korean, and Vietnamese (FOCCUS, Inc. USA, 2013). The inventory is also available in Braille and audio versions for those who are visually and/or hearing impaired. REFOCCUS is available in both English and Spanish.

FOCCUS has also been adapted for those with different religious backgrounds. The wording of questions related to values, spirituality, and religion differs based on the version being used. The Catholic, Christian Orthodox, and Christian Non-denominational versions use terms and language specific to these groups, respectively. The general edition does not make reference to a specific religion and uses generic language regarding values and beliefs. As noted earlier, couples that have different religious affiliations complete the interfaith questions.

FOCCUS was written for those who can read at the 6th-grade reading level. The Alternate Edition of FOCCUS is written at the 3rd-grade level and may be suitable for those with developmental disabilities or for those where English is not their primary language.

Evidence-based Research and Evaluation

When FOCCUS was initially developed, the inventory was evaluated for its psychometric properties by an independent firm, SRI Research Center, Inc. (Markey & Micheletto, 1997). SRI discovered that the **internal reliability** for the various categories ranged from .86 to .98, which demonstrates good internal reliability. It also found evidence for the **construct validity** for FOCCUS.

Another study by Williams and Jurich (1995) demonstrated the **predictive validity** of FOCCUS. In this study, couples that completed FOCCUS 4–5 years earlier were contacted and assessed for their marital status and marital quality (if still married). Couples were then classified into high- or low-quality marriages based on their marital status and marital quality. Using the FOCCUS scores, a discriminant function analysis was able to accurately predict for 74% of the couples whether they had a high- or low-quality marriage after 4–5 years.

When the subscale for cohabitation was developed, the Gallup Organization evaluated its psychometric properties (Markey & Micheletto, 1997). Construct validity was established for the subscale and it had acceptable internal reliability (Kuder-Richardson = 0.79).

In 2012, a study was conducted to evaluate and revise the FOCCUS inventory. These findings resulted in the new 4th edition of FOCCUS being created (FOCCUS, Inc. USA, 2013). The **content validity** of FOCCUS inventory was assessed by having Archdiocesan priests in Omaha, FOCCUS office staff, and sociologists in the field of marriage and family evaluate the instrument (Schiffbauer, personal communication, June 6, 2014). This led to the addition, deletion, and revision of multiple items. A subsequent pilot study of the revised inventory demonstrated that it had good internal reliability (Cronbach's alpha = 0.92).

Some recent research has also evaluated how effective FOCCUS is for preparing couples for marriage. The results of a 2013 survey by FOCCUS (n = 3,287 respondents) revealed that individuals found taking FOCCUS to be a helpful experience (Schiffbauer, personal communication, June 6, 2014). Ninety-six percent of individuals reported that FOCCUS facilitated discussion of important topics with their future mate, and 91% stated that taking FOCCUS helped them prepare for marriage.

A study among United Kingdom couples preparing for marriage found some evidence that taking the FOCCUS may contribute to couples developing a more elaborated understanding of marital commitment (Burgoyne, Reibstein, Edmunds, & Routh, 2010). It should be noted that this finding is based on a small sample size of individuals.

Another study in the United Kingdom by Spielhofer et al. (2014) evaluated couples preparing for marriage that either took FOCCUS or a workshop called Preparing Together. Qualitative interviews with couples that completed FOCCUS indicated that couples found the experience valuable because it helped them identify and discuss differences in their relationship (p. 43). Whereas only 31% of the couples reported that the Preparing Together workshop was "quite relevant/ useful," 63% of those who had FOCCUS reported the experience as being "quite relevant/useful." Based on the interviews with couples, this appears to be due to the fact that FOCCUS provided individualized feedback for couples and a safe place to discuss differences (p. 44). Using a pre- and post-test design (with no control group), the study documented a significant change in relationship quality after completing FOCCUS, with a modest **effect size** of d = 0.22. There was not a significant change in well-being or communication. Another benefit of couples taking FOCCUS was that it made them more receptive to seeking counseling or relationship support in the future (p. 53). In fact, couples that took FOCCUS were more receptive to seeking relationship support than those who took the Preparing Together workshop, even though pretest scores were similar for both groups. The positive experience of meeting with a facilitator face-to-face, which mirrors the counseling format, could account for this difference.

Professional Preparation and Training Issues

To purchase and administer FOCCUS, individuals are required to obtain training and certification as a facilitator (FOCCUS, Inc. USA, n.d.). FOCCUS facilitators can be either licensed professionals or lay individuals. However, lay individuals must be associated with an approved FOCCUS organization (e.g., church, family life office) to become a facilitator. Individuals interested in becoming facilitators must attend a one-day workshop provided by a certified FOCCUS Trainer, or receive the training online. The training instructs individuals on how to administer FOCCUS and interpret the results. It also provides guidance on how to use the feedback effectively to help couples examine and discuss their relationship. FOCCUS facilitators are also required to have the FOCCUS *Facilitator Manual*, which provides supplemental information and questions that can be used to make couple discussions more effective. Individuals who only want to use REFOCCUS do not need to become a trained FOCCUS facilitator.

Conclusion

FOCCUS is an excellent tool that couples preparing for marriage can benefit from taking. By providing individualized feedback, FOCCUS can encourage a couple to more deeply explore their relationship in areas that are important to building a successful marriage. The use of facilitators can help create a safe place for couples to explore their expectations and possible differences. Research is emerging that provides evidence for the reliability and validity of the instrument, but also documents the potential value to couples that take FOCCUS. The developers of FOCCUS have also created REFOCCUS, an inventory that can be used by married couples for enrichment.

Key Points

- The FOCCUS inventory is a tool used to help engaged couples prepare for marriage, while REFOCCUS is used with married couples for enrichment.
- FOCCUS and REFOCCUS provide couples individualized feedback in a number of different areas that are important to marriage.
- FOCCUS and REFOCCUS should not be used as tests, but rather as tools for encouraging couples to explore and discuss their relationship.
- Trained facilitators are used to administer FOCCUS and provide feedback to couples.
- Current research suggests that FOCCUS is a valid and reliable instrument and that couples find the process of taking FOCCUS to be beneficial.
- FOCCUS is available in different languages and religious versions and has special sets of questions for interfaith couples, cohabitating couples, remarried couples, and couples with children.

Discussion Questions

1. What is *not* an appropriate use of FOCCUS when working with couples?
2. What are two key differences between the FOCCUS and REFOCCUS inventories?
3. What is the role of the facilitator when using the FOCCUS inventory?
4. What are the four types of couples for which special issues scales have been developed for FOCCUS?

5. What are the ways in which FOCCUS has been adapted for couples of various cultural and religious backgrounds?

Additional Resources

For more information about FOCCUS or REFOCCUS, contact:
FOCCUS, Inc. USA
Nazareth Hall
3300 North 60th Street
Omaha, NE 68104 3402
877-883-5422 or 402-827-3735
Website: http://www.foccusinc.com

References and Further Readings

Burgoyne, C., Reibstein, J., Edmunds, A., & Routh, D. (2010). Marital commitment, money and marriage preparation: What changes after the wedding? *Journal of Community and Applied Social Psychology, 20*, 390–403.

FOCCUS, Inc. USA. (2013). *FOCCUS facilitator manual* (4th ed.). Omaha, NE: Author.

FOCCUS, Inc. USA. (n.d.). *FOCCUS Pre-Marriage Inventory and REFOCCUS Marriage Enrichment Inventory website.* Retrieved from http://www.foccusinc.com

Larson, J., Newell, K., Topham, G., & Nichols, S. (2002). A review of three comprehensive premarital assessment questionnaires. *Journal of Marital and Family Therapy, 28*, 233–239.

Markey, B., & Micheletto, M. (1997). *FOCCUS facilitator manual* (2nd ed.). Omaha, NE: FOCCUS, Inc.

Spielhofer, T., Corlyon, J., Durbin, B., Smith, M., Stock, L., & Gieve, M. (2014). *Relationship Support Interventions Evaluation.* London: Department of Education. Retrieved June 6, 2014, from https://www.gov.uk/government/uploads/system/uploads/attachment_data/file/275240/RR315_-_Relationship_Support_Interventions_Evaluation_210114.pdf

Williams, L., & Jurich, J. (1995). Predicting marital success after five years: Assessing the predictive validity of FOCCUS. *Journal of Marital and Family Therapy, 21*, 141–153.

10

RELATE ASSESSMENT

Vicki L. Loyer-Carlson

LEARNING GOALS

- Identify the four relationship contexts covered by the RELATE Questionnaire.
- Become aware of RELATE research that provides understanding about factors such as the impact of family of origin and the role of different types of conflict on relationship satisfaction.
- Become familiar with multiple ways that RELATE can be used by lay persons, applied professionals such as therapists and teachers, and research professionals.
- Understand four basic propositions upon which RELATE is based.

Introduction

The perfect match. These words work well when folding socks. They do not work as well to describe people who are dating. Despite the claims of matchmaking services, tests cannot determine whether a couple has a "perfect" fit. Tests can assess relationship satisfaction and stability, and the likelihood of being stable within a period of time into the future.

RELATE is an assessment tool for use in building strengths and unearthing challenges in intimate relationships by assessing satisfaction and stability, values, habits, and more. Particularly useful for relationships which may have some permanency (such as seriously dating, engaged, or married couples) the RELATE subscales provide important feedback. RELATE has a more than 30-year history, a solid design, and a simple format. Within minutes of taking RELATE, the couple will receive a RELATE report that provides an assessment of strengths and challenges, interpretation guidance in the context of a body of current research, and norms based on a large data set. The multiple scales in the assessment are calculated to create a picture of the couple and their similarity based on perceived attitudes, behaviors, and values allowing professionals to predict with some accuracy the couple's likelihood of later satisfaction in their relationship. The purpose of this chapter is to introduce RELATE as a relationship assessment instrument by providing an overview of the theoretical foundation and history upon which it is based, to describe its scales and subscales, and to review its contribution to empirical literature. This chapter also provides a guide to the ways RELATE is used by the lay respondent, the applied professional, and to the research professional.

History

RELATE began more than 30 years ago as the **Marital Inventories** (Yorgason, Burr, & Baker, 1980). As teams of researchers and practitioners worked to increase the predictive ability and the user friendliness of the instrument, the Marital Inventories evolved to become the PREParation for Marriage Instrument (**PREP-M**, Holman, Busby, & Larson, 1989) and then became the RELATionship Evaluation Questionnaire (**RELATE**, Holman, Busby, Doxey, Klein, & Loyer-Carlson, 1997).

The RELATE Institute (formerly the Marriage Study Consortium) is dedicated to developing research and outreach tools for use directly with the public and to gather relationship information about personal characteristics, couple characteristics, self and family history, and interaction patterns that influence relationships. Since the early 1990s, the members of the **RELATE Institute (RI)** have used the findings of RELATE research to bring couple education to couples around the world. Written in several languages (e.g., English, Spanish, German), and used as an integral part of some couples' programs (e.g., CoupleCARE of Australia [Halford et al., 2006], RELATE With Your Mate of Arizona [Loyer-Carlson & Busby, 2003]), RELATE has had wide and lasting impact.

Couples who agree more on values, attitudes, and preferences tend to be more satisfied with each other. Couples are seen to be competent in providing relationship information and in receiving results from information they provide. RELATE couples are respected to manage their own information and are given feedback about the relationship areas that show strengths and needs for growth. Over 270 items represent over 60 scales that assess relationships in areas that couples often do not identify as important early in their relationships. Providing detailed explanations about each area and providing guidance for discussion via both Summary and Detailed Reports provide thorough feedback to the couple. Couples print out their reports and use them as a guide in conversations, can revisit their results online, and are provided with suggestions for further study and links to trained facilitators when needed. (To see a copy of the RELATE Report you can go online to www.RELATE-Institute.org/about/FAQ. Click the sentence "Can

I see a sample report from a relationship evaluation?" Next, click "See a sample PDF RELATE report now.")

A number of Internet questionnaires have emerged over the past decade, but the RI was one of the first professional assessments that was developed and delivered online. RELATE is a user-friendly, research-based, relationship assessment tool that has been used to educate professionals, individuals, and couples about the qualities that occur in successful relationships. The goal of RI has been to make it as easy to access a quality assessment as the matchmaking services have made it to access lay assessments, but with the integrity and quality of the professional-only questionnaires. Complimentary tokens were provided at workshops and trainings for professionals to experience RELATE and its reports so that users could understand the value, and limitations, of the "snapshot" that is taken when an individual answers a questionnaire and the importance of understanding that information in context to fully develop that snapshot.

Professional-only accounts. As RELATE became better known more professionals found use for RELATE in their classrooms and their clinical practices. Professionals needed to be able to see clients' profiles to prepare treatment plans and group activities, and to compare their clients to clients in other demographics. Professional accounts were created for professors, Certified Family Life Educators, and licensed mental health professionals. To be awarded a professional account documentation of appropriate education in relationships, certification or licensure, and ethical practice standards were required. Clients were notified that those tokens allowed specific professionals access to their information. Professionals were then able to establish data bases of their respondents, and were able to conduct research with their own samples. A brief RELATE was developed for program leaders to assess their participants' change over time.

Dissemination. RELATE information was, and still is, disseminated primarily through traditional academic avenues such as peer-reviewed journals, books, and conferences. The RELATE Institute remains dedicated to the development and testing of a framework of healthy premarital and early marital relationships. RELATE was built and advertised with the energy of faculty, graduate students, marriage and family therapists, and clergy in the field of marriage and family therapy, and has been found and used by tens of thousands of users since its original appearance.

Theoretical Foundation

The framework for RELATE is based on the comprehensive review of research on premarital predictors of marital quality by Larson and Holman (1994), longitudinal research by Holman and associates (Holman, 2001), and research conducted by Gottman and colleagues (Gottman, 1994, 1999). Karney and Bradbury's (1995) review of longitudinal predictors of marital quality and stability support RELATE's areas of emphasis in the marital (as opposed to premarital) arena.

Stahmann and Hiebert's (1997) review of unique areas of concern for remarrying individuals and couples forms the basis for the RELATE-RS (Remarriage Supplement). The specific items used in RELATE either came from research instruments that have demonstrated adequate reliability and validity, or were created and tested by the developers of RELATE based on research, theory, or clinical experience (Holman, 2001).

From a practical perspective, RELATE is founded upon four basic propositions:

Proposition I: People continue to do what is rewarding and avoid that which is costly. As Harold Kelley (1979) theorized in his Theory of Interdependence, rewards and costs are modified as relationships develop. We like people who are similar to ourselves and find rewarding relationships where we believe our partners are flexible and kind, and who make decisions that are in our best interest.

Proposition II: People are dynamic and relationships evolve: History and context, however, is stable. Relationship assessments represent a "snapshot" of where couples are in their relationship at the moment they are taking the test. Some things in that picture will change over time. There are basic parts of that picture that will remain the same. Some parts can become less prominent, but they will always be there.

Areas of family background, history of abuse and trauma, and questions of ethnicity, religiosity, and socioeconomics are all factors that have impact on the couple directly and indirectly. Even in situations where an individual has created an adult life that is much different from her/his history, the history remains part of the individual, and therefore part of the partnership.

Proposition III: Discourse is healing. Providing respondents with comprehensive feedback about their relationship and instructions for discussion is healing. The costs and rewards in the relationship are a factor of the level of couple agreement rather than on any one specific style of interaction. Consequently, the experts on the relationship are the couple, and the experience is different than one would have if the couple were to require expert assistance. This is an important aspect of RELATE: Ultimately, couples themselves are responsible for understanding and working on their relationships, and for asking for help when they need it.

Proposition IV: People can be fallible. With self-administered questionnaires, there are at least three areas of fallibility: self-presentation errors, defensiveness, and lack of awareness that comes out of ethnocentrism. The first challenge, self-presentation, is that people tend to want to present themselves well. Particularly when the respondents have been students for a period of time (such as college students), the respondents are concerned with earning an "A" in their relationship. RELATE is not a relationship "test" and cannot provide "grades"–passing or otherwise. There is value in the information that comes from comparing each partner's response to the other. For respondents who are concerned about matching well and receiving a "high score," the accuracy of RELATE compromised. The RELATE Report illustrates what each person brings to the relationship and the ways in which the couple operates. Couples who cannot be honest in their answers, or who collaborate to create a higher agreement level than would occur otherwise, will not benefit as much from the RELATE Report.

Second, the process of productive discourse between the couple in the areas of agreement and disagreement is enriching. Healthy discourse can be cut short by defensiveness. For those times that couples are unable to achieve healthy discourse, professionals are able to coach effective communication skills. The process of discussing the various questions in RELATE provides an intervention of sorts and couples can turn to family life educators, clergy members, or therapists to help them learn a conversational style that can be used throughout their relationship.

Last is the issue of lack of awareness that comes out of ethnocentrism. Areas of social living, such as role behavior that is shared and agreed upon within a culture, are difficult to see by people within that same culture. The same behavior that is considered flexible in one culture may be considered inflexible by the next: This is a cultural issue. In couples who are relatively new there is often the challenge that the cultural lens has yet to be truly tested. Often new couples have fewer serious issues or arguments come up that are based on original belief systems. Differences in meaning are seen in the RELATE Report such that the respondent and the partner report on the same behaviors: Jane answers about Jane's behavior and Jim answers about Jim's behavior.

Needs Assessment and Target Audience

Young, premarital adults who can be assessed before their relationships become permanent and before they settle into destructive patterns of conflict, and the professionals who work with them, were the target audience of RELATE. The need for the instrument to be truly available to this population required that it be affordable, interesting, attractive, and able to measure couple relationships on multiple dimensions. The result was online versions of **READY** (for single adults) and RELATE (for persons in a relationship) for use by lay persons and for the convenience of applied and research professionals. It is one of the lowest-priced research-based instruments available in the profession. It does not require professional facilitation, and respondents can receive their own Summary Report that contains clear instructions for interpretation and questions for further self study. Overall, the benefits of RELATE for respondents and clinicians alike is simplicity, availability, and low cost, meeting the needs of our target audience.

The Scales and Subscales of RELATE

There are four relationship contexts that are explored in RELATE: The individual, the family, the cultural, and the couple. RELATE begins with the *individual context*, a focus on personality and values, from the perspective of the self and from the perspective of the partner. The report shows four graphs so that the perceptions of self and the perceptions of others' perceptions of self can be easily seen. This individual context contains characteristics that are more enduring and less likely to change, or will never change (such as your birthday), no matter who your partner is. It contains information specifically about you, your expectations, and your lifetime experiences. These scales highlight what you bring to the relationship in your personal characteristics (biological self, gender, race, age), personal interactions styles (emotional maturity, self-esteem, depression (happiness), flexibility, calmness, sociability, kindness, and substance abuse), and beliefs and attitudes (personal autonomy, spirituality, gender roles).

As the picture broadens, family background becomes more important. *Family context* involves past and present family relationships and the partner's past and present family relationships. Several questions address the family structures or experiences while the partners were growing up, how the family members interacted with each other, and how the partners interact with their families today. Not surprisingly, the family that one grew up in greatly influences the expectations, habits, and fears that are brought with partners to their close relationships today. Parents are the ultimate authority in a family, so the family context in RELATE consists of the style and quality of the parent's couple relationship, and the relationship of each parent with the children. In the family background section there are also questions about the types of stressors and trauma that each family endured.

Race and ethnicity fundamentally influences experiences and expectations. This comprehensive assessment of relationships includes an exploration of the cultural context that the partners bring to the relationship. Culture, religion, celebrations, and prohibitions are all culturally based phenomena and are explored in RELATE as the *cultural context*. The cultural context includes beliefs and values supported by the social systems with which the family interacts; the workplace, the schools, and the places of worship that the family may visit. These systems surround families and individuals and provide ways of thinking about events and decisions that may be different from thoughts and feelings of members of other social groups.

Relationships also create a unique interactional environment. The ways that partners speak with one another, the information they exchange, their ideas of fun, finances, and friendships all make up the *couple context* and are explored in the RELATE assessment. The couple context is the most important area to consider when evaluating a relationship. In the end all the other areas of context are only important insofar as they influence the way that the couple act and feel. The couple context is the relationship of the present, where everything from the past is either recreated in the current pattern of acting or discarded for something better.

RELATE report delivers reliable, validated results. The scales of RELATE have reliability scores between 0.70 and 0.90 for both internal consistency and test-retest calculations. Validity results are equally impressive, with educators, clinicians, and researchers alike supporting RELATE as a sound instrument for forecasting marital satisfaction (Busby, Holman, & Taniguchi, 2001).

TABLE 10.1 Directions for Taking RELATE

---

1. Go to www.relate-institute.org.
2. Click **SIGN UP** next to **NEW USER** on the home page.
3. Enter information to sign up for your new account.
4. Click **SIGN UP**.
5. A page will come up telling you a verification email will be sent to the email address provided.
6. Click **CONTINUE**.
7. When asked, "Are you currently in a couple relationship? (e.g. seriously dating, engaged or married)," click **YES**.
8. Click **BEGIN**.
9. Complete sections A–H, answering ALL the questions. A segment takes approximately 5–7 minutes to complete. Click forward arrows after each segment.

   NOTE: Leaving questions blank will show incomplete graphs and missing data on the Report. You can retake any segment by clicking on that icon. However, once you pay for your report, you will not be able to change any answers.

10. After completing section H, you will be asked if you want to finalize your report. Click **PROCEED**.
11. The next page will inform you that your report is not yet purchased. Click on **PURCHASE REPORT**.
12. Select a payment method: either pay with credit card or pay with token.
13. Next, you can either view your report or add a partner.
14. Add your partner:
    a. You will need your partner's username.
    b. Enter a random fact so your partner can correctly identify you.
    c. Log out.
    d. Your partner should then log into his/her account, go under the "Reports" tab, and select to confirm partner request.
    e. YOU HAVE 30 DAYS TO ADD A PARTNER.
15. To view your report click the "Reports" tab at the top of the page, then select "View Report." It may take a couple minutes to download to your computer.

At this point, the history, theoretical framework, and scales of RELATE have been described. Consider going online and taking the RELATE or READY before you read on to the research results for studies using RELATE data, and programs that integrate the use of RELATE. The instructions for logging on to RELATE are in the section titled "*Directions for taking RELATE.*"

Curriculum and Program for Individuals and Couples

RELATE is intended to be used independently, or as an adjunct to professional services. It is not intended to be limited to a single specific program. In the event that a couple or individual take RELATE or READY on their own, they would go to the website (Relate-Institue.org) and select the questionnaire that they would be best suited for: *RELATE* if they are currently in a relationship, and *READY* if they are not. Within a few minutes of completing their assessment they will receive a summary report of their relationship and/or relationship style. The summary is complete with interpretation guidelines and suggestions for discussions and follow-up in each of over 60 areas known to affect satisfaction in intimate relationships.

When RELATE is used in premarital counseling with a clinician or clergy, the report is easily divided into four sections, lending itself to four 2-hour sessions. First, focus on background and contextual factors such as the family that each member has come from. Whether the members of the couple's family experience divorce, addiction, mental illness, or other sources of conflict and or stress will influence how members of the couple see relationships and the strategies they may have learned to deal with difficulties. The next session focuses on individual traits and behaviors such as emotional health, interpersonal skills, and physical health. In this section attention is paid to the couple's perceptions of the other's personality characteristics, particularly their perception of the other's kindness and flexibility. Getting a sense of the overriding sentiment in the relationship (positive or negative) is an important part of this session. Next, a close look at the couple interactional processes focuses on similarities in values, attitudes, beliefs as well as relationship goals for sex, procreation, and conflict styles. Finally, the last session focuses on problem areas detected in RELATE such as substance abuse, destructive conflict styles, mood or impulse control disorders, or conflicts with members of the social network that may impact the relationship satisfaction (Larson & Holman, 1994). The Summary Profile provides all of the data needed for these four sessions, and further information can be obtained by examining the Detailed Report that is also available with the Summary Report, and provides the answers given by the respondents to each question. There are answers, however, that are not reported back to the couple in consideration of the individual, such as history of physical and sexual abuse. For those areas the results are available as summary graphs and couples are encouraged to work with a professional to further investigate those areas. The couple and the clinician can decide whether the couple only receive the reports and bring them into their session, the clinician receive the report and present it to the couple, or both the clinician and the couple receive the report when it is ready. Professional RELATE accounts can be set up to allow the professional to access all reports submitted by their clients.

Evidence-based Research and Evaluation

With over 270 items that make up more than 60 scales and subscales, it is not surprising that RELATE covers a great deal of relationship information. RELATE was designed to focus on relationship satisfaction and stability, and to stimulate productive discussions between members of a couple in each of those areas. For program planning, the scales of RELATE are extremely helpful. For example, when couples both believe that their own personal characteristics (such as kindness and flexibility) are better than those of their partner's, they are more likely to experience worse relationship outcomes. On the other hand, couples in which both individuals rate their partner substantially higher than they rated themselves have the highest relationship outcome scores in the large cross-sectional sample (Busby, Holman, & Niehuis, 2009). Those data on each couple are available in the Summary Report in the first graph on page 3, or in the detailed summary on page 20 under "Individual Characteristics." In terms of empathy, the single most important factor was the female's view of her partner's empathy (Busby & Gardner, 2008). This means that programs should include conversations with the couple about how they view one another at different times in their relationship. It encourages partners to challenge negative perceptions of the other that are often present in dissatisfied relationships. Regarding money and finance, RELATE research has shown that the materialism of a wife is related to a husband's marital satisfaction, but the husband's materialism does not have the same effect (Dean, Carroll, & Chongming, 2007). This has implications for programming regarding couples' finances.

Many relationship programs are designed to stop cycles of violence that can occur in families. From RELATE data we find that family of origin violence influence a partner's overall perceptions of the family environment, but is not as important as the negative communication and aggression that may exist between partners (Busby, Holman, & Walker, 2008). Negative family of origin experiences influence adults in terms of more negative attitudes toward relationships, but those expectations can be improved by more positive experiences in the present (Busby, Gardner, & Taniguchi, 2005). Overall, personal values result from religion, sex, birth position, father's education, and perceived quality of the home environment (Busby & Holman, 1989). Despite a potential value of commitment, negative unresolved experiences do increase relationship anxiety and are associated with avoidance issues in relationships (Draper, Holman, Grandy, & Blake, 2008). These RELATE studies support the importance of working through family of origin issues, particularly those that cause reactivity, as a step in the preparation for marriage (Holman & Busby, 2011).

Conflict is another issue that permeates couple distress. Couples where both partners are validating, or at least one member was validating, were likely to be more satisfied and stable. Mismatched couples where even one partner reported hostile rating for either partner is a serious concern and a referral should be considered. Avoidant couples can be functioning well although additional assessment is recommended regarding their investment in the relationship (Busby & Holman, 2009).

Sexual activity also affects the couple relationship: The longer a couple waited to become sexually involved the better their sexual quality, relationship communication, relationship satisfaction, and perceived relationship stability was in marriage. The point of initiation of sexual activity within the couple relationship may indicate that commitment and security are issues to address with the couple (Busby, Carroll, & Willoughby, 2010).

Program Goals and Objectives

There is no one program that is associated with RELATE. The objectives of RELATE fit the needs of many applied programs. The assessment can be completed within an hour, it provides information known to affect relationship functioning, and is entirely confidential. Many programs and practices need tools that can be used to meet their specific needs. The ability to tailor interventions to specific clients, or groups of clients, is an advantage of using RELATE. As opposed to offering all couples standardized treatment, a tailored program increases the appeal and accessibility of education for diverse couples. For example, including conflict negotiations in the curriculum has been identified as an element that consistently adds to the effectiveness in premarital programs (Carroll & Doherty, 2003), and RELATE can highlight the part of conflict negotiation that would provide the couple with the most benefit. RELATE has been used for experiential groups such as "Sweetheart" weekends and equine-assisted couple's education and therapy. For example, RELATE is a central feature of *RELATE with your Mate*, a couple's education and enrichment program (Loyer-Carlson & Busby, 2003). Couples receive tokens for RELATE when they sign up for the Sweetheart Weekend and are asked to complete RELATE at least one week prior to the weekend so the Reports can be reviewed by the group leader. The program is then tailored to the specific needs of the couples who are attending. For example, if the reports indicate a need for communication training, more time is spent on communication education and activities. If, however, the report indicates trauma and difficulties such as depression or anxiety, more time is spent addressing those issues, and group leaders are aware of potential triggers and challenges. Similarly, equine-facilitated psychotherapy is a powerful experiential therapy, and in the Family Therapy Practice Center of Southern Arizona (FTPCaz) Relationship series (Loyer-Carlson & Simon-Heldt, 2012), prior to a couples' equine experience, they are asked to complete RELATE so that the therapist can plan the activity that would be the most helpful to the client.

RELATE has been used for many years as an adjunct to instruction in university classrooms as well. Students take RELATE at the beginning of the semester, and as each area of relationships is studied, for example, the conflict styles articulated by John Gottman (avoidant, validating, volatile, escalating) (see Busby & Holman, 2009), students review their RELATE results that graph their style and write a short essay on the content area and how the factor operates in their own lives.

Professional Preparation and Training Issues

There is no special training needed to interpret the RELATE. For those couples wanting to explore their relationship further, certified family life educators, licensed or certified marriage and family therapists, and clergy members have the background to explore the results because the items and the scales are based on empirical research and theory. Stahmann and Hiebert (1997) emphasized that prior to helping clients with RELATE, practitioners need to take RELATE themselves, carefully going through the results so that they have a personal understanding of the Report. Professionals particularly benefit from the Detailed Report and should study the items and raw data for each of the subscales to understand the diagnostic criteria that are available. Providers are cautioned to only work within their specific areas of competency and licensing, and to not make claims outside of the scope of the instrument.

Steps for interpreting RELATE: Sensitivity, Snapshot, and Summarize. Dr. Jeffry Larson has led numerous training sessions on interpreting RELATE with couples. He estimates that the average couple will require a 60–75 minute feedback session, while a distressed couple will require two or more sessions for an effective interpretation. He offers the general advice that clinicians begin the session with *Sensitivity* to each person's feelings and interpretations during the session, and to encourage the couple to see the results as a *Snapshot* of their relationship. Marriage education is less likely to produce fears and stigmas than therapy (Larson, 2004), and therapist-directed interventions were not as effective as semi-independent programs (Busby, Ivey, Harris, & Altes, 2007). Coaching even low-intensity activities of talking about major issues in the relationship is valuable to couples' ownership of their relationship health (Duncan, Childs, & Larson, 2010). Larson suggested that the professional should offer education regarding each of the subscales of the RELATE, and at the same time help the couple to clarify their feelings and their own interpretations of the meaning of the scales. Finally, the couple should *Summarize* the results of their interpretation to further highlight the personal meaning rather than having the professional summarize for them. Specific steps and guidelines that Larson (2004; 2011) offered are: (1) prior to the interpretation session, review the reports and note the unique strengths and challenges of the couple; note any areas of concern that may require referrals such as depression or anxiety; (2) engage the couple in discussion around their relationship history and status, and talk with them about their goals in taking RELATE; remind them that RELATE does not predict the future, and that the value is in discussion and developing new insights; (3) if RELATE results do not look accurate, go back to the detailed responses in case the respondent misunderstood the question or made an error when answering the question. The results graphs are set with three colors: red (challenge area), white (worthy of discussion), and green (strength area). Discuss each of the areas, using the Summary graph at the end to set goals for improvement.

The RELATE report is intended to be kept as a relationship reference that the couple can refer back to at any time. Clinicians are cautioned to take particular care with RELATE and carefully assess whether they should keep the RELATE in their client files. If the clinician decides to keep copies of RELATE, a decision should be made about how the results of the instrument will be protected, consistent with HIPPA regulations and record-keeping laws and statutes in your state.

To assess progress in relationship skill building, RELATE can be taken more than one time. RELATE can be taken alone (e.g., READY), with the same partner, or with a new partner.

Cultural Implications

A major value of RELATE is in the discussion it stimulates. Because there is no one profile of couples that RELATE ranks as better than another, and because of the large amount of time that is spent on context and values, it is an effective instrument to use with most cultures. There is evidence, however, that not all of the areas tested in RELATE are effective for all cultures (Martinson, 2000; Parra-Cardona & Busby, 2006). Linguistically, however, when RELATE is translated into another language, it is done so using a modified serial approach in translation. This process is done in several stages, including first translating the questionnaire by committee, then assessing the clarity and equivalence of the items. Next, the questionnaire is back-translated before it is field-tested. When those steps are completed, RELATE is assessed for reliability and finally the results are interpreted (Carroll, Holman, Segura-Bartholomew, Bird, & Busby, 2001). This was initially completed with the Spanish version of RELATE, rendering the Spanish version to be equivalent to the original English version.

Conclusion

The purpose of this chapter was to introduce RELATE by providing an overview of the theoretical foundation and history upon which it is based, to describe its scales and subscales, and to review its contribution to empirical literature. This chapter also provided a guide to the ways RELATE is used by the lay respondent, the applied professional, and to the research professional. RELATE is based on comprehensive research reviews of premarital predictors of marital quality and stability and operates with four propositions: (1) people continue to do what is rewarding and avoid that which is costly, (2) people are dynamic and relationships evolve but history and context are stable, (3) discourse is healing, and (4) people can be fallible. There are four relationship contexts that are explored in RELATE: the individual, the family, the cultural, and the couple. The RELATE questionnaire contains over 270 items that make up more than 60 scales and subscales, represented in bar graphs and summarized in over 30 pages of graphs and explanations, provided directly to the respondents. There is no one program that is associated with RELATE and the objectives of RELATE fit the needs of many applied programs. There is no special training needed to interpret the RELATE, although persons are encouraged to take RELATE themselves and study the reports before attempting to help others with their reports.

Key Points

- RELATE is a product of over 30 years of research and development.
- The RELATE Report is generated in minutes after both members of the couple have taken RELATE.
- Couples who agree more on values, attitudes, and preferences tend to be more satisfied with each other.
- Sample RELATE Reports are available in the FAQ section of RELATE (www.relateinstitute.org/about/FAQ).
- The RELATE framework is based on a comprehensive research review of premarital and marital predictors of marital qualities.
- Guided discussions of RELATE Results between members of the couple are healing, and suggestions for those discussions are provided in the Report.

Discussion Questions

1. RELATE is designed to be used by individuals and couples to assess their relationships without the assistance of a couple's therapist or educator. What are the benefits of such an instrument? Are there any dangers in couples being able to access their own relationship reports?
2. Research indicates that a negative family of origin experience does not directly affect the couple relationship, but does so more through anxiety or avoidance in close relationships. Why then would you want to measure family of origin or personal history in a relationship evaluation?
3. RELATE is a research instrument and is designed to assist couples in learning about their relationships. Can RELATE be used as a "matchmaking" tool for dating websites? Why or why not?

References and Further Readings

Busby, D., Carroll, J., & Willoughby, B. (2010). Compatibility or restraint: The effects of sexual timing on marriage relationships. *Journal of Family Psychology, 24,* 766–774.

Busby, D., & Gardner, B. (2008). How do I analyze thee? Let me count the ways: Considering empathy in couple relationships using self and partner ratings. *Family Process, 47,* 229–242.

Busby, D., Gardner, B., & Taniguchi, N. (2005). The family of origin parachute model: Landing safely in adult romantic relationships. *Family Relations, 54,* 254–264.

Busby, D., & Holman, T. (1989). The influence of background variables and quality of the home environment on values: A path analysis. *Family Perspective, 23,* 203–216.

Busby, D., & Holman, T. (2009). Perceived match or mismatch on the Gottman conflict styles: Associations with relationship outcome variables. *Family Process, 48,* 531–545.

Busby, D., Holman, T., & Niehuis, S. (2009). The association between partner enhancement and self-enhancement and relationship quality outcomes. *Journal of Marriage and Family, 71,* 449–464.

Busby, D., Holman, T., & Taniguchi, N. (2001). RELATE: Relationship evaluation of the individual, family, cultural, and couple contexts. *Family Relations, 50,* 308–316.

Busby, D., Holman, T., & Walker, E. (2008). Pathways to relationship aggression between adult partners. *Family Relations, 57*(1), 72–83.

Busby, D., Ivey, D., Harris, S., & Altes, C. (2007). Self-directed, therapist-directed, and assessment-based interventions for premarital couples. *Family Relations, 56,* 279–290.

Busby, D., & Loyer-Carlson, V. (2003). *Pathways to marriage: Premarital and early marital relationships.* Boston, MA: Allyn & Bacon.

Carroll, J., & Doherty, W. (2003). Evaluating the effectiveness of premarital prevention programs: A meta-analytic review of outcome research. *Family Relations, 52,* 105–118. doi:10.1111/j.1741-3729.2003.00105.x

Carroll, J., Holman, T., Segura-Bartholomew, G., Bird, M., & Busby, D. (2001). Translation and validation of the Spanish version of the RELATE questionnaire using a modified serial approach for cross-cultural translation. *Family Process, 40,* 211–231.

Dean, L., Carroll, J., & Chongming, Y. (2007). Materialism, perceived financial problems, and marital satisfaction. *Family and Consumer Sciences Research Journal, 35,* 260–281.

Draper, T., Holman, T., Grandy, S., & Blake, W. (2008). Individual, demographic, and family correlates of romantic attachments in a group of American young adults. *Psychological Reports, 103,* 857–872.

Duncan, S., Childs, G., & Larson, J. (2010). Perceived helpfulness of four different types of marriage preparation interventions. *Family Relations, 59,* 623–636.

Gottman, J. (1994). *Why marriages succeed or fail.* New York, NY: Simon & Schuster.

Gottman, J. (1999). *The marriage clinic: A scientifically based marital therapy.* New York, NY: W.W. Norton.

Halford, W., Moore, E., Wilson, K., Dyer, C., & Farrugia, C. (2006). *CoupleCARE: A guidebook for life partners.* Bown Hills QLS, Australia: Australian Academic Press.

Holman, T. (2001). *Premarital prediction of marital quality or breakup: Research, theory, and practice.* New York, NY: Kluwer Academic/Plenum.

Holman, T., & Busby, D. (2011). Family of origin, differentiation of self and partner, and adult romantic relationship quality. *Journal of Couple and Relationship Therapy, 10,* 3–19.

Holman, T., Busby, D., Doxey, C., Klein, D., & Loyer-Carlson, V. (1997). *Relationship Evaluation (RELATE).* Provo, UT: Marriage Study Consortium.

Holman, T., Busby, D., & Larson, J. (1989). *PREParation for marriage* (questionnaire). Provo, UT: Brigham Young University.

Karney, B., & Bradbury, T. (1995). The longitudinal course of marital quality and stability: A review of theory, methods and research. *Psychological Bulletin, 19*(1), 3–34.

Kelley, H. (1979). *Personal relationships: Their structures and processes*. Hillsdale, NJ: Lawrence Erlbaum Associates.

Larson, J. (2004). Innovations in marriage education: Introduction and challenges. *Family Relations, 53*, 421–424.

Larson, J. (2011). *RELATE Interpretation Session Guidelines*. Limited Circulation. Jeffry_Larson@byu.edu

Larson, J., & Holman, T. (1994). Premarital predictors of marital quality and stability: An applied literature review. *Family Relations, 43*, 228–237.

Loyer-Carlson, V., & Busby, D. (2002). *RELATE User's Guide*. Boston, MA: Allyn & Bacon. www.relateinstitute.org

Loyer-Carlson, V., & Busby, D. (2003). *RELATE With Your Mate* Handbook. (Program funded by a grant from the State of Arizona, Limited Circulation available from first author).

Loyer-Carlson, V., & Simon-Heldt, S. (2012). *Equine facilitated psychotherapy: It is what it is: Relationships workshop*. Tucson, AZ: Roger's Bandalero Ranch.

Martinson, V. (2000). Albanian family-of-origin and adult children's relationship quality. Thesis, Brigham Young University, Provo, Utah.

Parra-Cardona, J. R., & Busby, D, (2006). Exploring relationship functioning in premarital Caucasian and Latino/a couples: Recognizing and valuing cultural differences. *Journal of Comparative Family Studies, 37*, 345–359.

Stahmann, R., & Hiebert, W. (1997). *Premarital and remarital counseling*. San Francisco, CA: Jossey-Bass.

Yorgason, B., Burr, W., & Baker, T. (1980). *Marital Inventories* (questionnaire). Provo, UT: Brigham Young University.

PART IV

Evidence-based Practices in Skills-based Programs

11

RELATIONSHIP ENHANCEMENT PROGRAM AND MASTERING THE MYSTERIES OF LOVE

Robert F. Scuka

LEARNING GOALS

- The reader will gain an understanding of the theory of deep empathy and the application of the special Identification Mode of empathy.
- The reader will be able to identify the various versions of the RE and MML programs and their target audiences.
- The reader will be able to identify and describe the 11 RE skills.
- The reader will understand the different delivery options for the RE and MML programs.
- The reader will become acquainted with the results of some of the most important RE research studies, including two studies that showed additional gains at follow-up compared to post-test.
- The reader will become aware of opportunities for training and certification in the RE program or one of the MML programs.

Introduction

The **Relationship Enhancement (RE) model** was one of the first psychoeducational skills-training programs developed to help couples and families have better relationships. Bernard Guerney, Jr. and colleagues at Pennsylvania State University developed the initial formulation of RE during the late 1960s and early 1970s. Their collective work was published as *Relationship Enhancement: Skill-Training Programs for Therapy, Problem Prevention, and Enrichment* (Guerney, 1977). The core conviction behind the creation of RE was that the primary source of family distress was a deficit of good relationship skills rather than overt psychopathology. Hence, the goal was to develop a systematic way of teaching and helping couples and families learn good relationship skills. The name *Relationship Enhancement* gave perfect expression to the desired outcome.

From the beginning, RE was conceived simultaneously as a therapy with a psychoeducational component (Scuka, 2005) and a psychoeducational program to be offered in an educational, non-therapeutic setting such as a weekend workshop or multiweek program format (Guerney & Scuka, 2010). The skills-training component is identical in RE Therapy and the RE Program. What distinguishes RE Therapy is the elaboration of advanced techniques designed to effectively manage and deepen the therapy process. These include **troubleshooting, becoming, doublebecoming**, and **laundering**. There also are basic teaching and coaching skills applied in both RE Therapy and the RE Program that are designed to deepen a couple's or family's **dialogue process**. These include **instructing, structuring, demonstrating, modeling, prompting, positive reinforcement**, and **drawing out underlying positives** (cf. Scuka, 2005, for detailed descriptions).

Theoretical Foundations and History

The heart and soul of the RE model is Carl Rogers's person-centered approach that focuses on the centrality of emotion to human experience and the crucial role that empathy, non-judgmental acceptance, and respect play in personal healing. But if the Rogerian focus on emotion and empathy represent the foundation of RE, then skill-building approaches derived from learning theory, and behavioral modification techniques derived from behavioral theories, constitute the guiding methodology of the RE model. By systematically integrating elements of these different theoretical perspectives, Guerney achieved two things simultaneously. First, he took Rogers's use of empathy as a skill used by a therapist to facilitate personal insight and healing in a client and extended it to a skill that is taught to clients so as to facilitate mutual understanding and interpersonal healing in their relationships. Second, he developed a systematic way of teaching people empathy and other relationship skills so as to maximize the effective learning and integration of those skills. Following the principles of learning theory, the skills teaching methodology in RE employs three core components: didactic teaching to provide a conceptual frame of reference, demonstration and modeling of the RE skills to provide a model of desired behaviors, and intensive supervision and coaching of the learners' practice and employment of the skills in order to provide an opportunity for experiential integration of the skills.

On the basis of empirical research and extensive clinical and educational program experience, the RE model has evolved from three skills to the current 11 skills. The three original, core skills taught in RE are expressive skills to share one's experience, feelings, concerns and desires, subjectively and respectfully; empathic skills that facilitate listening to and understanding others more deeply; and discussion and negotiation skills that follow a structured dialogue process. Problem-solving skills to help couples devise creative, win–win solutions, self-change skills to reduce unwanted behaviors, and helping others change skills to support others in implementing their agreements were added over time to meet those specific needs. Coaching skills are designed to help partners skillfully manage their dialogue process when mistakes get made, while conflict management skills help partners exit from cycles of hostility and blame. Generalization skills encourage family members to employ the basic skills in daily life with one another and in other relationships, while maintenance skills reinforce longer-term use of the skills while nurturing the relationship. Finally, forgiveness skills have been introduced to help overcome alienation and foster healing.

The central role of empathy in RE. The hallmark of RE skills-training is its emphasis on the crucial role of empathy in fostering mutual understanding, compassion, and healing in relationships. But the emphasis in RE is on what is called *deep empathy* (cf. Scuka, 2005), which involves "reading between the lines" of what the expresser literally expresses for him- or herself in order to connect experientially with and identify the deeper layers that are implied in what the person was able to express about his or her experience, perspective, feelings, concerns, desires, values, or goals. The goal for the empathizer in the verbal empathy, then, is not simply to repeat back what the expresser literally expressed—which after a while becomes monotonous and counterproductive—but to include in one's verbal acknowledgment of the expresser's perspective whatever one was able to pick up on through one's reading between the lines. In this manner, the empathizer in effect gives back to the expresser what could be described as an enhanced version of what that person was able to express for him- or herself. In approaching empathy in this way, the empathizer accomplishes three things simultaneously: one understands the expresser better; one leaves the expresser *feeling* understood; and one potentially helps the expresser understand his or her own experience better.

In addition, RE has developed a specialized way of having intimate partners empathize with one another that is referred to as the **Identification Mode** of empathy (cf. Scuka, 2005). In the Identification Mode of empathy, the empathizer imaginatively steps into the shoes of the partner, imagines oneself being the other person experiencing things the way the other person experiences them, and then represents the partner's experience using the first person pronoun *I*, speaking as though the empathizer *were* the partner. There are two profound advantages to doing verbal empathy in this specialized way. First, it empowers the empathic imagination so that the empathizer is enabled to give a more spontaneous, deeper, and richer empathic representation of the partner's experience. Second, by the empathizer reenacting the partner's experience in this way, the partner is enabled to imaginatively watch his or her experience unfold before his or her eyes. This in turn enables the partner to gain what is called "observational distance" from his or her experience, which has the effect of taking that person into an even deeper connection with and understanding of his or her experience. This way of providing empathy is a powerful gift that one partner can give the other partner, and is taught in all versions of the RE program.

Needs Assessment and Target Audience

RE has been used with a wide variety of populations and across levels of problem severity, including primary prevention programs and programs designed to reduce the effects of existing problems. The original research on RE was done with a majority of the participants in the lowest two levels of the Hollingshead Socio-Economic/Educational Status Index. In addition, this initial research was based on as many rural as urban participants.

In order to make RE even more accessible to as many people as possible, two new formats of the RE Program have been created. The first is an audio version of the original RE Program for people who may have limitations around their ability to read (Guerney, 1994). Second, and even more important, the RE Program has been rewritten to simplify the presentation of the RE skills at a 5th-grade reading level. This *Mastering the Mysteries of Love* (MML) version of the RE Program, which was first published in 2004, also has added experiential learning exercises to make the program more engaging for program participants (Guerney & Ortwein, 2011a). The central motivation and goal in creating this new MML version of the RE program was to maximize the program's accessibility to relatively disadvantaged populations, including low-income, poorly educated, homeless, or incarcerated individuals, couples, or families. The latest edition of MML has introduced a new skill into the RE model, namely the Forgiveness skill, which is designed to foster healing and reconciliation in relationships where there has been a significant betrayal or the inflicting of interpersonal harm.

With the assistance of federally funded grants that have been available nationwide since 2004 under the Building Strong Families Project, the Healthy Marriage Initiative, and the Pathways to Responsible Fatherhood Grants, MML has extended the range and reach of RE immensely. Indeed, over the past 10 years, in partnership with over 85 organizations, MML has been used with over 40,000 individuals or couples in marriage preparation or relationship enrichment programs nationwide. MML's ability to be implemented so widely has been assisted by the creation of its own leadership training manual (Guerney & Ortwein, 2011b) and numerous DVD resources, as well as by the creation of a very highly structured training process and ongoing support for the implementation of MML in local settings.

The accessibility of the MML version of RE has been extended even further into special target audiences by the creation of three additional adaptations of the MML program, each with its own participant manual and leadership training guides. *Love's Cradle* is for new or soon-to-be parents, and combines the RE skills with issues related to being a couple and adjusting to parenting (Guerney & Ortwein, 2008a). It also includes four seven-hour modules around the topics of trust, marriage, money, and complex family relationships. Love's Cradle also has its own accompanying DVD (Ortwein, 2005).

Ready for Love is for singles or individuals in a relationship who are to unable to attend with their partner (Guerney & Ortwein, 2008b). Ready for Love combines the RE skills with experiential learning activities built around core topics such as the qualities of good relationships, boundaries, emotional safety, and the biology of love. Additional topics include components of trust, healing, and forgiveness, the effects of adult relationships on children, and how to approach one's partner when one desires him or her to make a change.

Mastering the Mysteries of Stepfamilies combines the RE skills with special topics focused on the unique and challenging dynamics of stepfamilies (Landrum, Ortwein, & Guerney, 2009a). Topics include stepfamily boundaries, bio-parent/child and stepparent/stepchild bonds, ways to maintain a successful relationship with the other bio-parent, effective discipline in a stepfamily, old and new family traditions, and nurturing the new marriage.

The most recent iterations of RE and MML have been adaptations created for Catholic and Protestant churches. Mastering the Mysteries of Sacramental Love: A Relationship Enhancement Program for Catholic Couples (MMSL) combines RE skills in the MML format with Catholic teaching on sacramental marriage (Ortwein & Guerney, 2011). Each RE skill is introduced with biblical references and linked to Catholic teaching on marriage in a manner designed to give couples needed tools to live their faith. In-class learning activities combine lectures, group discussions, experiential activities, and couple dialogues. Participants practice each concept and skill in class and are encouraged to carry over the concepts and skills into practical applications at home. The 24-hour program can be taught in its entirety or a module can be taught independently. It can be presented in a weekend or weekly format.

CoupleTalk: Cracking the Code to an Amazing Relationship (Flecky & Flecky, 2014) is a new 10-session, video-based recreation of the RE skills designed to make RE even more accessible and user-friendly by taking advantage of the most up-to-date video and instructional tools to create an experiential program that engages participants while they learn. CoupleTalk contains two parts: Part 1—Cracking the Code to a Deeper Connection, and Part 2—Cracking the Code to Handling Conflict. Each part contains five sessions of video-based instruction, demonstrations, and interactive exercises together with a workbook for each participant. Part 1 is focused on the core communication skills and dialogue process, while Part 2 is focused on how to manage disagreements, handle strong emotions, and repair a relationship when it has been damaged. Another feature of *CoupleTalk* is that the RE skills are set in a scriptural context, in order to make this version of RE attractive for use in Protestant church settings. In addition, *CoupleTalk* makes RE more accessible than ever because the program does not require a trained leader, but is structured and organized through the videos themselves. *CoupleTalk*, therefore, can be used independently in small groups, large classes, weekend retreats, or by a couple in their own home.

Program Goals and Objectives

The heart of the learning and integration process in RE is the couple's or family's use of expressive and empathic skills in the context of a structured dialogue process. This process is where the couple or family has the opportunity to engage one another around whatever issues need to be addressed, but in a manner designed to minimize defensiveness and maximize the opportunity for positive communication and, as relevant, constructive problem solving. The fundamental goal, however, is to foster deepened emotional connection and, as relevant, healing in the relationship. In the process, RE fosters the reconfiguration of participants' patterns of interaction away from dysfunctional, alienating patterns that create anxiety and lead to emotional insecurity, distancing, and disengagement, and toward more positive, relationship-nurturing patterns of interaction that encourage emotional security, trust, openness, and active engagement while also fostering participants' capacity to show and receive love.

Another objective of RE, especially as embodied in the generalization and maintenance skills, is to help couples and families integrate the RE skills and dialogue process into their daily lives on a long-term basis, with the hope that this leads to continued improvement in their relationships. In this way, RE incorporates a problem prevention component by equipping couples and families with the skills to solve future challenges successfully on their own.

Curriculum and Other Program Issues

The RE and MML programs can be offered in a number of different formats: two-day (weekend), multisession (weekly), combined one-day and multisession (weekly), and an abridged one-day format. The first three formats typically are 14–16 hours long, whereas the one-day format would last for 7–8 hours. In each of the first three formats each of the 11 RE skills is introduced through a mini-lecture, which is followed, as appropriate, by a live or video demonstration, a practice exercise, an experiential exercise, and/or a couple's dialogue. In the one-day format, typically five or six of the skills are introduced. One advantage of the multisession and combined formats is that they permit the incorporation of home assignments between sessions in order to reinforce participants' learning. Regardless of the format, intensive coaching of participants' exercises and dialogues is fundamental to the longer-term success in their mastery and integration of the RE skills and dialogue process. Participant feedback has convinced some organizations to add booster sessions and/or home visits to their presentation of the RE Program, MML, and Love's Cradle. The goal in each case is to help participants maintain their gains from attending the program.

Cultural Implications

The RE and MML programs have been used in numerous foreign countries and have been translated into a number of languages. Scuka has personally led RE trainings in Korea and El Salvador, where the original RE Program is being offered on a regular basis with Korean and Spanish translations of the RE Program manual. In addition, there is an Institut Francophone de Relationship Enhancement (IFRE) in France, where RE trainings and workshops for couples are offered in French on a regular basis, utilizing a French translation of the original RE Program manual. IFRE also has been quite successful in bringing the RE Program into business settings in France. The original RE Program manual also has been translated into German, Greek, and Mandarin.

The MML program manual and leader's guide, and the Love's Cradle program manual and leader's guide, have been translated into Spanish and are being used extensively in Latino communities and churches throughout the United States. In addition, Latino communities have the benefit of Spanish-language video resources for MML and Love's Cradle. The MML program manual and leader materials also have been translated into Korean under the auspices of the Korean Churches for Community Development, and are being used in Korean-American communities in the U.S. In addition, the MML program is being used in a Native American project in Montana, and there are several projects using MML that center in the African-American community in the U.S.

Under the auspices of the U.S. Committee for Refugees and Immigrants, special attention also has been given to the needs of various refugee and immigrant groups through the translation and creative revisioning of the RE skills into volumes with the general title of *Relationship Enhancement® for Refugees and Immigrants*. Translations for these refugee and immigrant communities have been done in Spanish, Arabic, Burmese, Farsi, Karen, Napali, Somali, and Tigrinya (Guerney, Ortwein, & Amin, 2009), and they are being actively used in those communities under the leadership of trained program leaders and certified MML Program Trainers. Additional translations of MML have been made into Chinese, Hmong, and Vietnamese.

The conclusion to be drawn from all the translations that have been done of the original RE Program and the MML version of the RE program, together with their extensive use in a number of countries and various ethnic or linguistic communities in the U.S., is that RE is an eminently adaptable program that in principle can be used effectively in virtually any ethnic or linguistic community. The primary reason is that RE is a skills-based rather than a content-based program, which makes it relatively easy to adapt to different cultural settings.

Evidence-based Research and Evaluation

The RE model has a strong empirical research base that encompasses both RE Therapy and the RE Program. From the 1970s through the 1990s, 32 empirical research studies were conducted involving RE. Some of the research was done on the educational program version of RE and some was done on the therapy application of RE. The most comprehensive summary of 25 of the research studies on RE is to be found in Accordino and Guerney (2002). A more limited summary of the most important research studies, but in more descriptive detail, is to be found in Scuka (2005).

Validation of the superior effectiveness of RE can be found in a meta-analytic study by Giblin, Sprenkle, and Sheehan (1985), which demonstrated the comparative superiority of RE to 13 other models. The average effect size across all relationship approaches included in this meta-analysis was .44, whereas the average effect size for RE was a robust .96. One important conclusion of this study was that more structured approaches that emphasize skills training and behavioral practice, as opposed to discussion, had superior outcomes. A second meta-analysis conducted by Hahlweg and Markman (1988) confirmed the superior effectiveness of RE with an even higher effect size of 1.14.

Five of the RE research studies involved direct comparison with another therapy model or psychoeducational program, and in each case RE was found to be at least as effective as the other models on some of the outcome measures and superior to the other model on at least one or more of the outcome measures. In one study comparing the RE Program to a no-treatment condition and the Couples Communication (CC) program (Brock & Joanning, 1983), RE was shown at post-test to be more effective at increasing marital communication (including the expression of affection) and marital satisfaction. Then, at 3-month follow-up, the outcomes for RE couples were superior to the outcomes for CC couples on all variables. Another significant aspect of this study is that the most distressed RE couples who entered this study experienced greater gains than the most distressed CC couples, and those RE couples maintained their gains at follow-up.

A second study compared a Premarital RE (PRE) program with an Engaged Encounter (EE) program (Sams, 1983). The programs were led by volunteer couples trained to lead each of the programs. From pre-test to post-test, the couples attending the PRE program showed greater gains than the couples attending the EE program in the areas of empathy skills, expressive skills, and their ability to solve problems effectively. The implication of the study, in line with the observation of Giblin and his colleagues referenced above, is that the skills-training components of the PRE program compared to their relative absence in the EE program accounted for the superior outcomes for those attending the PRE program.

In another study involving mother–daughter dyads, RE was compared to a no-treatment group and a Traditional Treatment (TT) group that essentially was an unstructured open communication group (Guerney, Coufal, & Vogelsong, 1981). The no-treatment dyads showed virtually no improvement, while the TT dyads showed improvement only in the general satisfaction of their relationships. By contrast, participants in the structured RE group showed significant improvement in all areas measured: empathy, expressive skills, general communication patterns, and the general quality of their relationships.

A follow-up study sought to evaluate the comparative effectiveness of a booster program at reinforcing gains from the original interventions (Guerney, Vogelsong, & Coufal, 1983). Both RE booster group participants and RE participants from the original study who did not participate in the RE booster group gained more than their TT group counterparts on measures of empathy, expressiveness, and general relationship quality, again reinforcing the superiority of the RE intervention. In addition, RE booster group participants gained more than non-participants in the RE booster group, thus validating booster sessions as a way to maintain gains. But the most significant result was that follow-up testing of the non-participants in the RE booster group showed gains on all measures compared to post-test rather than the typically expected decrease. This result demonstrates not only that RE can foster a longer-term maintenance of gains even in the absence of a booster intervention, but that the positive effects of RE treatment may continue to increase long past the termination of treatment.

A similar longer-term positive increase in gains at follow-up compared to post-test was found in another RE research study (Griffin & Apostal, 1983). Couples who participated in a six-week RE Program significantly increased their functional differentiation of self and the quality of their marital relationships at post-test. At one-year follow-up, not only were these gains maintained, but additional gains in differentiation of self were found that had not been present at post-test. This outcome indicates that RE can result in long-term positive change in couples even after the conclusion of their participation in the RE Program.

The latter two studies provide the strongest evidence in support of the effectiveness of RE. Not only did each of these two studies substantiate the maintenance of gains over time for the RE participants but, even more significantly, both studies also documented that the RE intervention had a continuing positive influence resulting in an increase in gains at follow-up. This is an unexpected but positive result. The usual research expectation is that at follow-up there will be some reversion toward pre-test levels compared to post-test, as the positive effects of the original intervention gradually wear off. The fact that the mother–daughter dyads that did not participate in booster sessions nonetheless showed additional gains on all measures is an impressive result. Both of these results offer powerful testimony to the long-term effectiveness of RE as an intervention.

The skills-training component of RE, including its emphasis on reinforcing behaviors that increase participants use of the skills on an ongoing basis, is a likely explanation for these positive outcomes. The result, as reflected in both studies, is that participants benefitted from the self-reinforcing gains derived from the skills-learning and the ensuing transformation of their patterns of interaction. In sum, RE succeeds not only at helping people change their patterns of behavior, but also succeeds at preserving those changes and even succeeds in fostering a continuation of positive change beyond their participation in RE.

The *Mastering the Mysteries of Love* version of RE has been used with over 40,000 people in marriage preparation and/or relationship enrichment programs nationwide over the past 10 years. A preliminary report presented at the National Association for Relationship and Marriage Education annual conference (Larsen-Rife & Early, 2011) points to the process factors that influenced positive outcomes for the 2,940 participants who attended the MML program in California. The three components assessed were presentation time, skills practice time, and discussion time. Not surprisingly, skills practice time was found to be the most influential program component, followed by presentation time, with discussion time having virtually no impact on positive outcomes. Time spent in practice was associated with improved problem solving at post-test, improved communication at 30-day follow-up, and improved relationship satisfaction at post-test, 30-day follow-up, and 6month follow-up.

The *Love's Cradle* program also has been used extensively around the country. For example, under the auspices of a federal grant award, Bethany Christian Services offered the program in the Atlanta area as an initial 14-hour weekend program, with six months of follow-up support, including home visits. Program findings were presented by Wimmer and Gibbs (2011). Follow-up surveys of 24.4% of the original 394 attending couples who agreed to participate in the research study revealed statistically significant improvements in communication and conflict resolution, with an average effect size of .65 or better. In addition, 87% of women and 90% of men expressed increased satisfaction with their primary intimate relationship, while 69% of mothers reported that their relationship felt stable.

Preparation and Training Issues

Each of the six major RE programs has its own unique leader's manual tailored to the specifics of that program in order to facilitate and systematize the training of RE or MML Program Leaders. These include *Couples' Relationship Enhancement® Program: Leader's Manual* (Scuka, Nordling, & Guerney, 2009); *Mastering the Mysteries of Love: Leader's Guide* (Guerney & Ortwein, 2011b); *Love's Cradle: Leader's Guide* (Ortwein & Guerney, 2008a); *Ready for Love: Leader's Guide* (Ortwein & Guerney, 2008b); *Mastering the Mysteries of Stepfamilies: Leader's Guide* (Landrum, Ortwein, & Guerney, 2009b); and *Mastering the Mysteries of Sacramental Love* (Ortwein, 2011).

It is important to note that an empirical research study by Most and Guerney (1983) validated that non-professional lay people can be effectively trained to become highly proficient RE Program Leaders, as measured and rated by RE Program Trainers, and as rated by couple participants in the RE Program. The reason this is important is that it vastly increases the number of couples who can be offered the RE Program or one of the MML-based programs nationwide and internationally because the pool of potential program leader trainees is not limited to mental health professionals. This is what has happened with the extensive training of new Certified RE Program and MML Program Trainers over the past decade, who in turn train hundreds of program leaders nationwide.

As part of the systematic training of program leaders for the five MML-based programs, prospective leaders typically attend the MML program as a partici- pant before attending a two-day leader/facilitator training. In this way, prospective leaders gain first-hand experience of the core MML program and the RE skills by first experiencing them as participant learners. This helps future leaders bet- ter understand some of the questions or challenges that other participants may have when they attend the given program. This in turn strengthens their ability to more effectively lead their chosen program and coach participants during their exercises and dialogues.

Another important consideration in the training of RE or MML Program Leaders is for them to understand the clear boundaries between providing skills training and coaching versus providing therapy. This is especially crucial given that the majority of individuals trained to become RE or MML Program Leaders are not mental health professionals. Program leaders therefore are taught that their role in working with couples or families is to focus strictly on helping participants master the skills that make up the RE or MML program, and they are not to give advice on participants' substantive issues or delve into participants' potentially deeper levels of emotion. At the same time, program leaders are trained to recog- nize when an individual or couple may benefit from a referral to a mental health professional, and are provided protocols around how to do that.

Once an individual or couple gains sufficient experience leading the RE Pro- gram or one of the MML-based programs, they become eligible to enter into an extended training process leading to formal certification as a Trainer of Leaders for the RE Program or one of the MML-based programs. The training process involves the trainee receiving supervision of his or her live or video presentation of an actual RE or MML workshop, co-leading a two-day leader/facilitator training with a certified program trainer in order to receive on-the-spot and post-training supervision, and independently planning and conducting one's own leader/facili- tator training that is video-taped for supervision. This extended training process ensures a high level of fidelity to the continued promulgation of the RE model.

The longer-term goal is to create self-sufficient, localized training centers that can continue independently to train new program leaders and certify new trainers of leaders. To this end, many of the initial leader/facilitator trainings are offered on-site in a variety of agency and community settings in order to encourage and facilitate successful local implementation of the chosen RE or MML pro- gram. Local implementation of the various programs is also facilitated by ongoing supervision, consultation, and technical assistance as needed.

Finally, the cultural adaptability and reach of RE into different linguistic/cul- tural communities has been facilitated by the certification of trainers who then are able to present the RE Program Leadership Training or one or more of the MML Leadership Training Programs in their respective languages of Spanish, French,

Korean, Chinese, Hindi, Swahili, Armenian, Farsi, Bosnian, Arabic, or Burmese. In addition, the MML Program is being led by trained leaders who are able to present the program in their native languages of Somali, Mai Mai, Nepali, Amharic, Spanish, and Swahili.

Conclusion

RE is one of the most effective psychoeducational skills-training programs. The research supporting its effectiveness is extensive and compelling. Furthermore, the MML version of RE has made the RE skills and dialogue process more accessible to a wide audience and has benefited countless individuals and couples over the past decade. The *Love's Cradle* program has helped fledgling parents nurture their adult relationship during one of the most challenging transitions any couple can face. The *Ready for Love* program has helped single people and people in relationships whose partner is unable to attend benefit from the skills training so as to improve their current or future intimate relationship. The ability to take Ready for Love into prison settings offers an emotional boost to those individuals who are looking forward to being able to be reunited with a loved one. The *Mastering the Mysteries of Stepfamilies* program provides a welcome resource to newly constituted families that are struggling with questions of allegiances, boundaries, and new relationships that represent unchartered waters. The *Mastering the Mysteries of Sacramental Love* program provides Catholic parishes access to RE in a manner that links RE skills to a religious faith perspective. The new *Couple Talk* program, with its video-based instructional approach that does not require a trained leader to present it, is likely to make the RE skills even more widely accessible. All told, the "family" of RE and MML programs offers a comprehensive set of resources to help people have the best possible relationships that they can have.

Key Points

- RE is a psychoeducational skills-training program designed to help couples and families create and maintain fulfilling and successful relationships.
- RE combines a Rogerian emphasis on empathy with skills-building approaches derived from learning theory in order to create a systematic way of helping people successfully integrate communication and other skills into their relationships.
- The RE dialogue process is designed to facilitate deepened emotional connection and to foster healing in a relationship that has suffered serious injury.
- The extensive research on RE has consistently demonstrated is effectiveness, including its superior effectiveness when directly compared to other approaches.
- RE and its MML version have extensive video resources to support the training of program leaders and for use in workshops with program participants.

- RE and MML have been successfully adapted into numerous and diverse cultural settings, including adaptations for refugee and immigrant groups, as evidenced by the existence of 15 foreign-language translations and the training of leaders who can lead the programs in their native languages.

Discussion Questions

1. What was the core conviction behind the creation of the RE program?
2. What are the three core principles of learning theory incorporated into the teaching of RE skills?
3. What are the three original, core skills taught in RE and MML?
4. What factors likely explain the superior outcomes of RE in research studies compared to other approaches?
5. What was the principal goal in creating the MML version of RE, and what are its distinguishing features?
6. What are the unique features and advantages of the CoupleTalk adaptation of the RE program?

Additional Resources

In addition to the original RE program and the five MML program manuals and leader's guides already referenced, information on available resources, including training and program videos, as well as training and certification opportunities, are available at the following websites:

- For the original RE Program, please visit www.nire.org
- For the *Mastering the Mysteries of Love* version of the RE program, *Love's Cradle, Ready for Love, Mastering the Mysteries of Stepfamilies*, and *Mastering the Mysteries of Sacramental Love*, please visit www.skillswork.org
- For information on translations of the RE Program under the auspices of the U.S. Committee for Refugees and Immigrants, please visit www.refugees. org/healthyfamilies
- For the new video-based *CoupleTalk* program, please visit www.Couple Talk.com

References

Accordino, M., & Guerney, B., Jr. (2002). The empirical validation of Relationship Enhancement couple and family therapies. In D.J. Cain & J. Seeman (Eds.), *Humanistic psychotherapies: Handbook of research and practice* (pp. 403–442). Washington, DC: American Psychological Association.

Brock, G., & Joanning, H. (1983). A comparison of the Relationship Enhancement Program and the Minnesota Couple Communication Program. *Journal of Marital and Family Therapy, 9*, 413–421.

Flecky, D., & Flecky, A. (2014). *Couple Talk: Cracking the code to an amazing relationship* [DVDs and Manuals]. Fullerton, CA: Relationship Research Foundation.

Giblin, P., Sprenkle, D., & Sheehan, R. (1985). Enrichment outcome research: A meta-analysis of premarital, marital and family interventions. *Journal of Marital and Family Therapy, 11*, 257–271.

Griffin, J., Jr., & Apostal, R. (1983). The influence of Relationship Enhancement training on differentiation of self. *Journal of Marital and Family Therapy, 19*, 267–272.

Guerney, B., Jr. (1977). *Relationship Enhancement: Skill-training programs for therapy, problem prevention, and enrichment.* San Francisco, CA: Jossey-Bass.

Guerney, B., Jr. (1994). Relationship Enhancement audio program [Audio cassette]. Silver Spring, MD: IDEALS.

Guerney, B., Jr., Coufal, J., & Vogelsong, E. (1981). Relationship Enhancement versus a traditional approach to therapeutic/preventative/enrichment parent-adolescent program. *Journal of Consulting and Clinical Psychology, 4*, 927–939.

Guerney, B., Jr., & Ortwein, M. (2008a). *Love's Cradle: Building strong families through Relationship Enhancement®.* Frankfort, KY: Relationship Press.

Guerney, B., Jr., & Ortwein, M. (2008b). *Ready for Love: Relationship Enhancement® for singles and solos.* Frankfort, KY: Relationship Press.

Guerney, B., Jr., & Ortwein, M. (2011a). *Mastering the Mysteries of Love: A Relationship Enhancement program for couples* (5th ed.). Frankfort, KY: Relationship Press.

Guerney, B., Jr., & Ortwein, M. (2011b). *Mastering the Mysteries of Love: Leader's guide* (5th ed.). Frankfort, KY: Relationship Press.

Guerney, B., Jr., Ortwein, M., & Amin, G. (2009). *Relationship Enhancement® for refugees and immigrants: Illustrated participant manual* (2nd ed.). Arlington, VA: U.S. Committee for Refugees and Immigrants. (Translations available in Arabic, Burmese, Farsi, Karen, Nepali, Somali, Tigrinya.) Available at www.refugees.org/healthyfamilies

Guerney, B., Jr., & Scuka, R. (2010). *Relationship Enhancement: A program for couples* (4th ed.). Frankfort, KY: Relationship Press.

Guerney, B., Jr., Vogelsong, E., & Coufal, J. (1983). Relationship Enhancement versus a traditional treatment: Follow-up and booster effects. In D. Olson & B. Miller (Eds.), *Family studies review yearbook* (Vol. 1, pp. 738–756). Beverly Hills, CA: Sage Publications.

Hahlweg, K., & Markman, H. (1988). Effectiveness of behavioural marital therapy: Empirical status of behavioural techniques in preventing and alleviating marital distress. *Journal of Consulting and Clinical Psychology, 56*, 440–447.

Landrum, N., Ortwein, M., & Guerney, B., Jr. (2009a). *Mastering the Mysteries of Stepfamilies: A Relationship Enhancement program for success.* Frankfort, KY: Relationship Press.

Landrum, N., Ortwein, M., & Guerney, B., Jr. (2009b). *Mastering the mysteries of stepfamilies: Leader's guide.* Frankfort, KY: Relationship Press.

Larsen-Rife, D., & Early, D. (2011, June). *What really works for marriage education.* Presentation given at the National Association for Relationship and Marriage Education Annual Conference, Houston, TX.

Most, R., & Guerney, B., Jr. (1983). The empirical evaluation of the training of lay volunteer leaders for premarital Relationship Enhancement. *Family Relations, 32*, 239–251.

Ortwein, M. (2005). *Instructional video to accompany Love's Cradle and Mastering the Mysteries of Love* [DVD]. Frankfort, KY: Relationship Press.

Ortwein, M. (2011). *Mastering the Mysteries of Sacramental Love: A Relationship Enhancement program for Catholic couples.* Frankfort, KY: Relationship Press.

Ortwein, M., & Guerney, B., Jr. (2008a). *Love's Cradle: Leader's guide.* Frankfort, KY: Relationship Press.

Ortwein, M., & Guerney, B., Jr. (2008b). *Ready for Love: Leader's guide*. Frankfort, KY: Relationship Press.

Ortwein, M., & Guerney, B., Jr. (2011). *Mastering the Mysteries of Sacramental Love: A Relationship Enhancement program for Catholic couples*. Frankfort, KY: Relationship Press.

Sams, W. (1983). *Marriage preparation: An experimental comparison of the Premarital Relationship Enhancement (PRE) and the Engaged Encounter (EE) programs*. Unpublished doctoral dissertation, Pennsylvania State University. Ann Arbor, MI: ProQuest University Microfilms International, Dissertations Publishing, ProQuest document ID 303278776.

Scuka, R. (2005). *Relationship Enhancement therapy: Healing through deep empathy and intimate dialogue*. New York, NY: Routledge.

Scuka, R., Nordling, W., & Guerney, B., Jr. (2009). *Couples' Relationship Enhancement® program: Leader's manual*. Bethesda, MD: IDEALS.

Wimmer, J., & Gibbs, A. (2011). FRAME-Works: Relationship Enhancement for unmarried parents. In Office of Family Assistance (OFA)(Ed.), *The impact of healthy marriage programs on low-income couples and families: Program perspectives from across the United States* (pp. 18–26). Washington, DC: U.S. Department of Health and Human Services, Administration for Children and Families. Retrieved from http://www.healthy marriageinfo.org/resource-detail/index.aspx?rid=3920#analysis

12

THE PREVENTION AND RELATIONSHIP EDUCATION PROGRAM (PREP) FOR INDIVIDUALS AND COUPLES

Laurie A. Tonelli, Marcie Pregulman, and Howard J. Markman

LEARNING GOALS

- The reader will have an understanding of the theory and research leading to the development of PREP.
- The reader will be able to identify a variety of audiences who may benefit from the PREP intervention and be knowledgeable about the various versions of PREP available.
- The reader will be equipped with information about the goals of PREP and will be well informed of the content areas covered and skills developed in the PREP curriculum.
- The reader will be aware of potential obstacles to implementing PREP and resources to handle them effectively.
- The reader will be acquainted with findings from a great deal of research suggesting benefits of PREP with a diversity of populations.
- The reader will be apprised of PREP trainings offered to professionals and laypersons.

Introduction

Every couple faces issues that have the potential to decrease satisfaction and possibly destroy their relationship. The **Prevention and Relationship Education Program [PREP]** (Markman, Stanley, & Blumberg, 2010) helps couples develop the skills they need to better address the inevitable conflict they will face and teaches couples ways to protect, preserve, and restore positive connections.

PREP initially stood for the Premarital Relationship Enhancement Program, and then changed to the Prevention and Relationship Enhancement program.

Finally, the acronym obtained its current meaning, Prevention and Relationship Education Program. The founders of PREP (Howard Markman and his colleagues) were some of the first to conduct longitudinal studies to assess factors that predict marital distress and divorce. Previously, most research was limited to factors associated with *already* distressed marriages, making it impossible to determine what variables were responsible for the *development* of that distress. The creators of PREP analyzed how couples handled conflict and discovered that response to disagreements was one of the best predictors of relationship success (Markman, 1979, 1981). Therefore, helping participants learn and practice constructive communication behaviors and conflict resolution skills was, and still is, a major focus of PREP.

Theoretical Foundations and History

PREP is based on **cognitive-behavioral theory** and research and also draws from family developmental and systems theories (Markman & Floyd, 1980; Markman, Floyd, Stanley, & Lewis, 1986). The founders of PREP acknowledge the many stressors acting on contemporary couples including transgenerational factors, individual personality preferences, environmental influences, and elements impacting the couple's evolving family system (i.e., their expectations and communication patterns) (Markman et al., 1986). The developers of PREP also recognize the importance of other expected and unexpected family life cycle stressors (e.g., transition to parenthood).

The PREP model assumes that these stressors, if not balanced with adequate couple supports and resources, can derail a relationship. The overriding objective for the creators of PREP was to develop a program that would bolster the supports necessary for a couple's relationship to thrive. This goal led them to focus on developing supports more susceptible to change (e.g., communication and expectations) rather than those factors that were static (e.g., personality and transgenerational issues). Exploring and modifying beliefs and expectations are targets of the PREP intervention because they are frequently sources of conflict in relationships. As PREP evolved, more emphasis was placed on positive connections (e.g., fun, friendship, sensuality) and deeper meanings (e.g., commitment, forgiveness, core beliefs), commensurate with research in the field.

Needs Assessment and Target Audience

The need for an effective intervention that could help prevent divorce prompted the development of PREP. The creators of PREP acknowledged the growing rate of divorce and the enormous social and financial costs associated with it, including personal distress, physical and mental disorders, disruption of lives, and of course, its impact on children (Markman, Floyd, & Dickson-Markman, 1982). PREP was designed to reduce relationship distress and dissolution in marriage (Markman et al., 1986) and, as its name suggests, was developed as a preventative

TABLE 12.1 Versions of the Prevention and Relationship Education Program

Programs for Individuals

Name of Program	Description	Length	Target Audience
PREP 7.0	Described in this chapter.	12 hours	Couples in committed relationships
Within Our Reach	Activity-based curriculum that helps couples build on their strengths and teaches them relationship skills and decision-making strategies that allow them to establish safer and more stable unions benefiting them and their children.	2 to 32 hours	Non-traditional couples with children, often low-income
A Nuestro Alcance	This is the Spanish version of *Within Our Reach.*	32 hours	Spanish-speaking couples
PREP for Strong Bonds	This curriculum addresses issues common to all couples (e.g., communication, stress, support) in addition to those specific to military families (e.g., deployment and reintegration).	15 hours	Military couples
Christian PREP	This curriculum incorporates all concepts of PREP with a Christian emphasis, including addressing the practice of faith and prayer in couple relationships.	2–12 hours	Christian couples
2 Hour PREP	This curriculum uses the foundational lessons from PREP to give participants key skills and principles from the program.		Couples in committed relationships whose time constraints prevent them from participating in the more comprehensive program
Within My Reach	This curriculum gives individuals tools to interact and make decisions that allow for healthy relationships including setting personal and relationship goals.	15 hours	Single women and men, often low-income
On My Shoulders	This is an interactive curriculum designed to build on men's strengths and provide them with skills to establish and maintain healthy relationships, especially with their children.	21 hours	Fathers

Got Your Back	This curriculum helps military men and women improve understanding and decision making in their relationships, aiding individuals to see how their decisions and actions can help them realize their most important life goals.	6.5 hours	Military personnel
Walking the Line	This curriculum addresses relationship issues unique to inmates including improving their relationships and communication in them and managing their expectations before and after their release from confinement.	17 hours	Inmates

Note. More information about the various versions of PREP may be found at www.prepinc.com

intervention. The founders of PREP recognized the transition to marriage as a pivotal point in the family life cycle and an ideal time for implementing change because negative patterns in a couple's relationship were not yet ingrained (Markman & Floyd, 1980; Markman et al., 1986). Accordingly, PREP was originally intended for couples planning to marry. However, the relationship education provided by PREP has since been found to be useful with a wide array of individuals and couples.

As a result of its proven benefits, PREP has been increasingly used in a variety of forms with diverse populations. Engaged and married couples from differing socioeconomic backgrounds, married military couples, couples expecting a child, unmarried couples with children, couples with health issues, college students in dating relationships, international couples, and men and women in prison are just a few of the audiences targeted to receive the PREP intervention (Halford & Bodenmann, 2013; Markman & Rhoades, 2012). In addition, some of the groups to whom PREP has been successfully implemented comprise individuals (rather than couples) who may not be in a relationship. These participants included young mothers, single fathers, incarcerated men and women, and single individuals in the military (Markman & Rhoades, 2012; Markman et al., 2009). Various versions of PREP targeted to specific populations are presented in Table 12.1.

PREP's expanded audience also includes those less likely to seek traditional relationship therapy. Broadly stated, PREP was developed to be a "friendly" alternative to couple therapy. It is a viable option for couples, individual members of a couple, or individuals seeking relationship education who face barriers associated with traditional therapy (e.g., stigma, costs, locations of services). Many aspects of PREP appeal to those wanting an alternative to traditional counseling. These include the format of PREP (structured sessions occurring over a finite period of time); PREP does not require participants to share intimate feelings; PREP is present/future oriented (as opposed to some therapies that require individuals to discuss the same issues over and over); and PREP is goal driven.

PREP's aims of preventing relationship distress and divorce, and its focus on handling conflict in a constructive manner, is useful for any individual or couple seeking to improve their chance of having a healthy and stable relationship. This means the target audience of PREP includes those in almost any stage of their relationship.

Program Goals and Objectives

The overarching goal of PREP is to increase relationship satisfaction by providing an understanding of healthy and happy relationships and the factors that contribute to them. As a result, participants are taught skills and principles that will help them create and maintain satisfying and healthy relationships. PREP, like other evidence-based relationship education programs, assumes that protecting and preserving positive connections in relationships is associated with beneficial outcomes in the future (Markman, Rhoades, Stanley, Ragan, & Whitton, 2010). Therefore, positive connections are targets of intervention and include fun, support, romance, sensuality, and friendship (Markman, Stanley, & Blumberg, 2010). Communication is also targeted because problems in communication frequently lead to marital distress (Gottman, 1994; Karney & Bradbury, 1995; Markman, 1981). Accordingly, participants are equipped with practical communication techniques that allow them to constructively manage conflict in their relationships. Principles fundamental to good relationships are also covered including those related to expectations, commitment, and forgiveness.

In addition to improving and protecting healthy relationships, one goal of PREP (and PREP-related) programs is to help individuals recognize characteristics of unhealthy relationships. By providing information about the ingredients of both successful (e.g., positive connections) *and* unsuccessful relationships (e.g., danger signs), participants can make informed decisions that allow them to establish better outcomes in their relationships, or at times, lead them to end a maleficent relationship.

Curriculum and Other Program Issues

Curriculum. The PREP curriculum is **manualized** and the material is presented in a series of short lessons often followed by guided skill practices. While the core concepts of PREP are present in every version, some material is differentiated to best meet the specific needs of the audience (see Table 12.1). The curriculum covered in this section is from *PREP 7.0*, the most recent version of the original PREP program presented in the book *Fighting for Your Marriage* (Markman, Stanley, & Blumberg, 2010).

Introduction. The introduction provides participants with a summary of what couples will learn in the workshop. Research indicating positive outcomes associated with relationship education and PREP is discussed, along with the benefits of a healthy relationship.

Communication Danger Signs. Communication danger signs are one of the first things taught to participants. These negative communication behaviors are especially problematic and can lead to the erosion of affection, respect, commitment, sex, and friendship. Danger signs include escalation, negative interpretation, invalidation, and withdrawal. The PREP program teaches individuals and couples to identify these destructive communication styles and stop negative behaviors when they are present.

Couples also need a way to exit conversations when they are not going well. The concept of "Time Out" or "Taking A Break" is presented in this module to provide a way for participants to deescalate and refocus, thereby preventing potential danger signs from developing.

Honey, Let's Talk (Good Communication). During this lesson, one of the most important skills of PREP, the **Speaker Listener technique**, is taught to participants. Emphasis is placed on couples learning to effectively talk to one another when their typical ways of communicating fail. Participants also learn that they can use the Speaker Listener technique proactively when they need to address difficult issues in a future conversation. However, this reflective listening tool is different from other programs because the primary goal of the Speaker Listener technique is to help participants avoid the identified danger signs and handle conflict constructively. Two positive outcomes, understanding and the feeling of being understood, are often associated with the Speaker Listener technique, but are not its main objective. Instead, the Speaker Listener technique provides participants with rules of safe communication (e.g., speak for yourself, don't mind read).

The Speaker Listener technique is introduced to participants by a PREP leader and video exemplars are used to demonstrate successful attempts of its implementation. Each participant is given a "floor," a small square piece of cardstock resembling a floor tile with the rules of the Speaker Listener technique listed on it. Because it is a cornerstone of PREP, it is practiced throughout the program, starting with easy conversations about non-confrontational issues and eventually progressing to address areas of concern in a relationship. Ultimately, the goal is for participants to learn to talk to their partners using safe and effective techniques that reduce the likelihood of escalation and tension.

Events and Hidden Issues. The terms *event, issue*, and *hidden issue* are all defined during this lesson. Events are the day-to-day happenings that couples argue about the most. They are often seemingly unimportant actions like leaving the toilet seat up, not putting the cap on the toothpaste, or leaving the gas tank on empty. Issues are key problem areas often triggered by events—parenting, chores, relationships with relatives, cleanliness, timeliness, religion, and arguments over money all fall into this category. Hidden issues are deeper concerns that frequently manifest in arguments about issues and events. They are sometimes unknown to the individual and include control, caring, trust, respect, and commitment. Hidden issues are often emotionally charged and are best resolved with open, safe, and clear communication. Because most individuals deal with these issues only in the context of arguments over events, and are often unaware of the underlying problems causing tension, the Speaker Listener technique is highly beneficial. For this reason, PREP participants are educated through instruction and videos about how the Speaker Listener technique can help them deal with difficult issues in a constructive manner.

Fun and Friendship. A good relationship program would not be complete without a unit on fun and friendship. The major objective of this lesson is to demonstrate the importance of these qualities and show couples how to foster a healthy relational environment that is free of conflict. During this unit participants learn specific strategies on how to strengthen their friendship and have more fun together while protecting that time from conflict.

You, Me and Us. This module emphasizes the unique qualities of individuals and the recognition that each person brings his or her own strengths and weaknesses to any relationship. Individuals explore their own personalities and also examine their partner's. Participants are then asked to recognize both areas of concern and those that are healthy and edifying. The lesson emphasizes the importance of refraining from preemptive judging and is driven by a quiz called Colors of Personality.

Also in this unit, the importance of expectations and how they influence relationships is discussed. Participants examine their own individual expectations and their origin. The PREP curriculum emphasizes the importance of open communication about these expectations to ensure honesty and understanding.

Stress and Relaxation. Inevitably, most people will deal with stress at some point in their lives. This module underscores the necessity of learning to handle stress in a healthy way to protect relationships from its negative effects. Suggestions are given for reducing stress and activities are taught that individuals can implement during stressful periods.

Problem solving. This lesson guides participants through a problem-solving model. Although the founders of PREP believe it is often unnecessary for partners to agree on a solution (simply talking about it safely and fully can be enough), they acknowledge that in certain circumstances it may be necessary for a couple to resolve an issue. In fact, participants often come to a relationship education program with a specific problem they want to address. Therefore, participants are shown exemplar videos of couple discussions that demonstrate steps that often result in effective resolution. This problem-solving model can be used when couples feel it is necessary to find a solution to a problem.

Forgiveness. This lesson focuses on forgiveness in relationships and participants are provided information on ways to work through the process. During this session, individuals receive instruction on how to effectively ask for, and extend, forgiveness to their partner.

Supporting Each Other. There are many different ways of supporting and encouraging relationship partners. This module helps individuals recognize how they prefer to be supported and encouraged. Practicing the newly learned Speaker Listener technique, they also explore their partner's preferences. They use the rules of the technique and focus on listening, paraphrasing, and being supportive without problem solving or giving advice.

The Sensual/Sexual Relationship. Differences between sensuality and sexuality are identified in this lesson. Often other prominent issues in relationships are associated with a decrease in the frequency of sensual and sexual touch. Ways to preserve sensuality and communicate safely about differences in desires are explored. This unit also discusses, although not in great detail, the differences between healthy sexual relationships and ones where sexual abuse is present.

Sharing Hearts. During Sharing Hearts, participants learn about "xyz" statements. This activity provides a structured way for individuals to express their needs and desires to their partners in a specific and meaningful way. They also learn about different ways to express love and the lesson emphasizes that their own preferences may not be the same as their partner's. Ultimately, participants are encouraged to express love in the way that is most appreciated by their partner.

Ground Rules. Ground rules summarizing the key points of the program are reviewed in this module. Ground rules are presented as an agreement between partners outlining how they will maintain respect and protect their relationship. Participants are reminded of the importance of agreeing to use the skills learned in order to shield their relationship from the possible dangers of conflict. During this time, couples are also encouraged to make fun, friendship, and sensuality priorities in their relationship.

Commitment. Commitment is an important theme of the PREP program. According to the founders, commitment is the foundation of a lasting relationship and what solidifies a couple during difficult circumstances. Commitment is explained as having two meanings: constraint and dedication. Constraints keep individuals in relationships regardless of their personal dedication to them. Buying a house together, having kids, and a shared bank account are all examples of constraints. Dedication is the more positive connotation associated with commitment. It refers to the desire of individuals to sacrifice and invest in their relationships and seek the welfare of their partners. Research suggesting how these concepts influence stability and satisfaction in relationships is examined and lends credibility to the claims of PREP.

Program Issues

Because of the modular format of PREP, it is easily modified to accommodate time constraints and can be taught to suit its audience. Some programs utilize the format of the classic PREP in its entirety (12 hours), while others use pieces of the program. In addition, there are versions of the PREP program (e.g., *Within Our Reach,* Stanley et al., 2006) that are longer than the traditional template (see Table 12.1). Given the didactic nature of the PREP program, many couples (sometimes hundreds) can learn and benefit at the same time. Thus, PREP is frequently administered in retreat and workshop form. However, professional therapists and coaches also use it in traditional therapy and even in over-the-phone relationship counseling (see loveyourrelationship.com for information on PREP-based phone counseling).

Despite the flexibility of the program, administering PREP does present some challenges. Individuals are frequently unfamiliar with relationship education and are not aware that the PREP program is available. In addition, many couples will divorce without ever seeking professional help (Doss, Rhoades, Stanley, & Markman, 2009). Even when they do seek assistance, some couples often wait until the marriage or relationship has suffered a tremendous amount of harm, thus making repairs far more difficult than they would be if the couple had sought services earlier. Another challenging issue associated with implementing PREP is "getting people in the room." Committing to attending and completing the program is especially difficult because it usually involves both partners and there are frequently barriers that prevent couples from being able to take a relationship class/workshop or go on a retreat. Common barriers include work, childcare, location, cost, spiritual convictions, and finding a leader with whom they can relate.

However, the different versions of PREP available (Table 12.1) address many of these issues. Although all versions cover core concepts related to the programs goals and objectives, modifications have been made to address unique audiences. For example, *Christian PREP* (Stanley, Trathen, & McCain, 1999) is available to clergy responsible for relationship education in religious organizations. One version of PREP is available for military personnel and another for prison inmates. Some versions of PREP are for individuals in relationships who are participating without a partner while others address issues faced by engaged or married couples with children. There are also several variations of PREP that have been tweaked to address socioeconomic status.

More specifically, *Within My Reach* (Pearson, Stanley, & Kline, 2005) and *Within Our Reach* (Stanley et al., 2006) are PREP curriculum aimed at individuals with low income. Similar to other versions of PREP, *Within Our Reach* targets individuals who are currently in a relationship and has been used by men participating in the *Fatherhood Relationship and Marriage Education (FRAME)* project, a federally funded community-level study (Markman et al., 2009). *Within Our Reach* provides individuals with skills to handle conflict in an effort to create a better environment for children. In addition, the curriculum helps couples identify barriers to meeting relationship goals and overcoming foreseeable obstacles. It also equips couples with coping strategies to deal with stressors unique to their circumstances (e.g., severe financial strain, community involvement, etc.).

Within My Reach addresses the needs of individuals who may not necessarily be in a relationship at the time of the workshop. While the curriculum is designed to help those participants in viable relationships, it is also useful for individuals who are single because it clearly presents characteristics of healthy and unhealthy relationships. This enables all participants to make better relationship decisions in future. Moreover, the curriculum provides information and skills aimed at improving co-parenting with an ex-partner and balancing the needs of parents and children (Rhoades & Stanley, 2011).

Current technology is creating options to help overcome some of the obstacles to relationship education. Relationship Coaches provide PREP to individuals and couples using telephones or digital communication technology such as Skype. Additionally, there are some Internet-friendly programs and webinars that provide relationship education to individuals and couples. An example of this is **ePREP**, a 90-minute self-directed version of PREP. In spite of the limited time exposed to PREP principles, researchers found that dating couples who participated in ePREP training exhibited better relationship and mental health outcomes than couples who did not receive the intervention (Braithwaite &

Fincham, 2007, 2009). Versions of ePREP will soon be available online (see PREPinc.com) for both couples and individuals. In addition, there will be an Internet-based PREP program intended for, but not limited to, foster and adoptive parents (see PREPinc.com and fosterparentcollege.com).

Cultural Implications

The success of PREP is not limited to a small segment of culture and its principles have been implemented and well received in the United States and abroad. In the United States, its developers have ensured that it has been taught to a diverse population of individuals and couples. These include men and women from distinct organizational cultures like the Army and Navy. In addition, participants from different ethnic and cultural backgrounds such as Native Americans, Hispanic/Latino, Asian, Jewish, and Christian have all received PREP training. And, as previously stated, the PREP curriculum has been used extensively with different socioeconomic populations. In fact, PREP has been part of interventions delivered to couples with low income in two large-scale federally funded research projects: Building Strong Families (BSF, see Wood, McConnell, Moore, Clarkwest, & Hsueh, 2010) and Strengthening Healthy Marriages (SHM, see Hsueh et al., 2012).

The BSF study looked at the impact of relationship education on individual and relationship outcomes of unmarried couples expecting a child at eight different sites in the United States. The study compared couples that received an intervention with those who had not and found small but positive effects in couples who participated in the Oklahoma intervention where a version of PREP combined with a parenting program was delivered (Devaney & Dion, 2010). Because of these results many low-income individuals in Oklahoma now receive the PREP intervention (it has become a state-supported program) and during a span of 10 years over 300,000 people were served in Oklahoma with versions of PREP.

Likewise, Strengthening Healthy Marriages studied the effects of relationship education on low-income married couples with children at eight sites in the United States. Three of the sites compared a version of PREP (*Within Our Reach*, Stanley et al., 2006) to a control group who received no intervention. One-year follow-up data on over 1,000 couples who received the intervention indicated promising outcomes. Small but important differences were found between low-income couples who did and did not receive *Within Our Reach*. Significantly fewer couples in the group that received *Within Our Reach* reported that their relationship was in trouble and the men in those couples reported significantly less physical assault (Rhoades, 2015).

Outside of the United States, PREP has been used in parts of Estonia, Chile, Israel, Denmark, Sweden, Norway, South Korea, South Africa, Russia, China, Germany, and Colombia. The curriculum has been translated to several languages including Spanish, German, Chinese, Russian, Swedish, Norwegian, and Estonian.

The founders are aware that adaptations of the PREP format and curriculum are necessary to respond with sensitivity to cultural norms and they emphasize the importance of partnering with experts who understand the complexities of the culture in formulating such modifications (Markman et al., 2009). Adaptations based on cultural rules and expectations associated with gender, romantic relationships, and marital norms are sometimes in order. For example, when training professionals in Israel in a conservative religious community, the Sensuality and Sexuality lesson had to be adapted. Usually during that unit, couples are encouraged to hold hands while walking or when they are together in public areas. They are also encouraged to embrace or even kiss each other when coming home or leaving for the day. Yet in this Israeli community those suggestions would be inappropriate.

Still, much of the relationship education provided by PREP transcends culture. Because most people hope to enjoy healthy satisfying relationships and nearly all individuals experience conflict in relationships, the PREP curriculum is relevant across cultures.

Evidence-based Research and Evaluation

There is a large body of research that supports the use of PREP. Couples who participate in it generally display better communication, report higher levels of satisfaction in their relationships, exhibit greater relationship stability, and experience improved individual functioning (Halford & Bodenmann, 2013; Markman & Rhoades, 2012; Wadsworth & Markman, 2011). While interpreting results of a relationship education program are complex, and findings are at times mixed, couples who have received PREP show short-term gains in relationship satisfaction (Halford & Bodenmann, 2013), less negative communication, and more positive communication when followed up five years after marriage (Markman, Rhoades, Stanley, Ragan, & Whitton, 2010). These results are important to note because communication problems are a major risk factor for marital distress (Gottman, 1994; Karney & Bradbury, 1995; Markman, 1981). Therefore, changing communication and conflict patterns is an important measure of an intervention's success (Wadsworth & Markman, 2011).

Research shows that certain populations may benefit more than others from relationship education. Halford and Bodenmann (2013) suggest that while all couples benefit to some extent from relationship education, couples with high modifiable risks (i.e., issues involving communication, dyadic coping, problem solving, and/or self-regulation) may benefit most (both immediately following the intervention and over time). Evidence of the usefulness of PREP with high-risk samples has also been found in couples where infidelity has occurred (Allen, Rhoades, Stanley, Loew, & Markman, 2012) and with couples with a history of parental divorce or violence (Halford, Sanders, & Behrens, 2001).

Interestingly, PREP may provide valuable information that leads to beneficial breakups in some high-risk couples. Markman, Rhoades, Stanley, and Peterson

(2013) looked at divorce rates in a sample of couples who married in religious organizations and either received PREP or some other premarital intervention from their religious organization's naturally occurring services. They found that couples who evidenced more negative communication before marriage were more likely divorce if they had received PREP. A similar trend was found in couples who reported premarital aggression, where a larger number of couples that received PREP intervention eventually divorced. Markman et al. (2013) noted the importance of ascertaining the potential benefits of divorce, as some may end a maleficent relationship (i.e., those marred by negative communication patterns and aggression). Markman et al. (2013) pointed to the possibility that participants' increased understanding of danger signs in those poor relationships may have been acquired through the PREP training.

The benefits of PREP extend beyond the couple relationship and impact other members of the family as well. In a large, federally funded study (Family Expectations) of relationship education, researchers found that couples participating in PREP, combined with a program called Becoming Parents (Jordan, Stanley, & Markman, 1999), were more likely to stay together and had higher levels of happiness, support, affection, and fidelity. Participants were also better at parenting than couples in the control group (Devaney & Dion, 2010). Positive parenting outcomes have also been found with a version of PREP administered to parents with low income. Fathers who participated in the program reported an increase in their parenting alliance with their wives, which was associated with more involvement in parenting their children (Rienks, Wadsworth, Markman, Einhorn, & Moran, 2011). Furthermore, children of parents who received the modified version of PREP showed less internalizing and externalizing symptoms than children whose parents did not participate. These differences appeared to be related to changes in parenting and parent coping (Wadsworth, Santiago, Einhorn, Moran, Rienks, & Markman, 2011).

The impact of PREP on parenting is currently being studied at the University of Denver. Couples who received PREP before they married were assessed prior to their wedding and at yearly intervals for the past 15 years. Assessments include self-report and observational measures of couple and individual functioning. These couples are now participating in a family research assessment where the couple brings their oldest child to participate in the interview. Consistent with previous assessments, self-report and observational measurements are made of the couple's communication. Observational measures of parents communicating with their child are also obtained. During the family interview, the mother and father separately discuss a problem area in their relationship with their child. By assessing communication between parent and child, it is possible to see the effects of PREP on the way these individuals communicate with one another. In addition, the relationship between parental communication and important child functioning outcomes may also be examined.

Future directions for research have been delineated (Markman & Rhoades, 2012) and PREP contributors recognize the importance of going beyond positive outcomes to better understand the mechanisms and moderators of these results (Wadsworth & Markman, 2011). Where results have been mixed, it is essential to explore the possible reasons. For example, are there certain characteristics of a couple or individual that prevent PREP from being effective? With which populations is PREP most useful? Such research will not only ensure the efficacy of PREP, but also inform the relationship education field as a whole.

Professional Preparation and Training Issues

Professionals must learn PREP from a PREP master trainer. These trainings are typically three days in length. Booster trainings and consultation are offered by webinar, allowing for the option for PREP-trained leaders to refresh their skills from an office or home. After acquiring the training, professionals can utilize most of the PREP educational tools and programs.

Many therapists, counselors, and clergy are trained in PREP. These professionals offer PREP workshops and retreats or use pieces of the program (e.g., Speaker Listener technique) in their counseling practices. Laypersons may also be trained to deliver PREP. As mentioned previously, PREP is a manualized relationship program. Therefore, curriculum is outlined in the Leader Manual and indicates what the leader should communicate to participants during each lesson. Videos of couples demonstrating many of the concepts covered are an integral part of the curriculum. The thorough curriculum facilitates the process of training laypersons to be PREP leaders. Laypersons and professionals seeking PREP training should possess good relationship skills, some organizational skills, and be fairly adept at public speaking.

PREP-trained leaders teach the curriculum by focusing on major points and concerns, facilitating discussion, answering questions, and providing guided practice of the skills taught. PowerPoint slides, videos, audios, and animations are part of the PREP curriculum and supplement the lessons. A participant manual is available to leaders as well. The manual offers notes to participants corresponding to the main points of the lessons. Finally, leaders may train paraprofessionals as coaches, depending on a number of issues, including the goal of the particular program, time constraints, and costs. PREP coaches help participants practice the skills taught by the leader and answer participants' questions about the material presented in the lessons.

Conclusion

The Prevention and Relationship Education Program is a well-researched cognitive-behavioral relationship education program whose goal is to help individuals and couples create and maintain satisfying and healthy relationships. PREP accomplishes this goal by equipping participants with practical communication techniques that allow them to constructively manage conflict in their relationships. Principles fundamental to good relationships are also covered including those related to fun, friendship, sensuality, expectations, commitment, and forgiveness.

The PREP curriculum is manualized and leaders are trained to deliver short lessons, facilitate discussion, answer questions, and provide guided practice of the skills taught. PowerPoint slides, videos, audios, and animations are part of the PREP curriculum and supplement the lessons.

PREP has been used in many forms with diverse populations. Research in the United States and internationally suggests that PREP is an effective relationship education program. Participants generally display better communication, report higher levels of satisfaction in their relationships, and exhibit greater relationship stability.

Key Points

- PREP is a cognitive-behavioral relationship education program whose goal is to help individuals and couples create and maintain satisfying and healthy relationships.
- The PREP curriculum is designed to educate participants about characteristics of healthy and unhealthy relationships, and equip them with communication skills to constructively manage inevitable conflict in their relationships.
- Many versions of PREP are available to meet the specific needs of a variety of populations.
- PREP is a well-researched relationship education program. Findings from studies with diverse populations suggest its efficacy, as participants generally display better communication, report higher levels of relationship satisfaction, and exhibit greater relationship stability.
- The manualized format of PREP and the many visual supplements available allow for its easy implementation by professionals and laypersons.

Discussion Questions

1. Why did the founders of PREP think it was so important to develop a program that could help couples handle conflict in their relationships?
2. Originally, PREP was targeted at couples planning to marry. Today, its audience is far more differentiated. Who does this audience now include?
3. How do the different versions of PREP address the unique concerns of each audience?
4. What are some of the key concepts covered in the PREP curriculum and how is a focus on communication woven throughout?
5. What modifications may need to be made to PREP to adequately address the cultural background of participants? In what ways does the PREP curriculum transcend culture?
6. What benefits of PREP are evidenced in research? What are the findings regarding PREP's impact on marital satisfaction, communication, breakup, mental health, and parenting?
7. How can someone be trained to deliver PREP?

Additional Resources

PREPinc.com
LoveYourRelationship.com
www.nrepp.samhsa.gov

References and Further Readings

Allen, E., Rhoades, G., Stanley, S., Loew, B., & Markman, H. (2012). The effects of marriage education for Army couples with a history of infidelity. *Journal of Family Psychology, 26*, 26–35. Retrieved from http://dx.doi.org/10.1037/a0026742

Braithwaite, S., & Fincham, F. (2007). ePREP: Computer based prevention of relationship dysfunction, depression and anxiety. *Journal of Social and Clinical Psychology, 26*, 609–622.

Braithwaite, S., & Fincham, F. (2009). A randomized clinical trial of a computer based preventive intervention: Replication and extension of ePREP. *Journal of Family Psychology, 23*, 32–38.

Devaney, B., & Dion, R. (2010). *15-Month impacts of Oklahoma's Family Expectations Program.* Washington, DC: Mathematica Policy Research.

Doss, B., Rhoades, G., Stanley, S., & Markman, H. (2009). Marital therapy, retreats, and books: The who, what, when and why of relationship help-seeking. *Journal of Marital and Family Therapy, 35*, 18–29.

Gottman, J. (1994). *What predicts divorce?* Hillsdale, NJ: Lawrence Erlbaum Associates.

Halford, W., & Bodenmann, G. (2013). Effects of relationship education on maintenance of couple relationship satisfaction. *Clinical Psychology Review, 33*, 512–525. Retrieved from http://dx.doi.org/10.1016/j.cpr.2013.02.001

Halford, W., Sanders, M., & Behrens, B. (2001). Can skills training prevent relationship problems in at-risk couples? Four-year effects of a behavioral relationship education program. *Journal of Family Psychology, 15*, 750–768. Retrieved from http://dx.doi.org/10.1037//0893-3200.15.4.750

Hsueh, J., Alderson, D., Lundquist, E., Michalopoulos, C., Gubits, D., Fein, D., & Knox, V. (2012). *The Supporting Healthy Marriage Evaluation: Early impacts on low-income families.* Washington, DC: Administration for Children and Families, Office of Planning, Research, and Evaluation.

Jordan, P., Stanley, S., & Markman, H. (1999). *Becoming parents: How to strengthen your marriage as your family grows.* San Francisco, CA: Jossey-Bass.

Karney, B., & Bradbury, T. (1995). The longitudinal course of marital quality and stability: A review of theory, methods, and research. *Psychological Bulletin, 118*, 3–34.

Markman, H. (1979). The application of a behavior model of marriage in predicting relationship satisfaction for couples planning marriage. *Journal of Consulting and Clinical Psychology, 47*, 743–749.

Markman, H. (1981). The prediction of marital success: A five-year follow-up. *Journal of Consulting and Clinical Psychology, 49*, 760–762.

Markman, H., & Floyd, F. (1980). Possibilities for the prevention of marital discord. *The American Journal of Family Therapy, 8*(2), 29–48.

Markman, H., Floyd, F., & Dickson-Markman, F. (1982). Toward a model for the prediction and primary prevention of marital and family distress and dissolution. In S. Duck (Ed.), *Personal relationships 4: Dissolving personal relationships* (pp. 233–261). London, UK: Academic Press.

Markman, H., Floyd, F., Stanley, S., & Lewis, H. (1986). Prevention. In N. Jacobson & A. Gurman (Eds.), *Clinical handbook of marital therapy* (pp. 173–195). New York, NY: Guilford Press.

Markman, H., & Rhoades, G. (2012). Relationship education research: Current status and future directions. *Journal of Marital and Family Therapy, 38,* 169–200. doi:10.1111/j.1752-0606.2011.00247.x

Markman, H., Rhoades, G., Stanley, S., & Peterson, K. (2013). A randomized clinical trial of the effectiveness of premarital interventions: Moderators of divorce outcomes. *Journal of Family Psychology, 27,* 165–172. doi:10.1037/a0031134

Markman, H., Rhoades, G., Stanley, S., Ragan, E., & Whitton, S. (2010). The premarital communication roots of marital distress: The first five years of marriage. *Journal of Family Psychology, 24,* 289–298. doi:10.1037/a0019481

Markman, H., Rienks, S., Wadsworth, M., Markman, M., Einhorn, L., Moran, E., Glojek, M., Pregulman, M., & Gentry, L. (2009). Adaptation: Fatherhood, Individual, and Islamic Versions of PREP. In S. Callan & H. Benson (Eds.), *What works in relationship education: Lessons learned from academics and service deliverers in the United States and Europe* (pp. 67–74). Doha, Qatar: Doha International Institute for Family Studies and Development.

Markman, H., Stanley, S., & Blumberg, S. (2010). *Fighting for your marriage.* San Francisco, CA: Jossey-Bass.

Pearson, M., Stanley, S., & Kline, G. (2005). *Within My Reach leader's manual.* Denver, CO: PREP for Individuals, Inc.

Rhoades, G.K. (2015). The effectiveness of the Within Our Reach relationship education program for couples: Findings from a federal randomized trial. *Family Process,* online. doi:10.1111/famp.12148

Rhoades, G., & Stanley, S. (2011). Using individual-oriented relationship education to prevent family violence. *Journal of Couple and Relationship Therapy, 10,* 185–200.

Rienks, S., Wadsworth, M., Markman, H., Einhorn, L., & Moran, E. (2011). Father involvement in an ethnically diverse low-income sample: Baseline associations and changes resulting from preventive intervention. *Family Relations, 60*(2), 191–204. doi:10.1111/j.1741-3729.2010.00642.x

Stanley, S., Markman, H., Jenkins, N., Rhoades, G., Noll, L., & Ramos, L. (2006). *Within Our Reach leader's manual.* Denver, CO: PREP Educational Products, Inc.

Stanley, S., Trathen, D., & McCain, S. (1999). *Christian PREP manual for leaders: Prevention and Relationship Enhancement Program.* Denver, CO: Christian PREP, Inc.

Wadsworth, M., & Markman, H. (2011). Where's the action?: Understanding what works and why in relationship education. *Behavior Therapy, 43,* 99–112. doi:10.1016/j.beth.2011.1.006

Wadsworth, M., Santiago, C., Einhorn, L., Moran, E., Rienks, S., & Markman, H. (2011). Preliminary efficacy of an intervention to reduce psychosocial stress and improve coping in low-income families. *American Journal of Community Psychology, 48,* 257–271.

Wood, R., McConnell, S., Moore, Q., Clarkwest, A., & Hsueh, J. (2010). *The Building Strong Families Project. Strengthening unmarried parents' relationships: The early impacts of Building Strong Families.* Washington, DC: Administration for Children and Families, Office of Planning, Research, and Evaluation.

13

EPL AND ITS ADAPTATIONS

Research and Implementation in Germany and Beyond

Ann-Katrin Job, Franz Thurmaier,
Joachim Engl, and Kurt Hahlweg

LEARNING GOALS

- Learn about differences between the German and the U.S. system in psychosocial interventions.
- Know about the key role of communication and problem-solving skills in couple prevention.
- Learn about the similarities and differences between the German couple relationship enhancement programs:
  EPL *Ein Partnerschaftliches Lernprogramm* ("A Couples' Learning Program")
  KEK "Constructive Marriage and Communication"
  KOMKOM "Communication-Competence Training in Couple Counseling"
  TTT "Talk Talk Talk and More" for adolescents.
- Know about approaches to disseminate preventive interventions (trainer trainings, recruitment of couples, training fees, student trainer trainings) and to ensure high-quality program conduction.
- Learn about the worldwide reach and cultural implications of EPL and KEK.

Introduction

At the beginning of a committed relationship, almost all couples report high levels of relationship satisfaction (Fowers, Lyons, & Montel, 1996). However, the mean level of couples' relationship satisfaction typically declines each year over at least

10 years (Glenn, 1998), and is particularly notable after the birth of the first child (Doss, Rhoades, Stanley, & Markman, 2009).

For many couples the erosion of relationship satisfaction leads them to seek divorce: Couple researchers consentaneously report divorce rates about 50 percent among American, and 40 to 45 percent among German, Swiss, English, or Australian first marriages (e.g., Hahlweg, Baucom, Grawe-Gerber, & Snyder, 2010). Of these, about 50 percent occur in the first eight years of marriage (BiB—Federal Institute of Population Research, 2014) and, in addition, there is even a higher separation rate of unmarried couples than of married ones (e. g., Callan, Benson, Coward, Davis, Gill, Grant, Percival, & Rowthorn, 2006; Ermisch & Francesconi, 2000). Accordingly, not only the partners but also many children and adolescents are affected by their parents' divorce.

Why are these findings important? Relationship conflict, separation, and divorce rank among the most severe, commonly occurring stresses that adults experience. Moreover, they are related to numerous negative health, social, and economic consequences for the partners as well as for their children (for a review see, e.g., Hahlweg, Baucom, Grawe-Gerber, & Snyder, 2010). Instead of giving another summary on these findings, this chapter reviews risk factors for relationship distress and disruption, and provides a brief overview of the German approach to prevention. Subsequently, *Ein Partnerschaftliches Lernprogramm* **EPL** (*A Couples' Learning Program*; Hahlweg, Markman, Thurmaier, Engl, & Eckert, 1998) is presented, a primarily German, couples' relationship education (CRE) program, and its advancements within the last 25 years. Research findings on the efficacy, effectiveness, and dissemination of EPL and its subgroup-specific adaptations are described. Finally, future trends, potentials, and challenges are discussed.

The German Approach to Prevention

Approximately, 81 million people live in Germany, of these about 36 million are married, and about 5.6 million are cohabiting (corresponding to 18 million married, and 2.8 million cohabiting couples; BiB—Federal Institute of Population Research, 2014).

With regard to religiousness, the current situation in Germany differs considerably from other countries (e.g., the United States). First of all, there are two main religious communities in Germany: In 2011, about 34 percent of the German population reported to belong to the Evangelical Church and only about 28 percent to the Catholic Church (Statista, 2014). Moreover, there were further minority communities, e.g., Buddhists, Muslims, and Jews (total percentage of minority members: about 5 percent of the population). Second, about one third of the German population (33 percent) is unaffiliated with any religion. Accordingly, with regard to prevention, the influence of the churches is quite small, although, within the German Catholic Church, couples are obligated to participate in pre-marriage education before they get married. Apart from that, preventive couple intervention is mostly subsidized and offered by private or public institutions such as counseling centers.

Participation fees for preventive interventions significantly differ depending on the respective intervention, the provider, and the financial support for programs and participants. Because the German health care system only covers costs for most medical and dental checks as well as for several preventive physiotherapeutic treatments, but not preventive interventions with a psychological focus, participation fees usually need to be paid by the participants themselves.

In Germany, there is no representative data available to estimate the dissemination of preventive programs. Yet, in 2004, Lösel, Schmucker, Planckensteiner, and Weiss (2006) tried to investigate the current status of preventive programs in Germany. Referring to a nationwide survey, the estimated annual number of preventive interventions was about 200,000. Most of these interventions were mother-child groups and were offered by family education facilities; less than 1,500 aimed to strengthen and sustain intimate relationships. With regard to participation fees, Lösel et al. (2006) found that about 90 percent of all interventions were subsidized by public funds, however, only about 37 percent were free of charge. Further, 65 percent of all interventions were self-developed by the provider and only very few were evidence-based: Although most of the programs regularly used subjective trainer evaluations for quality assurance, only 1.4 percent were evaluated systematically in controlled research studies.

These results highlight the enormous deficit of psychosocial prevention research in Germany. They also call attention to the gap between research and practice: Politicians as well as public services in Germany prefer to promote new approaches as well as programs for as many participants as possible, instead of supporting the dissemination of evidence-based programs. Additionally, the Lösel et al. (2006) study indicated the increased demand for preventive interventions in general, but also for preventive couple interventions, especially in light of the increasing divorce rates.

The Link between the Quality of Dyadic Interactions and the Course of Relationships

During the last decades substantial research has been conducted to identify **risk factors** for relationship deterioration and breakup (for a detailed review see Markman, Rhoades, Stanley, Ragan, & Whitton, 2010). It has consistently been shown that sociodemographic variables, such as the partners' religious affiliation, the (non-)existence of children in a relationship, or (un)employment, facilitate couples' separation, or make it more difficult. However, these factors are not decisive for why partners become dissatisfied. Instead, couple researchers report that psychological factors primarily cause relationship impairment, and among these, especially the partners' communication and problem-solving skills (Karney &

Bradbury, 1995) as well as their dyadic coping competencies (their ability to cope with individual and couple stress in their everyday life).

Strengthening couples' relationship skills is a main aim when thinking of treating and preventing relationship distress (Fawcett, Hawkins, Blanchard, & Carroll, 2010). In the context of prevention, the idea is to support couples at an early stage of their relationship and teach them interpersonal competencies to manage future challenges so that they can sustain long-term relationship satisfaction (Halford, Markman, & Stanley, 2008).

These considerations have already been taken into account by developing relationship and marriage education (RME) programs, among these EPL (e.g., Hahlweg et al., 1998) and, to mention just two more, the *Prevention and Relationship Education Program PREP* (see chapter 12) and the *Couples Coping Enhancement Training CCET* (see chapter 14).

Ein Partnerschaftliches Lernprogramm (EPL) "A Couples' Learning Program"

EPL (e.g., Hahlweg et al., 1998) is a research-based RME program, adapted from PREP (e.g., Markman, Floyd, Stanley, & Stoorasli, 1988, and chapter 12) in 1987. Since then, EPL has been shown to significantly improve couples' long-term communication and problem-solving skills in different settings. Currently, it is the most empirically supported RME program in Europe.

Program goals and objectives. The first goal of EPL is to decrease the frequency of negative and to increase the frequency of positive exchange between partners during conflict discussions and to solve relationship topics more effectively (Job & Hahlweg, in press). Moreover, the second goal is to encourage and assist couples to talk about expectations and values in key areas of their relationship to enable the partners to learn more about each other and their common life. As PREP, EPL in particular, is a **primary prevention** program that addresses all couples who are generally satisfied with their relationship and who, until now, have no or only few relationship conflicts. If there are already recurring and unsolved conflicts between partners, it is more difficult for a couple to engage in new skills and, in the long run, not to slip back into old communication habits. In Germany, EPL is mainly offered to young couples and couples with a short relationship duration in the context of pre-marriage education.

Curriculum and other program issues. EPL can be delivered individually or in groups, either in five to six weekly sessions of approximately 2 to 2.5 hours' duration or at a weekend meeting (typically Saturday to Sunday afternoon). Group sizes vary from two to six couples with one to three qualified trainers for each group. The couples meet as a group for the lecture portions of the sessions but meet alone and work with a trainer for all other aspects of each session. As a result of the steady supervision of partner conversations by the EPL trainers, the couples learn to use the communication and problem-solving skills instantaneously and not only before and after the exercises (Job, Engl, Thurmaier, & Hahlweg, 2014). Table 13.1 gives an overview on the contents of the six EPL sessions. Within the training, partners are not expected to share personal information with other couples in the group because talking about personal issues is only performed with each other in a separate room.

Evidence-based research on EPL. Altogether, participants are usually highly satisfied with EPL. In the following, empirical findings on program efficacy in different target populations are summarized. For reasons of readability, only

TABLE 13.1 A Couples' Learning Program EPL: Content of the Six Sessions of the Communication and Problem-solving Program

	Content
Session 1	To facilitate teaching, in Session 1 trainers show a short video of a relationship conflict as an example for dysfunctional couple communication. With the help of this video, the couples develop communication skills, five for the speaker (e.g., speaking for oneself, staying on topic) and five for the listener (e.g., active listening, paraphrasing). For the rest of the session, each couple practices the application of these skills while discussing a positive relationship topic.
Session 2	Session 2 is devoted to the expression of negative feelings which can occur within conflict discussions and to the way the partner should respond to such self-disclosures. After a first role-play, the couples have the chance to talk about an own topic.
Session 3	In Session 3 a structured five-step problem-solving scheme is introduced, and the couple applies this scheme to one of their current relationship problems: First, they discuss the topic by using the newly learned communication skills; second, there is a brainstorming on conflict solutions; third, the partners evaluate each option; fourth, they agree on a solution (or on a compromise); and fifth, plan the initial implementation steps.
Session 4	Session 4 is devoted to the effects that expectations can have on a relationship. Based on separately completed questionnaires, the partners are prompted to talk about complex terms (e.g., trust or friendship) by using their own examples (e.g., "Yesterday, I felt deep trust when you embraced me after I had ... ").
Session 5	Session 5 is devoted to communication in the sexual domain, stressing the fact that ineffective or nonexistent communication about sexual needs and wishes may lead to sexual dissatisfaction. Through the exercise, couples are encouraged to talk about sex-related terms (e.g., eroticism, fantasy, orgasm) and to link these terms to their own experiences.
Session 6	Depending on the couples' needs, in Session 6 different topics can be discussed such as the meaning of a Christian marriage; the preferred position of the relationship in the partners' everyday life, or parenthood.

significant results are reported; for more detailed information refer to the original research articles.

Premarital education with EPL. In a first evaluation study, the efficacy of EPL was investigated in the context of premarital education within the Catholic Church (EPL I; Hahlweg et al., 1998). The study had a quasi-experimental design: 64 couples participated in EPL while 32 couples participated in traditional Catholic, similarly time-consuming premarital prevention program or received no intervention. On average, couples were 28 years of age and reported a mean relationship duration of three and a half years. Ninety percent of the couples planned to get married within the next month, 71 percent had at least a high school education, and 80 percent were Catholic. At pre-assessment, there were neither significant differences between EPL and control couples, nor between the control couples themselves (traditional premarital vs. no intervention).

At the 5-year follow-up the divorce rates differed significantly between groups: 16 percent for the control versus 4 percent for the EPL couples. EPL couples also demonstrated significantly greater use of positive verbal and nonverbal behavior (namely self-disclosure, positive solution, and acceptance of partner) than controls. In contrast, control couples displayed significantly greater use of negative verbal behavior (e.g., criticism, disagreement, and justification), and nonverbal negative behavior than EPL spouses (Thurmaier, Engl, & Hahlweg, 1999).

EPL for moderately dissatisfied couples. In a second study, EPL was used as an indicated prevention program for couples who self-identify with some symptoms of distressed relationships but who do not identify themselves as being in need of couple therapy. In a randomized waitlist control group design (EPL II; Kaiser, Hahlweg, Fehm-Wolfsdorf, & Groth, 1998), 67 couples with a minimum relationship duration of three years were recruited. Of these 71 percent reported to be dissatisfied with their relationship. After the training, EPL II couples reported significantly fewer relationship problems and showed significantly greater skills in positive verbal and nonverbal communication and fewer negative verbal communication behaviors than control couples (inter-group effect sizes: ES_{verbal} = 0.65, $ES_{nonverbal}$ = 0.35). At 1- year follow-up, EPL II couples reported significantly fewer problem areas in comparison to pre-assessment and no changes in couple satisfaction compared to post-assessment, supporting the short-term effectiveness and stability of changes of the EPL II.

The conclusions from the Kaiser et al. (1998) study were further supported by another uncontrolled study (EPL II-B; Braukhaus, Hahlweg, Kroeger, Groth, & Fehm-Wolfsdorf, 2003). In this investigation, the effectiveness of adding two booster sessions with each couple individually, one and three months after the EPL II training, was investigated. A total of 62 couples took part in the study. At post-assessment, the positive findings of the Kaiser et al. (1998) study could be replicated. Furthermore, at 1-year follow-up, couples with booster sessions reported significantly higher marital satisfaction ratings and fewer problem areas than couples receiving the EPL II weekend program only ($ES_{EPL\ II}$ = .13/.12 vs.

$ES_{EPL\ II-B}$ = .41/.40). Following these results, booster sessions additionally seem to be effective in enhancing the long-term effectiveness of preventive interventions.

EPL long-term results. Hahlweg and Richter (2010) investigated an 11-year follow-up of the EPL II and EPL II-B sample. They report divorce rates of 28 percent for EPL couples compared to 53 percent for controls (couples who initially did not participate in any intervention). Of all couples who were still cohabitating after 11 years (EPL and control group), 75 percent reported a high relationship satisfaction.

Recently, a 25-year follow-up of the EPL I study was investigated (Engl, 2014). Although the results have not yet been published, first results seem promising. Even after 25 years, 33 EPL and 11 control couples could again be contacted. This corresponds to a dropout rate of about only 39 percent over 25 years. With regard to the divorce rates, the authors still found a significant difference: 4.9 percent in the married EPL couples (those who got married after their participation in the training) versus 26 percent in the married control group couples (who did not take part in EPL). Moreover, from pre-assessment to 25-year follow-up, the martial satisfaction of the EPL couples declined significantly less than the marital satisfaction of the control couples ($p < .01$). Besides, about 60 percent of the EPL couples reported to still use the EPL communication skills "often" or "very often." In summary, the studies document many short- and long-term positive effects for couples after having participated in EPL.

KEK "Constructive Marriage and Communication"

A first adaptation of EPL is *Konstruktive Ehe und Kommunikation* **KEK** ("**Constructive Marriage and Communication**"; Engl & Thurmaier, 2002), a selective preventive couple intervention. Selective preventive interventions target subgroups of the population who have an elevated risk for developing a problem. KEK, in particular, addresses couples who are cohabitating for at least two years and who want to deepen their relationship. Compared to newlywed couples, couples with a longer relationship duration are more likely to be dissatisfied with their relationship (e.g., Glenn, 1998) and, therefore, are at an elevated risk for developing relationship problems. As EPL, KEK is preventive which means that it does not address couples who are distressed and in need of couple therapy.

Program goals and objectives. On the one hand, within KEK, couples are also taught communication and problem-solving skills which they can use to resolve conflicts and daily stresses more efficiently. On the other hand KEK has more cognitive elements than EPL (Engl & Thurmaier, 2002). In particular, it involves exercises to facilitate (a) self-reflection (e.g., of one's own conflict behavior or one's own stake in a contentious issue), (b) perception (e.g., to correctly interpret the partner's nonverbal stress indicators), and (c) individual coping strategies (e.g., to modify one's own internal dialog). Moreover, detailed information is given on psychological mechanisms of couple interactions (e.g., on the "vicious circle of communication").

Curriculum and other program issues. KEK is based upon EPL but has been expanded with regard to contents as well as to methodological aspects, and time scheduling. It comprises 7 sessions at 3 hours each and is conducted in two extended weekend meetings (Friday to Sunday). Group size is up to four couples with two qualified and supervised trainers, ideally one male and one female trainer (Engl & Thurmaier, 2002).

KEK trainings have a gradual manner: The first four units, of which Sessions 1 to 3 are identical to EPL (cf. Table 13.1), serve to transfer basic knowledge and to teach couples communication and problem-solving skills. After having started with simple and unproblematic topics within the first exercises, partner conversations slowly turn towards more controversial issues. Furthermore, in Session 4, the couples' attention is directed to positive partner characteristics and skills to promote mutual recognition and praise. At the second weekend, in units 5 to 7, the couples go on practicing the application of the newly learned skills and are assisted to develop new communication habits for their everyday life (e.g., fixed dates for couple conversations). Furthermore, couples work out skills to handle changes within the relationship more effectively and to sustain individual and dyadic resources. If possible, there should be about three weeks between the two KEK training blocks so that the couples have the chance to gain first experiences with the skills in their everyday life. Table 13.2 gives more information on the KEK Sessions 4 to 7.

Evidence-based research on KEK. Engl and Thurmaier (2002) demonstrated the efficacy of KEK in a longitudinal study over three years. A total of 48 couples took part in KEK; further 25 couples participated in another, similarly time-consuming, Catholic marriage intervention. At pre-assessment, in both groups, the couples had on average been married for about 12 years and reported to have two children at school age. Of the couples, two thirds were dissatisfied with their relationship. Post-intervention, results showed that KEK couples communicated significantly more positively and less negatively with their partner than control couples (inter-group effect sizes ES = .71–.91). Furthermore, there was a significant increase in relationship satisfaction (ES = .72) and a significant decrease in the number of relationship conflicts in the KEK couples compared to controls (ES = 1.26). Physical and psychological problems significantly decreased in both groups. Results remained stable up to three years follow-up. None of the KEK couples got divorced within this period of time, less than 5 percent reported to have separated. Apparently, KEK positively affected couples' long-term relationship behavior and the way to experience their everyday life.

Following EPL and KEK: Add-on trainings for satisfied couples. Couples, who already participated in EPL or KEK but want to continue to work on their relationship, have the chance to participate in an *APL—Refreshment Training* or in *SPL—Stress Management with Couples' Learning Program*.

APL—Refreshment Training. The goal of APL is to provide couples more time to exercise the use of the communication and problem-solving skills and to impart

TABLE 13.2 Content of the KEK Sessions 4 to 7 and, respectively, the KOMKOM Sessions 4 to 8

	Content
KEK and KOMKOM Session 4	Session 4 focuses on the expression of positive feelings. Reciprocal, positive interactions between partners—not only verbally, but also actively—help to sustain and strengthen love and respect for each other. Therefore, the partners' attention is called to their partners' positive characteristics as well as to different ways of stimulating and pampering each other. They reflect and talk about why they love each other and exchange information on good things they can do for each other.
KOMKOM Session 5	Session 5 is devoted to "emergency strategies." In preparation of serious couple conflicts, partners talk about their individual experiences and behaviors in so-called emergency situations. In emergency situations, which are highly stressful, one or both partners are not able to adhere to specific communication skills anymore; but, if both partners know what is going on with each other, they can be more empathic and maybe even prevent further escalation.
KEK Session 5 KOMKOM Session 6	To facilitate the implementation of the newly learned communication and problem-solving skills in their everyday life, in Session 6, couples are assisted to develop new communication habits. They talk about preconditions for discussions on relationship topics, such as time, place, and content as well as facilitative and aggravating behaviors.
KEK Session 6 KOMKOM Session 7	In Session 7, couples are encouraged to look more closely at their relationship: They are assisted to reflect and talk about former positive as well as negative relationship changes and developments, and to set new goals for re-orientation. According to experience, important topics are sexuality, professional life, and family.
KEK Session 7 KOMKOM Session 8	Session 8 is devoted to "relationship strengths." Couples (as well as counselors and therapists) often tend to focus on weaknesses. In doing so, they risk to lose track of the satisfying parts of their relationship. Therefore, partners first self-reflect on and then talk about "What are the strengths of our relationship?" and "What do I/does my partner contribute to this?" This last exercise often gets quite intensive and encourages couples to keep positive and vivid conversations even in the long run.

knowledge on how to cope with more difficult relationship topics, such as emergency situations, ways to strengthen resources, or work-life balance. APL is delivered in groups of up to four couples and takes three sessions of about 2.5 hours each. APL trainers are trained in KEK (see Section 7.1) or passed an additional APL training course.

SPL—Stress Management with Couples' Learning Program. SPL is another add-on training that focuses on the partners' individual and dyadic stress management skills. Within SPL (four sessions at 2.5 to 3.5 hours), couples practice how to effectively use relaxation techniques, such as *Progressive Muscle Relaxation* (Jacobson, 1929) and *Mental Focus* (Benson, Beary, & Carol, 1974). Moreover, they get psycho-education on stress development as well as on stress management, and develop individual problem-solving and emergency strategies for high-conflict situations. SPL trainers are also trained in KEK (see Section 7.1) or passed an additional SPL training course.

KOMKOM "Communication-Competence Training in Couple Counseling"

Another adaptation of EPL is *Kommunikations-Kompetenz-Training in der Paarberatung* **KOMKOM** ("**Communication-Competence Training in Couple Counseling**"; Engl & Thurmaier, 2005) that had been developed after KEK not only produced positive effects in satisfied but also in dissatisfied couples. KOMKOM is an intensive communication training tailored to the special needs of couples in the context of relationship and marriage counseling who complain about communication and problem-solving difficulties. Accordingly, KOMKOM is a program addressing couples who identify themselves as maritally distressed in need of couple therapy or counseling.

Program goals and objectives. The idea of developing KOMKOM was to provide a program to supplement and enrich the common choice of interventions in couple and marriage counseling. As EPL and KEK, KOMKOM is a cognitive-behavioral intervention, thus, it does not only aim to teach couples basic communication and problem-solving skills, but also dyadic competencies to better manage everyday stresses and to cope with (re-)occurring relationship problems (Engl & Thurmaier, 2005). Furthermore, couples learn to develop and practice relationship-friendly communication habits. By focusing on existing relationship strength and resources, relationship problems and areas of conflict are reflected, and positive changes are encouraged.

Curriculum and other program issues. Different from most of the other interventions in the context of couple counseling, KOMKOM is time-limited. It is divided in eight units, each about two hours when working with a single couple or about three hours when working with a group of up to four couples (Engl & Thurmaier, 2005). KOMKOM can be offered weekly or at two extended weekend meetings with two trainers for each group (again ideally one male and one female trainer). The sessions are the same as in KEK but with one additional session on "emergency strategies" (see Table 13.2, Session 5). After having exercised the use of the communication and problem-solving skills, couples are taught self-reflection and stress coping competencies to enable changes in their attitude towards their partner as well as their relationship. The goal is to get partners away from unreflected and unfair accusations and instead to gain a differentiated perception of one's own part in relationship conflicts. The couples' positive experiences with an increased dyadic communication during KOMKOM facilitate changes in the partners' attitudes towards each other as well as enable long-lasting improvements.

Evidence-based research on KOMKOM. The short- and long-term results of KOMKOM are quite promising. In a first correlative study (Engl & Thurmaier, 2005), 36 couples (mean age: 40 years, mean relationship duration: 14 years) took part in KOMKOM. Of these 86 percent were married at pre-assessment, 78 per cent at least had one child, and all couples reported a low relationship quality. Two weeks after having taken part in KOMKOM (one couple (3%) doped out), both male and female partners were significantly more satisfied with their relationship (*ES* ≥ 0.61). Moreover, still at 3-year follow-up, significant improvements were found for communication quality (*ES* = 0.53–0.89), the reduction in the number of relationship conflicts (*ES* = 0.77) as well as for diverse relationship quality measures (*ES* = 0.50–0.70), e.g., with regard to the couples' shared leisure time, sexuality, and child raising. Male and female partners equally benefited from KOMKOM and were highly satisfied with the program contents. Considering these results, within the context of couple counseling in Germany, to date, KOMKOM produced the best short- and long-term results of all.

TTT "Talk Talk Talk and More," Communication and Problem-Solving Training for Adolescents

Talk Talk Talk and More (TTT; Köthke, Köthke, & Zimmermann, 2015) is the latest adaptation of EPL not addressing couples but adolescents aged 15 to 21 years. It was developed at the University of Braunschweig where it is frequently conducted by supervised student trainers with secondary school pupils.

Program goals and objectives. The goal of TTT is to teach adolescents communication and problem-solving skills which they can use to better resolve conflicts, not only with an intimate partner but in all social relationships, e.g., with family, friends, or at school, and to improve their social skills.

Curriculum and other program issues. TTT comprises five sessions at 1.5 to 2 hours each and can be offered weekly or at a weekend meeting (Saturday to Sunday afternoon). As for the other trainings of the "EPL family," there are two TTT trainers and four to eight participants in each group. The first four TTT sessions are similar to the ones in EPL (cf. Table 13.1); solely, the focus is on communication in various situations not only with an intimate partner. Therefore, to better adapt the program to adolescents, some exercises were supplemented with regard to the choice of topics, e.g., homework, parental time limits, and conflicts between friends. Moreover, the fifth EPL session ("sexuality") was replaced by exercises to act in a self-confident way. First, information are given on "What are social skills?" (e.g., skills to become accepted, to be self-confident, to say no, or to admit weaknesses) and on "How do we develop social skills?" (by watching others, by trial and error). Afterwards, participants work out advantages and disadvantages of aggressive, insecure, and self-confident behavior and then practice self-confident behaviors in role-plays.

Evidence-based research on TTT. First results of an experimental waitlist control group study with 107 grammar school pupils (74 girls, 33 boys; mean age: 16.9 years) and 22 student trainers indicate that participants are highly satisfied with TTT (Köthke et al., 2015). With regard to the efficacy, participants showed a significant increase of communicational knowledge as well as communication skills. Only two pupils (2 percent) preliminarily dropped out of the training.

Professional Preparation and Training Issues

How to become a trainer? Prospective trainers (in the following called trainees) should already be experienced in working with couples and / or groups. Each of the "EPL-family" trainer trainings addresses another target population: (1) EPL trainer trainings address psychologists, educationists, and theologians; (2) KEK trainer trainings solely address well-experienced EPL trainers; (3) KOMKOM trainer trainings address psychotherapists and couple counselors in the context of marital, family, and life counseling; and (4) TTT trainer trainings address qualified employees in family education, especially teachers, counselors as well as social educationists who want to expand their knowledge in working with adolescents.

The trainer trainings of EPL, KEK, KOMKOM, and TTT each take 2 x 3 days. At the beginning, all trainees get the respective training manual, followed by the two training blocks that usually take place at intervals of three to four weeks and are both quite intensive: In groups of twelve to sixteen trainees and three to four supervisors, the use of the communication and problem-solving skills are extensively practiced. The trainer trainings primarily schedule exercises in small groups of up to four trainees with one supervisor each. Additionally, in the second training block, further training elements such as the lecture parts, and how to cope with negative or critical acknowledgments of participants, are practiced. For EPL, KEK, and KOMKOM trainers who want to conduct TTT, there is a special, intensive one-day workshop. During this workshop, the already experienced trainers practice TTT trainer skills by primarily focusing on the distinction between the TTT and the EPL approach.

Following the training blocks, EPL, KEK, and TTT trainees need to pass an accreditation workshop to get an official certificate allowing them to conduct trainings. During this examination supervisors evaluate the trainees' trainer skills. The minimum requirements to successfully pass the examination are:

1. Full attendance of the training blocks.
2. Ability to quickly follow couple discussions and to intervene instantly but not with regard to the content of the couple conversation: Trainers need to

be able to protect partners (or adolescents) from a negative course of conversation and to promote positive conflict behavior. Trainees who do not respond appropriately (e.g., too late, confusing, castigatory, or not at all) and / or who are not able to reinforce positive approaches of conflict behavior do not obtain the certificate.

3. Group leader behavior: Presentation of the EPL, KEK, or TTT concept as defined by the standardized manual. In dealing with the participants, the trainees should convey appreciation, acceptance, as well as encouragement.

There is no accreditation workshop for KOMKOM because the psychotherapists and couple counselors are usually very well experienced in working with couples. In very rare cases, KOMKOM trainees are advised to not conduct trainings. Regardless of the program focus, all trainers are obligated to undergo annual supervision. Supervision takes place in groups, is often free of charge, and takes about one day. New trainers usually provide their first trainings with well-experienced trainers; no additional supervision is regularly provided.

Participant recruitment and training fees. In EPL and KEK, a lot of couples take part upon recommendation of former participants. Additionally, both trainings are promoted through provider websites, newspaper articles, flyers, information events, and through a series of DVDs on couple communication (see also Section 7.5). Participation fees locally differ between 65 to 150 euro (about between .85 to 2.05 dollars) per couple for EPL and to about 250 euros (about 3.40 dollars) for KEK. While a lot of EPL and KEK trainings for couples are subsidized by the Catholic Church, trainer trainings, trainer supervision, and training materials are subsidized by the German Ministry of Family Affairs Senior Citizens, Women and Youth (http://www.bundesregierung.de/Webs/Breg/EN/FederalGovernment/Ministries/BMFSFJ/_node.html).

As defined by the target population of KOMKOM (see Section 5), participants are couples who came to see a marital, family, and life counselor about communication and problem-solving difficulties. The training is mainly offered in Catholic marriage counseling centers and therefore usually has a low fee or is even free of costs. However, costs for KOMKOM trainings offered by private providers such as out-patient psychotherapists are considerably higher and differ significantly among one another.

TTT trainings are usually promoted and offered in secondary schools, in local youth centers, or youth counseling centers. Adolescents are invited to participate on a voluntary basis; most TTT trainings are free of charge.

The Braunschweiger dissemination approach: EPL student trainer trainings. To enlarge the number of EPL trainers in Germany and thus, to enhance the accessibility of evidence-based CRE for couples, a new dissemination approach was started at the University of Braunschweig, by teaching select students of psychology in EPL (Job, Mattei, Vasterling, & Hahlweg, in press). The student's licensing includes a 4-day workshop (also consisting of working through the EPL manual and intensive, supervised role-play training in groups of four trainees). The workshop is followed by a 2.5 hour accreditation workshop as well as the conduction of two EPL trainings in groups of two trainees and up to four couples under close supervision. It was found that the students self-rated expertise of being a couples' trainer significantly increased from pre- to post-assessment (before vs. after the student trainer training; $ES = 1.59$). Furthermore, following participation, couples were highly satisfied with EPL and rated their students' trainers expertise as being high (Job, et al., in press). With regard to the short-term effectiveness, Job and Hahlweg (2015) found that whether couples benefitted from EPL was dependent on the spouses' relationship satisfaction at pre-assessment: Male and female partners with a low relationship satisfaction were about twice as likely to benefit from EPL compared to spouses with a moderate to high relationship satisfaction (men: 65% vs. 39%; women: 69% vs. 33%). At the same time, spouses with a low relationship satisfaction were at the highest risk to still be dissatisfied at 3-month post-assessment (men/women: 73% / 74%), compared to spouses who were moderately satisfied (34% / 37%), and especially those who were highly satisfied (4.8% / 8.5%). These results indicate that, although about two thirds of the dissatisfied couples on average benefitted from EPL, over 70 percent were still dissatisfied three months after participation. Apparently, the EPL was effective for a lot of dissatisfied couples, but not effective enough. With regard to satisfied couples the authors reasoned that, although a lot of them decreased with regard to their relationship satisfaction ($ES \leq 0$), it was not merely negative, because most of them were still happy after training. Accordingly, Job and Hahlweg (2015) suggest not to analyze couple samples as a whole but dependent on the spouses' initial relationship satisfaction. In total, the results of the new dissemination approach show that EPL student trainer trainings seem to be promising for increasing the number of EPL trainers and to ensure high-quality trainings.

Worldwide number of trainers and couples reached by EPL, KEK, KOMKOM, and TTT. As summarized in Table 13.3, the current number of trainers in Germany and abroad as well as the number of couples reached by the EPL, KEK, KOMKOM, and TTT significantly differ, depending on the respective program. Because there is no national statistic systematically recording the number of annually realized couple trainings in Germany, estimated numbers of the program authors are being reported.

DVD series Successful Communication to Keep Love Alive. The idea of the DVD series *Successful Communication to Keep Love Alive* has been developed by two of the EPL authors, Joachim Engl and Franz Thurmaier (2007). By using the DVDs, couples have the chance to make themselves familiar with the contents and goals of EPL at home. To date, three DVDs with renowned actors have been released. Of these, the first focuses on a young couple (just moving in together), the second on a middle-aged couple (about 40 years of age, two school-aged children), and the third one on a(n) (almost) retired couple (partners living together for many years, grown up children, grandchildren). Depending on the target

TABLE 13.3 Worldwide Number of Trainers, Number of Conducted Trainings, and Couples Reached by EPL, KEK, KOMKOM, and TTT Estimated by the Responsible Developers Joachim Engl and Franz Thurmaier, or respectively, Tanja Zimmermann (July 2014).

	EPL	*KEK*	*KOMKOM*	*TTT*
Approximate number of trainers living in Germany	1,500	410	484	151
Approximate number of trainers living abroad	150, mostly in Austria and Switzerland, but also in Brazil, Italy, Belgium, France, Latvia, Sweden, Slovenia, and the Czech Republic	50, mostly in Austria, Switzerland, Slovenia, and Brazil	—	—
Estimated number of trainings per year	250	150	100	15
Estimated number of participating couples (for TTT) adolescents) per year	1,000	600	300	120 adolescents (no couples)

audience, on each DVD, a handful of typical couple conflicts are re-enacted with diverse outcomes for each scene, e.g., open conflict, clarification, or resignation. After having watched an initial scene, couples can choose between outcomes. Audio comments help to identify communication errors and to find or develop adequate alternatives. Moreover, additional booklets with detailed explanations and suggestions for each scene are also available.

The three DVDs are also used within trainings of the EPL family: On the one hand, to identify communication errors from which the communication skills are derived, and on the other hand, to watch the clarification of a couple conflict to immediately observe the use of the identified communication skills.

In Bavaria, all marrying couples receive a copy of the DVD for young couples at the Bureau of Vital Statistics. Apart from that, the costs for the DVDs amount to 10 euros each (about 13.50 dollars).

Cultural Implications of EPL, KEK, KOMKOM, and TTT

Most of the EPL and KEK as well as all KOMKOM and TTT trainers have originally been trained in Germany by using the German versions of the standardized training manuals. For EPL and KEK, there are also trainer trainings sporadically offered in Austria, Switzerland, and South Tyrol (German-speaking part of Italy). Moreover, EPL and KEK participant materials and handouts are available in foreign languages, e.g., in English, Mongolian, Portuguese, Spanish, and Slovene. The EPL training manual itself is available in German and Slovenian; an EPL workbook was translated into Croatian, Czech, Polish, and Spanish. Because, to date, KOMKOM and TTT have exclusively been conducted and disseminated in Germany, training materials and handouts are only available in German.

For EPL and KEK, there are no specific requirements except for equality between spouses, and there are also no necessary cultural adaptations of one of the two programs: Many years of implementation experiences have shown that couples from diverse cultural backgrounds appear to get along well with the EPL and KEK training contents and exercises. However, couples sometimes differ with regard to addressed topics, e.g., while German couples more often talk about leisure time, Brazilian couples more frequently talk about fidelity. Furthermore, depending on particular characteristics of language, trainer interventions sometimes differ between cultures, e.g., between Germany and Austria (by coaching the couples, Austrian trainers significantly more often apply the subjunctive mode). Because trainers and participants typically are from the same cultural background, these specifics usually do not pose a problem at all. Some trainers even offer bilingual trainings in English/German or Spanish/German.

Conclusion

In summary, EPL and its adaptations are short-term interventions, but provide a significant and long-lasting benefit for couples in terms of strengthening and sustaining healthy relationships. Thereby EPL, KEK, and KOMKOM each address couples at different stages of their relationship from young and satisfied couples to couples with a longer relationship duration, and couples who already self-identify with some symptoms of relationship distress. The latest adaptation, TTT, even tries to reach adolescents and to teach them interpersonal communication and problem-solving skills.

The special aspect about the EPL family is its model for quality assurance: Depending on the respective program, people who are interested in becoming a trainer first need to take part in one or even several standardized training courses and pass an examination to get licensed (except for KOMKOM). Moreover, they need to commit themselves to regular supervision. These procedures ensure long-term high-quality trainings.

Developing an effective program is only half of the battle. The other half requires successful program dissemination as well as a framework to maintain the high quality of program implementation. For the EPL developers, this is a coexisting challenge even after 25 years. Prevention efforts usually depend on financial grants to promote and organize interventions. Unfortunately, in Germany, research findings are usually of secondary importance. All too often, new programs as well as programs for as many participants as possible are preferentially provided with financial resources. Anyhow, thinking of EPL and its adaptations, the developers succeeded to find continuing funding, to tailor the training to different subgroups of couples and even to adolescents as well as to continuously ensure high-quality trainings.

Nevertheless, there are still good reasons for cautious optimism: Despite having the largest dissemination compared to other evaluated couple interventions, to date, EPL is far from having a significant impact on German divorce rates. Only few couples hear about EPL or its adaptations and even less actually participate in a training. In the United States, 80 to 90 percent of couples who get divorced did not make use of any form of couple counseling or couple therapy (Halford, Markman, Kline, & Stanley, 2003). Reasons for not seeking help are diverse (Doss, Atkins, & Christensen, 2003): On the one hand, couples report they did not think anything was wrong in their relationship and therefore were not motivated to seek help; on the other hand, couples who are already dissatisfied often think it is "too late" for their relationship to improve. Further self-reported barriers are a lack of knowledge about or doubts upon the effectiveness of available services, a general preference to solve problems on their own coming along with a fear of stigmatization, high treatment costs as well as logistic challenges such as a lack of time or child care. To summarize, it is hard to convince couples who are experiencing problems to seek help, and it is even harder to convince people not experiencing difficulty to seek services ("Honeymoon phase") (Job & Hahlweg, 2015). Therefore, in the future, we particularly need more efforts to promote preventive couple intervention to reach as many couples as possible and to motivate them to make use of available services by reducing barriers of participation. In this context, it has repeatedly been recommended to create an organization and structure on the national level to oversee the development and dissemination of couple interventions (Job, Bodenmann, Baucom, & Hahlweg, 2014). If that's the case, EPL and its adaptations definitely show great promise for positively influencing couples' long-term relationship developments.

Key Points

- There is a substantial need for prevention of chronic relationship dissatisfaction and breakup; both are associated with negative health, social, and economic consequences.
- With the aim of strengthening couples' relationship skills, several relationship enhancement (CRE) programs have been developed.
- In Germany, there is an enormous deficit of psycho-social prevention research and even a larger gap between research and practice.
- The communication and problem-solving training *Ein Partnerschaftliches Lernprogramm* EPL ("A Couples' Learning Program") is the most empirically supported CRE program in Europe.

- KEK "Constructive Marriage and Communication," KOMKOM "Communication-Competence Training in Couple Counseling," and TTT "Talk Talk Talk and More" for adolescents are evidence-based group-specific adaptations of EPL.
- Prospective trainers need to attend standardized trainer trainings and accreditation workshops as well as annual supervision after being accredited.
- Within a new approach to more effectively disseminate EPL, students with a major in psychology are taught to become accredited trainers.
- EPL and KEK participant materials are also available in foreign languages, e.g. in English, Spanish, and Slovene.
- Future research should focus on the broad dissemination and implementation of CRE programs.

Discussion Questions

1. Why do we need couple relationship enhancement programs?
2. What was the core conviction behind EPL and its adaptations?
3. What are the main differences and similarities between EPL and its adaptations?
4. What are the program goals and objectives of EPL and its adaptations?
5. What are the core skills taught in EPL and its adaptations?
6. What factors likely explain the superior outcomes of the EPL family in research studies?
7. How is the quality of the EPL family trainings being assured?

References

Benson, H., Beary, J.F., & Carol, M.P. (1974). The relaxation response. *Journal for the Study of Interpersonal Processes, 37*, 37–46.

BiB—Federal Institute of Population Research (2014). *Ehedauerspezfische Scheidungsziffern (Marriage duration specific divorce rates)*. Retrieved May 20, 2014, from http://www.bib-demografie.de/SharedDocs/Glossareintraege/DE/E/ ehedauerspezifische_scheidungsziffer.html

Braukhaus, C., Hahlweg, K., Kroeger, C., Groth, T., & Fehm-Wolfsdorf, G. (2003). The effects of adding booster sessions to a prevention training program for committed couples. *Behavioural and Cognitive Psychotherapy, 31*, 325–336.

Callan, S., Benson, H., Coward, S., Davis, H., Gill, M., Grant, H., Percival, D., & Rowthorn, R. (2006). *Breakdown Britain: Fractured families*. London: Social Policy Justice Group.

Doss, B., Atkins, D., & Christensen, A. (2003). Who's dragging their feet? Husbands and wives seeking marital therapy. *Journal of Marital and Family Therapy, 29*, 165–177.

Doss, B., Rhoades, G., Stanley, S., & Markman, H. (2009). The effect of the transition to parenthood on relationship quality: An 8-year prospective study. *Journal of Personality and Social Psychology, 96*, 601–619.

Engl, J. (2014). *Arbeitsbericht 2013 (Work report 2013)*. Institut für Forschung und Ausbildung in Kommunikationstherapie e.V., München.

Engl, J., & Thurmaier, F. (2002). Kommunikationskompetenz in Partnerschaft und Familie. In B. Rollett & H. Werneck (Hrsg.), *Klinische Entwicklungspsychologie der Familie* (S. 326–350) *(Clinical development psychology of family)*. Göttingen, Hogrefe.

Engl, J., & Thurmaier, F. (2005). KOMKOM—ein hochwirksames Kommunikationstraining in der Eheberatung (KOMKOM—a highly effective communication training in couple counseling). *Beratung aktuell, 1*, 22–40.

Engl, J., & Thurmaier, F. (2007). *Ein Kick mehr Partnerschaft. Gelungene Kommunikation . . . damit die Liebe bleibt. Eine interaktive DVD zum Gelingen von Beziehungen (A kick for the relationship. Successful communication to keep love alive)*. Munich, Germany: Institute of Research and Training in Communication Therapy.

Engl, J., & Thurmaier, F. (2012). *Damit die Liebe bleibt. Richtig kommunizieren in mehrjährigen Partnerschaften*. Bern: Huber (ISBN: 978-3-456-85087-0)

Ermisch, J., & Francesconi, M. (2000). Cohabitation in Great Britain: Not for long, but here to stay. *Journal of the Royal Statistical Society, Series A, 163*(2), 153–171.

Fawcett, E., Hawkins, A., Blanchard, V., & Carroll, J. (2010). Do premarital education programs really work? A meta-analytic study. *Family Relations, 59*, 232–239.

Fowers, B., Lyons, E., & Montel, K. (1996). Positive marital illusions: Self-enhancement or relationship enhancement? *Journal of Family Psychology, 10*, 192–208.

Glenn, N. (1998). The course of marital success and failure in five American 10-year cohorts. *Journal of Marriage and Family, 60*, 269–282.

Hahlweg, K., Baucom, D., Grawe-Gerber, M., & Snyder, D. (2010). Strengthening couples and families: Dissemination of interventions for the treatment and prevention of couple distress. In K. Hahlweg, M. Grawe-Gerber, & D. Baucom (Eds.), *Enhancing couples: The shape of couple therapy to come* (pp. 3–30). Göttingen: Hogrefe.

Hahlweg, K., Grawe-Gerber, M., & Baucom, D. (Eds.). (2010). *Enhancing couples. The shape of couple therapy to come*. Göttingen: Hogrefe.

Hahlweg, K., Markman, H., Thurmaier, F., Engl, J., & Eckert, V. (1998). Prevention of marital distress: Results of a German prospective-longitudinal study. *Journal of Family Psychology, 12*, 543–556.

Hahlweg, K., & Richter, D. (2010). Prevention of marital instability and couple distress: Results of an 11-year longitudinal follow-up study. *Behaviour Research and Therapy, 48*, 377–383.

Halford, K., Markman, H., Kline G., & Stanley, S. (2003). Best practices in couple relationship education. *Journal of Marital and Family Therapy, 29*, 385–406.

Halford, W., Markman, H., & Stanley, S. (2008). Strengthening couples' relationships with education: Social policy and public health perspectives. *Journal of Family Psychology, 22*, 497–505.

Jacobson, E. (1929). *Progressive relaxation*. Oxford, UK: University of Chicago Press.

Job, A-K., Bodenmann, G., Baucom, D., & Hahlweg, K. (2014). Neuere Entwicklungen in der Prävention und Behandlung von Beziehungsproblemen bei Paaren: Aktueller Forschungsstand und zukünftige Herausforderungen (New developments in the prevention and treatment of relationship problems in couples: Current research and future challenges). *Psychologische Rundschau, 65*, 11–23.

Job, A-K., Engl, J., Thurmaier, F., & Hahlweg, K. (2014). Das Kommunikationstraining »Ein Partnerschaftliches Lernprogramm (EPL)« für Paare—Überblick über den Praxis- und Forschungsstand (The communication training "A Couples Learning Program" for couples—Overview on the state of practice and research). *Report Psychologie, 2*, 58–69.

Job, A.-K. & Hahlweg, K. (in press). Preventing couple distress: Long term outcome and international dissemination. In S. Walper, E.-V. Wendt, & F. Schmahl, *Preventing couple distress: Long term outcome and international dissemination.* Dordrecht, Netherlands: Springer Science + Business Media.

Job, A-K., & Hahlweg, K. (2015). *Don't forget about the beginning: Effectiveness of a German couples' relationship education program depending on the partners' initial relationship satisfaction.* Manuscript submitted for publication.

Job, A-K., Mattei, M., Vasterling, I., & Hahlweg, K. (2015). *Kompetente Trainer—Zufriedene Paare: Effektivität einer Ausbildung für Studierende der Psychologie im Kommunikationstraining "Ein Partnerschaftliches Lernprogramm EPL" (Satisfied couples—Professional trainers: Effectiveness of a student training course in "A Couples' Learning Program EPL"). Verhaltenstherapie,* in press.

Kaiser, A., Hahlweg, K., Fehm-Wolfsdorf, G., & Groth, T. (1998). The efficacy of a compact psychoeducational group training program for married couples. *Journal of Consulting and Clinical Psychology, 66,* 753–760.

Karney, B., & Bradbury, T. (1995). The longitudinal course of marital quality and stability: A review of theory, method, and research. *Psychological Bulletin, 118,* 3–34.

Köthke, N., Köthke, T., & Zimmermann, T. (2015). *"Talk, Talk, Talk and More." Evaluation eines Kommunikations- und Kompetenztrainings für Jugendliche ("Talk, Talk, Talk and More." Evaluation of a communication and social competence training for adolescents).* Manuscript submitted for publication.

Lösel, F., Schmucker, M., Planckensteiner, B., & Weiss, M. (2006). *Bestandsaufnahme und Evaluation von Angeboten im Elternbildungsbereich. Abschlussbericht* [Survey and evaluation of educational measures for parents]. Erlangen Nürnberg: Universität Erlangen-Nürnberg.

Markman, H., Floyd, F., Stanley, S., & Stoorasli, R. (1988). Prevention of marital distress: A longitudinal investigation. *Journal of Consulting and Clinical Psychology, 56,* 210–217.

Markman, H., Rhoades, G., Stanley, S., Ragan, E., & Whitton, S. (2010). The premarital communication roots of marital distress and divorce: The first five years of marriage. *Journal of Family Psychology, 24,* 289–298.

Schindler, L., Hahlweg, K., & Revenstorf, D. (2013). *Partnerschaftsprobleme: So gelingt Ihre Beziehung. Handbuch für Paare.* 4. Auflage. Heidelberg: Springer. (ISBN: 13 978-3-642-29008-4)

Statista—The Statistics Portal. (2014). *Gehören Sie einer Kirche oder Religionsgemeinschaft an und wenn ja, welcher? (Do you belong to a religious community and if yes, which one?).* Retrieved June 30, 2014, from http://de.statista.com/statistik/daten/studie/179440/umfrage/zugehoerigkeit-zu-einer-religionsgemeinschaft/

Thurmaier, F., Engl, J., & Hahlweg, K. (1999). Eheglück auf Dauer? Methodik, Inhalte und Effektivität eines präventiven Paarkommunikationstrainings. Ergebnisse nach 5 Jahren (Marital happiness forever? Methods, content, and efficacy of a premarital prevention program—5 year results). *Zeitschrift für Klinische Psychologie, 28,* 64–62.

14

THE COUPLES COPING ENHANCEMENT TRAINING (CCET)

Guy Bodenmann

LEARNING GOALS

- Understand the impact of extra-dyadic stress on couples' functioning and realize the meaning of this type of stress for relationship education programs.
- Be familiar with the concept of dyadic coping and the role dyadic coping plays in relationship functioning and moderating negative effects of extra-dyadic stress on couples' interaction.
- Know specific components of the CCET, mainly psycho-education regarding the role of stress for couples, communication training, problem-solving training, and the 3-phase method.
- Understand the goals of the 3-phase method and how the provider works with the couple by prompting stress-related self-disclosure, active listening, and support provision.

Introduction

In the 1990s, a new line of research emerged when different researchers began to investigate the effects of **stress** and **coping** on marriage. This research yielded new ideas for relationship education (RE) programs as well as couple therapy. The findings from this line of research provide the theoretical and empirical background for **Couples Coping Enhancement Training (CCET)** that was developed in 1994.

A significant body of research shows that everyday stress (Lazarus & Folkman, 1984) is consistently negatively associated with relationship satisfaction, quality, and stability (for overview see Randall & Bodenmann, 2009; Story & Bradbury,

2004). In particular, extra-dyadic stress (i.e., stress originating from outside the relationship such as stress at the workplace or stress with neighbors) affects relationship satisfaction negatively by spilling over to the couple relationship prompting intra-dyadic stress (i.e., interpersonal tensions and arguments), and thereby a decrease in relationship satisfaction (Bodenmann, Ledermann, & Bradbury, 2007; Bodenmann & Cina, 2006; Falconier, Nussbeck, & Bodenmann, 2013; Frye & Karney, 2006; Ledermann, Bodenmann, Rudaz, & Bradbury, 2010; Neff & Karney, 2004; Repetti, 1989; Repetti, Wang, & Saxbe, 2009). These studies yield empirical evidence for the stress–divorce model (Bodenmann et al., 2007).

Theoretical Foundations and History

The **stress–divorce model** assumes that harmful spill-over effects of extra-dyadic stress on close relationships are due to: (1) a lack of time that couples experience in times of stress along with less shared experiences, weakening the feeling of we-ness and intimacy; (2) a decrease in the quality of dyadic communication (e.g., more criticism, contempt, belligerence, defensiveness, withdrawal, and less positivity); (3) a higher likelihood of health problems (both psychological or physical) as well as (4) greater appearance of partner's difficult personality traits (e.g., rigidity, intolerance, dominance, etc.) that become more obvious in times of stress. However, the model also postulates that the negative impact of extra-dyadic stress on relationship functioning is not deterministic, and can be buffered by individual and **dyadic coping** (Bodenmann et al., 2007). Above all, dyadic coping plays an important role, once stress spills over to the couple.

Dyadic coping, or the way couples manage stress together, is a concept that has received increased attention in the last two decades (e.g., Acitelli & Antonucci, 1994; Bodenmann, 1995, 1997; Cutrona & Gardner, 2006; Revenson, Kayser, & Bodenmann, 2005). Among different models of dyadic coping, the systemic-transactional model (STM; Bodenmann, 1995, 2005) has received most attention. Couples Coping Enhancement Training (CCET) is grounded in this model. STM postulates that if one partner is stressed then both partners are affected (mutual interdependence). Accordingly, couples have a vital interest in coping together with these demands. A large body of research consistently demonstrates the important role of dyadic coping in predicting relationship satisfaction (e.g., Bodenmann, Pihet, & Kayser, 2006; Herzberg, 2013; Levesque et al., 2014; Pasch & Bradbury, 1998; Papp & Witt, 2010), stability (Bodenmann & Cina, 2006) as well as individual well-being (Bodenmann, Meuwly, & Kayser, 2011).

Both partners' satisfaction, well-being and personal functioning are associated with the quality of couple's dyadic coping. A systematic review showed that dyadic coping is not only associated with relationship satisfaction of couples in the community, but also couples dealing with cancer (Traa, van Ounden, Bodenmann, & Den Oudsten, 2014). Other studies indicate that dyadic coping plays a moderating role in that it buffers the impact of daily stress on verbal aggression (Bodenmann, Meuwly, Bradbury, Gmelch, & Ledermann, 2010) or relationship satisfaction (Falconier et al., 2013; Merz, Meuwly, Randall, & Bodenmann, 2014). Along similar lines, Meuwly et al. (2012) reported that the more one partner is engaged in positive dyadic coping, the faster the other partner's cortisol recovery from extra-dyadic stress. Bodenmann and his colleagues noted that an enhancement of couple's positive dyadic coping after participation in CCET coincides with an improvement of relationship satisfaction (Bodenmann, Bradbury, & Pihet, 2009; Bodenmann, Hilpert, Nussbeck, & Bradbury, 2014). The aim of fostering dyadic coping in CCET is sound and reasonable in light of these findings.

Program Goals and Objectives

The fact that the quality of dyadic communication often decreases when partners are stressed means that it is often not sufficient to teach couples only communication skills. Instead partners should realize that when partners experience bad moods (e.g., withdrawn or hostile), it is often because they have been subjected to hard and stressful situations, and their mood is not related to their partner but to these negative circumstances (no negative attribution towards partner but towards external conditions). Thus the partner who is not experiencing a bad mood should ask the one who is what happened, why they are in this poor temper. By asking, the partner invites the other to communicate about his/her stress experience and thus learns about what happened to the other and what this meant to the partner. This can be taught in RE by helping couples enlarge their repertoire of dyadic coping competencies. Accordingly, CCET's objectives are: (1) teach couples about the impact of extra-dyadic stress on couple's functioning, (2) improve the appraisal of partner's stress experience in both partners (enhancement of mutual stress perception), (3) improve the way partners communicate with one another about the stress that they experienced (enhancement of stress communication by means of the **funnel method**, see below), and (4) improve the dyadic coping repertoire of a couple (enhancement of dyadic coping) which leads to a higher feeling of we-ness, mutual intimacy, trust, and love.

Needs Assessment and Target Audience

The CCET is offered as primary prevention for all couples interested in building a strong relationship. However, couples aware of the negative impact of stress on their intimate relationship and suffering from first signs of crisis can also benefit from CCET workshops. Recently, adapted forms of the CCET are also offered to couples becoming parents (CCET combined with Couple CARE for parents, Halford, Petch, & Creedy, 2010), dual career couples (Merz et al., 2014), and couples dealing with financial strain (TOGETHER; Falconier, 2014).

Curriculum and Other Program Issues

The CCET is 15 hours in length and consists of five units. Typically, CCET is offered as a weekend workshop, but it can be conducted as a series of 5 weekly sessions lasting 3 hours each. CCET workshops are usually conducted in groups of 4–8 couples, with a ratio of 2 couples per provider. Although there are different modes of delivery (combined with DVD or without) the efficacy of the program is similar (Merz et al., 2014). The different units of the CCET are presented below.

Unit 1: Stress and its impact on close relationships. Participants learn that stress is a dynamic process whereby a specific demanding situation triggers cognitive appraisals that go along with specific stress emotions. As each partner may appraise the same situation differently and, as a result, experience different emotions, this insight may lead to a better understanding why different emotions in similar situations are experienced by the partners. The goal of this input is to increase couples' awareness of the need to communicate overtly how one feels in a specific situation of stress. This process is illustrated in several exercises, and participants increase their awareness of their own stress level in everyday life.

Unit 2: Enhancing dyadic coping. The enhancement of dyadic coping includes the training of several skills. First, couples are trained to adequately and explicitly communicate their own stress within a deepened emotional self-disclosure process by means of the funnel method as part of the 3-phase method. Second, couples learn to better perceive and understand the partner's stress by empathic joining. Third, the enhancement of positive dyadic coping is focused, especially emotion-focused supportive dyadic coping in an attempt to support the partner in his/her emotion regulation, problem solving, or joint dyadic coping. The training of these skills is done by means of the *3-phase method.*

The first phase of the 3-phase method lasts approximately 30 minutes and consists of the emotional stress exploration described with a metaphor of a funnel. This "funnel method" describes an activity where one partner (partner A) begins at the top of the funnel with a factual description of a recent example of a stressful situation not related to the couple (e.g., something that happened at work), and works his/her way to the bottom of the funnel where he/she speaks about the deeper aspects of the stressful event and explores a personal schema that is activated by the event. Starting with a short narrative description of the situation, partner A is prompted by the trainer to go deeper into his/her emotions, thoughts, and perceptions that are linked with the stressful event and is helped to explore which personal schema (e.g., attachment, perfectionism, control, dependency) might be involved in the stressful event. In a soft and warm voice, the provider encourages and coaches the individual in the process of emotional exploration with short, open-ended questions, such as "How did you feel?" "What happened to you?" "What did this mean to you?" "Why was this so stressful?" Simultaneously, the provider coaches partner B to listen and summarize important aspects of what partner A is saying and to ask open-ended questions if clarification is needed.

Through this process both partners get a clear understanding of deeper aspects of the stressful event. For example, being late for an important appointment may at first trigger general emotions, such as anger, frustration, or embarrassment. By further exploring this event, (i.e., progressing further down the funnel), the stressed person touches upon core beliefs like being perceived as unreliable, incompetent, or untrustworthy. Such appraisals of one's self may lead to activation of emotions, such as guilt, shame, anxiety, or sadness, and reveal a personal schema (not being worthy, not being in control, not being loved, not being perfect). This process of emotional exploration allows both partners to understand that these stress emotions are a logical consequence of one's own appraisals and the activation of a relevant schema (Gruen, Folkman, & Lazarus, 1988; Park & Folkman, 1997). The deeper understanding of the meaning of the stressful event for partner A by partner B is the central aim of the first phase of the 3-phase method.

In the second phase of the 3-phase method (10 minutes) partner B is asked to provide positive supportive dyadic coping that matches the level of emotional self-disclosure demonstrated by partner A. At this point, partner B is aware of the meaning that the stressful event holds for partner A and is able to express empathy and interest. He/she also may provide other forms of emotion-focused supportive dyadic coping, such as helping to positively reframe the situation, promoting a sense of solidarity with the partner, telling the partner how he/she is appreciated, pointing out the partner's quality and strengths, helping the partner to slow down and to relax, or helping the partner to actively find solutions for the problem. In this phase partner A listens but does not offer any evaluative comments in response to partner B.

In the third phase of the 3-phase method (5 minutes) partner A is invited to tell partner B how satisfied he/she was with the support provided by partner B. He/she tells how helpful the support was and what else might have helped him/ her to feel better. This feedback enhances the sense of being adequately supported.

Upon completion of this phase, the partners reverse roles, and partner B then describes a stressful event, and partner A is actively listening and offering dyadic coping. During the course of the CCET, it is important that both partners are involved in both roles, so they can experience what it is like to describe their stress-related emotions and to offer support and receive support.

By engaging in the 3-phase method the partners learn to effectively provide supportive dyadic coping in a way that truly meets the needs of the other. At the same time they strengthen the feeling of "we-ness" (cohesion, intimacy, solidarity, and mutual trust within the relationship).

Unit 3: Integrating fairness, equity, and boundaries. Couples need a clear consensus of fairness and equity to maximize the effects of dyadic coping for both partners. Otherwise, an imbalance can lead to feelings of dependency, resentment, or dominance (Walster, Traupmann, & Walster, 1978). Relationship boundaries are important to help couples establish the primacy of their relationship, an idea that is congruent with the notion of one's partner being one's first line of support

(Revenson, 1994). Thus, the couples are sensitized to these issues and learn to differentiate between supportive dyadic coping, on one hand, and creating dependency or giving undesired support on the other hand. By increasing their awareness of fairness and mutuality (i.e., dyadic coping as a form of mutual giving and receiving) and having both partners engage in emotional self-disclosure, the couple invests in all three forms of dyadic coping (i.e., supportive, common, and delegated dyadic coping). The aim of dyadic coping is to offer support in a form that is needed and most useful. It is not intended to take advantage of a partner's stress to strengthen one's own position in the relationship. Then the concept of fairness and boundaries is expanded into the general context of daily life, and both partners engage in an analysis of boundaries in relation to other important persons (children, parents, and friends), so they can become aware of stress caused by boundary violations of others. By means of maps and exercises, both partners assess and come to understand equity within the relationship both in terms of where it is and what might be improved. Additionally, they analyze their relationships to other persons and the influence that these other relationships exert upon their partnership.

Unit 4: Enhancing dyadic communication. This module of CCET is similar to the PREP program (see chapter 12) and is mainly dedicated to improving communication skills through supervised role plays (Markman, Renick, Floyd, Stanley, & Clements, 1993). Additionally, through a presentation by the provider, participants learn to distinguish between constructive communication behaviors (e.g., active listening, making compliments, showing interest, reconciliation) and dysfunctional communication behaviors (criticism, defensiveness, contempt, belligerence, and withdrawal). Here, the couples are introduced to categories of problematic communication as developed by Gottman (1994) through video demonstrations. Each partner is asked to assess these problematic communication styles in his/ her own behavior by means of a short questionnaire. Then the couples are introduced to more effective ways of discussing differences through the widely used speaker-listener technique and trained in this through supervised role plays (ratio two couples per provider).

Unit 5: Enhancement of problem solving. Training in problem solving is conducted in the format of a supervised exercise (ratio two couples per provider) and involves a six-step procedure that is derived from the PREP (Markman et al.,1993). The six steps are describing the problem; brainstorming to explore as many solutions as possible; choosing the best solution; planning to solve the problem in everyday life by implementing this solution; and evaluating the solution.

Professional Preparation and Training Issues

A high degree of standardization of the program is ensured through the use of a detailed and highly structured manual for trainers and a thorough instruction program for the trainers delivering the program. Each provider receives

35 hours of training over a 5-day period and 20 hours of group supervision. Before delivering the program, providers have to pass an exam and are licensed for two years.

Evidence-based Research and Evaluation

CCET has been evaluated in different randomized controlled trials as well as studies on effectiveness. Findings on consumer satisfaction revealed that 85% of women as well as men rate the training as *good* to *very good*, another 10% as *moderately good*, and 5% as *not helpful*.

Bodenmann and his colleagues, in a 2-year follow-up study including 73 couples attending a CCET workshop and 73 couples without intervention, found a significant improvement of relationship satisfaction, communication skills, dyadic coping, and well-being in couples attending CCET (e.g., Bodenmann, Pihet, Shantinath, Cina, & Widmer, 2006; Pihet, Bodenmann, Cina, Widmer, & Shantinath, 2007; Widmer, Cina, Charvoz, Shantinath, & Bodenmann, 2005).

Ledermann, Bodenmann, and Cina (2007), in a randomized controlled trial (RCT) where 50 couples attending CCET were compared to 50 couples in a waiting-list control condition within a 1-year follow-up, documented a significant improvement of CCET couples with regard to relationship quality (couple's communication, dyadic coping). Effects were stable within the 1-year-follow-up, however, were weaker after 6 months and 1 year, compared to 2 weeks after the workshop.

In a 4-month follow-up-study the short-term efficacy of the CCET with 157 couples in a business context was evaluated. Forty-one couples participated in CCET, 44 couples in individual-oriented stress management training, and 46 couples formed the waiting-list control group. Couples attending CCET outperformed the other groups in individual and dyadic coping, communication as well as burn-out symptoms (Schär, Bodenmann, & Klink, 2008).

In a 6-month follow-up study the efficacy of a CCET DVD was assessed with 88 couples forming the intervention group (DVD group), another 77 couples receiving the DVD and a telephone coaching, and another 99 couples forming the waiting-list control condition. Both CCET formats (working alone on the DVD and DVD with telephone coaching) improved relationship satisfaction as well as communication and dyadic coping (Bodenmann et al., 2014).

A 6-month follow-up study with 159 dual earner couples examined the efficacy of different formats of the CCET. Forty couples received a shortened version (DVD plus 8 hours workshop), 39 couples a compact version (12 hours workshop), 39 couples the classic version (15 hours workshop), and 41 couples formed the waiting-list control condition. The RCT shows that all formats are equally effective in improving dyadic coping and communication (Merz, Nussbeck, Halford, Schär, & Bodenmann, under review). The different studies are summarized in Table 14.1.

TABLE 14.1 Summary of Evaluation Studies

Author	Participants	Intervention	Measures	Key Findings
Bodenmann et al. (2006) Widmer et al. (2005)	$N = 146$ couples	18 hours of CCET compared with non-intervention control group (matched couples)	Self-report relationship quality and dyadic coping, Observed communication and dyadic coping behavior	Couples in the CCET condition improved significantly more than control couples within the follow-up of 24 months. Effect sizes ranged between .10 to .80 in self-report measures and .10 to 1.50 in observed behavior.
Ledermann, Bodenmann, & Cina (2007)	$N = 100$ couples	18 hours of CCET, compared with no intervention control (RCT)	Self-report relationship satisfaction, couple communication, dyadic coping	CCET produced moderate to large effect sizes in relationship satisfaction, effects attenuated somewhat by 12 months.
Schär, Bodenmann, & Klink (2008)	$N = 168$ couples	15 hours of CCET compared with individual stress training and control group (RCT)	Self-reported communication, dyadic coping, well-being, burn-out	CCET outperformed the individual training and the control condition. CCET improved dyadic communication, dyadic coping as well as well-being and reduced the likelihood for burn-out within 5 months.
Bodenmann et al. (2014)	$N = 264$ couples	CCET DVD was compared to DVD with telephone coaching and control condition (RCT)	Self-reported relationship satisfaction, communication, dyadic coping, well-being, happiness	Both CCET DVD conditions outperformed control couples. Effect sizes ranged from .23 to .47. The more intensively the couples worked with the DVD, the stronger the effects.

Study	N	Design	Measures	Results
Merz, Nussbeck, et al. (under review)	N = 159 couples	Three formats of CCET, varying regarding length, compared to waiting-list control group (RCT)	Self-reported communication, dyadic coping	All three formats were equally effective and improvement of communication and dyadic coping was higher in CCET conditions than control group. Effect sizes ranged from .37 to .60. The more stressed couples were, the stronger the effects.
Falconier (2014)	N =18 couples	Pilot study on TOGETHER (pre-post-follow-up 3-month measure)	Self-reported relationship satisfaction, financial strain, dyadic coping	Partners' financial strain could be reduced as well as male's negative communication. On the other side, both partners' financial management skills and dyadic coping strategies regarding financial strain could be improved as well as male's relationship satisfaction.

Cultural Implications

The CCET is successfully used in different Western countries (e.g., U.S., France, Italy, Germany, Spain, Switzerland), reflecting that the program is appropriate for Western cultures. As the program is based on research in those countries, the cultural dimension is considered. CCET has, however, not been offered in Eastern cultures. Currently, an adaptation of CCET for Chinese couples is being developed.

Conclusion

The Couples Coping Enhancement Training (CCET) is an evidence-based relationship education program, based upon stress and coping theory and research in couples on the one hand and cognitive-behavioral methods on the other hand. A core element is the 3-phase method aiming at enhancing stress-related self-disclosure and dyadic coping. As compared to other programs, CCET focuses principally on the impact of extra-dyadic stressors on couples' functioning and how couples can successfully cope together as a couple with daily hassles or severe stressors. CCET is offered as relationship education in universal, selective as well as indicated prevention. Its effectiveness has been examined in several RCT studies.

Key Points

- CCET is a standardized, manualized evidence-based relationship education program used in universal prevention as well as indicated and selective prevention (couples becoming parents, dual career couples).
- The program has a length of 15 hours and is usually offered as a weekend workshop.
- CCET is based on stress and coping research in couples and tries to attenuate the negative impact of extra-dyadic stress on couples functioning.
- The training of specific skills such as dyadic communication, dyadic problem solving, and dyadic coping is a main component of CCET. Exercises are supervised by a licensed CCET provider with a ratio of 2 to 1 (two couples per provider), allowing a profound learning of skills.
- Within the skills training the 3-phase method plays a particular role. This method allows partners to learn how to adequately communicate their emotional stress experience to the partner and how to better understand the personal schema that was triggered by the event (phase 1). In phase 2 partners learn to adequately support each other and to match support with specific needs of the partner. In phase 3 partners give a personalized feedback on the quality of the support and specific wishes. This method allows to improve dyadic coping, which revealed to be an important predictor of relationship satisfaction and stability.

- The program has been evaluated in different RCT studies showing positive effects of the program with regard to relationship satisfaction, skill improvement, well-being, and sexual desire. The program also improves child well-being and reduces child behavioral problems by improving their parents' relationship quality. Effects are more or less established for a duration of two years.

Discussion Questions

1. What was the core conviction behind the creation of the CCET?
2. Why is stress and coping, especially dyadic coping, emphasized in CCET?
3. What is the original core method of the CCET?
4. What are the principal goals of this method?
5. What is the rationale of the unit on equity and fairness?

Additional Resources

The CCET manual and workshop materials (PowerPoint slides, questionnaires, worksheets) are available in German, French, and English (guy.bodenmann@psychologie.uzh.ch). The DVD in German can be ordered from www.paarlife.com.

References and Further Readings

Acitelli, L., & Antonucci, T. (1994). Gender differences in the link between marital support and satisfaction in older couples. *Journal of Personality and Social Psychology, 67*, 688–698. doi:10.1037/0022–3514.67.4.688

Bodenmann, G. (1995). A systemic-transactional conceptualization of stress and coping in couples. *Swiss Journal of Psychology / Schweizerische Zeitschrift Für Psychologie / Revue Suisse De Psychologie, 54*, 34–49.

Bodenmann, G. (1997). Dyadic coping—a systemic-transactional view of stress and coping among couples: Theory and empirical findings. *European Review of Applied Psychology, 47*, 137–140.

Bodenmann, G. (2005). Dyadic coping and its significance for marital functioning. In T. Revenson, K. Kayser, & G. Bodenmann (Eds.), *Couples coping with stress: Emerging perspectives on dyadic coping* (pp. 33–49). Washington, DC: American Psychological Association.

Bodenmann, G., Bradbury, T., & Pihet, S. (2009). Relative contributions of treatment-related changes in communication skills and dyadic coping skills to the longitudinal course of marriage in the framework of marital distress prevention. *Journal of Divorce and Remarriage, 50*, 1–21. doi:10.1080/10502550802365391

Bodenmann, G., Charvoz, L., Bradbury, T., Bertoni, A., Iafrate, R., Giuliani, C., Banse, R., & Behling, J. (2007). The role of stress in divorce: A retrospective study in three nations. *Journal of Social and Personal Relationships, 24*, 707–728. doi:10.1177/0265407507081456

Bodenmann, G., & Cina, A. (2006). Stress and coping among stable-satisfied, stable-distressed and separated/divorced Swiss couples. *Journal of Divorce and Remarriage, 44*, 71–89. doi:10.1300/J087v44n01_04

Bodenmann, G., Hilpert, P., Nussbeck, F., & Bradbury, T. (2014). Enhancement of couples' communication and dyadic coping by a self-directed approach: A randomized controlled trial. *Journal of Consulting and Clinical Psychology.* doi:10.1037/a0036356

Bodenmann, G., Ledermann, T., & Bradbury, T. (2007). Stress, sex, and satisfaction in marriage. *Personal Relationships, 14,* 551–569. doi:10.1111/j.1475-6811.2007.00171.x

Bodenmann, G., Meuwly, N., Bradbury, T., Gmelch, S., & Ledermann, T. (2010). Stress, anger, and verbal aggression in intimate relationships: Moderating effects of individual and dyadic coping. *Journal of Social and Personal Relationships, 27,* 408–424. doi:10.1177/0265407510361616

Bodenmann, G., Meuwly, N., & Kayser, K. (2011). Two conceptualizations of dyadic coping and their potential for predicting relationship quality and individual well-being. *European Psychologist, 16,* 255–266.

Bodenmann, G., Pihet, S., & Kayser, K. (2006). The relationship between dyadic coping and marital quality: A 2-year longitudinal study. *Journal of Family Psychology, 20,* 485–493. doi:10.1037/0893–3200.20.3.485

Bodenmann, G., Pihet, S., Shantinath, S.D., Cina, A., & Widmer, K. (2006). Improving dyadic coping in couples with a stress-oriented approach: A 2-year longitudinal study. *Behavior Modification, 30,* 571–597. doi:10.1177/0145445504269902

Cutrona, C. & Gardner, K. (2006). Stress in couples: The process of dyadic coping. In A.L. Vangelisti & D. Perlman (Eds.), *The Cambridge handbook of personal relationships* (pp. 501–515). New York, NY: Cambridge University Press.

Falconier, M. (2014). TOGETHER—A couples' program to improve communication, coping, and financial management skills: Development and initial pilot-testing. *Journal of Marital and Family Therapy.* doi:10.1111/jmft.12052

Falconier, M., Jackson, J., Hilpert, P., & Bodenmann, G. (In revision). Dyadic coping and relationship satisfaction: A meta-analytic review of studies using the dyadic coping inventory.

Falconier, M., Nussbeck, F., & Bodenmann, G. (2013). Immigration stress and relationship satisfaction in Latino couples: The role of dyadic coping. *Journal of Social and Clinical Psychology, 32,* 813–843. doi:10.1521/jscp.2013.32.8.813

Frye, N., & Karney, B. (2006). The context of aggressive behavior in marriage: A longitudinal study of newlyweds. *Journal of Family Psychology, 20,* 12–20. doi:10.1037/0893–3200.20.1.12

Gottman, J. (1994). *What predicts divorce?* Hillsdale, NJ: Erlbaum.

Gruen, R., Folkman, S., & Lazarus, R. (1988). Centrality and individual differences in the meaning of daily hassles. *Journal of Personality, 56,* 743–762.

Halford, W., Petch, J., & Creedy, D. (2010). Promoting a positive transition to parenthood: A randomized clinical trial of couple relationship education. *Prevention Science, 11,* 89–100. doi:10.1007/s11121-009-0152-y

Herzberg, P. (2013). Coping in relationships: The interplay between individual and dyadic coping and their effects on relationship satisfaction. *Anxiety, Stress and Coping, 26,* 136–153. doi:10.1080/10615806.2012.655726

Lazarus, R., & Folkman, S. (1984). *Stress, appraisal, and coping.* New York, NY: Springer.

Ledermann, T., Bodenmann, G., & Cina, A. (2007). The efficacy of the Couples Coping Enhancement Training (CCET) in improving relationship quality. *Journal of Social and Clinical Psychology, 26,* 940–959. doi:10.1521/jscp.2007.26.8.940

Ledermann, T., Bodenmann, G., Rudaz, M., & Bradbury, T. (2010). Stress, communication, and marital quality in couples. *Family Relations, 59,* 195–206. doi:10.1111/j.1741-3729.2010.00595.x

Levesque, C., Lafontaine, M., Caron, A., Flesch, J., & Bjornson, S. (2014). Dyadic empathy, dyadic coping, and relationship satisfaction: A dyadic model. *Europe's Journal of Psychology, 10*, 118–134. doi:10.5964/ejop.v10i1.697

Markman, H., Renick, M., Floyd, F., Stanley, S., & Clements, M. (1993). Preventing marital distress through communication and conflict management trainings: A 4-and 5-year follow-up. *Journal of Consulting and Clinical Psychology, 61*, 70–77.

Merz, C., Meuwly, N., Randall, A., & Bodenmann, G. (2014). Engaging in dyadic coping: Buffering the impact of everyday stress on prospective relationship satisfaction. *Family Science, 5*, 30–37. doi:10.1080/19424620.2014.927385

Merz, C., Nussbeck, F., Halford, K., Schär, M., & Bodenmann, G. (Under review). The effects of dose, mode of delivery and couple ... ... the outcomes from Couples Coping Enhancement Training (CCET).

Meuwly, N., Bodenmann, G., Germann, J., Bradbury, T., Ditzen, B., & Heinrichs, M. (2012). Dyadic coping, insecure attachment, and cortisol stress recovery following experimentally induced stress. *Journal of Family Psychology, 26*, 937–947. doi:10.1037/a0030356

Neff, L., & Karney, B. (2004). How does context affect intimate relationships? Linking external stress and cognitive processes within marriage. *Personality and Social Psychology Bulletin, 30*, 134–148. doi:10.1177/0146167203255984

Papp, L., & Witt, N. (2010). Romantic partners' individual coping strategies and dyadic coping: Implications for relationship functioning. *Journal of Family Psychology, 24*, 551–559. doi:10.1037/a0020836

Park, C., & Folkman, S. (1997). Meaning in the context of stress and coping. *Review of General Psychology, 1*, 115–144.

Pasch, L., & Bradbury, T. (1998). Social support, conflict, and the development of marital dysfunction. *Journal of Consulting and Clinical Psychology, 66*, 219–230.

Pihet, S., Bodenmann, G., Cina, A., Widmer, K., & Shantinath, S. (2007). Can prevention of marital distress improve well-being? A 1 year longitudinal study. *Clinical Psychology and Psychotherapy, 14*, 79–88. doi:10.1002/cpp.522

Randall, A., & Bodenmann, G. (2009). The role of stress on close relationships and marital satisfaction. *Clinical Psychology Review, 29*, 105–115. doi:10.1016/j.cpr.2008.10.004

Repetti, R. (1989). Effects of daily workload on subsequent behavior during marital interaction: The roles of social withdrawal and spouse support. *Journal of Personality and Social Psychology, 57*, 651–659.

Repetti, R., Wang, S., & Saxbe, D. (2009). Bringing it all back home: How outside stressors shape families' everyday lives. *Current Directions in Psychological Science, 18*, 106–111. doi:10.1111/j.1467-8721.2009.01618.x

Revenson, T. (1994). Social support and marital coping with chronic illness. *Annals of Behavioural Medicine, 16*, 122–130.

Revenson, T., Kayser, K., & Bodenmann, G. (2005). *Couples coping with stress: Emerging perspectives on dyadic coping.* Washington, DC: American Psychological Association. doi:10.1037/11031-000

Schär, M., Bodenmann, G., & Klink, T. (2008). Balancing work and relationship: Couples coping enhancement training (CCET) in the workplace. *Applied Psychology, 57*, 71–89. doi:10.1111/j.1464-0597.2008.00355.x

Story, L., & Bradbury, T. (2004). Understanding marriage and stress: Essential questions and challenges. *Clinical Psychology Review, 23*, 1139–1162. doi:10.1016/j.cpr.2003.10.002

Traa, M. J., De Vries, J., Bodenmann, G., & Den Oudsten, B. L. (2014). Dyadic coping and relationship functioning in couples coping with cancer: A systematic review. British Journal of Health Psychology. doi: 10.1111/bjhp.12094

Walster, E., Traupmann, J., & Walster, G.W. (1978). Equity and extramarital sexuality. *Archives of Sexual Behavior, 7*, 127–142. doi:10.1007/BF01542062

Widmer, K., Cina, A., Charvoz, L., Shantinath, S., & Bodenmann, G. (2005). A model dyadic coping intervention. In T. A. Revenson, K. Kayser, & G. Bodenmann (Eds.), *Couples coping with stress: Emerging perspectives on dyadic coping* (pp. 159–174). Washington, DC: American Psychological Association.

15

RELATIONSHIP ATTACHMENT MODEL (RAM) PROGRAMS

Pick and Links

John Van Epp and Morgan Van Epp Cutlip

LEARNING GOALS

- Gain an overview of the five interactive dynamic bonds of the Relationship Attachment Model (RAM) and how the RAM provides a picture of both relationship development for new relationships and relationship maintenance for established relationships.
- Learn the two major aspects of the PICK program for singles during relationship development: the five key areas to explore in a dating relationship that foreshadow what a partner will be like in a committed or marriage relationship, and an application of the RAM for building a relationship in a healthy and safe way ("safe zone").
- Understand the guiding principle in the LINKS program for couples that ensures successful relationship maintenance: couples regularly assessing their relationship with the RAM and setting practical goals to strengthen and balance the deficits in each of the five dynamic bonds represented by the RAM.
- Learn the rationale for the PICK program for singles and the LINKS program for couples.
- Learn the four objectives of the PICK program, and the four objectives of the LINKS program.
- Explore the cultural implications of the RAM and the two programs based on the RAM, PICK and LINKS.
- Understand the empirical support of the objectives of the PICK and LINKS programs.
- Learn the steps for becoming a certified instructor in both the PICK and LINKS programs.

Introduction

One of the most essential human needs is forming and maintaining close relationships (Baumeister & Leary, 1995; Worthington, 2005). The presence or absence of close relationships has been found to have serious consequences for one's happiness, mental health, mortality, suicidality, and overall life experience (Baumeister & Leary, 1995; Goldsmith, 2007; McAdams & Bryant, 1987; Qualter & Munn, 2002). And when one spans the myriad of human relationships, the most influential relationship, arguably is the marital relationship. Research has found that this relationship has similar and consistent, if not even more benefits than other close relationships. For instance, being married has been shown to serve as a protective factor against stress, depression, alcohol consumption, and overall psychological and somantic health problems and illnesses (Kamp Dush & Amato, 2005; Waite & Gallagher, 2000; DeLongis, Folkman, & Lazarus, 1988).

The protective effect of marriage is not guaranteed by status alone, however. Rather the *quality* of one's relationship bond contributes beneficial or harmful effects beyond those gained from just the marital status (Brown & DiMeo, 2007; DeLongis, Folkman, & Lazarus, 1988; Waite, Luo, & Lewin, 2008). In a review of marriage research from the 1990s to 2005, Worthington (2005) concluded that "beneath these (research) findings, we discover the buried treasure. The *emotional bond between couples is the golden thread* that holds partners together. Marital success is not most importantly about how partners behave with each other. It is more about the emotional bond between them and about healing threats to that bond" (p. 261, italics added).

Worthington's conclusion suggested that to focus only on couples' *behaviors* (e.g., interactional skills) was akin to missing the forest for the trees. In other words, the **skills-deficiency emphasis**—couples just needing to develop behavioral skills in interpersonal communication and conflict management—was itself deficient. Although there is definite value in helping couples sharpen these skills, the broader concepts of relationship bonds seem to remain abstract and undefined. Clients often know relationship terms like *love, trust, commitment, mutuality, reciprocity, forgiveness, support,* and so on but lack concrete conceptualizations of what these terms looked like in real life. In addition, a couple's mastery of specific communication skills does not automatically translate into a successful management of their overall relationship.

Theoretical Foundations and History

So in 1986, based on my clinical experiences and a review of the literature and theories of love, intimacy, and attachment, I (i.e., John Van Epp) developed an interactive, visual representation of the major constructs that seemed to constitute all relationships (Van Epp, 1997, 2006; Van Epp Cutlip, Futris, Van Epp, & Campbell, 2008). The **Relationship Attachment Model (RAM,** see Figure 15.1) looks like the face of an equalizer with up–down sliders and suggests that relationships comprise five major constructs referred to as dynamic bonds: know, trust, rely, commit, and touch.

These five constructs independently exist, with their ranges providing unique contributions to the experience of connection in relationships. The interactions of these five constructs create various feelings, experiences of vulnerability and resilience, closeness and distance, and relationship states. Additionally, each construct or dynamic bond represented by the RAM has a reciprocal nature within relationships. There is an extent to which one knows another and is also known by that person; there is an extent that one trusts another and is trusted; relies on someone and is relied upon, and so on. Therefore, the RAM can measure individuals' evaluation of self (how I know you, trust you, rely on you, etc.), other (how I believe you know me, trust me, rely on me, etc.), and the overall relationship (the degree we know each other, trust each other, rely on each other, etc.).

A primary strength of the RAM is its outward simplicity. Although the RAM is a conceptual model that integrates major psychological theories and extensive social and psychological research, to a layperson the model can be understood with little to no explanation beyond the presentation of a picture. Thus, the RAM has intuitive meaning "as is" without much explanation and can be personalized to reflect the strengths and weaknesses of a specific relationship because the five dynamic bonds can be moved into constellations that represent different

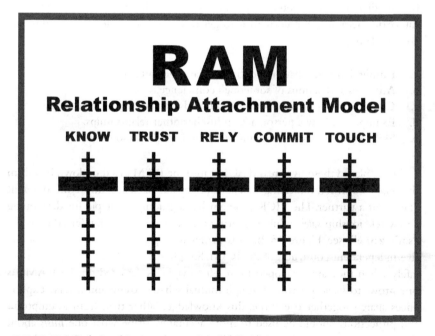

FIGURE 15.1 Relationship Attachment Model (RAM)

relationship experiences. Since its original design, the RAM has been evaluated in both qualitative and quantitative studies, validating the five independent constructs and their interactive power to describe relationship types and experiences (Cutlip, 2013).

The RAM provides the framework for the two relationship education programs: **PICK** a Partner (Premarital Interpersonal Choices and Knowledge) and Couple **LINKS** (Lasting Intimacy through Nurturing, Knowledge and Skills). The former, also known by the title, *How to Avoid Falling for a Jerk or Jerkette*, used the RAM to understand relationship development and partner selection. The latter applied the RAM to relationship maintenance, providing couples with an interactive pictorial representation of the various fluctuations that occur in their relationships and the skills needed to successfully navigate through these relationship experiences. In many ways, these two programs are two halves of close relationships with PICK providing a plan for the selection of a partner and the building of a new relationship (part one), and LINKS describing a plan for the sustainment and ongoing resiliency of an already developed relationship (part two).

PICK was developed in 1996 when I was teaching marriage and family assessment at Ashland Theological Seminary in addition to my full-time private practice. I remember thinking that the extensive research about premarital predictors of marital outcomes needed to be organized and translated into the language of my clients. And so I categorized several hundred articles into five categories that best predicted what a potential partner would be like in marriage. These five categories became the crucial areas to get to know and explore about someone you are dating:

a.   Family dynamics that predict future marriage patterns.
b.   Attitudes and actions of someone's conscience.
c.   Compatibility potential between you and the person you are dating.
d.   Examples of how a person acts in his/her other relationships.
e.   Skills a person has in communication and conflict resolution.

I then placed these five areas (FACES) into the RAM as a dropdown box from the *know* construct, indicating that it is important to get to know the different "faces" of a partner. The PICK program has a guiding principle for developing a new relationship *safely* while exploring the faces of a partner, referred to as the "**safe zone**" (see Figure 15.2). This principle explains the interactions of the five independent constructs of the RAM. Simply stated, relationships grow more safely when they are developed from left to right as depicted on the RAM. As one grows to *know* a partner through mutual self-disclosure and diverse experiences shared together over time, this knowledge, rather than from assumptions and projections, should be used to more accurately shape what one *trusts* about that partner. Trust and reliance should interact and grow together, with the degree of trust setting the ceiling for the ways one chooses to *rely* on another, and the ways that a partner proves to be reliable reinforcing or revising one's trust. As these three grow together, there is a greater security and lower vulnerability in giving oneself in *commitment* and sexual *touch* to that partner. Or, to state the "safe zone" another way: It is risky to go farther in sexual touch than the level of what you know or trust about someone; and there are clear vulnerabilities to forming a commitment beyond the ways the other person has proven reliable, or to look to the other person to meet your needs beyond your proven trust, or to trust a partner significantly more than what you know about that partner. Therefore, the PICK program packages key areas to get to know about a partner and the relationship skills that can build a safe and healthy relationship all in this one visual model, the RAM. In practical language, this program can help singles follow their hearts without losing their minds.

Shortly after writing PICK, the RAM was used as the framework for the LINKS curriculum but with a different guiding principle focused on relationship maintenance. Life will inevitably impact relationships causing changes in the levels of the five bonding dynamics portrayed in the RAM. Relationship experiences represented by these fluctuations or imbalances on the RAM often have inherent vulnerabilities; however, the real danger is not becoming imbalanced, but *staying* imbalanced. Therefore, the sessions in LINKS unpack each of the five dynamic

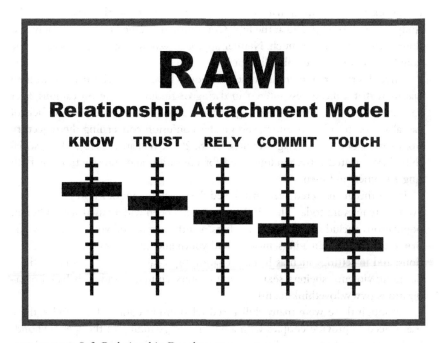

FIGURE 15.2 Safe Relationship Development

constructs of the RAM and their respective skills, and then provide a couple with a plan (called "huddles") to regularly meet together and assess where they are out of balance in their RAM profile and then to set small goals to strengthen their relationship in those specific areas.

Needs Assessment and Target Audience

Programs for couples have been the primary area of emphasis throughout most of the adult relationship education movement. Couples do need help in their relationships in preparation for marriage. However, it makes sense to provide materials for singles *long before* they become engaged. This was the rationale for the development of PICK.

Almost 15 years ago, Glenn and Marquardt (2001) wrote *Hooking Up, Hanging Out, and Hoping for Mr. Right*, a report in the Institute for American Values. This report was based on telephone interviews with a nationally representative sample of 1,000 college women, and in-depth conversations with 62 women on 11 campuses over 18 months. They found that women were confused about the dating-mating game on campus. There were few remaining rituals that let women know where they stand. Traditional dating had been replaced by "hanging out." Only 50 percent of senior women had been asked out on six or more dates in their four years at college. And yet, 63 percent of the college women expected to meet their future husband on campus. The two most common practices were casual sex with no emotional involvement or constant togetherness, which the study referred to as "joined at the hip." Commitment seemed to come in only two doses—too little or too much. Neither approach was very successful because the couples in both types usually did not last.

Since this report, numerous studies and books have been written about women *and* men that indicate less interest in dating or finding a mate on campus, later ages at first marriage but younger ages at first cohabitation, increased numbers of casual sex on into late twenties, and greater confusion concerning the trajectory from singlehood to marriage (Freitas, 2008, 2013; Williams, 2013). These social shifts have created a tremendous need for education and intervention for both single women and men.

It was this unanswered need that fueled the development of PICK and makes it even more relevant today. The PICK program has been widely used with different populations including military members, youth, parents of youth, never-been-marrieds, single-again adults, incarcerated youth and adults, low-income populations; and in settings such as healthy relationship coalitions, educational settings, domestic violence shelters, sexual assault centers, churches, and faith-based organizations (www.lovethinks.com).

Although there were many skill-based relationship courses for couples, there was a need to provide couples with a better understanding of the specific bonds in their relationship and a plan for managing these relational bonds through the natural ups and downs of life. In this approach, relationship skills are viewed as a means to the end goal of strengthening the dynamic bonds of a couple's relationship. By defining the relational bonds with the RAM, couples better understand the purpose of working on specific skills, and are more empowered to intentionally manage their relationship.

Therefore, the core of the LINKS course is to teach couples how to intentionally "run their relationship" by regularly assessing their current strengths and vulnerabilities with the Relationship Attachment Model and then set short-range relational goals in the five dynamic bonds represented in the RAM. When the levels of these dynamic bonds are high, feelings of love and closeness are maximized. Empowering couples to manage the bonds of their relationship is vital because maximizing feelings of love and closeness is central for the health and longevity of close relationships (Bachand & Caron, 2001; Robinson & Blanton, 1993; Holmberg, Orbuch, & Veroff, 2004; Ponzetti, 2005). In addition, strong love feelings have been shown to be the first and foremost predictor for whether a couple belonged to a high or low well-being group with higher well-being associated with greater love (Riehl-Emede, Thomas, & Willi, 2003). The RAM framework then provides couples a simple yet comprehensive method of assessing and maintaining their feelings of love through the management of the five dynamic bonds of their relationship.

The LINKS program has been widely used with populations similar to the PICK course including civilian couples, military members, incarcerated individuals, and low-income populations; and in settings such as healthy relationship coalitions, domestic violence shelters, churches, and faith-based organizations.

Each program has over 10,000 certified instructors with more than 500,000 participants having completed the respective course throughout the United States, Singapore, South America, Europe, and South Korea. The instructor and participant materials are available in English, Spanish, and Mandarin.

Program Goals and Objectives

The PICK program has four major objectives. First, it is designed to increase a participant's confidence and knowledge about the dating and partner selection process. Gardner, Giese, and Parrott (2004) argued that many relationship attitudes and behavior patterns are developed well before adulthood and engagement, when most couples attend premarital prevention programs.

Second, the PICK program is intended to increase one's judgment and discernment of a dating partner and what needs to be explored in order to better understand the character of a person. Long-standing research has supported that couples which are better acquainted before marriage have significantly higher rates of marital quality (Birtchnell & Kennard, 1984; Grover, Russell, Schumm, & Paff-Bergen, 1985; Kurdek, 1991, 1993), and experience fewer problems when they face the inevitable difficulties of marriage (Grover et al., 1985).

The third objective of the PICK program is to increase intentionality in pacing a new, developing relationship. This includes slowing down the speed of sexual involvement which has been associated with lower rates of cohabitation and higher marital quality outcomes.

The fourth and final objective of the PICK program is to increase intentionality about setting boundaries in trust-building, dependencies, and sexual touch. Stanley (2003) argued that one of the primary reasons premarital education has value is because it slows couples down and fosters greater deliberation. Singles seem to do better with a plan in order to have a conscious, intentional approach to dating and mate selection.

The LINKS program also has four major objectives. The first objective is to increase communication skills and positive communication experiences. Staying in the know with another is incredibly important to maintaining a close, bonded relationship, whether it be a marital relationship or close friendship (Amato & Previti, 2009).

The second objective is to increase feelings of satisfaction and love within the relationship. Murray, Holmes, and Griffin (1996) and Fowers, Lyons, Montel, and Shaked (2001) found that satisfaction in marriage was related to maintaining an idealistic rather than a realistic perception of one's spouse. Overall, individuals were happier in their relationships when they idealized their partners and their partners idealized them. In addition, strong feelings of love and closeness is strongly predictive of relationship health and longevity (Robinson & Blanton, 1993; Holmberg, Orbuch, & Veroff, 2004; Ponzetti, 2005).

Third, the LINKS program is designed to increase confidence for positively resolving conflicts. Long-standing research has found that marital distress can be prevented by developing positive communication and skills in conflict management (Gottman & Krokoff, 1989; Markman, Floyd, Stanley, & Storaasli, 1988; Markman, Renick, Floyd, Stanley, & Clements, 1993).

The fourth objective is to increase the understanding and behaviors of relationship maintenance. While communication skills are important in marriage, many couples who divorce state reasons other than communication problems. Among studies on why couples divorce, Amato and Previti (2009) found that "growing apart" was the fourth most common reason for divorce. Similarly, Bodenmann et al. (2006) found that "loss of love" was the most significant contributor to both men's and women's decision to divorce. The LINKS course has the primary objective of empowering couples with a plan to manage their love by assessing their relationship in each of the five dynamic bonds of the RAM and then setting goals for enhancing their relational experience in each of the five areas.

Curriculum and Other Program Issues

One of the unique features of the PICK and the LINKS curricula is that the content of both courses is *chunked* in the RAM. The word "**chunking**" comes from a landmark 1956 study by George A. Miller, in which he integrated information processing theory with learning theory to describe how a collection of elements having strong associations with one another become packaged or chunked as a single item, resulting in greater recall. I found that most singles and couples who attended other relationship classes recalled and practiced only one or two significant components from the curriculum just 3–6 months later. One explanation for this may be due to the fact that the sessions of most courses are topical without any clear association or connection between them—in other words, the curriculum expects the *participant* to chunk the content together in a meaningful and memorable whole.

However, in the first session of both PICK and LINKS, the participants learn the RAM as a single unit, quickly memorizing the five "sliders" representing the dynamic bonds in a relationship. As a result, each subsequent session simply unpacks the details of a chunked concept that they have already memorized and associated with familiar, concrete experiences. In fact, PICK program participants memorize both the RAM and the FACES in session 1 because the content of the FACES is chunked within the RAM. This packaged structure increases learning and retention, enabling participants to remember and therefore use what they gained from their classes.

In addition, because most couples only seemed to follow through on one activity from an entire course, the LINKS course pinpoints just one primary takeaway all participants are encouraged to practice on a weekly or biweekly basis. However, this one takeaway, called *huddles*, captures all of the content of the course because it is a RAM-based format for couples to use in a 20-minute meeting to assess how they are doing in their communication and talk times (know); their attitudes toward, apologies to, and appreciations of each other (trust); the ways they work together and support each other, and mutually meet each other's needs/wants in the 10 areas of intimacy (rely and touch). The conclusion of this huddle is for couples to set some simple and practical goals to achieve before their next huddle (commit), thus strengthening all of the major bonds in their relationship on a regular basis and improving the overall trajectory of their relationship.

The PICK and LINKS programs also have similarity in the facilitation of the respective course material and the balance between the course content and practical, interactive activities. Although there are some portions that are lecture, the primary style of facilitation is to guide participants in discussions by using questions from the participant workbooks that are explained and expanded in the instructor lesson plans. In addition, there are many activities which participants do within small groups. For instance, in the LINKS course, 3–4 couples sit at each table with couples taking turns engaging in an interactive exercise or practicing a relationship skill in front of their table group. Benefits of this approach include mutual accountability, comradery, role modeling, and positive feedback from peers. Afterwards, the instructor processes most of these table activities by asking for a volunteer to stand, introduce a partner from their table, and share what he or she really liked about what that partner had said/did in the activity. This approach to processing activities generates a positive environment, provides encouraging feedback to couples that can increase a sense of pride in their relationship, and helps the volunteers to practice restatements, a basic communication skill.

The PICK program also utilizes many table group activities (with 5–9 individuals at each table). A few of the many activities include discussing questions assigned from the participant workbooks, making a family tree of what participants would like to repeat, not repeat, and revise in their future marriage from their own family of origin, making posters of the specific personality characteristics, values, and lifestyle preferences that should be explored in a dating relationship with indications of what would be considered deal-breakers or non-negotiables, and writing out individual goals for improving one's dating relationships and emotional management. The instructor often facilitates processing of the group activities by having volunteers from groups explain to the rest of the class what they generated in their group interaction. This creates an opportunity for participants to teach and learn from each other, increasing the ownership of the material.

Both PICK and LINKS have numerous workbooks for specific populations with only minor alterations to the content of the overall courses. The various workbooks of the PICK course include the basic adult 5-lesson, the young adult 5- or 10-lesson, the military 5-lesson, the faith-based 10-lesson, and the domestic violence 5-lesson. The workbooks for the LINKS course include the basic 5-lesson, the military 5-lesson, and the faith-based 10-lesson. Program materials for both PICK and LINKS come in English, Spanish, and Chinese languages.

The concepts of *relationship development* and partner selection are elucidated from the RAM in the five sessions of the PICK program outlined in *Table 15.1*. The first session provides an overview of the RAM; the second and third sessions expand what one needs to get to know and explore about a partner (FACES); the fourth and fifth sessions continue to move through the RAM with the former explaining trust and rely, and the latter exploring commitment and touch.

TABLE 15.1 PICK a Partner Program Session Descriptions

Session	Title and Description	RAM Dynamic
1	**A bird's eye view of dating** Participants learn to identify the characteristics of difficult partners in dating relationships, review the major social shifts affecting dating practices, cultivate a belief in the need for partner-selection education, develop an understanding of what makes a relationship safe, gain a formula for getting to know a dating partner, and differentiate between healthy and unhealthy relationships by using the RAM.	**Know**

Session	Title and Description	RAM Dynamic

2   **You can't marry Jethro without gettin' the Clampetts**   **Know**
Participants discover how falling in love can create
tunnel vision and the factors that reinforce this
common experience; they define and describe the
necessary ingredients for effectively changing negative
or unhealthy past personal patterns; they learn
the first two of the five areas they need to **know**
about a dating partner: first, the understanding of a
dating partner's **F**amily background is developed by
exploring the ways participants have been shaped by
past family experiences; second, the importance of the
conscience for positive marital outcomes is explained,
with a practical plan for examining during the dating
process the **A**ttitudes and actions that reflect one's
conscience.

3   **The ingredients for a lasting relationship**   **Know**
Participants continue to explore the last three areas to get
to **know** about a prospective partner: first, they discuss
the importance of **C**ompatibility in three key areas:
personality, values, and lifestyles; second, they generate
Examples of the relationship patterns with others that are
vital to examine in a dating partner; and finally, they learn
and practice the **S**kills of healthy communication and
conflict resolution.

4   **Why is it that expectations lead to disappointments?**   **Trust/Rely**
Participants learn a practical definition of **trust** and how
trust can be developed in safe ways, and what it means
to **rely** on another; they deepen their understanding
and self-reflection of three common causes of
unhealthy relationship patterns; they generate examples
of eight characteristics of a trustworthy/reliable person;
and develop a practical approach for determining the
pace of investing trust and reliance on a prospective
partner.

5   **Put the horse before the cart**   **Commit/ Touch**
Participants generate the qualities of ideal **commitment**,
the risks of staying committed too long in an
unhealthy dating relationship, and the differences in the
commitment to marry versus cohabit; they examine some
of the potential risks of cohabitation; they learn about
the emotional and physical bonding effects of sexual
chemistry and **touch**; and they examine some of the
ways that sexual practices before marriage impact marital
outcomes.

The LINKS program also teaches the RAM, but applies it to couples in committed relationships with an emphasis on *relationship maintenance*. Each of the five sessions develop the concepts, skills, and practical activities of one of the dynamic bonds of the RAM. Couples practice using the RAM as a format for assessing their relationship and setting goals in regular meetings called "huddles." The five sessions of the LINKS program are described in Table 15.2.

TABLE 15.2 LINKS Session Descriptions

Session	Title and Description	RAM Dynamic
1	**Relentlessly pursuing intimacy** Couples learn the RAM and how it helps to visualize the bonds of closeness and intimacy in their relationships; they cultivate an understanding and desire to become *relationship managers* who put continued effort in building and *running* the closeness and intimacy in their relationships; they develop an understanding of what makes a relationship safe and how a relationship develops vulnerabilities; they discuss their talk times and the need to "stay in the **know**" in their relationship; and they learn and practice the components of healthy communication.	**Know**
2	**Respectfully cultivating trust** Couples discuss the meaning of **trust**; they learn what it means to live with a partner in the home and a partner in one's head (how to keep a good attitude toward a partner); they generate the ways that a negative attitude toward a partner can develop into deep resentments, and practical plans of reframing and solution-oriented approaches for getting out of a resentment and back to a positive attitude; they develop a plan and visual picture for how to successfully handle conflicts; they explore causes of a broken trust, its impact, and the processes of forgiving and rebuilding trust.	**Trust**
3	**Reciprocally meeting needs** Couples develop the belief that mutual need fulfillment will strengthen the bond of marriage and deepen the character of each partner; they discuss the ways they **rely** on each other and work toward an agreement on the roles and division of responsibilities in their marriage and family; they establish a regular plan for handling their finances in mutually agreeable ways; they learn the 10 top activities that foster intimacy in the togetherness of a relationship; and they conduct a relationship meeting called a huddle	**Rely**

Session	Title and Description	RAM Dynamic
	in which they use the RAM to evaluate their communication (*know*), attitudes toward, appreciations of, and apologies to each other (*trust*), support of each other and mutually fulfilling activities with the top 10 list (*rely* and *touch*), and set some practical goals to achieve before their next huddle (*commit*).	
4	**Resiliently charting your course** Couples discuss ideal **commitment** in marriage, and the ways that they carry each other in their hearts; they learn a practical definition of commitment and the ways that it increases resiliency in a marriage relationship; they learn a model of resiliency and then use it to discuss times that they successfully worked through challenges in resilient ways.	Commit
5	**Romantically renewing your union** Couples gain working definitions of the sex drive and sexual arousal; they generate a list of causes of change in the sexual drive or sexual arousal; they explore differences between their sex drives and what creates arousal, and set practical goals for growing in their sexual relationship; they discuss their affectionate **touch**, romantic times, and set goals for new adventures; they identify six topics to discuss about their sexual relationship.	Touch

Cultural Implications

There is very little research on the marriages of ethnically diverse populations, or how they understand the concepts of love, trust, reliance, commitment, and intimacy (Madathil & Benshoff, 2008). So it is possible that the way the RAM and the constructs that constitute the RAM are perceived may vary among individuals of different cultures. However, the RAM has resonated with all cultures that have been exposed to it in the PICK and LINKS programs. For instance, both relationship education programs have been translated into Spanish and Mandarin and have been used extensively among Spanish- and Chinese-speaking individuals and couples. Additionally, both programs have been funded and promoted by the government in Singapore, a predominantly Chinese population (see www.lovethinks.com).

However, it is possible that someone of a different cultural background may use different terms for the constructs in the RAM and/or place varying levels of importance on them. For example, the importance placed on "chemistry" or "intimacy" was discussed by unmarried 22- to 29-year-olds in India who are set to have either arranged or self-selected marriages. These individuals placed importance on intimacy and chemistry but felt that in arranged marriages the progression and development of intimacy would occur after commitment (Netting, 2010). While this finding is not completely different from what the PICK course asserts, the understanding of the constructs of *touch* and *commitment* may be defined and valued differently.

PICK is designed to address numerous issues in dating and mate selection that have occurred with the rise of individualism predominately from the influence of Western culture. Therefore, cultures that continue to practice arranged marriages would most likely believe that parents are responsible for some of what the PICK attributes to the agenda of singles. Another example is that the role of sex among collectivist cultures seems to be prioritized differently than among individualistic cultures. Specifically, collectivist cultures view the primary function of sex as an existential responsibility toward the preservation of the human species. The second function is connected to pleasure and the third function of sex is relational (Smith & Montilla, 2010).

However, the apparent universality of the five constructs of the RAM provide potential cultural applications of the PICK and LINKS programs in which cultural nuances can actually be depicted on the RAM. An example of this was a PICK training I conducted in Singapore which included a number of professional marriage matchmakers. Their culture did not practice strict arranged marriages, but it did have a tradition of singles seeking guidance and accountability with a professional matchmaker. They modified some of the material in the course to be used in their consultations with singles, but found the RAM to be an excellent visual that had the potential of depicting what they would consider healthy and unhealthy relationship development. So their guiding principles for the RAM were a little different than what was in the PICK course, but the same constructs or dynamic bonds described in the RAM also occurred in their relationships.

The lack of research on love, marriage, and its related constructs among ethnically diverse populations warrants significant further study. Additionally, future research on the PICK and LINKS courses should explore the applicability of those courses and the RAM with ethnically diverse populations.

Evidence-based Research and Evaluation

The PICK program has been evaluated among several different populations, including single Army soldiers, youth, singles-again, and low-income populations. The findings of these evaluations have demonstrated that the PICK program increases confidence and knowledge about the dating and partner selection process, increases judgment and discernment of a dating partner, increases intentionality in pacing a new relationship, and increases boundary setting in new relationships.

The PICK program has been used in military settings and specifically within the Army's Strong Bonds Program since 2001. Van Epp et al. (2008) conducted a quasi-experimental study among single Army soldiers to evaluate the effectiveness of PICK using a retrospective pre-post design and control group. The study included 272 single Army soldiers at Fort Jackson and the Defense Language Institute; 123 participants voluntarily completed the PICK program and questionnaire and 149 completed the control group questionnaire. Findings demonstrated that the participants of the PICK program espoused healthier beliefs about marriage following completion of the course. The program participants also reported that they felt more knowledgeable about how to choose a healthy partner and more confident about how to develop a relationship in a safe way. Finally these participants reported an increase in their relationship development skills and knowledge.

A retreat format of the PICK program was also evaluated among 86 4-H youth from urban and rural counties (Brower, MacArthur, Bradford, Albrecht, & Bunnell, 2012). The participants were, on average, 16.6 (SD = 1.24) years old and predominantly female (71%). A retrospective pre-post test design was used and the results indicated that the participants demonstrated a significant increase in their relationship development skills, a positive and significant increase in listening and conflict resolution skills, and an increase in relationship problem-solving skills.

Finally, ongoing evaluation efforts of the PICK program are being conducted for the Atlanta, Georgia, offices of Bethany Christian Services, an international adoption agency with adoption and family services in 15 countries (Bethany Christian Services, 2014). To date, over 228 participants have been taught the PICK program in the Atlanta region. Of these participants, 89% are African American and 58% had an income less than 5,000 per year. The evaluation efforts include a true pre-post test design with 3-month follow-up. The results have found that the program participants have shown a significant increase in placing importance on the key areas to get to know about a future partner, a significant increase in relationship development skills, and an increase in positive beliefs about marriage. At the 3-month follow-up, participants reported significant and continuing effects of the PICK program as well as positive behavioral changes such as ending harmful relationships, making an effort to get to know their partners more deeply, enforcing sexual boundaries, enforcing boundaries in how much they trust their partner, limiting how much they rely on a partner early in the relationship, talking with friends about the PICK course, increasing awareness of things they want to improve in their relationships, and making positive changes in their relationships.

The LINKS course is part of an ongoing examination by Marriage Works! Ohio, a grant-funded coalition of diverse organizations united to help build healthy families throughout the Miami Valley of Ohio by providing marriage and relationship education for couples (Marriage Works! Ohio, 2014). The participants of the LINKS program completed a pre-test in addition to a retrospective pre- and post-test evaluation and the comparison group only completed the pre-test. A total of 138 participants were in the program group and 285 were in the comparison group. A comparison between the comparison and program group revealed significant differences in ethnicity and yearly income. Specifically, there was a higher proportion of African Americans (72% vs. 27%) and Caucasians (63% vs. 37%) in the comparison group and a higher proportion of Hispanics in the program group (36% vs. 64%; χ^2 = 9.77; p <. 05). Additionally, a higher proportion of those earning $39,999 or less came from the comparison group (χ^2 = 34.79; p < .001). There were no significant differences in age, level of education, or gender.

The latest results of the LINKS evaluation suggested that participants reported a significant positive increase in relationship skills and relationship satisfaction. Relationship skills were assessed using a 10-item scale that asked the participants how frequently they used various communication and conflict resolution skills on a Likert-type scale ranging from *almost never to very frequently* (α = 0.89). This scale was developed specifically to assess the effectiveness of the LINKS program with Marriage Works! Ohio in collaboration with the developer of the LINKS program. The comparison group completed the same measure and the program group completed a pre-test in addition to a retrospective pre-post assessment.

Results indicated that there was no significant difference between the comparison group scores and the program group pre-test scores. There also was no significant instructor effect found, which suggests that results were consistent regardless of who taught the course. Furthermore when looking at the composite scores, there was not a significant difference between the program group's pre-test scores and their retrospective pre-scores (pre-test M = 28.51 SD = 5.85; retrospective pre-test M = 28.30 SD = 5.95, t (124) = −0.43, p = 0.67). However, when the individual pre-test and retrospective pre-test scores were examined, each of the scores was significant in that participants rated that they used healthy communication and conflict resolution skills more often on the pre-test than they did on the retrospective pre-test.

When comparing the program group's pre-test scores to the post-test scores, the results found a significant program effect, indicating more frequent use of healthy communication and conflict resolution skills following the delivery of the LINKS program (pre-test M = 28.19 SD = 6.00; post-test M = 37.28 SD = 5.80, t (130) = −16.46, p < .0001). Furthermore, all but one item ("*do you and your partner fix a conflict with only sex*") showed statistically significant improvement in the expected direction following the delivery of the LINKS program. If the results had been presented using the retrospective pre- and post-test scores, all items would have been significant in the expected direction. The retrospective pre-test score and true pre-test score on the item "*how often do you and your partner fix a conflict with only sex*" suggest that participants underestimated how often they use sex to fix a conflict prior to taking the LINKS course.

Relationship satisfaction was measured using a 17-item scale on which participants rated their level of satisfaction with various areas of their relationship on a 6-point Likert-type scale ranging from *very dissatisfied to very satisfied* (α = 0.95). This scale was developed specifically for use at the coalition in Dayton in collaboration with the developer of the LINKS program. The comparison group completed the same scale. The scale assessed specific areas of the relationship and the participant's level of satisfaction with those areas, for example, overall relationship satisfaction, how much time the couple spends together, trust in the partner, how affection is shown, the sexual relationship, and equity in the relationship. These areas were measured because they are specific areas that are discussed in the LINKS program.

There were no significant differences between the program and comparison group on pre-test scores. Multivariate analyses, however, revealed a significant program instructor effect F (17, 170) = 1.33 (p < .01; partial = η^2 .16). While this is not surprising given that 13 different instructors taught the LINKS program, the effect size would be classified as small (Cohen, 1977).

Overall, there was a significant program effect on the pre- and post-test scores, indicating more relationship satisfaction following the delivery of the LINKS program (pre-test M = 68.73 SD = 17.04; post-test M = 77.34 SD = 13.50, t (131) = −6.09, p < .0001). Furthermore, each item showed statistically significant improvement in the expected direction following the delivery of the LINKS program.

To date, the evaluations of the PICK and LINKS programs have been positive. Overall, the PICK program has demonstrated that it increases participants' knowledge and confidence about the dating and partner selection process, increases judgment and discernment of a partner and what needs to be explored when getting to know a partner, increases intentionality when pacing a relationship, and increases boundary setting in a developing relationship. The LINKS course has been shown to increase positive relationship behaviors such as healthy communication, conflict resolution skills, and the behaviors of relationship maintenance. Furthermore, the LINKS course has been shown to increase participants' overall relationship satisfaction as well as satisfaction with specific areas of the relationship.

Professional Preparation and Training Issues

Both the PICK and LINKS programs have two methods of instructor certification: live training and out of the box training. For *Live training*, each participant must purchase the course Instructor Certification Packet (ICP) in addition to attending the live training by Dr. Van Epp or a Master Instructor. And for *Out of the box training*, each participant must purchase an Instructor Certification Packet, watch the instructor certification DVD course, and complete an online test. The Instructor Certification Packet (ICP) for PICK and LINKS contains the same arrangement of materials, but for the respective courses. The only exception is that the PICK ICP includes a copy of the book, *How to Avoid Falling in Love with a Jerk*. An ICP includes a:

1. DVD instructor certification course by Dr. Van Epp
2. DVD course of Dr. Van Epp teaching the program to participants
3. Instructor lesson plans
4. PowerPoint presentation that is synchronized with the lesson plans
5. Sample workbook
6. Relationship Attachment Model trifold board (2' × 3') to use when facilitating a class.

Once certified, instructors receive discounts on workbook orders and gain access to a password-protected section of the website, www.lovethinks.com. Each program has its own "instructor section" that includes numerous free downloads for instructors to use when teaching the course. Some of the free materials include supplemental lessons on specific topics, additional lesson plans for specific versions (i.e., faith-based lesson plans, Spanish lesson plans, abbreviated lesson plans), additional PowerPoints for different versions (i.e., military, faith-based, youth), suggestions to supplement each session, delivery format possibilities, additional group activities, and promotional posters and brochures.

Conclusion

PICK and LINKS are two relationship education programs that utilize the Relationship Attachment Model (RAM) as a framework for their sessions because all of the content in these programs is chunked within the five constructs of the model (know, trust, rely, commit, and touch). PICK applies the RAM to *relationship development* and partner selection, embedding the five areas to explore in a relationship (FACES) in the "know" construct. The safe zone, a guiding principle about the interaction of the five constructs in the RAM, is used to explain the way to build a new relationship with minimal vulnerability.

The LINKS program is like a sequel to PICK because it applies the RAM to *relationship maintenance*. Maintaining a relationship is essential because life will naturally impact one's relationship, resulting in fluctuations of closeness. However, the guiding principle for couples to successfully maintain closeness in their relationship is to regularly assess these fluctuations by creating a profile with the five constructs in the RAM, and then set small goals to strengthen the dynamic bonds which are deficit. Each session of the LINKS program unpacks one of the five dynamic bonds of the RAM, explaining the concepts and practicing the skills that strengthen that bond in a close relationship. The primary takeaway of LINKS is a regular meeting (*huddles*) in which couples use the RAM to assess their relationship and set goals to keep strengthening their bonds of closeness.

Key Points

- The five interactive dynamic bonds of the Relationship Attachment Model (RAM) provide a picture of both relationship development for new relationships and relationship maintenance for established relationships.
- The PICK program for singles describes two major aspects of romantic relationship development: the five key areas to explore in a dating relationship that foreshadow what a partner will be like in a committed or marriage relationship, and an application of the RAM for building a relationship in a healthy and safe way ("safe zone").
- The guiding principle for successful relationship maintenance in the LINKS program is for couples to regularly assess their relationship with the RAM and to set practical goals to strengthen and balance the deficits in each of the five dynamic bonds represented by the RAM.
- The rationale for providing a plan for partner selection in the PICK program is based on several major social shifts.
- The PICK program has been empirically shown to increase confidence in dating and partner selection, understanding of the necessary areas to explore in a potential partner, intentionality in pacing a new relationship, and boundary setting in key areas of relationship development.
- The LINKS program has been empirically shown to increase communication skills, feelings of satisfaction and love, confidence for positively resolving conflicts, and the understanding and behaviors of successful relationship maintenance.
- All of the content of both the PICK and LINKS programs are chunked in the RAM which enhances the participants' memorization and application of the content of the programs.
- The instructor facilitation techniques for both PICK and LINKS includes small group exercises and discussion, activities, class discussions, and brief lectures.
- The RAM has been positively received by several ethnically diverse populations which has provided a culturally relevant framework for the content of the PICK and LINKS programs.
- The steps for becoming a certified instructor can be accomplished by attending a live training or distant learning at home.

Discussion Questions

1. What does Worthington mean by the golden thread that holds partners together?
2. How does the RAM portray relationship bonds?
3. What is the unique core of the LINKS course and how can this help couples with their relationship?
4. What are two objectives of the PICK course?
5. What are two objectives of the LINKS course?

6. What is the concept of chunking and how does it apply to the PICK and LINKS programs utilizing the RAM as a framework for categorizing the content of the courses?
7. What are the benefits of how the LINKS course engages couples in small table group activities, and how does the instructor process those activities?
8. What are some ways that the RAM can be used to help explain cultural differences when using PICK or LINKS in diverse settings?
9. What are eight positive outcomes of participants of the PICK program?

References and Further Readings

Amato, P., & Previti, D. (2009). People's reasons for divorcing: Gender, social class, the life course, and adjustment. *Journal of Family Issues, 24*, 602–626.

Bachand, L., & Caron, C. (2001). Ties that bind: Qualitative study of happy long-term marriages. *Contemporary Family Therapy, 23*, 105–121.

Baumeister, R., & Leary, M. (1995). The need to belong: Desire for interpersonal attachments as a fundamental human motivation. *Psychological Bulletin, 117*, 497–529.

Bethany Christian Services. (2014). *Bethany Christian Services: Relationship Education Evaluation Summary.* Atlanta, GA: Cutlip, M.

Birtchnell, J., & Kennard, J. (1984). Early and current factors associated with poor-quality marriage. *Social Psychiatry, 19*, 31–40.

Bodenmann, G., Charvoz, L., Bradbury, T., Bertoni, A., Iafrate, R., Giuliani, C., Banse, R., & Behling, J. (2006). Attractors and barriers to divorce: A retrospective study in three European countries. *Journal of Divorce and Remarriage, 45*, 1–23.

Brower, N., MacArthur, S., Bradford, K., Albrecht, C., & Bunnell, J. (2012). Got dating: Outcomes of a teen 4-H relationship retreat. *Journal of Youth Development: Bridging Research and Practice, 7*(1), 118–124.

Brown, R.L., & DiMeo, J. (2007). Research Report Institute of Insurance and Pension Research. University of Waterloo, Ontario, Canada.

Busby, D., Carroll, J., & Willoughby, B. (2010). Compatibility or restraint? The effects of sexual timing on marriage relationships. *Journal of Family Psychology, 24*, 766–774.

Cohen, J. (1977). Statistical power analysis for the behavioral sciences. New York, NY: Routledge.

Cutlip, M. (2013). *A qualitative examination of the Relationship Attachment Model (RAM) with married individuals.* Doctoral dissertation. Retrieved from ProQuest Dissertations and Theses. (Accession Order No. akron1365099833).

DeLongis, A., Folkman, S., & Lazarus, R.S. (1988). The impact of daily stress on health and mood: Psychological and social resources as mediators. *Journal of Personality and Social Psychology, 54*, 486–495. doi:10.1037/0022-3514.54.3.486

Fowers, B., Lyons, E., Montel, K., & Shaked, N. (2001). Positive illusions about marriage among married and single individuals. *Journal of Family Psychology, 15*, 95–109.

Freitas, D. (2008). *Sex and the soul: Juggling sexuality, spirituality, romance and religion on America's college campuses.* New York, NY: Oxford University Press.

Freitas, D. (2013). *The end of sex: How hookup culture is leaving a generation unhappy, sexually unfulfilled, and confused about intimacy.* New York, NY: Basic Books.

Gardner, S., Giese, K., & Parrott, S. (2004). Evaluation of the Connections: Relationships and marriage curriculum. *Family Relations, 53*, 521–527.

Glenn, N., & Marquardt, E. (2001). *Hooking up, hanging out, and hoping for Mr. Right: College women on dating and mating today.* New York, NY: Institute for American Values.

Gobet, F., Lane, P., Croker, S., Cheng, P., Jones, G., Oliver, I., & Pine, J. (2001). Chunking mechanisms in human learning. *Trends in Cognitive Sciences, 5*, 236–243.

Goldsmith, E. (2007). Stress fatigue and social support in the work and family context. *Journal of Loss and Trauma, 12*, 155–169.

Gottman, J., & Krokoff, L. (1989). Marital interaction and satisfaction: A longitudinal view. *Journal of Consulting and Clinical Psychology, 57*, 47–52.

Grover, K., Russell, C., Schumm, W., & Paff-Bergen, L. (1985). Mate selection processes and marital satisfaction. *Family Relations, 34*, 383–386.

Holmberg, D., Orbuch, T., & Veroff, J. (2004). *Thrice-told tales: Married couples tell their stories.* Mahwah, NJ: Lawrence Erlbaum.

Kamp Dush, C., & Amato, P. (2005). Consequences of relationship status and quality for subjective well-being. *Journal of Social and Personal Relationships, 22*, 607–627. doi:10.1177/026540750506438

Kurdek, L. (1991). Predictors of increases in marital distress in newlywed couples: A 3-year prospective longitudinal study. *Developmental Psychology, 27*, 627–636.

Kurdek, L. (1993). Predicting marital dissolution: A 5-year prospective longitudinal study of newlywed couples. *Journal of Personality and Social Psychology, 64*, 221–242.

Madathil, J., & Benshoff, J. (2008). Importance of marital characteristics and marital satisfaction: A comparison of Asian Indians in arranged marriages and Americans in marriages of choice. *Family Journal: Counseling and Therapy for Couples and Families, 16*, 222–230.

Markman, H., Floyd, F., Stanley, S., & Storaasli, R. (1988). Prevention of marital distress: A longitudinal investigation. *Journal of Consulting and Clinical Psychology, 56*, 210–217.

Markman, H., Renick, M., Floyd, F., Stanley, S., & Clements, M. (1993). Preventing marital distress through communication and conflict management training: A 4- and 5-year follow-up. *Journal of Consulting and Clinical Psychology, 61*, 70–77.

Marriage Works! Ohio. (2014). *Marriage Works! Ohio: Relationship Education Evaluation Summary.* Dayton, OH: Cutlip, M.

McAdams, D., & Bryant, F. (1987). Intimacy motivation and subjective mental health in a nationwide sample. *Journal of Personality, 55*, 395–413. doi:10.1111/j.14676494.1987.tb00444.x

Miller, G. (1956). The magical number seven, plus or minus two: Some limits on our capacity for processing information. *Psychological Review, 63*, 81–97.

Murray, S., Holmes, J., & Griffin, D. (1996). The self-fulfilling nature of positive illusions in romantic relationships: Love is not blind, but prescient. *Journal of Personality and Social Psychology, 71*, 1155–1180.

Netting, N. (2010). Marital ideoscapes in 21st-century India: Creative combinations of love and responsibility. *Journal of Family Issues, 31*, 707–726. doi:10.1177/0192513X09357555

Ponzetti, J. (2005). Family beginnings: A comparison of spouses' recollections of courtship. *Family Journal: Counseling and Therapy for Couples and Families, 13*, 132–138.

Qualter, P., & Munn, P. (2002). The separateness of social and emotional loneliness in childhood. *Journal of Child Psychology and Psychiatry, 43*, 233–244. doi:10.1111/14697610.00016

Riehl-Emede, A., Thomas, V., & Willi, J. (2003). Love: An important dimension in marital research and therapy. *Family Process, 42,* 253–267.

Robinson, L., & Blanton, I. (1993). Marital strengths in enduring marriages. *Family Relations, 42,* 38–45.

Sassler, S., Addo, F., & Lichter, D. (2012). The tempo of sexual activity and later relationship quality. *Journal of Marriage and Family, 74,* 708–725.

Smith, R., & Montilla, R. (2010). Recovering intimacy with Latino couples: Cultural, religious and gender considerations. In J. Carlson & L. Sperry (Eds.), *Recovering Intimacy in Love Relationships: A Clinician's Guide.* New York, NY: Routledge.

Stanley, S. (2003). Strengthening marriages in a skeptical culture: Issues and opportunities. *Journal of Psychology and Theology, 31,* 224–230.

Teachman, J. (2003). Premarital sex, premarital cohabitation, and the risk of subsequent marital dissolution among women. *Journal of Marriage and Family, 65,* 444–455.

Van Epp, J. (1997). *The Relationship Attachment Model.* Unpublished manuscript.

Van Epp, J. (2006). *How to avoid marrying a jerk: The foolproof way to follow your heart without losing your mind.* New York, NY: McGraw Hill.

Van Epp Cutlip, M., Futris, T., Van Epp, J., & Campbell, K. (2008). The impact of the PICK: A partner relationship education program on single Army soldiers. *Family and Consumer Sciences Research Journal, 36,* 328–349.

Waite, L., & Gallagher, M. (2000). *The case for marriage: Why married people are happier, healthier, and better off financially.* New York, NY: Doubleday.

Waite, L., Luo, Y., & Lewin, A. (2008). Marital happiness and marital stability: Consequences for psychological well-being. *Social Science Research, 38,* 201–212.

White, R., Cleland, J., & Carael, M. (2000). Links between premarital sexual behavior and extramarital intercourse: A multi-site analysis. *AIDS: Journal of the International AIDS Society, 14,* 2323–2331. Retrieved from http://journals.lww.com/aidsonline/pages/results.aspx?txtKeywords=White,%20R.,%20Cleland,%20J

Williams, A. (2013, January 11). The end of courtship. *New York Times,* p. ST1.

Worthington, E. (2005). Repairing the emotional bond: Marriage research from 1997 through early 2005. *Journal of Psychology and Christianity, 24,* 259–262.

16

YOUTH-FOCUSED RELATIONSHIP EDUCATION

Relationship Smarts Plus and Love Notes

Marline E. Pearson and Kay Reed

LEARNING GOALS

- Acquire an understanding of the history and catalysts for the recent emergence of youth-focused relationship education.
- Identify the links between the relationship needs and deficits of youth and risky behaviors—especially risky sexual behaviors.
- Recognize that relationship patterns, attitudes, expectations, and behaviors established in the teen years typically continue into early adulthood and beyond.
- Connect the dots between youthful relationship patterns and the rise in non-marital births and fragile families among young adults.
- Be familiar with the goals and key components of the comprehensive relationship education programs *Relationship Smarts PLUS* and *Love Notes*.
- Appreciate the importance of building skills, as well as employing lively, culturally relevant activities, popular media, music, and youth-generated narratives and scenarios to engage youth.
- Become acquainted with evaluation research on *Relationship Smarts PLUS* and *Love Notes*.

Introduction

This chapter focuses on **Relationship Smarts PLUS**, an evidence-based relationship skills curriculum for teenagers 13–18 years of age, and **Love Notes: Making Relationships Work** ("Love Notes"), its adaptation for older teens and young adults (16–24 years). Since *Love Notes* is developed for older youth, including young parents, it contains many of the same relationship concepts of *Relationship Smarts PLUS*, but has a stronger focus on sexual decision making and planning for sexual choices. *Relationship Smarts PLUS* is based on the results of a five-year, federally funded, rigorous evaluation with 8,000 teenagers conducted by Jennifer Kerpelman, Ph.D., at Auburn University (Kerpelman, Pittman, Adler-Baeder, Stringer, Eryigit, Cadely, & Harrell-Levy, 2010; Kerpelman, Pittman, Adler-Baeder, Eryigit, & Paulk, 2009; Kerpelman, 2007; Adler-Baeder, Kerpelman, Schramm, Higginbotham, & Paulk, 2007; Adler-Baeder & Kerpelman, 2005). Both *Relationship Smarts PLUS* and *Love Notes* are included on the National Registry of Evidence Based Programs and Practices (NREPP), a service of the Substance Abuse and Mental Health Administration (SAMHSA). *Love Notes* is currently in the fourth year of a major federal (U.S.) pregnancy prevention evaluation study in the Tier II track of innovative approaches (principal investigators: Becky Antle and Anita Barbee at University of Louisville).

Theoretical Foundations and History

The idea of relationship education for youth on an evidenced-based platform is relatively new. Although it makes intuitive sense to educate youth on forming and maintaining healthy romantic relationships, until recently curricula were not available and there were few schools, community-based youth-serving organizations, or religious support settings where it was given serious attention. By the early 2000s that began to change. A brief history of the emergence of youth-focused relationship education curricula follows.

By the 1990s, empirical research and programs on adult relationships and marriage were more widespread and available to the public. A big boost came in 1997 with the formation of **Coalition of Marriage, Family, and Couples Educators** (CMFCE) that brought together researchers, program developers, and practitioners. CMFCE made research and skill-based education widely available to couples and curated information out of the research labs and clinical offices into user-friendly and affordable form for adult couples. CMFCE inspired many of us to ask, *Why not start younger with healthy relationship education?* That idea became ever more pressing with the realization that many young people had fewer and fewer models of healthy relationships and healthy marriages.

But perhaps the strongest impetus for developing youth relationship education programs came from a growing sense (especially from those who work with and teach at-risk youth) that there was a missing piece in prevention work. Yes, many youth receive drug education, sex education, and pregnancy/STI-HIV prevention programs. Some youth also receive services to help them with school completion, substance abuse, and other issues, including those referred to family services, foster care, and the juvenile justice system.

Despite these important interventions and prevention programs, poor love choices have an uncanny way of derailing the progress a young person might otherwise make. There was a growing belief among early pioneers in youth relationship education that young people's love lives were not neutral—they had the capacity to help or hinder youth as they move toward adulthood.

Many who work with youth know that an important social determinant of risky behaviors is found in troubled pasts and troubled relationships—especially in family, but also among peers and romantic partners. Indeed, the Adverse Childhood Experiences (ACE) Study has offered compelling correlations between a number of adverse childhood experiences and risky sexual behaviors (Felitti, Anda, Nordenberg, Williamson, Spitz, Edwards, Koss, & Marks, 1998). Scientific studies aside, most of those working with youth can attest to the reality that poor relationship choices often go hand in hand with poor sexual choices. Yet, how to form and maintain healthy relationships, *despite one's past or one's lack of models*, is an area of primary prevention that is not addressed, or addressed only superficially. We teach about sex, but little about the larger context in which sex occurs—relationships.

Addressing sexual behaviors primarily within a health context of risks and protection came into question. Bio-reproductive and contraceptive and condom information and access, while essential, do not automatically translate into usage. Likewise, teaching refusal or negotiation skills alone does not necessarily translate into the *motivation* to engage those skills to refuse, delay, or to negotiate the consistent use of protection while of high school age or beyond.

A revealing statistic to consider in this regard is that while the U.S. has made significant progress in bringing down *teenage* pregnancy rates (overall over 50% since 1990 (Kost & Henshaw, 2012; Santelli, Lindberg, Finer, & Singh, 2007), among older youth (over 19 and into the 20s) there has been an almost equal increase (41%) during the same time in unplanned pregnancies among older youth (Mosher, Jones, & Abma, 2012). And even with the overall decline in unplanned pregnancy among teenagers, there are serious disparities in rates among minority and disadvantaged teens.

Maybe something important is missing that can help explain the disparities. And maybe this missing piece explains why the conventional health-based approaches are not remembered all that well beyond the high school age years as unplanned pregnancies are growing dramatically among those in their early 20s, and especially those with less education. Just waiting until one is older to have an unplanned pregnancy is not without serious risks. Unplanned pregnancy among young adults is linked to relationship turbulence, reduced likelihood of moving into a stable union, poorer relationship quality, and worsened child outcomes (Suellentrop, 2008).

Here is a story that helps illustrate that the missing piece might have something to do with a knowledge and skills deficit in forming healthy relationships. It is about two 18-year-old girls in a well-respected youth development program targeting at-risk teens. These girls had been with the program for four years, since about age 14. They had had the best of prevention education. They were thoroughly knowledgeable about STIs/HIV, pregnancy, contraceptives and condoms and had access to them. They had been educated about date rape and dating violence. They had drug education, help with school and with conflict with parents. In fact, these girls became the star peer educators, even producing materials for teens themselves. In short, they had had the best of what prevention efforts and comprehensive sex education had to offer. They were considered success stories for the program. But, at age 18, both girls found themselves pregnant—one with a guy who was already out of the picture before the child's birth and the other in an unhealthy relationship. Something was missing.

There was little these two girls retained from these educational programs that was truly positive and proactive. They had no "North Star" for their intimate lives—no vision of or expectation for a healthy relationship, no knowledge or skills for how to build one, how to handle the chemistry of attraction, or for choosing partners wisely. They had no "North Star" for meaningful sex, commitment, nor any understanding of how an unplanned pregnancy outside of a committed healthy adult union carries serious risks for child and parents.

These two girls had been taught what to avoid, what to say "no" to, and how to protect themselves with condoms and contraceptives. But they lived in a world of lowered expectations for sex, for love, for commitment, and for partners. They had no models of healthy romantic relationships, no idea of how to choose a partner, and no idea how to build and maintain a healthy relationship.

If the popular culture says sex is no big deal, and establishing a committed union /marriage before babies is no big deal, and that fathers don't really matter; and if youth haven't been encouraged to think about a context for sex that is personally meaningful and protective of health *and heart*, then why not slide quickly into relationships and why not slide into sex? And why not have a baby before establishing a healthy union/marriage?

The developers of youth-based relationship education want to assist youth in cultivating a "North Star" for healthy romantic relationships, and to help them understand and practice the skills needed to realize them. Relationship skill education supports youth in making wiser sexual choices that are protective of their meaningful aspirations. Comprehensive relationship education can support youth in navigating the terrain of youthful romantic relationships and in making real decisions, versus *sliding*, when it comes to partners, relationships, sex, and the timing of family formation.

More and more school and community programs dedicated to youth development and pregnancy prevention have embraced *Relationship Smarts PLUS* and *Love Notes* as critical pieces to their missions. For example, youth and workforce development organizations such as *Youth Build U.S.A.* (with 225 affiliates across the U.S.) and *Opportunities Industrialization Centers of South Florida* have embraced *Relationship Smarts PLUS* and *Love Notes* as an important part of their programming. These organizations have seen how troubled love lives and unplanned pregnancies derail the youth they work with despite the gains they make in other areas of their lives. Additionally, they understand that the "soft skills" of emotional intelligence and self-regulation help young people succeed in the workplace. While focusing on romantic relationships, the skills learned in *Love Notes* are frequently generalized to various sites with positive results.

Similarly some schools have fully integrated *Relationship Smarts PLUS* and *Love Notes* into their health and sex education classes, as well as into their school-age parent programs. The states of Georgia and Utah have integrated *Love Notes* and *Relationship Smarts PLUS* into their *Personal Responsibility and Education Program* (PREP). They are adding relationship skills to their programming because they have found that young people who seek intimacy with a partner do not understand that true intimacy is more than physical. When they do understand how relationships develop and how intimacy is more than physical, they will often make different decisions about their sexual behaviors.

The *Strengthening Relationships/Strengthening Families* program run by Texas State University uses *Love Notes* with its young parents in addition to its usual parenting classes. They understand that relational turbulence is often the cause of Adverse Childhood Experiences (ACES) in children and that once young parents understand how their love lives impact their children, then their relational behaviors change (Toews & Yazedjian, 2012).

Some community colleges, knowing that troubled relationships and unplanned pregnancy are leading reasons for leaving school, have picked up relationship education programs such as *Love Notes* as part of their student success initiatives, for example Madison Area Technical College's *Gateway to College* (2014a) and *TRiO Student Support Services* (2014b).

"You cannot," wrote Jonathan Swift, "reason a person out of something he has not reasoned into." To endure, life lessons must be adopted from within. These two evidenced-based programs advance that process—addressing positive youth development, life skills, dating violence, and pregnancy prevention all within a robust framework of building knowledge and skills for developing and maintaining healthy relationships.

Theoretical foundations. *Relationship Smarts PLUS* and *Love Notes* are based upon three behavioral theories/approaches: (1) **Theory of Reasoned Action/ Planned Action**: focuses on addressing beliefs and values that influence decisions young people make about relationships, sexual behavior, and personal development; (2) **Social Learning Theory**: addresses beliefs about likely results of actions; aims to increase confidence, and behavioral capability to take action; and (3) a **Youth Development perspective**: emphasizes providing youth with the actual resources and skills they need to experience healthy development. The emphasis is on building skills—building confidence, the self-awareness, and the ability to put the skills in action.

Needs Assessment and Target Audience

The target audience for *Relationship Smarts PLUS* is teens in the 8th to 12th grade. *Love Notes* is geared to older teens and young adults (16–24 years of age) including young parents. Although most of the content of both curricula is highly relevant for all youth, it is especially engaging for disadvantaged and minority youth, particularly, young males. Both curricula are used in school and after-school settings, community-based youth-serving organizations, and other institutional settings such as juvenile corrections, as well as programs serving young parents.

Youthful romantic relationships are a subject of importance to all those concerned with adolescent development and their successful transition to adulthood. The start of romantic relationships marks a key developmental step in adolescence. The majority of teens of high school age have been involved in a romantic relationship (Carver, Joyner, & Udry, 2003), and almost one-half of high school-aged teens report that they have had at least one sexual experience (Centers for Disease Control and Prevention, 2008). Recent research notes that how teens define these relationships, how they navigate them, and how they communicate within them influence when teens first have sex or whether they use condoms and contraceptives (Ford, Sohn, & Lepkowski, 2001; Girodano, Manning, & Longmore, 2005; Manlove, Ryan, & Franzetta, 2007). That, in turn, relates to a youth's likelihood of having or fathering a child.

Importantly, the *habits of heart* take root during adolescence. The relationship patterns, attitudes, expectations, and behaviors established in the teen years are likely to continue into early adulthood and beyond (Furman & Shaffer, 2003; Carver, Joyner, & Udry, 2003). Will those relationships be healthy or unhealthy, safe or dangerous? Will they be linked with risky sexual behaviors or an unplanned pregnancy? The answers to these questions will have a strong bearing not only on school completion and employment, but on the well-being of the next generation of children.

It is time to connect the dots between teen relationships and sexual behaviors and the dramatic increase of fragile families (defined as families formed with the birth of a child to unmarried parents). This trend towards more and more fragile families has dramatically increased child poverty. Research has documented that fragile family circumstances are often associated with increased relationship transitions and turbulence, multiple partner fertility and family complexity, and poorer child outcomes (McLanahan & Carlson, 2002). This troubling trend can be partially addressed through healthy relationship skills programs, such as Oklahoma's *Building Strong Families* (BSF) project (Campbell & Wood, 2002). But, an important opportunity is lost if we wait for engagement or marriage to offer relationship and marriage education (RME); similarly if we wait until the birth of the first child.

But there is more in terms of needs assessment. The most powerful evidence of need comes from youth themselves. Numerous surveys of youth from all socio-economic groups have indicated a strong desire for attention to relationships. MEE Productions (2002) with the National Campaign to Prevent Teen and Unplanned Pregnancy produced *This Is My Reality*, an important national report on the attitudes, behaviors, and needs of urban minority youth. This production provides an inside look at Black youth's views on sex, relationships, marriage, pregnancy, and parenthood. A common refrain from youth in the report: "Talk to us about emotional risks, not just health risks." In an exit survey of a recent pregnancy prevention/condom negotiation initiative for older foster youth, attention to relationships was listed as a top unmet need. Teen focus groups convened to gather needs and interests for New York State's public health teen website, *Act for Youth*, found relationships to be the number one stated need. That 90 percent of high school seniors say that having a good marriage and family life is "extremely important" speaks to the need to address healthy relationship development (Schulenberg, Bachman, Johnston, & O'Malley, 1994).

The income and ethnic-racial disparities in teen pregnancy rates may also be a signal for innovation. Parental relationship instability is linked to the social determinants of teenage relationship and sexual behaviors. Given the declines in marriage and increases in unmarried childbearing, multiple partner fertility, and family complexity (particularly among those with less education and income) there is a need for greater attention to helping youth form and maintain healthy relationships.

Finally, the needs of young parents must be examined and addressed. Currently they get no help on their relationships whatsoever. Yet, there is an abundance of research on the connection between the quality and stability of the parental/couple relationship, parenting capacity, and child well-being. Eighty-two percent of young unmarried parents are romantically involved at the time of birth and have high hopes for a future with marriage (McLanahan, Garfinkel, & Waller, 1999; McLanahan & Beck, 2010). Most will fail. These young people need help learning the skills and strategies for healthy relationships; they need frameworks to assess the viability and safety of their relationships. They also need to learn how to choose partners more wisely next time and how to build a healthy relationship. Young parents have a critical need for relationship skills to communicate and handle conflict to co-parent effectively whether they stay together or not.

Program Goals and Objectives

Relationship Smarts PLUS and *Love Notes* are designed to build knowledge and skills for healthy relationships. Both represent a holistic and innovative approach to youth development, dating violence, and pregnancy prevention. These goals, typically in separate programs, are integrated within a comprehensive healthy relationship skills program. Both curricula build assets and strengthen protective factors while appealing to young peoples' aspirations.

The basic goals are to deepen self-awareness and future orientation; to learn what healthy relationships are and aren't, and to build the knowledge and skills for forming and maintaining healthy relationships. The emphasis on healthy relationship skills supports wiser sexual decision making and a protective capacity to avoid or exit unhealthy and unsafe relationships. New messages on pregnancy prevention that address child well-being and timing of family formation strengthen its prevention goals.

Finally, the Teen-Parent Connection activities (*Relationship Smarts PLUS*) and Trusted Adult Connection activities (*Love Notes*) provide a serious way to continue the conversations on these very important topics outside the program with caring adults in a youth's life.

Goals and Objectives

Relationship education directed at youth share similar goals and objectives:

1. Deepen self-knowledge and future orientation; employ trauma-informed strategies to examine one's past to identify personal growth and development goals, as well as clarify values and relationship expectations.
2. Decrease faulty relationship beliefs; develop a better understanding of the building blocks and components of healthy relationships.
3. Increase the ability to assess relationships; recognize unhealthy and/or dangerous relationships.
4. Develop efficacy in employing healthy relationship skills; in particular, research-based communication and conflict management skills.
5. Decrease disrespect and violence in relationships; cessation of unhealthy relationships.
6. Increase confidence and efficacy for engaging in conscious decision making and negotiation regarding relationships, sex, and the timing of family formation.
7. Delay first time sex; delay/wait longer in subsequent relationships.
8. Increase use of contraception and condoms when sexually active.
9. Increase well-being of youth.

Curriculum and Other Program Issues

Relationship Smarts PLUS contains 12 lessons designed for 8th to 12 graders. *Love Notes*, designed for 16- to 24-year-olds, including young parents, contains 13 lessons with a stronger focus on self-awareness and personal development, sexual decision making and planning for sexual choices, and family formation and parenting. These curricula are delivered entirely through activities that are informative, upbeat, fun, and engaging. Activities include drawing, sculpture, music, film, short videos, stories, poetry, role-plays, and skills practice to provide more engaging and effective learning. An interactive workbook allows youth to apply concepts to their personal lives. Both programs are successful in engaging males as well as females. The "Parent-Teen Connection" activities (*Relationship Smarts PLUS*) and the "Trusted Adult Connection" activities (*Love Notes*) for each lesson are designed to convey core material to parent or trusted adults. They serve as catalysts for conversations with caring adults on these very important issues. These connection activities provide a way to partner with parents and adults and mentors in helping youth navigate the choppy waters of youthful relationships. Activity cards, workbooks, DVDs, YouTube clips, PowerPoint slideshows for each lesson, posters, and suggested music videos and songs are available along with the instructor manual.

Relationship Smarts PLUS begins with two lessons on self-awareness, future orientation, and planning. Topics include maturity, values identification, life mapping, goal setting, and handling peer pressure.

- Lesson 1: Who Am I and Where Am I Going?
- Lesson 2: Maturity Issues and What I Value

The next five lessons focus on understanding and handling the chemistry of romantic attraction, the building blocks of healthy relationships and choosing partners wisely, ways to assess relationships, how to employ a decision-making framework, breaking up and dating violence prevention.

- Lesson 3: Attractions and Infatuation
- Lesson 4: Principles of Smart Relationships
- Lesson 5: Is It a Healthy Relationship?
- Lesson 6: Decide, Don't Slide
- Lesson 7: Dating Violence and Breaking Up

The two lessons that follow draw on communication and conflict management skills adapted for youth from the leading research-based program (PREP, see chapter 12 in this book) for adult couples. Teens examine the patterns in their own families of origin, learn to recognize the communication danger signs, and practice a complete package of skills for better communication and the safe handling of conflict.

- Lesson 8: Communication and Healthy Relationships
- Lesson 9: Communication Challenges and More Skills

The next two lessons focus on sexual decision making. Youth are inspired by stories, poetry, music, and film to identify sexual values, boundaries, and pacing for intimate involvement that are personally meaningful. They also practice refusal, negotiation, and assertiveness skills and draw on the healthy relationship skills they have learned. Then they are challenged to examine unplanned pregnancy through the eyes of a child; to consider the serious issues of unplanned pregnancy and the importance of making clear decisions about the timing of family formation.

- Lesson 10: Sexual Decision Making
- Lesson 11: Unplanned Pregnancy through the Eyes of a Child

The final lesson addresses teens and social media. This lesson challenges young people to make meaningful and informed choices about their use of social media.

- Lesson 12: Teens, Technology, and Social Media

Love Notes shares many concepts with *Relationship Smarts PLUS* with additional content on understanding yourself, pregnancy/STI prevention, family formation and co-parenting issues. There are additional DVDs and scenarios written specifically for an older youth audience that is more likely to be sexually active, including some who are raising a child.

Before addressing relationships, *Love Notes* focuses on self-examination to better understand how one's past influences one's present and to identify personal growth and development goals. In these first three lessons youth learn that healthy relationships start with the individual.

- Lesson 1: Relationships Today: defining a vision; possibility of making choices; importance of support (trusted adult).
- Lesson 2: Knowing Yourself: learning about personality style (*COLORS Personality Tool*), examining one's past and how it affects one's present; making decisions for future personal development.
- Lesson 3: My Expectations—My Future: clarifying relationship expectations; setting goals.

The following five lessons help young people, including pregnant and parenting youth, learn about healthy relationships through topics such as the chemistry of attraction, ingredients and the sequence of building blocks for healthy relationships, a deeper look at the dimensions of intimacy and how it develops, and a realistic concept of love. Youth learn what's important to find out about a person, acquire a set of guiding principles for good relationships, use an intentional, "deciding, not sliding" approach for relationship decisions, and acquire a clear assessment model for healthy and unhealthy relationships. They also learn how to deal with break-ups and move forward with special tips for parents. There is a special focus on recognizing abusive behaviors, setting high standards, and practicing skills to prevent and halt disrespectful behavior.

- Lesson 4: Attractions and Starting Relationships: understanding the brain chemistry of romantic attraction, relationship dynamics, and stages of relationships.
- Lesson 5: Principles for Smart Relationships: guiding principles for friendships and romantic relationships.
- Lesson 6: Is It a Healthy Relationship?: framework for assessing the health of a relationship.
- Lesson 7: Dangerous Love: awareness of warning signs and behaviors of abusive behavior, practice in drawing the line of respect early on, safe exiting; breaking up safely, and tips for moving forward.

- Lesson 8: Decide, Don't Slide: relationship building blocks and decision-making model.

The next two lessons focus on sexual decision making and sexual planning. Youth are inspired by stories, poetry, music, and film to identify sexual values and boundaries. They are encouraged to make decisions about the context and pacing (i.e., timing) of sexual involvement. They also practice refusal, negotiation, and assertiveness skills drawing on the healthy relationship skills they have learned. They develop informed plans for their sexual choices after receiving medically accurate information on STIs/HIV, pregnancy and contraception through engaging media and interactive activities.

- Lesson 9: Sexual Decision Making: identifying values and boundaries, defining a context and pacing for sex, developing self-efficacy in communication, negotiation, and assertiveness about sex.
- Lesson 10: Let's Plan for Choices: medically accurate knowledge of STIs, pregnancy, and contraception, develop personal plans for sexual choices, practice negotiation, assertiveness, refusal, and safe exit skills.

The next two lessons offer a state-of-the-art communication and conflict management skills package for maintaining healthy relationships adapted for youth from the leading research-based program for adult couples (PREP, University of Denver). Youth become aware of patterns that harm relationships, assess their own patterns in relationships, and practice a set of skills for effective communication, anger and emotional regulation. They learn how to recognize issues that underlie arguments and how to talk through difficult issues, and engage in problem solving.

- Lesson 11: What's Communication Got to Do with It?
- Lesson 12: Communication Challenges and More Skills

In the final lesson, youth are engaged in a deeper exploration of the consequences of unplanned pregnancy and relationship instability for children. They will also examine the role of fathers in family formation and barriers to father involvement along with co-parenting challenges. Youth develop personal success plans for education, employment, relationships, and parenting.

- Lesson 13: Unplanned Pregnancy through the Eyes of a Child

Cultural Implications

Both programs work very well with diverse and at-risk youth, but much of the content is relevant to any young person. PowerPoint slides are laden with images that represent diverse youth, including those of diverse sexual orientation. The suggested scripts in the facilitator manual have language that is LGBTQ inclusive, as is the language in scenarios for activities. Both curricula were written with the help of a large group of teens and young adults (male and female) of diverse backgrounds to provide culturally relevant contexts. These young people not only wrote most of the activity scenarios, but also contributed poetry, quotes, and narratives. Two films from *Scenarios USA*, written by teens (one, by Latino and the other by African-American teens) are included in *Love Notes* (one is included in *Relationship Smarts PLUS*). These scripts were then produced by award-winning Hollywood filmmakers. Numerous organizations and schools serving vulnerable youth have reported that both curricula are well received by their youth.

Evidence-based Research and Evaluation

As noted at the outset, *Relationship Smarts PLUS* was evaluated with 8,000 high school students in a five-year federally funded evaluation with a team of researchers led by Jennifer Kerpelman, Ph.D. of Auburn University. Using both quasi-experimental and experimental designs, the evaluators' plan was to study the course for one year, then tweak the content and approach, evaluate that revised approach a second year, test that, and so forth for four years of instruction. In the first two years, Family and Consumer Science teachers taught the program in their classes. In the last two years, health teachers taught the program. The fifth year of the study was reserved for final data collection. After each wave of data collection, the results were published in a peer-reviewed journal. In addition, other researchers have studied *Relationship Smarts PLUS* in different contexts (Kerpelman et al., 2010; Kerpelman et al., 2009; Kerpelman, 2007; Adler-Baeder et al., 2007; Adler-Baeder & Kerpelman, 2005).

Research outcomes of the *Relationship Smarts PLUS* curricula instruction cluster in three main areas: (1) a reduction in verbal aggression; (2) a reduction in faulty relationship beliefs; and (3) an improvement in conflict management skills. Each outcome and its related finding is detailed in Table 16.1.

Study strengths. Most of the measures used in the studies are well established and have good psychometric properties. The intervention is based on a strong theoretical foundation. Training was provided to the teachers to deliver the intervention. Overall, analyses were appropriate, and in one study, sophisticated growth curve modeling was used to capture differences between the intervention and control groups over time.

Study limitations. The psychometric properties of some instruments are based on research conducted with college students, not the study population. Neither study adequately monitored fidelity; that is, it is unclear whether teachers implemented all program modules as intended. Attrition and missing data were high in both studies, particularly for the 1- and 2-year follow-up surveys administered in one study when half the participating students had graduated from high school. For that study, the amount of data imputed at 2-year follow-up to compensate for high attrition makes it difficult to draw firm conclusions. In the other study, the

Table 16.1 Evaluation Results

Outcome 1: Verbal Aggression

Description of Measures	Verbal aggression was measured using a revised version of the Conflict Tactics Scales (CTS2) which consisted of 4 items.
Key Findings	Compared with the control group, the intervention group had a significant decrease in use of verbal aggression from pre- to post-test ($p = .02$).
Studies Measuring Outcome	Adler-Baeder, F., et al. (2007). The impact of relationship education on adolescents of diverse backgrounds. *Family Relations, 56*, 291–303.
Study Designs	Quasi-experimental
Quality of Research Rating	2.7 (0.0–4.0 scale)

Outcome 2: Relationship Beliefs

Description of Measures	Relationship beliefs were measured using 3 subscales of the Relationship Beliefs Scale (RBS). The aggression beliefs subscale included 2 items; a faulty relationship beliefs subscale included 5 items; and a realistic relationship beliefs subscale included 4 items. In a second study, three subscales were created to measure theoretically based faulty relationship beliefs: one and only (e.g., There is only one true love out there who is right for me to marry), love is enough (e.g., In the end, our feelings of love should be enough to sustain a happy marriage), and cohabitation (e.g., Living together before marriage will improve our chances of remaining happily married). Each subscale included 4 items at pre- and post-test and 1 item (see example above) at 1- and 2-year follow-up. Students completed the pre-test before intervention and the post-test after intervention.
Key Findings	Compared with control group, intervention group had a significant increase in realistic relationship beliefs from pre- to post-test ($p = .03$). In study 2, intervention group students had significant improvement from pre- to post-test on all three subscales (i.e., love is enough, one and only, cohabitation) in comparison with control group ($p < .001$ for all subscales). Results were maintained at 1-year follow-up but not 2-year follow-up.
Studies Measuring Outcome	Adler-Baeder, F., et al. (2007). The impact of relationship education on adolescents of diverse backgrounds. *Family Relations, 56*, 291–303. Kerpelman, J., et al. (2009). Evaluation of a statewide youth-focused relationships education curriculum. *Journal of Adolescence, 32*, 1359–1370. Kerpelman, J., et al. (2010). What adolescents bring to and learn from relationship education classes: Does social address matter? *Journal of Couple and Relationship Therapy, 9*, 95–112.

(Continued)

Table 16.1 Continued

Outcome 2: Relationship Beliefs

Study Designs	Experimental, Quasi-experimental
Quality of Research Rating	2.7 (0.0–4.0 scale)

Outcome 3: Conflict Management Skills

Description of Measures	Conflict management skills were measured using an 8-item subscale of the Interpersonal Competence Questionnaire (ICQ).
Key Findings	Students were randomly assigned to a group implementing the intervention or a group providing regular class curriculum. Intervention group students did not have significant improvement in perceived conflict management skills in comparison with control group at any post-intervention assessment. However, intervention group had significant improvement in perceived conflict management skills compared to the control group from pre-test through 1-year follow-up ($p < .01$) in a subsample analysis that controlled for the influence of social and economic factors.
Studies Measuring Outcome	Kerpelman, J., et al. (2009). Evaluation of a statewide youth-focused relationships education curriculum. *Journal of Adolescence, 32,* 1359–1370.
	Kerpelman, J., et al. (2010). What adolescents bring to and learn from relationship education classes: Does social address matter? *Journal of Couple and Relationship Therapy, 9,* 95–112.
Study Designs	Experimental
Quality of Research Rating	2.8 (0.0–4.0 scale)

Adapted from *SAMHSA's National Registry of Evidence-based Programs and Practices* Relationship Smarts PLUS (RS+) website: http://www.nrepp.samhsa.gov/ViewIntervention.aspx?id=280

relevance of diversity and other potentially confounding variables was discussed but remained largely unaddressed in analyses.

Ongoing research and recognition. In addition to the extensive research conducted by Kerpelman, Adler-Baeder, and their colleagues, *Love Notes* (Pearson, 2012) is currently in the fourth year of the major federal (U.S.) pregnancy prevention evaluation study in the Tier II track to test innovative approaches. Preliminary findings are interesting. Youth were randomly assigned to one of three groups. One group received a community-building program (control group), another received Reducing the Risk, a health-based pregnancy/STI prevention program (experimental group), and the third group received *Love Notes* (experimental group). Both experimental groups are showing more abstinence and usage of condoms or contraception if sexually active. However, those in *Love Notes* who were sexually active were only doing so in safe relationships. So it is not just using protection as in "safer sex," but they are more discerning, i.e., sexually active only in safe relationships (Barbee & Antle, in press). *Relationship Smarts PLUS*, and *Love Notes* as an adaptation, are listed on the National Registry of Evidence-based Programs and Practices (NREPP), a service of the Substance Abuse and Mental Health Administration (SAMHSA/CDC).

Professional Preparation and Training Issues

Instructors must have the capacity to create an open and trusting environment with the participants, which will make deep and meaningful conversations possible. Instructors should also model healthy relationship behaviors of respect, good communications, and emotional control. Given the personal nature of the sensitive topics covered in the materials, instructors must be prepared to handle issues that arise with students or be able to refer them on to others who can help.

Instruction in *Relationship Smarts PLUS* and *Love Notes* rely on participant involvement in activities that bring the lessons home. Comfort with leading activities that include current media, music, and videos is essential.

Hands-on teacher training is available for *Relationship Smarts PLUS* and *Love Notes*. Although not required, this preparation will help instructors implement the materials more quickly, consistently, and effectively. Experience shows that even a few hours of training gives teachers the confidence, motivation, and tools for success.

Conclusion

There are compelling reasons to address the romantic lives of youth. There are serious deficits in terms of models, scripts, expectations, and knowledge and skills for forming healthy relationships. Poor love choices can derail young peoples' lives with regards to school completion, employment, parenting, and health. We must move beyond a narrow health framework of bodies, sexual risks, and protection as the primary way in which to address the love lives of youth. We need to embrace the whole person—heart and health. And we must acknowledge that the two are inextricably linked. For our most vulnerable youth, this is especially important. As adult models and guides for stable and healthy relationships and marriages are in short supply, we cannot afford to have the popular media and peer culture provide all the scripts and guides for navigating romantic relationships. To build a culture of healthy and stable adult unions/marriage we must start with youth.

Key Points

- The catalysts for youth-focused RE was the emergence of research- and skills-based marriage education, as well as the growing recognition that youth increasingly lack models and guidance for building healthy relationships.

- Those in youth prevention work are beginning to see the limitations of a purely health "risks and protection" model.
- Relationship education can address some of the social determinants of risky behaviors and build important protective assets like the skills to form and maintain healthy relationships.
- "Habits of the heart" take root during the teen years and continue into adulthood. We lose an important opportunity if we wait until adulthood to offer relationship and marriage education.
- Youth-focused relationship education can help address the patterns, attitudes, expectations, and behaviors that link to the rise in non-marital births among those in their 20s.
- The basic components of a youth-focused relationship program include:
  - Knowing Yourself
  - Relationship Knowledge, Guides, and Assessment Frameworks
  - Research-based Communication and Conflict Management Skills
  - Linking Relationship Education to Sexual Decision making
  - Looking at the big picture—consequences for children from relationship instability and unplanned pregnancies.
- *Relationship Smarts PLUS* has completed a rigorous evaluation in the state of Alabama with 8,000 diverse teams. *Love Notes* is in year four of a five-year federal grant testing innovative approaches to pregnancy prevention.

Discussion Questions

1. How was the emergence of marriage education programs related to the subsequent development of youth-focused relationship education?
2. How can building healthy relationship knowledge, guides, and skills reduce risky sexual behaviors? What are the benefits of integrating these two separate fields (i.e., youth relationship education and sexuality/pregnancy prevention education)?
3. Why should we not wait until adulthood or engagement before we offer research- and skills-based marriage education?
4. How do the deficits youth face regarding relationships (e.g., models, guides, knowledge, skills) relate to the rise of non-marital and unplanned births among those in their 20s and early 30s?
5. What are the five components of a comprehensive youth-based relationship program? What are the overall goals?
6. How have *Relationship Smarts PLUS* and *Love Notes* been evaluated?

Additional Resources

Act for Youth: http://www.actforyouth.net/
Child Trend Research Briefs: http://www.childtrends.org/our-research/
Dibble Institute: http://www.dibbleinstitute.org/
Fragile Family and Child Wellbeing: http://www.fragilefamilies.princeton.edu/
Middle Ground on Sex Ed: http://www.dibbleinstitute.org/Documents/ZMGSE-50.pdf

StayTeen: http://stayteen.org/
The National Campaign: http://thenationalcampaign.org/
UGA Cooperative Extension Impact Report on Relationship Smarts PLUS: http://www.fcs.uga.
edu/docs/RS_State_Impact_Report_2013.pdf

References and Further Readings

Adler-Baeder, F., & Kerpelman, J. (2005). Looking towards a healthy marriage: School-based relationships education targeting youth. *Technical report prepared for the Alabama Department of Child Abuse and Neglect Prevention*, Auburn, AL: Auburn University. Retrieved from www.dibbleinstitute.org/Documents/Love_school_relations.pdf

Adler-Baeder, F., Kerpelman, J., Schramm, D., Higginbotham, B., & Paulk, A. (2007). The impact of relationship education on adolescents of diverse backgrounds. *Family Relations, 56*, 291–303.

Barbee, A., & Antle, B. (In press). Enhancement of Love Notes: Building healthy relationship skills, reducing teen dating violence and preventing teen pregnancy and STI transmission. *Journal of Couple and Relationship Therapy*.

Campbell, N., & Wood, R. (2002). *Building Strong Families*. Retrieved from www.building strongfamilies.info/index.htm

Carver, K., Joyner, K., & Udry, J. (2003). National estimates of adolescent romantic relationships. In P. Florsheim (Ed.), *Adolescent romantic relations and sexual behaviors: Theory, research, and practical implications* (pp. 23–56). Mahwah, NJ: Lawrence Erlbaum Associates.

Centers for Disease Control and Prevention. (2008). *Youth Risk Behavior Surveillance Survey— United States, 2007*. Atlanta, GA: Centers for Disease Control and Prevention.

Felitti, V., Anda, R., Nordenberg, D., Williamson, D., Spitz, A., Edwards, V., Koss, M., & Marks, J. (1998). Relationship of childhood abuse and household dysfunction to many of the leading causes of death in adults: The Adverse Childhood Experiences (ACE) Study. *American Journal of Preventative Medicine, 14*, 245–258.

Ford, K., Sohn, W., & Lepkowski, J. (2001). Characteristics of adolescents' sexual partners and their association with use of condoms and other contraceptive methods. *Family Planning Perspectives, 33*, 100–105, 132.

Furman, W., & Shaffer, L. (2003). The role of romantic relationships in adolescent development. In P. Florsheim (Ed.), *Adolescent romantic relations and sexual behavior: Theory, research, and practical implications* (pp. 3–22). Mahwah, NJ: Lawrence Erlbaum Associates.

Futris, T., Sutton, T., & Richardson, E. (2013). An evaluation of the Relationship Smarts PLUS program on adolescents in Georgia. *Journal of Human Sciences and Extension, 1*, 2–15. See http://www.dibbleinstitute.org/NEWDOCS/Georgia-evaluation-RQplus.pdf

Giordano, P., Manning, W., & Longmore, M. (2005). The romantic relationships of African American and white adolescents. *The Sociological Quarterly, 46*, 545–568.

Kerpelman, J. (2007). Youth focused relationships and marriage education. *The Forum for Family and Consumer Issues, 12*(1), online. Retrieved from ncsu.edu/ffci/publications/2007/v12-n1-2007 spring/index-v12-n1-may-2007.php

Kerpelman, J., Pittman, J., & Adler-Baeder, F. (2008). Identity as a moderator of intervention-related change: Identity style and adolescents' responses to relationships education. *Identity, 8*, 151–171.

Kerpelman, J., Pittman, J., Adler-Baeder, F., Eryigit, S., & Paulk, A. (2009). Evaluation of a statewide youth-focused relationships education curriculum. *Journal of Adolescence, 32*, 1359–1370.

Kerpelman, J., Pittman, J., Adler-Baeder, F., Stringer, K., Eryigit, S., Cadely, H., & Harrell-Levy, M. (2010). What adolescents bring to and learn from relationship education classes: Does social address matter? *Journal of Couple and Relationship Therapy, 9*, 95–112.

Kost, K., & Henshaw, S. (2012). *U.S. teen pregnancies, births, and abortions, 2008: National trends by age, race, and ethnicity.* New York, NY: Guttmacher Institute. Retrieved from www. guttmacher.org/pubs/USTPtrends10.pdf

Madison Area Technical College. (2014a). *Gateway to College.* Madison, WI: Madison Area Technical College. See madisoncollege.edu/gateway-to-college

Madison Area Technical College. (2014b). *TRiO-SSS.* Madison, WI: Madison Area Technical College. See madisoncollege.edu/trio-sss

Manlove, J., Ryan, S., & Franzetta, K. (2007). Contraceptive use patterns across teens' sexual relationships: The role of relationships, partners, and sexual histories. *Demography, 44*, 603–621.

McLanahan, S., & Beck, A. (2010). Parental relationships in fragile families. *Future Child, 20*(2), 17–37. Retrieved from http://www.futureofchildren.org/futureofchildren/ publications/docs/20_02_02.pdf

McLanahan, S., & Carlson, M. (2002). Welfare reform, fertility, and father involvement. *The Future of Children, 12*(1), 146–165.

McLanahan, S., Garfinkel, I., & Waller, M. (1999). The Fragile Families and Child Well-being Study. *Public Policy Institute of California,* p. 6. Retrieved from repec.ppic.org/content/ pubs/op/OP_1199MWOP.pdf

MEE Productions Inc. (2002). *This is my reality—The price of sex: An inside look at Black youth sexuality and the role of the media.* Philadelphia, PA. See www.meeproductions.com/

Mosher, W., Jones J., & Abma J. (2012). Intended and unintended births in the United States: 1982–2010. *National Health Statistics Reports,* no. 55, p. 8. Hyattsville, MD: National Center for Health Statistics.

Pearson, M. (2012). *Love Notes v2.0: Relationships, sex, and parenting for "at risk" young adults.* Berkeley, CA: The Dibble Institute. Retrieved from www.dibbleinstitute.org/ love-notes-2/

Pearson, M. (2013). *Relationship Smarts PLUS 3.0.* Berkeley, CA: The Dibble Institute. Retrieved from http://www.dibbleinstitute.org/love-u2-relationship-smarts-plus-new/

Santelli, J., Lindberg, L., Finer, L., & Singh, S. (2007). Explaining recent declines in adolescent pregnancy in the United States: The contribution of abstinence and improved contraceptive use. *American Journal of Public Health, 97*, 150–156.

Schulenberg, J., Bachman, J., Johnston, L., & O'Malley, P. (1994). *Historical trends in attitudes and preferences regarding family, work, and the future among American adolescents: National data from 1976 through 1992: Monitoring the Future.* Occasional Paper 37, p. 22. Ann Arbor, MI: Institute for Social Research, University of Michigan.

Suellentrop, K. (2008). Science Says #34: Unplanned Pregnancy and Family Turmoil. Washington, DC: *The National Campaign to Prevent Teen and Unplanned Pregnancy.* Retrieved from https://www.dibbleinstitute.org/Documents/SS34_FamilyTurmoil.pdf

Toews, M., & Yazedjian, A. (2012). *Strengthening relationships/Strengthening families.* San Marcos, TX: Texas State University. Retrieved from www.ccf.txstate.edu/Projects/ Current-Projects/Strengthening-Relationships—Strengthening-Families.html

Trella, D. (2009). *Relationship Smarts: Assessment of an adolescent relationship education program.* National Center for Family and Marriage Research, Working paper series WP-09–12. Bowling Green, OH: Bowling Green State University. Retrieved from http://www. dibbleinstitute.org/Documents/LU2_wp09-12.pdf

Whitehead, B., & Pearson, M. (2006). *Making a Love Connection: Teen Relationships, Pregnancy, and Marriage.* Washington, DC: National Campaign to Prevent Teen and Unplanned Pregnancy.

PART V

Evidence-based RME and Diverse Groups

17

RELATIONSHIP EDUCATION WITH SAME-SEX COUPLES

Sarah W. Whitton

LEARNING GOALS

- Become aware of the unique challenges faced by same-sex couples, which might be addressed with relationship education.
- Understand the need for culturally sensitive relationship education programs designed specifically for same-sex couples.
- Learn about the Strengthening Same-Sex Relationship Programs (Male and Female Versions) and the initial evidence supporting their efficacy.
- Learn about how healthy same-sex relationship education is being used within larger online efforts to promote the sexual and general health of LGBT youth.

Introduction

There are sizeable numbers of **same-sex couples** living in Western nations today. According to data from recent national Censuses, same-sex couples represent 4–10 of every 1,000 couple households in the United States, Canada, Australia, Ireland, and New Zealand (Australian Bureau of Statistics, 2012; Gates & Cooke, 2013; Statistics Canada, 2012). This translates into around 650,000 same-sex couples in the U.S.; 44,000 in Canada; and 34,000 in Australia. As societal acceptance of **sexual minorities** increases and legal recognition of same-sex relationships becomes more widely available, the number of same-sex couples is likely to rise. Indeed, while a publically declared committed relationship was generally not possible for sexual minorities of past generations, the vast majority (over 80%) of lesbian and gay youth today expect to be monogamously partnered after age 30 (D'Augelli, Rendina, & Sinclair, 2007). Consequently, relationship educators are increasingly likely to encounter same-sex couples seeking services. It is important that culturally sensitive relationship education programs are available for these couples.

Characteristics of Same-sex Couples

In general, same-sex couples and heterosexual couples are highly similar across many relationship dimensions, including satisfaction, communication patterns, intimacy, equality, and conflict (Kurdek, 2004; Peplau & Fingerhut, 2007). Moreover, the core relationship processes (e.g., communication, conflict resolution skills, commitment) that predict couple outcomes appear to be consistent across couple type (e.g., Kurdek, 2005). This similarity suggests that the models of relationship functioning that underpin relationship education efforts, despite being grounded in research on different-sex couples, may be fairly generalizable to same-sex couples. However, it cannot be forgotten that same-sex couples live within a broader social context that stigmatizes same-sex attractions and sexual behavior. From an **ecological systems perspective** (Bronfenbrenner, 1979), which highlights the impact of broader culture's attitudes and ideologies on individuals and their close relationships, this heterosexist social climate fundamentally affects the relationships of lesbian, gay, bisexual, and transgendered **(LGBT)** individuals. Minority stressors, including discrimination, rejection by loved ones, and pressure to conceal one's sexual minority identity, not only negatively influence individual well-being (Meyer, 2003), but also present unique challenges to initiating and maintaining romantic partnerships. Models of risk and resilience in same-sex couples (Green, 2004) highlight three primary areas of unique risk: heterosexism, including legal denial of and social pressures to conceal one's same-sex relationships; lack of socially prescribed norms to guide same-sex partners in relations with each other, their children, relatives, and others; and low levels of social support from family. Marriage inequality is one salient example of the unique challenges faced by same-sex couples. Despite rapid increases during the past decade in the number of nations and U.S. states that allow same-sex marriage, it is still only legal in 17 countries and in certain states within Mexico and the U.S. (as of April 2015, 36 U.S. states). As a result of marriage prohibitions in the United States, only about a third of U.S. cohabiting same-sex couples have a legally recognized relationship (Gates, 2013), though many of the unmarried couples would marry if they could (Reczek, Elliott, & Umberson, 2009). Consequently, countless same-sex couples are denied the many benefits that marriage confers, including tangible legal and financial benefits as well as social and community acknowledgment and support (Nagle, 2010).

The unique challenges faced by same-sex couples appear to have negative consequences for both individual and relationship health. Adults in same-sex partnerships report poorer health than do those in different-sex marriages (Denney, Gorman, & Barrera, 2013; Liu, Reczek, & Brown, 2013). This resonates with the general health disparities experienced by sexual minorities, who report disproportionately high rates of physical and mental health problems (Conron, Mimiaga, & Landers, 2010). Same-sex couples also break up sooner and more often than different-sex couples. For example, in a U.S. sample, 19% of male same-sex couples and 24% of female same-sex couples ended their relationships within 12 years versus 15% of married different-sex couples (Kurdek, 2004). Similarly, longitudinal data from the Netherlands indicate that same-sex relationships dissolved 11.5 times more often than married different-sex couples (Kalmijn, Loeve, & Manting, 2007). Lack of legal recognition likely accounts for some of the increased instability of same-sex relationships, as marriage generally decreases risk for relationship dissolution. However, cohabiting same-sex couples also have higher odds of break-up than non-married, cohabiting different-sex couples (Kalmijn et al., 2007; Lau, 2012). Further, married same-sex couples in Norway and Sweden divorce at higher rates than married different-sex couples (Andersson, Noack, Seierstad, & Weedon-Fekjær, 2006). Together, these findings suggest that same-sex couples face challenges to long-term stability beyond those associated with lack of access to legal marriage and may remain at risk for dissolution even as same-sex marriage becomes more widely available.

The heightened risk for break-up among same-sex couples has important public health implications. The end of a romantic relationship is associated with a host of negative physical and mental health outcomes for the partners (e.g., Rhoades, Kamp Dush, Atkins, Stanley, & Markman, 2011) as well as their children (Amato, 2000), which is highly relevant given that one-fifth of U.S. same-sex couples are parenting children (Gates & Cooke, 2013). Conversely, the well-documented mental and physical health benefits of heterosexual marriage (Waite & Gallagher, 2000) suggest that healthy, long-term same-sex relationships may promote health among sexual minorities. Some research supports this notion. Relationship involvement is associated with higher well-being in lesbian women (Wayment & Peplau, 1995) and, among sexual minority adults in cohabiting relationships, relationship satisfaction is associated with fewer depressive symptoms (Whitton & Kuryluk, 2014). Further, support provided by a same-sex romantic partner buffers individuals from the negative effects of stress (Graham & Barnow, 2013). Together, these findings suggest that efforts to promote same-sex relationship health and stability, including culturally sensitive relationship education programs, hold promise for reducing the disproportionate rates of mental health issues in LGBT individuals.

The Strengthening Same-Sex Relationships (SSSR) Programs

The **Strengthening Same-Sex Relationships (SSSR) programs** for male couples (Buzzella & Whitton, 2009) and female couples (Whitton, Scott, & Buzzella, 2013) are evidence-based relationship education programs designed specifically for same-sex couples. The following sections of this chapter will describe: (1) the rationale for developing relationship education programs specifically for same-sex couples, (2) preliminary research conducted to inform the culturally sensitive adaptation of existing relationship education curriculum, (3) the SSSR program content and format, and (4) research to date evaluating the SSSR programs.

Program Rationale

As described throughout this volume, relationship education programs use a preventive approach to promote long-term relationship health by teaching participants the skills necessary to form and maintain healthy relationships and families. Evidence-based relationship education has been shown to positively impact different-sex relationships, improving couple communication and relationship quality (Hawkins, Blanchard, Baldwin, & Fawcett, 2008). There are several reasons to suggest that relationship education may be a particularly appropriate mode of intervention to support same-sex couples. First, the unique risks and elevated instability experienced by same-sex couples indicate that they represent a high-risk group who could particularly benefit from relationship education. Targeting same-sex couples would therefore be consistent with calls for a secondary prevention approach, in which relationship education is selectively offered to high-risk couples who are most likely to show benefits from participation (Halford, Markman, Kline, & Stanley, 2007). Second, the core relationship processes targeted in most relationship education programs (communication, conflict resolution skills, commitment) are predictive of same-sex couple outcomes (e.g., Kurdek, 2005), suggesting that relationship education to improve these processes is likely to also improve same-sex couple outcomes. Third, same-sex couples may be in particular need of relationship skills in order to successfully navigate the unique challenges they face (discrimination, lack of relationship norms, and poor family and community support). Finally, the preventive approach is less stigmatizing than couple therapy, which may be particularly important to sexual minorities who already experience considerable stigmatization.

Despite the potential for relationship education to benefit same-sex couples, established evidence-based programs (many of which are described in this volume), were developed for and tested on different-sex couples. It therefore cannot be assumed that these programs are appropriate, relevant, or helpful to same-sex couples. In general, interventionists must make certain that programs developed in one cultural context are acceptable when offered in another and do not have unintended harmful effects because of differences in cultural values, beliefs, or practices (e.g., APA, 2003; Castro, Barrera, & Martinez, 2004). Ideally, interventions should be adapted so that they are perceived as relevant, responsive, and culturally appealing to the new target population—thereby improving participant engagement and program acceptability—while maintaining fidelity to the core content that leads to positive outcomes (Kumpfer, Alvarado, Smith, & Bellamy, 2002). In the case of providing relationship education to same-sex couples, it is important to provide the "effective ingredients" of existing programs (e.g., communication skills training) while avoiding harmful program effects, such as inadvertently increasing minority stress and internalized negativity about same-sex couples by presenting material steeped in a heterosexist framework. Consistent with guidelines for culturally sensitive program adaptation (APA, 2003; Kumpfer et al., 2002), input from relationship educators and from same-sex couples themselves was gathered to inform the development of the SSSR programs.

Culturally Sensitive Adaptation of Relationship Education for Same-sex Couples

First, Whitton and Buzzella (2012) conducted a survey of couple therapists and researchers to assess their perceptions of whether same-sex couples benefit from existing relationship education programs, whether adaptation was necessary, and what specific adaptations might improve program acceptability. Respondents almost universally indicated that the core content of most existing relationship education programs (communication and conflict resolution, protecting positive couple connections, and commitment) were highly useful in work with same-sex couples. However, every one of the respondents who had delivered relationship education to same-sex couples reported having to adapt the material, primarily to remove **heterosexist bias** and avoid alienating their clients. In particular, they altered language (e.g., changing "spouses," "husbands," "wives," and "marriages" to "partners" and "relationships"), which was relatively easy to do for verbally communicated content but more difficult for printed materials. Program content emphasizing the importance of marriage and other symbols of commitment also required adaptation, as many legally or culturally sanctioned symbols are not available to same-sex couples. Most problematically, existing programs' supplemental materials (i.e., slides, workbooks, handouts, and instructional videos) depicted only different-sex couples. One respondent wrote: "they show only heterosexual couples and this is a big problem. Same-sex couples [do] not see themselves reflected in the videos." Another stated, "the main thing is that there needs to be video clips of same-sex couples." Respondents generally reported that same-sex couples had difficulty identifying with the heterosexual couples depicted in program materials, which interfered with their ability to learn the relationship skills and was experienced as alienating to some couples. Finally, survey findings indicated that several unique needs of same-sex couples were not addressed in existing curricula, most notably managing discrimination and stigma (including how and/or when to come out in various life contexts), the heightened need for relationship expectation negotiation (around such issues as monogamy and how/if to form a family with children), and building community and social support for the relationship.

Second, the development of SSSR was also informed by the perspectives of same-sex couples. Scott and Rhoades (2014) conducted focus groups with lesbian women to explore perceived barriers to participation in relationship education and desired content for relationship programs. Three major themes were identified regarding the women's perceived barriers to participating in relationship education. First, programs were perceived as unavailable for same-sex couples: participants stated that programs "are advertised for straight couples," are intended for couples getting married, and are offered primarily in religious settings that may not be accepting of sexual minorities. Second, participants reported concerns with comfort and safety, expressing uncertainty that group leaders or other participating (heterosexual) couples would be accepting of same-sex couples as well as fear of discrimination. One woman stated, "I definitely need to feel like I am accepted walking into a situation like that." Third, the participants expressed concerns that group leaders would not be competent or knowledgeable about lesbian couples and that program material would not be relevant to them. For example, one woman stated, "I'd be concerned that they would have a really rigid notion of what a successful relationship looks like [...] in a **heteronormative** way."

In the focus groups' responses to questions about the content that they would like to have included in relationship education programs, several common themes emerged: (1) learning ways to handle discrimination and legal challenges as a couple; (2) negotiating relationship disclosure, including differences between partners about how "out" to be to whom; (3) creating shared couple expectations for relationship development, division of labor, and relationship roles in the absence of societal norms or role models for long-term female same-sex couples; (4) communicating in ways that value emotional expression and foster intimacy; (5) family planning, including if and how to have children and how to parent existing children; and (6) maintaining a sexual intimacy over time, which participants felt would best occur in groups of female same-sex couples only.

Program Content and Format

The rich input from same-sex couples and the relationship educators described above was used to inform curriculum development for the Strengthening Same-Sex Relationships (SSSR) programs (Buzzella & Whitton, 2009; Whitton, Scott, & Buzzella, 2013). Separate versions were created for each gender so that participants would see couples similar to themselves in the program materials, could share experiences and form connections with other couples of the same gender make-up, and feel comfortable discussing sexual intimacy. This also allowed for specialization of program content by gender (e.g., sexual monogamy agreements for males, enhanced focus on building emotional intimacy and child-focused content for females). The SSSR programs were written to be free from heterosexist bias. Specifically, all language is appropriate for same-sex couples (e.g., "partner" vs. "spouse"; the gender of pronouns matches that of the participants), no assumptions are made regarding access to marriage or social approval, and the content is sensitive to behavioral diversity in same-sex relationships (e.g., flexible gender roles, negotiated non-monogamy). Program materials, including PowerPoint slides, example vignettes, participant workbooks, and video demonstrations of skills, all depict same-sex couples (female couples in SSSR-Female version, male couples in SSSR-Male version).

The SSSR Programs include five core content areas common to most skills-based CRE programs (Halford et al., 2007): (1) educating couples about key relationship processes that influence couple outcomes, (2) protecting positive relationship connections, (3) preventing or reducing destructive conflict, (4) promoting constructive communication, and (5) teaching couple-based problem-solving skills. These units were adapted to be culturally sensitive to same-sex couples (e.g., by removing heterosexist language and assumptions; depicting same-sex couples in supplementary materials) while retaining fidelity to the essential content. In addition, SSSR includes novel units designed to address the unique needs of same-sex couples (1) coping with minority stress and discrimination, which helps couples identify and replace maladaptive individual- and couple-level coping responses to discrimination and stigmatization (e.g., social withdrawal) (Hatzenbuehler, 2009), (2) building social networks that support the relationship, (3) creating a sense of stability (often in the absence of legal or social recognition on the relationship), and (4) negotiating clear relationship expectations in areas that commonly hold ambiguity for same-sex couples (e.g., non-monogamy sexual agreements, if and how to have children) (Green, 2004). In the Male program, the relationship expectations unit focuses on negotiating and honoring sexual agreements about monogamy, given the variety of sexual agreements that are common in male same-sex couples (Hosking, 2013) and the importance of clearly defined, mutually agreed-upon sexual agreements to men's sexual health and relationship well-being (LaSala, 2004). In contrast, this unit in the program for female couples focuses on relationship expectations regarding relationship disclosure and children (if and how to have children together; co-parenting issues), based on the focus group data (Scott & Rhoades, 2014) and the large percentage (30%) of female couples who live with children (Denney et al., 2013). Finally, SSSR-F includes one additional unit called "Advanced Communication Skills" which teaches skills for sharing emotions in ways that foster emotional safety and intimacy.

The SSSR-M and SSSR-F are 10-hour programs delivered in a group format, to groups of 3–6 couples. It is most commonly delivered over three weeks: an initial 6-hour weekend session covers the five core units to build couple adaptive processes, followed by two subsequent 2-hour weekday evening sessions, in which the new skills are applied to minority-specific topics (e.g., replacing maladaptive individual and couple coping strategies, negotiating relationship expectations, building social support networks). There is flexibility, however, in how the program is delivered. Other formats include two 5-hour weekend meetings or five 2-hour weeknight sessions. For each unit, facilitators present a short lecture with PowerPoint slides, typically including video demonstrations of the relationship skill. Couples are then given the opportunity to practice these skills with correct feedback from educators. Group discussion and sharing of ideas for how to handle particular stressors or implement particular skills is encouraged. Typically, SSSR is delivered by two co-facilitators, who may be supported by "coaches" who provide support and corrective feedback as couples practice the skills.

Program Evaluation

SSSR-Male version. Two pilot studies have evaluated SSSR-M, with three goals: (1) to assess program feasibility and acceptability, (2) to obtain preliminary efficacy data, and (3) to gather participant feedback to inform refinement of this program as well as same-sex relationship education more broadly. Both studies used a randomized waitlist control design. After enough couples were recruited to constitute a group (3–5 couples), each group was randomized to either immediate intervention or to a waitlist condition, in which couples received the program after a 4-week waiting period. Participants completed assessments at intake, post-waitlist (waitlist group only), post-treatment, and 3-month follow-up. Assessments included measures of specific risk factors targeted in the intervention (i.e., couple communication, perceived stress, social support for the relationship), as well as global relationship functioning (i.e., satisfaction and quality). At post-treatment, participants provided qualitative data on program acceptability.

The first study was conducted in 2009–2010 with a sample of 12 married or engaged couples in Boston (Buzzella, Whitton, & Tompson, 2012). Based on who responded to study advertisements, the sample was predominantly White (90%), highly educated (an average of 4 years of college), and highly satisfied with their relationships, but ranged widely in age (26–66 years) and relationship length (1.8–35 years). Results from the full sample ($n = 12$) indicated statistically significant improvements in couple communication behaviors, perceived stress, and relationship quality from pre- to post-intervention, representing medium- to large-sized effects (Cohen's $ds = 0.40$–0.80). Intervention effects were generally maintained at 3-month follow-up. Although the small sample size precluded formal statistical tests comparing treatment ($n = 7$) to waitlist ($n = 5$) data, participants who had attended the intervention reported somewhat better couple communication, lower perceived stress, higher relationship quality, and higher relationship satisfaction than those in the waitlist group. Together, these data provided preliminary support for SSSR-M's efficacy in promoting positive same-sex couple outcomes.

Study findings also supported the *acceptability* of SSSR-M. Participants reported high satisfaction with the program, which they rated as very helpful to their relationships and something that they would recommend to a friend. In the qualitative responses, participants frequently expressed appreciation that the program had clearly been designed for male same-sex couples rather than superficially adapted from a heterosexual relationship program, which conveyed that their same-sexuality was not an afterthought, kept them from having to translate heterosexual material, and highlighted the relevance of the material to their own relationships. Participants also liked that the group solely comprised male couples, which increased their comfort level and allowed them "to see other gay couples communicate." Common themes regarding how to improve the program were to offer more opportunities to connect with other couples and to give increased attention to couples' sexual relationship (the men reported that they would be quite comfortable doing so in a group of gay couples). In sum, this initial pilot study supported SSSR-M's feasibility, acceptability, and potential efficacy, as well as provided valuable feedback to inform program refinement. Based on these results, the program was refined primarily by: (1) adding additional opportunities for group discussion, sharing between couples, and out-of-group contact between couples, and (2) augmenting content focused on sex via the addition of an activity in which couples apply their new communication skills to a discussion of sexual agreements and preferences.

The refined program was evaluated in a second pilot study (Whitton et al., 2014). The research design was the same, with two differences: (1) the sample size was larger ($N = 20$ couples) to allow for statistical tests of program effects, and (2) analyses included observational measures of couple communication in addition to self-report measures. Participants were male same-sex couples in committed relationships of at least 6 months' duration. The sample was similar to the first study in terms of race (83% White; 13% Black), high education level, high relationship satisfaction, and widely ranging age (24–62 years) and relationship length (0.8–29 years). Couples who participated in the program showed significant improvements in targeted couple processes (self-reported and observed couple communication, perceived stress; medium effect sizes) as well as relationship functioning (satisfaction and quality; small effect sizes) from pre- to post-program. Perceived social support did not show pre- to post changes, but was significantly improved by follow-up. Observed improvements were generally maintained at 3-month follow-up, suggesting maintenance of program effects. However, despite the observed within-person improvements across intervention, program effects were generally not significant when compared to the waitlist control condition: Only observed positive communication was higher among participants who had completed the program than those who completed the waitlist. Therefore, we cannot confidently conclude that the program was effective in improving these couples' processes and outcomes. It is likely that the relatively small sample size limited power to detect effects, especially given ceiling effects observed in several variables. The men who volunteered to participate almost universally had satisfying relationships so that there was little room for improvement on relationship measures. In addition, waitlist couples showed small improvements in targeted relationship outcomes across the waiting period, which is not uncommon in trials of couple interventions (e.g., Cohen, O'Leary, & Foran, 2010). Future research using larger samples that provide greater power to detect effects is needed to examine whether SSSR-M is more effective than control conditions.

Furthermore, quantitative and qualitative data supported program acceptability. On a program satisfaction measure, participants rated the overall program and the individual units as very helpful to their relationships (Mean ratings above 6 on a 1–8 scale). In qualitative responses, participants commonly reported liking the strategies to communicate positively and avoid destructive communication, the individualized coaching from group leaders as they practiced new skills, and the material tailored specifically for male same-sex couples. Several participants mentioned that the program was empowering, raising their awareness of resources and equal right to quality programs. For example, one man said, "A lot of [hetero couples] are just given that sort of education . . . it just, it never really occurred to me . . . that that would be here for us." Commonly mentioned ways to improve the program included making the lecture portions of the program more exciting, addressing cultural differences (e.g., in how couples communicate), and further increasing the amount of interaction between couples, possibly by increasing group size (> 5 couples) and ensuring similarly in age across group members.

SSSR-Female version. The SSSR-F program is being evaluated in an ongoing, dual-site pilot study supported by the Lesbian Health Fund. The research design parallels that of the pilot studies of SSSR-M, using a randomized waitlist controlled design and mixed-methods data. In support of program feasibility and acceptability, there has been high interest in the program at both sites. Following fairly minimal advertisement of the study, we exceeded our planned sample size of 24 female same-sex couples, with 38 couples currently enrolled. Further, preliminary data from the first 16 couples to complete the program indicate high program satisfaction (*Mean* = 6.94 on a 1–8 scale). Qualitative responses indicate that female couples most liked the communication skills training, particularly the focus on how to enhance intimacy by communicating soft emotions (e.g., sadness, loneliness) rather than hard emotions (e.g., anger) and by attending to deeper relationship issues (e.g., trust). Participants frequently reported that they would have liked more interaction with the group (similar to the male participants in SSSR-M) as well as more specific ideas about how to get more connected to the local lesbian community. Initial efficacy estimates indicate pre- to post-program improvements in couples' self-reported negative and positive communication and stress (medium effect sizes), as well as relationship quality (small effect). In sum, these preliminary results suggest program feasibility, acceptability, and potential efficacy, and will be used to inform refinement of SSSR-F (e.g., by further increasing opportunities for participants to form and maintain connections with other couples in their group).

In sum, the SSSR programs are culturally sensitive adaptations of evidence-based relationship education programs. Male and female versions of SSSR show clear evidence of feasibility and acceptability. Data from pilot studies also provide preliminary support for program efficacy in building important relationship skills (e.g., communication) and relationship quality. Although it is not yet clear if program effects are significant in comparison to control conditions, observed pre- to post-program improvements are similar in size to those for existing, heterosexually focused programs (Hawkins et al., 2008). This suggests that adaptations of core relationship education content, which were made in the interest of eliminating heterosexist bias and improving relevance for same-sex couples, did not reduce program efficacy. Further, results to date also suggest the potential efficacy of novel program content designed specifically for same-sex couples (i.e., coping with minority stress and discrimination, garnering social support for the relationship, and clarifying ambiguous relationship expectations).

Healthy Relationship Education for LGBT Youth

Based on the promising data supporting the use of relationship education with adult same-sex couples, recent efforts have been made to provide healthy relationship education to LGBT adolescents via an Internet-based intervention (Mustanski, Greene, Ryan, & Whitton, 2014). These efforts parallel broader trends in the field to extend the reach of relationship education by providing it to individuals, adolescents, and people interested in online rather than in-person services. In particular, programs have been designed for individuals to attend alone, aiming to help partnered individuals stabilize and strengthen their current relationships (without having their partner present) and to help single individuals build skills that will support the development of healthy future relationships (Rhoades & Stanley, 2011). Relationship education programs have been successfully adapted for use with adolescents (Adler-Baeder, Kerpelman, Schramm, & Higginbotham, 2007), based on the view that it may be most effective to provide individuals with knowledge and skills to support healthy relationships during their teens as they begin dating and forming lasting patterns of relationship behavior. Finally, Internet-based delivery holds promise for large-scale dissemination of relationship education programs; many couples express preferences for online versus in-person resources (Georgia & Doss, 2013) and initial trials suggest that couples who participate in online relationship education learn and use relationship skills (Loew et al., 2012).

All of these innovations may be particularly helpful for LGBT youth, who as a consequence of the sexual prejudice they experience (Herek & McLemore, 2013) face unique challenges in developing their approach towards romantic and sexual relationships. Sexual minority teens often lack support from sources that typically provide knowledge and guidance in how to form and sustain healthy relationships, including parents, peers, schools, and community services (Kubicek, Beyer, Weiss, Iverson, & Kipke, 2010) and turn to the Internet to find this information (Mustanski, Lyons, & Garcia, 2011). To help address these issues, a brief healthy same-sex relationships curriculum was developed and delivered as part of an online sexual health promotion program for LGBT youth: The **Queer Sex Ed intervention** (QSE; Mustanski, Greene, Ryan, & Whitton, 2014). QSE is an Internet-based, multimedia intervention that aims to address the inequities in sexual health experienced by LGBT youth by providing comprehensive sexual health information (on understanding and accepting one's sexual orientation and gender identity, sexuality education, and safe-sex practices), including information on how to form and sustain healthy romantic relationships. To increase participant engagement, the program was moderated by an avatar, content was delivered in variety of formats (e.g., video, narrated text documents, anatomical images), and participants each generated three personalized sexual health improvement goals. The healthy relationships unit included content on communication skills (with video demonstration by teen same-sex couples), clarifying relationship expectations, maintaining positive and fun couple activities, and relationship safety.

In an initial evaluation of QSE, a sample of 202 LGBT youth (16 to 20 years old) completed QSEd as well as pre-test and post-test assessments. Findings supported the overall program's feasibility, acceptability, and preliminary efficacy (Mustanski et al., 2014). Over three fourths of participants completed the full intervention, spending on average 2 hours engaged with its content, and rated QSE very positively. There were small positive program effects on sexual orientation variables (e.g., internalized homophobia) and moderate effects on safer sex (e.g., contraceptive knowledge) outcomes. Specific to the healthy relationships content, self-reported couple communication skills improved significantly from pre- to post-intervention, and participants often noted the value of the relationships unit in their responses to open-ended questions about program acceptability. Example quotes include: "Loved the communication advice," and "It also helped to open up doors to healthy communication, which I've been having problems with in my relationships." In sum, these findings suggest that relationship education specifically tailored for LGBT youth and delivered online is feasible, highly acceptable, and possibly effective in building important relationship skills. More broadly, it supports the potential value of tailoring relationship education for adolescent sexual minorities, packaging it with other important content (e.g., sexual health), and using an online format to maximize reach.

Conclusion

Relationship education appears to hold promise for strengthening the relationships of LGBT people. Culturally sensitive relationship education programs for adult same-sex couples and for LGBT youth have been developed, are well liked by participants, and have shown preliminary evidence of efficacy in improving relationship skills. Continued evaluation of both types of program is warranted, including larger trials to more powerfully assess program efficacy. It will be important to assess if same-sex relationship education can be successfully delivered in community settings such as LGBT community centers, which can reach large numbers of diverse same-sex couples, provide an accepting and comfortable environment for sexual minorities, and have staff who are experienced in working with LGBT individuals. Further, dissemination of the same-sex relationship education programs to practicing clinicians and trainees might help with broader efforts to increase the numbers of marriage and family therapists who are adequately trained in evidence-based interventions for LGBT clients (Long & Serovich, 2003).

Key Points

- Same-sex couples, though similar to different-sex couples in many regards, face unique challenges that might be effectively addressed with relationship education.
- Qualitative and quantitative research suggests that existing mainstream relationship education programs contain considerable heterosexist bias and that same-sex couples would prefer programs designed specifically for them.
- The Strengthening Same-Sex Relationship Programs (Male and Female Versions) are recently developed culturally sensitive relationship education programs that teach core relationship skills and address the unique needs of same-sex couples. Data from pilot studies suggest these programs have high acceptability and show preliminary evidence of efficacy.
- A healthy same-sex relationship education curriculum for adolescents, delivered within a larger online effort to promote the sexual health of LGBT youth, has also shown promising results in a pilot study.

Discussion Questions

1. What are some of the unique challenges faced by same-sex couples? How might they be addressed with relationship education?
2. What are some of the problems that practitioners and LGBT individuals report regarding using traditional relationship education programs with same-sex couples?
3. In what ways are the Strengthening Same-Sex Relationship Programs adapted to be culturally sensitive to same-sex couples?

References and Further Readings

Adler-Baeder, F., Kerpelman, J., Schramm, D., & Higginbotham, B. (2007). The impact of relationship education on adolescents of diverse backgrounds. *Family Relations, 56,* 291–303.

Amato, P. (2000). The consequences of divorce for adults and children. *Journal of Marriage and Family, 62,* 1269–1287. doi:10.2307/1566735

American Psychological Association. (2003). Guidelines on multicultural education, training, research, practice, and organizational change for psychologists. *American Psychologist, 58,* 377–402.

Andersson, G., Noack, T., Seierstad, A., & Weedon-Fekjær, H. (2006). The demographics of same-sex marriages in Norway and Sweden. *Demography, 43,* 79–98. doi:10.2307/4137233

Australian Bureau of Statistics. (2012). *Same-sex couple families. Reflecting a Nation: Stories from the 2011 Census.* Retrieved June 9, 2014, from http://www.abs.gov.au/ausstats/abs@.nsf/Lookup/2071.0main+features852012-2013

Bronfenbrenner, U. (1979). *The ecology of human development.* Cambridge, MA: Harvard University Press.

Buzzella, B., & Whitton, S. (2009). *Strengthening Same-Sex Relationships: Male Version.* Unpublished Therapist Manual.

Buzzella, B., Whitton, S., & Tompson, M. (2012). A preliminary evaluation of a relationship education program for male same-sex couples. *Couple and Family Psychology: Research and Practice, 1,* 306–322. doi:10.1037/a0030380

Castro, F., Barrera, M., Jr., & Martinez, C., Jr. (2004). The cultural adaptation of prevention interventions: Resolving tensions between fidelity and fit. *Prevention Science, 5,* 41–45. Kluwer Academic-Plenum Publishers. doi:10.1023/B:PREV.0000013980.12412.cd

Cohen, S., O'Leary, K., & Foran, H. (2010). A randomized clinical trial of a brief, problem-focused couple therapy for depression. *Behavior Therapy, 41,* 433–446. doi:10.1016/j.beth.2009.11.004

Conron, K., Mimiaga, M., & Landers, S. (2010). A population-based study of sexual orientation identity and gender differences in adult health. *American Journal of Public Health, 100,* 1953–1960. doi:10.2105/AJPH.2009.174169

D'Augelli, A., Rendina, H., & Sinclair, K. (2007). Lesbian and gay youth's aspirations for marriage and raising children. *Journal of LGBT Issues in Counseling, 1,* 77–98.

Denney, J., Gorman, B., & Barrera, C. (2013). Families, resources, and adult health: Where do sexual minorities fit? *Journal of Health and Social Behavior, 54,* 46–63. doi:10.1177/0022146512469629

Gates, G. (2013). Demographics and LGBT Health. *Journal of Health and Social Behavior, 54,* 72–74. doi:10.1177/0022146512474429

Gates, G., & Cooke, A. (2013). *United States Census Snapshot: 2010.* Retrieved December 11, 2013, from http://williamsinstitute.law.ucla.edu/wp-content/uploads/Census 2010Snapshot-US-v2.pdf

Georgia, E., & Doss, B. (2013). Web-based couple interventions: Do they have a future? *Journal of Couple and Relationship Therapy, 12,* 168–185.

Graham, J., & Barnow, Z. (2013). Stress and social support in gay, lesbian, and heterosexual couples: Direct effects and buffering models. *Journal of Family Psychology, 27,* 569–578. doi:10.1037/a0033420

Green, R. (2004). Risk and resilience in lesbian and gay couples: Comment on Solomon, Rothblum, and Balsam (2004). *Journal of Family Psychology, 18,* 290–292. doi:10.1037/0893–3200.18.2.290

Halford, W., Markman, H., Kline, G., & Stanley, S. (2007). Best practice in couple relationship education. *Journal of Marital and Family Therapy, 29,* 385–406. doi:10.1111/j.1752–0606.2003.tb01214.x

Hatzenbuehler, M. (2009). How does sexual minority stigma "get under the skin"? A psychological mediation framework. *Psychological Bulletin, 135,* 707–730.

Hawkins, A., Blanchard, V., Baldwin, S., & Fawcett, E. (2008). Does marriage and relationship education work? A meta-analytic study. *Journal of Consulting and Clinical Psychology, 76,* 723–734. doi:10.1037/a0012584

Herek, G., & McLemore, K. (2013). Sexual prejudice. *Annual Review of Psychology, 64,* 309–333. doi:10.1146/annurev-psych-113011–143826

Hosking, W. (2013). Agreements about extra-dyadic sex in gay men's relationships: Exploring differences in relationship quality by agreement type and rule-breaking behavior. *Journal of Homosexuality, 60,* 711–733. doi:10.1080/00918369.2013.773819

Kalmijn, M., Loeve, A., & Manting, D. (2007). Income dynamics in couples and the dissolution of marriage and cohabitation. *Demography, 44,* 159–179. doi:10.2307/4137226

Kubicek, K., Beyer, W., Weiss, G., Iverson, E., & Kipke, M. (2010). In the dark: Young men's stories of sexual initiation in the absence of relevant sexual health information. *Health Education and Behavior, 37,* 243–263. doi:10.1177/1090198109339993

Kumpfer, K., Alvarado, R., Smith, P., & Bellamy, N. (2002). Cultural sensitivity and adaptation in family-based prevention interventions. *Prevention Science, 3,* 241–246. doi:10.1023/A:1019902902119

Kurdek, L. (2004). Are gay and lesbian cohabiting couples really different from heterosexual married couples? *Journal of Marriage and Family, 66,* 880–900.

Kurdek, L. (2005). What do we know about gay and lesbian couples? *Current Directions in Psychological Science, 14,* 251–254.

LaSala, M. (2004). Extradyadic sex and gay male couples: Comparing monogamous and nonmonogamous relationships. *Families in Society, 85,* 405–412.

Lau, C.Q. (2012). The stability of same-sex cohabitation, different-sex cohabitation, and marriage. *Journal of Marriage and Family, 74,* 973–990.

Liu, H., Reczek, C., & Brown, D. (2013). Same-sex cohabitors and health. *Journal of Health and Social Behavior, 54,* 25–45.

Loew, B., Rhoades, G., Markman, H., Stanley, S., Pacifici, C., White, L., & Delaney, R. (2012). Internet delivery of PREP-based relationship education for at-risk couples. *Journal of Couple and Relationship Therapy, 11,* 291–309. doi:10.1080/15332691.2012.718968

Long, J., & Serovich, J. (2003). Incorporating sexual orientation into MFT training programs: Infusion and inclusion. *Journal of Marital and Family Therapy, 29,* 59–67.

Meyer, I. (2003). Prejudice, social stress, and mental health in lesbian, gay, and bisexual populations: Conceptual issues and research evidence. *Psychological Bulletin, 129,* 674–697.

Mustanski, B., Greene, G., Ryan, D., & Whitton, S. (2014). Feasibility, acceptability, and initial efficacy of an online sexual health promotion program for LGBT youth: The Queer Sex Ed intervention. *Journal of Sex Research,* 1–11. doi:10.1080/00224499.2013.867924

Mustanski, B., Lyons, T., & Garcia, S. (2011). Internet use and sexual health of young men who have sex with men: A mixed-methods study. *Archives of Sexual Behavior, 40,* 289–300.

Nagle, J. (2010). *Same-sex marriage: The debate.* New York, NY: The Rosen Publishing Group.

Peplau, L., & Fingerhut, A. (2007). The close relationships of lesbians and gay men. *Annual Review of Psychology, 58,* 405–424. doi:10.1146/annurev.psych.58.110405.085701

Reczek, C., Elliott, S., & Umberson, D. (2009). Commitment without marriage. *Journal of Family Issues, 30,* 738–756.

Rhoades, G., Kamp Dush, C., Atkins, D., Stanley, S., & Markman, H. (2011). Breaking up is hard to do: The impact of unmarried relationship dissolution on mental health and life satisfaction. *Journal of Family Psychology, 25,* 366–374.

Rhoades, G., & Stanley, S. (2011). Using individual-oriented relationship education to prevent family violence. *Journal of Couple and Relationship Therapy, 10,* 185–200.

Scott, S., & Rhoades, G. (2014). Relationship education for lesbian couples: Perceived barriers and content considerations. *Journal of Couple and Relationship Therapy, 13,* 339–364. doi: 10.1080/15332691.2014.930704

Statistics Canada (2012). *Portrait of families and living arrangements in Canada. Families, households and marital status, 2011 Census of Population.* Catalogue no. 98-312 X2011001. Ottawa, ON: Ministry of Industry. Available at http://www12.statcan.gc.ca/census-recensement/2011/as-sa/98-312-x/98-312-x2011001-eng.pdf

Waite, L., & Gallagher, M. (2000). *The case for marriage* (p. 260). New York, NY: Doubleday Books.

Wayment, H., & Peplau, L. (1995). Social support and well-being among lesbian and heterosexual women: A structural modeling approach. *Personality and Social Psychology Bulletin, 21,* 1189–1199. doi:10.1177/01461672952111007

Whitton, S., & Buzzella, B. (2012). Using relationship education programs with same-sex couples: A preliminary evaluation of program utility and needed modifications. *Marriage and Family Review, 48,* 667–688. doi:10.1080/01494929.2012.700908

Whitton, S., & Kuryluk, A. (2014). Associations between relationship quality and depressive symptoms in same-sex couples. *Journal of Family Psychology, 28,* 571–576. doi: 10.1037/fam0000011

Whitton, S., Scott, S., & Buzzella, B. (2013). *Strengthening Same-Sex Relationships: Female Version.* Unpublished Therapist Manual.

Whitton, S., Weitbrecht, E., Kuryluk, A., & Buzzella, B. (2014). A small randomized clinical trial of a culturally adapted relationship education program for male same-sex couples. *Manuscript in Preparation.*

18

RELATIONSHIP AND MARRIAGE EDUCATION FOR LOW-INCOME COUPLES: STRENGTHENING STRESSED RELATIONSHIPS

Sage E. Erickson and Alan J. Hawkins

LEARNING GOALS

- Learn about the specific challenges and needs of low-income couples and create ideas of how to address these problems and overcome these challenges.
- Learn about the challenges in recruitment and retention in RME programs with low-income couples.
- Learn about the diversity of RME programs available to help low-income couples and where to access these resources.
- Learn about the initial evaluations investigating the effectiveness of RME programs for low-income couples.
- Ponder and speculate upon future directions for this research and the field.

Introduction

Becky is a mother of two living in Atlanta, GA. She has never been married but has two children from two different partners. Her current partner, Jeff, is alright, but sometimes he drinks too much and gets moody when he comes home from his multiple jobs. But, at least he has a job, Becky tells herself. Becky got pregnant at age fifteen and dropped out of high school. However, the guy didn't stay with her long and so her fairytale dreams were crushed pretty early in life. One day, she sees a flier for a relationship education class with free dinner one day a week. She decides to take it home and ask Jeff if he wants to go. "What's wrong with our relationship now?" he says. "I just want to make it better . . . think about getting married someday . . ."

she says. Somehow, she convinces Jeff to try it out, but she can tell they are both really nervous when they show up for the first time.

For many low-income couples like Becky and Jeff, forming and sustaining a healthy, long-term relationship is a struggle. In these disadvantaged populations, all the other problems of the day often overwhelm or dilute their desires to improve their relationship. Many of these couples struggle to know what "healthy" relationships look like because of the environment and family backgrounds they grew up in. However, despite these challenges, most couples still feel a strong desire to get married and have a happy, long-term relationship (Edin & Reed, 2005; Gibson-Davis, Edin, & McLanahan, 2005).

This raises a significant question: Can **Relationship and Marriage Education**, or **RME** (Halford, 2011), help low-income couples achieve their relationship aspirations? What are the special needs and challenges for these couples? How do we tailor RME classes for these couples? This chapter seeks to shed light on these questions and encourages the reader to ponder and develop answers for themselves on these issues. RME for low-income couples is fairly new—only about a decade old—so there are still many questions. Consequently, this is a fertile area for young researchers to contribute to the field with new ideas, out-of-the-box thinking, and rigorous research. This is also an important area for current public policy work because of the substantial tax dollars that go into addressing the effects of family instability (Scafidi, 2008).

Challenges and Barriers

RME has been shown to be generally effective with middle-class, white couples (Fawcett, Hawkins, Blanchard, & Carroll, 2010; Hawkins, Blanchard, Baldwin, & Fawcett, 2008). However, the lives of white, educated couples can be very different from low-income, disadvantaged couples. For example, a married, middle-class couple with a comfortable job and income might have challenges with parenting children, communication about sensitive subjects, and conflict resolution. However, they are not worried about where their next meal is going to come from, how to deal with an incarcerated ex-boyfriend/girlfriend, and whether they are going to get evicted next month because they can't pay the rent. Low-income couples often deal with these challenges and more and do not have the same amount of resources to manage these struggles.

Low-income couples face a variety of challenges: environmental, psychological, and emotional. Their environmental stressors can be unreliable transportation, no childcare, varying work schedules, and limited financial resources (Karney & Bradbury, 2005). Having multiple low-paying jobs with irregular schedules can make finding family time and/or attending a RME class very difficult. Even if the couple does find the time to come to a class, an old car that breaks down or no childcare could prevent their continuing attendance. Finally, limited financial resources places enormous stress on any relationship and can lead to conflict.

Other significant barriers to forming healthy relationships among low-income couples are psychological, such as the heightened risk for mental illness and problems associated with substance abuse (Carlson et al., 2014). Addictions to any substance can undermine the couple's relationship, trust, and financial goals. And, as a consequences of these addictions, many couples face incarceration of one spouse and the issues that arise with reentry and reintegration into the family, the community, and the workplace (Day, Acock, Bahr, & Arditti, 2005). Additionally, depression and mental illness, common in low income families, are associated with lower family functioning and can be barriers to couple satisfaction (Sarmiento & Cardemil, 2009).

Lastly, many low-income couples also have different emotional stressors than middle-class couples. Many low-income couples are not married and have uncertain futures together as a couple. Knobloch argues that being uncertain about your relationship makes people interpret comments, actions, or behaviors in a negative light and can lead to more negative communication (Knobloch, 2010). Thus, couples that are unsure about their relationships can have more negative interpretations and interactions because of the uncertainty. Moreover, some have speculated that cohabiting couples face a double dose of challenges: dating-couple issues (e.g., commitment, time together, discovering shared interests and hobbies) as well as married couple issues (e.g., household labor, gender roles, parenting) (Rhoades, Stanley, & Markman, 2012). With all of these environmental, psychological, and emotional challenges, can low-income couples be expected to gain from relationship education classes?

Because of these challenges, some speculate that we must help these couples first become financially stable and relieve some of these stressors *before* we can help them improve their relationships. The rationale is that these couples cannot focus on their relationships when they are worried about how to feed their families the next day and other problems (Johnson, 2012; Karney & Bradbury, 2005; Trail & Karney, 2012).

However, others believe that helping these couples improve their relationships will help them manage their stressors more effectively and help them improve their financial situations. This second opinion was held by Wade Horn, who initiated the U.S. government's support of relationship education for low-income couples as Assistant Secretary for Children and Families in the Administration for Children and Families (ACF). These efforts in 2002 became the ACF **Healthy Marriage Initiative (HMI)** funded through the **Temporary Assistance to Needy Families** (TANF) program. For more details about the ACF Healthy Marriages and Relationships Initiative, see National Healthy Marriage Resource Center (2010). The TANF program goals include the following: "reduce unwed childbirths, encourage the formation of two-parent families and reduce welfare dependency by encouraging marriage and work." With these goals in mind, the U.S. government funded many different community organizations to provide RME for low-income individuals and couples across the country.

Still others take a middle approach and believe that RME combined with other resources, like employment programs, substance abuse programs, and childcare, will be most effective in helping low-income couples. When a second round of federal funding for RME occurred in 2011, there was a greater emphasis on combining RME programs with other local resources in the community. In addition, President Obama has publicly acknowledged: "Expanding access to such [marriage and relationship education] services to low-income couples, perhaps in concert with . . . other services already available, should be something everybody can agree on" (Obama, 2008, p. 334).

Recruitment and Retention

How do we reach low-income couples? How do we encourage them to take the time to come to classes? How do we get them involved and excited and learning once they come? When it comes to low-income couples, practitioners have been using a "learn as you go" framework. Some people, however, have summarized their efforts and found several initial potential best practices to recruiting low-income couples.

In recruitment, there are two basic types: active and passive. **Active recruitment** encompasses speaking directly with the potential participants in face-to-face interaction. On the other hand, **passive recruitment** is nondirective and engages participants through the Internet, mailings, advertisements, and fliers. Ryan Carlson and a group of researchers set out to discover if there was a difference in active and passive recruitment methods for low-income couples. They found a gender difference: passive recruitment was better for women, but active recruitment was better for men (Carlson et al., 2014). Additionally, couples that were recruited passively required less effort to come to the initial intake appointment.

Others have found that recruiting multiple family members works more effectively than recruiting only one member of the family (Preloran, Browner, & Lieber, 2001). In the vignette above, recruiting *both* Becky and Jeff at the same time might have been more effective for Jeff's interest and reduced the pressure on Becky. However, usually we rely on recruiting one partner and having that partner tell the other about the program (Carlson et al., 2014). Some RME programs overcame this problem by recruiting during the hospital visit of the expectant mother (Wood, McConnell, Moore, Clarkwest, & Hsueh, 2012). Others postulate that most recruiting efforts should focus on men, because men need more convincing than women to come to RME classes (Carlson et al., 2012). Along these lines, the government is also funding responsible fatherhood programs in addition to healthy marriage programs (see https://hmrf.acf.hhs.gov/whats-new/

responsible-fatherhood/). Some of these programs include content on sustaining healthy relationships with the mother of their child.

Another effective method for recruitment is partnering with other agencies that normally serve these low-income populations (Hawkins & Ooms, 2012). Many RME programs have partnered with other local agencies and programs that offer employment help, job training, early childhood education (e.g., Head Start agencies), housing, and health care. These agencies have already established connections in the community and have already successfully contacted low-income couples. By being connected to these other agencies, RME programs have been able to gain access to low-income couples and, in turn, refer their participants back to these agencies for additional help.

However, once we interest low-income couples in coming to these programs, we still have the problem of retention: helping the couples to stay and complete the programs. Some have found that the use of incentives such as a free dinner, free childcare, and transportation vouchers have helped (Wood et al., 2012). Others find that cultural sensitivity in the curricula and the way in which the information is presented matters (Preloran et al., 2001). We will discuss this point more directly as we look at the different programs that have been developed specifically for low-income couples and how existing programs have been adapted to fit these couples' needs.

Researchers have also found that having a facilitator that is demographically similar to the participants may be important (Bradford, Adler-Baeder, Ketring, & Smith, 2012). Indeed, couples giving feedback in surveys and focus groups have expressed that they especially appreciate their relationship with the facilitator and with other couples they meet at the RME classes who are in similar situations. This leads us to suspect that one of the greatest factors in retention of couples in RME classes is the *relationships* that they form in those classes: both with the facilitator and with other couples. It might be that these new relationships formed at RME classes become a sort of support system. And these low-income couples might be especially in need of a support system—specifically one that is supportive of their couple relationship. Perhaps these couples do not get much support (encouragement for their couple relationship) from their extended families, work environments, or peer groups.

Additionally, when low-income couples are asked about what could be improved about these RME programs, they suggest several things: extending the services, having more reunion events or booster sessions, covering even more content, and making the programs more widely available (Dion et al., 2006, 2008). Thus, it seems like couples do enjoy these classes and want more of them.

However, despite these preliminary findings, recruitment and retention still remains a challenge for delivering RME to low-income couples (Hawkins & Ooms, 2012). Overall, not one set of incentives or recruitment and engagement efforts will work for every program. Each program needs to evaluate its target audiences in their communities and discover what will work best for them (Administration for Children and Families, 2014).

Overview of Existing Programs

As RME programs have shifted more attention to low-income couples, many existing programs revised their curricula to address this population and their unique challenges. For instance, the well-known PREP curriculum was adapted to Within Our Reach. Other adapted programs focusing on low-income couples include Family Expectations, Love's Cradle, Caring for My Family, For Our Future—For Our Family, and Loving Couples Loving Children (LCLC). (Programs used by the current grantees can be found at https://hmrf.acf.hhs.gov/programs/find-a-program/)

These curricula were adapted in at least two major ways: in content and in pedagogy. In content, they adapted these programs to fit the specific situations of low-income couples: their uncertain futures together as a couple, becoming parents before they became a couple, higher risk for aggression and domestic violence, and talking about money pressures. Some programs adapted the content to fit a certain ethnic culture (if they were serving a specific homogenous population) (Hawkins & Ooms, 2012). Additionally, because many of the couples have multiple children from multiple partners, co-parenting has become a substantive content element for most programs targeting low-income couples (Wood et al., 2012).

When it comes to domestic violence, some have voiced the opinion that RME programs might actually encourage those that are in unhealthy or violent relationships to stay together, thus endangering the victims (Ooms et al., 2006). Publicly supported programs, however, must develop a protocol for dealing with this issue (Bradford, Skogrand, & Higginbotham, 2011). Most protocol involve some kind of screening, as well as information about where participants can seek help for domestic violence problems. Furthermore, most curricula used in these programs address explicitly the topic of relationship violence as well as teach skills for more effective problem solving.

In pedagogy, program developers tried to adapt programs to be more hands-on, engaging, discussion-based, and less lecture-based. Most low-income couples do not have much education beyond high school. Thus, it would be harder for them to sit through a two-hour class where the facilitator lectures at the front of the room most of the time. Consequently, many programs have tried to adjust their educational style to provide for more videos, hands-on learning activities, and group and couple discussions.

Are We Reaching Low-income Couples?

When a program is initially started, sometimes it is difficult to reach the targeted population. With RME programs across the country, how many are reaching low-income couples? What are the demographic characteristics of these couples?

Recently, the Administration of Children and Families came out with a report summarizing the work that has been done and the demographics of those that have been served recently. According to the Healthy Marriage Participant Profile on ACF's website, they found that about 80% of the couples were at or below 200% of the federal poverty level (Administration for Children and Families, 2014). Furthermore, approximately half of the people taking RME classes had less than a high school education and only about half were employed. Although percentages differ dramatically by program, ACF has found significant racial and ethnic diversity among the participants in these programs: about 38% of participants were African American and 38% were Caucasian. By ethnicity, about 34% were Hispanic or Latino.

Some funded healthy marriage programs also collected information about the participants' romantic status and other family items. Approximately 70% of the couples were currently cohabiting and about 40% of the couples had children from previous relationships. This coincides with what we have expected about the challenges of low-income couple relationships: They can be uncertain about the future of their relationships and they often have children from previous relationships.

Assessment of RME for Low-income Couples

With the onset of the government's support of RME and its focus on low-income couples, people are concerned about its effectiveness. RME's effects on middle-income, white couples is quite robust, but would it work similarly for diverse, low-income couples?

While many researchers began their own studies on various programs, the government decided to conduct two large-scale studies on RME for low-income couples. These two studies, **Building Strong Families (BSF)** and **Supporting Healthy Marriage (SHM)**, became the focus of much public attention and controversy as the results began to unfold. The results from these studies were not overly positive: They found some small positive effects of RME, but they also found many null effects and a few slightly negative effects. Subsequently, many have wondered why they found such mixed results. Part of the reason might be that these studies were the first focused on low-income couples and as such should be considered a trial run that shows us how we need to improve. Another reason might be problems with program retention. In the BSF study, 40% of the treatment group (the group that received RME) did not come to a single class; only 10% of the treatment group received a strong dose of the intervention. This could bias results and mask the benefits that the attenders reaped from the RME classes.

While the results of the highly rigorous BSF and SHM studies were discouraging, many smaller studies were finding positive results with low-income couples (Cox & Shirer, 2009; Einhorn et al., 2008; Owen, Quirk, Bergen, Inch, & France, 2012; Stanley et al., 2005). Many ACF grantees also showed strong positive changes, especially in communication and conflict resolution (Administration for Children and Families, 2014). Why the mixed results?

A recent meta-analytic study set out to answer this question by analyzing all the RME studies with low-income samples. Hawkins and Erickson (in press) analyzed 22 control-group studies and 25 one-group/pre-post studies of RME programs targeted to lower-income individuals and couples. "Lower income" was defined as income less than twice the national poverty level. In control-group studies, they found that RME for diverse, lower-income couples has small, positive relationship effects on self-reports of relationship quality, communication, and domestic aggression with an overall effect size of $d = .061$ ($p < .01, k = 22$). More specifically, they found somewhat stronger effects for married couples ($d = .091$) than unmarried couples (i.e., cohabiting couples or dating couples, $d = -.016$). They also found that "near-poor" (1–2 times the poverty level) participants ($d = .074$) had more positive results than participants below the poverty level ($d = -.033$). Additionally, the RME programs produced greater positive effects when they had higher percentages of couples experiencing relationship distress at program entry (for < 25% distressed: $d = -0.033$; for 25%+ distressed: $d = 0.072$).

Furthermore, there were stronger effects for pre-post studies compared to control-group studies with an overall effect size of $d = 0.352$ ($p < .001, k = 25$). Looking at specific outcome variables in the pre-post studies, they found effect sizes were significant for communication skills ($d = 0.453$), relationship satisfaction/quality ($d = 0.362$), and co-parenting ($d = 0.251$) but not for relationship stability and relationship aggression. For the pre-post studies, they also found that ethnicity was a significant moderator, with studies with greater ethnic diversity finding more positive results for < 25%: $d = 0.099$; for 25%–49%: $d = 0.232$; for 50%+: $d = 0.450$).

Cultural Implications

So what does this study mean? The researchers found that relationship education does work for low-income couples, but the effects size are small for the most rigorous studies. Clearly, there is still much that needs to be improved for RME to be effective. It is encouraging, however, to find that programs serving racially and ethnically diverse couples showed greater improvement than programs with less diversity. It seems that many programs are succeeding in being culturally sensitive and engaging diverse audiences. It is also good to see that distressed couples appear to be benefitting from RME. Perhaps these distressed couples realize their need for change and are more motivated than other couples. Furthermore, these distressed couples may have limited access to relationship therapy services compared to financially better-off couples and thus appreciate the opportunity to learn from RME classes. Hence, RME programs may provide a valuable service to help distressed, lower-income couples who want to strengthen their relationships.

However, this meta-analysis suggests several areas for improvement. First, RME programs appear not to be as helpful to cohabiting couples as they are to married couples. Perhaps it is easier to work on one's relationship when there already is a high sense of commitment. Indeed, one study showed that without a strong commitment, relationship development is undermined (Stanley, Rhoades, & Whitton, 2010) and there may be less motivation to make use of the healthy relationship knowledge and skills. RME needs to improve its ability to help couples with less commitment and clarity about a future together to strengthen their relationships. Second, this meta-analysis suggests there are smaller effects for "very poor" participants versus "near-poor" participants. Does severe financial stress overwhelm healthy relationship skills? Or does financial stress simply prevent full attendance and engagement in the class? These are questions that still need to be answered.

Conclusion

There is obviously still a steep learning curve to climb as practitioners and researchers continue to discover what RME methods/classes/programs work best for low-income couples. While we seek to improve on current efforts and programs, we also urge practitioners to explore novel content, new pedagogies, creative delivery methods, and more effective recruiting. Should we continue using the same programs and curricula? Should we focus on learning skills or simply helping couples focus more on their relationships and families in their hectic lives? Could we use new technologies to teach about relationship education skills? Would a media campaign that saturates the society produce better results than classes?

Overall, this is a very new area of research. There is ample work for improvement and room for new ideas. Emerging practitioners and scholars may bring fresh ideas and energy to this important work to help low-income couples, like Becky and Jeff, whose story introduced this chapter, achieve their relationship aspirations. Greater success in this area will bless the lives of their children, and that is the ultimate purpose of this work.

Key Points

- RME programs need to consider the unique challenges that low-income couples face and endeavor to address these needs in their programs.
- RME programs need to carefully evaluate how they recruit and retain participants.
- Overall, researchers have found small, positive effects for RME programs with low-income couples.
- Significant improvements and creative new ideas are needed to make RME for low-income couples more effective.

Discussion Questions

1. How could we recruit more low-income couples? How do we help them to stay engaged in the program?
2. What should be taught in these RME programs? How can we incorporate new technology in educating low-income couples?
3. What new, creative ways can we use for educating low-income couples about healthy relationships?
4. What outcomes should we measure to evaluate these RME programs?

Program Highlight

The Alabama Healthy Marriage & Relationship Education Initiative (www.alabamamarriage.org)

> Supported by federal grants, Alabama offers a variety of RME classes for engaged couples, youth, single and married individuals. A large part of their focus is on RME classes for low-income couples. They coordinate with many local agencies in different counties in Alabama to offer their services. However, besides information about their classes, they also have many other interesting and engaging links on their website, like the Relationship Reality TV, which has small video clips of how couples deal with real problems. They have a guide specifically for unmarried parents called "Raising Your Child Together" and resources in "The Alabama Marriage Handbook." There are also links to "Love Notes" and ideas for fun activities to do as a couple.

References and Further Readings

Administration for Children and Families. (2014). The impact of healthy marriage programs on low-income couples and families: Program perspectives from across the United States. Retrieved from http://hmrf.acf.hhs.gov/resources/the-impact-of-healthy-marriage-programs-on-low-income-couples-and-families-program-perspectives-from-across-the-united-states/

Bradford, A., Adler-Baeder, F., Ketring, S., & Smith, T. (2012). The role of participant-facilitator demographic match in couple and relationship education. *Family Relations, 61*, 51–64. doi:10.1111/j.1741-3729.2011.00679.x

Bradford, K., Skogrand, L., & Higginbotham, B. (2011). Intimate partner violence in a statewide couple and relationship education initiative. *Journal of Couple and Relationship Therapy, 10*, 169–184.

Carlson, R., Daire, A., Munyon, M., Soto, D., Bennett, A., Marshall, D., & McKinzie, C. (2012). Examining recruitment follow-up phone calls and their influence on attendance for husbands and wives in a marriage and relationship education program. *Marriage and Family Review, 48*, 82–95. doi:10.1080/01494929.2011.627493

Carlson, R., Fripp, J., Munyon, M., Daire, A., Johnson, J., & DeLorenzi, L. (2014). Examining passive and active recruitment methods for low-income couples in relationship education. *Marriage and Family Review, 50*, 76–91. doi:10.1080/01494929.2013.851055

Cox, R., & Shirer, K. (2009). Caring For My Family: A pilot study of a relationship and marriage education program for low-income unmarried parents. *Journal of Couple and Relationship Therapy, 8,* 343–364. doi:10.1080/15332690903246127

Day, R., Acock, A., Bahr, S., & Arditti, J. (2005). Incarcerated fathers returning home to children and families: Introduction to the special issue and a primer on doing research with men in prison. *Fathering, 3,* 183–200. doi:10.3149/fth.0303.183

Dion, M., Avellar, S., Zaveri, H., & Hershey, A. (2006). *Implementing healthy marriage programs for unmarried couples with children: Early lessons from the Building Strong Families project: Final report.* Washington, DC: Mathematica Policy Research. Retrieved from http://www.mathematica-pr.com/publications/pdfs/healthymarriageprogram.pdf

Dion, M., Hershey, A., Zaveri, H., Avellar, S., Strong, D., Silman, T., & Moore, R. (2008). *Implementation of the Building Strong Families program.* Washington, DC: Mathematica Policy Research, Inc. Retrieved from http://www.mathematica-mpr.com/publications/PDFs/bsfimplementation.pdf

Edin, K., & Reed, J. (2005). Why don't they just get married? Barriers to marriage among the disadvantaged. *The Future of Children, 15,* 117–137.

Einhorn, L., Williams, T., Stanley, S., Wunderlin, N., Markman, H., & Eason, J. (2008). PREP inside and out: Marriage education for inmates. *Family Process, 47,* 341–356. doi:10.1111/j.1545-5300.2008.00257.x

Fawcett, E., Hawkins, A., Blanchard, V., & Carroll, J. (2010). Do premarital education programs really work? A meta-analytic study. *Family Relations, 59,* 232–239. doi:10.1111/j.1741-3729.2010.00598.x

Gibson-Davis, C., Edin, K., & McLanahan, S. (2005). High hopes but even higher expectations: The retreat from marriage among low-income couples. *Journal of Marriage and Family, 67,* 1301–1312.

Halford, W. (2011). *Marriage and relationship education: What works and how to provide it.* New York, NY: Guilford Press.

Hawkins, A.J. (2013). *The forever initiative: A feasible public policy agenda to help couples form and sustain healthy marriages and relationships.* North Charleston, SC: CreateSpace Independent Publishing Platform.

Hawkins, A., Blanchard, V., Baldwin, S., & Fawcett, E. (2008). Does marriage and relationship education work? A meta-analytic study. *Journal of Consulting and Clinical Psychology, 76,* 723–734. doi:10.1037/a0012584

Hawkins, A. & Erickson, S. (2015). Is couple and relationship education effective for lower income participants? A meta-analytic study. *Journal of Family Psychology, 29,* 59–68.

Hawkins, A., & Ooms, T. (2012). Can marriage and relationship education be an effective policy tool to help low-income couples form and sustain healthy marriages and relationships? A review of lessons learned. *Marriage and Family Review, 48,* 524–554. doi:10.1080/01494929.2012.677751

Johnson, M. (2012). Healthy marriage initiatives: On the need for empiricism in policy implementation. *American Psychologist, 67,* 296–308. doi:10.1037/a0027743

Karney, B., & Bradbury, T. (2005). Contextual influences on marriage: Implications for policy and intervention. *Current Directions in Psychological Science, 14,* 171–174. doi:10.1111/j.0963-7214.2005.00358.x

Knobloch, L. (2010). Relational uncertainty and interpersonal communication. In S. Smith & S. Wilson (Eds.), *New directions in interpersonal communication research.* (pp. 69–93). Thousand Oaks, CA US: Sage Publications, Inc.

National Healthy Marriage Resource Center. (2010). *Administration for Children and Families Healthy Marriage Initiative, 2002–2009.* Fairfax, VA: Author. Retrieved from http://www.healthymarriageinfo.org/about/faq/download.aspx?id=337

Obama, B. (2008). *The audacity of hope: Thoughts on reclaiming the American Dream* (Reprint ed.). New York, NY: Vintage.

Ooms, T., Boggess, J., Menard, A., Myrick, M., Roberts, P., Tweedie, J., & Wilson, P. (2006). *Building bridges between healthy marriage, responsible fatherhood, and domestic violence programs.* Washington, DC: Center for Law and Social Policy.

Owen, J., Quirk, K., Bergen, C., Inch, L.J., & France, T. (2012). The effectiveness of PREP with lower-income racial/ethnic minority couples. *Journal of Marital and Family Therapy, 38*(Suppl. 1), 296–307. doi:10.1111/j.1752-0606.2012.00294.x

Preloran, H., Browner, C., & Lieber, E. (2001). Strategies for motivating Latino couples' participation in qualitative health research and their effects on sample construction. *American Journal of Public Health, 91*, 1832–1841.

Rhoades, G., Stanley, S., & Markman, H. (2012). The impact of the transition to cohabitation on relationship functioning: Cross-sectional and longitudinal findings. *Journal of Family Psychology, 26*, 348–358. doi: 10.1037.a0028316

Sarmiento, I., & Cardemil, E. (2009). Family functioning and depression in low-income Latino couples. *Journal of Marital and Family Therapy, 35*, 432–445. doi:10.1111/j.1752-0606.2009.00139.x

Scafidi, B. (2008). *The taxpayer costs of divorce and unwed childbearing: First-ever estimates for the nation and for all fifty states.* New York, NY: Institute for American Values.

Stanley, S., Allen, E., Markman, H., Saiz, C., Bloomstrom, G., Thomas, R., Schumm, W., & Bailey, A. (2005). Dissemination and evaluation of marriage education in the Army. *Family Process, 44*, 187–201. doi:10.1111/j.1545-5300.2005.00053.x

Stanley, S., Rhoades, G., & Whitton, S. (2010). Commitment: Functions, formation, and the securing of romantic attachment. *Journal of Family Theory and Review, 2*, 243–257. doi: 10.1111/j.1756-2589.2010.00060.x

Trail, T., & Karney, B. (2012). What's (not) wrong with low-income marriages. *Journal of Marriage and Family, 74*, 413–427. doi:10.1111/j.1741-3737.2012.00977.x

Wood, R., McConnell, S., Moore, Q., Clarkwest, A., & Hsueh, J. (2012). The effects of building strong families: A healthy marriage and relationship skills education program for unmarried parents. *Journal of Policy Analysis and Management, 31*, 228–252.

19

RELATIONSHIP AND MARRIAGE EDUCATION FOR REMARRIED COUPLES AND STEPFAMILIES

Brian J. Higginbotham and Sheryl Goodey

LEARNING GOALS

- Learn about the diversity within, and unique challenges of, stepfamilies.
- Learn recruitment and retention strategies for stepfamily audiences.
- Learn about children participating in stepfamily RME.
- Learn how facilitator characteristics and skills contribute to ratings of stepfamily RME.
- Learn practical considerations for implementing stepfamily RME.

Introduction

Remarriages and **stepfamilies** have received increased attention in the past decade. The attention stems from the prevalence of divorce and repartnering and an interest in how unique issues in stepfamilies affect relationship quality (Sweeney, 2010). In addition to normative marital challenges, many couples in stepfamilies also face negative **cultural stereotypes** about their family structure, stepparenting responsibilities, and ongoing interactions with ex-partners (Ganong & Coleman, 2004). Addressing stepfamily specific issues can distract couples from attending to the enhancement of their own relationships and can, unintentionally, lead to increased conflict and dissolution (Schoen & Canudas-Romo, 2006). Fortunately, clinicians have noted that many of the problems commonly encountered by couples in stepfamilies stem from preventable or modifiable situations, not individual psychopathology (e.g., Visher & Visher, 1996). Consequently, scholars and family life educators have advocated for educational interventions as an effective mechanism to help prepare and assist couples with step-relationships (Adler-Baeder & Higginbotham, 2004; Lucier-Greer, Adler-Baeder, Ketring, Harcourt, & Smith, 2012).

Theoretical Foundations and History

There are various relationship and marriage education (RME) curricula marketed to couples in stepfamilies. Some explicitly utilize theory to guide their content, while others do not. For example, *Stepping Together* (Bosch, Gebeke, & Meske, 1992) uses family systems theory. *Smart Steps for Stepfamilies* (Adler-Baeder, 2007) draws upon ecological, systems, life course, and family strengths perspectives. Some curricula use theory to guide the design of the program. In *Learning to Step Together* (Currier, 1982) the author draws upon adult learning theory as the rationale for a variety of educational approaches, including lectures, discussions, role-plays, and exercises while *Skills Training for Stepparents* (Levant & Nelson, 1984) utilizes interpersonal process recall methods. (For a review of programs see Adler-Baeder & Higginbotham, 2004; and Whitton, Nicholson, Markman, & Pryor, 2008.)

Curriculum and Other Program Issues

It is important for practitioners to consider unique stepfamily issues in order to successfully meet the needs of their RME participants. Best practices involve the recognition of developmental differences between couples in first marriages without children and couples in remarriages and stepfamilies. Because of the added complexity in their lives, stepfamily RME should address both common and unique stressors for adults and children (e.g., Halford, Markman, Kline, & Stanley, 2003; Adler-Baeder & Higginbotham, 2004; Lawton & Sanders, 1994). Many of the issues that impact couple functioning are similar for all relationships. Good communication and conflict management, for example, are important, regardless of the family structure. However, general RME derived from the literature on first marriages offers an incomplete examination of the full range of factors related to couple functioning in remarriages (Adler-Baeder & Higginbotham, 2004). Consequently, when working with couples in stepfamilies, it is advisable to use a curriculum that has been developed specifically to meet their needs.

In a 2004 review of the research on factors that influence couple functioning in stepfamilies, the emergent themes included the importance of social support, validating the stepfamily experience, developing realistic expectations for stepfamily development, navigating (step)parent–(step)child relationships, prioritizing the couple relationship, and managing relationships with former partners (Adler-Baeder & Higginbotham, 2004). Without covering these topics, educators run the risk of leaving out important information and skills that stepfamily RME participants are seeking (see Higginbotham, Davis, Smith, Dansie, Skogrand, & Reck, 2012).

Adler-Baeder and Higginbotham (2004) reviewed the content and design of eight RME programs for stepfamilies. The coverage and approach of the curricula varied, but all addressed at least some of the factors unique to stepfamilies.

Few of the programs attended to children. Only one program provided classes concurrently for children while one other suggested attendance in some of the sessions. Consistent with a **family systems theory** (Nichols & Schwartz, 2001), couple functioning in stepfamilies could be enhanced by children participating in stepfamily RME and learning about stepfamily development while developing effective communication skills, conflict and anger management strategies.

Target Audience

Stepfamily RME generally targets couples with **step-relationships**. A couple with a step-relationship can be defined as a committed relationship between two adults where at least one of the adults has a child(ren) from a previous relationship(s). Married and engaged couples with step-relationships are often the primary focus of recruitment efforts. However, a large number of couples with step-relationships are not married (e.g., cohabitation unions). Consequently, many stepfamily RME programs, particularly those funded through public funds, can target all couples in step-relationships regardless of their marital status.

Stepfamily RME programs should consider the programmatic implications stemming from the diversity amongst stepfamilies (e.g., remarried couples, unions that include one spouse who has been married before and another who is entering his/her first marriage, cohabitating couples with children from previous unions, homosexual couples who would like to remarry but may not live in states that allow it). It has been suggested that participants may feel most comfortable in family life education with people of similar characteristics (e.g., Lengua, Roosa, Schupak-Neuberg, Michaels, Berg, & Weschler, 1992). For stepfamily RME specifically it has been proposed, "Although program content can be infused into general marriage education curricula for mixed-group participants, effectiveness will likely be enhanced if couples forming stepfamilies participate in a homogeneous group" (Adler-Baeder & Higginbotham, 2004, p. 455). Practitioners may wonder what degree of homogeneity is optimal. There are numerous and diverse possible partner combinations and the presence of 'yours, mine, or ours' children introduces additional variations (Ganong & Coleman, 2004). How targeted and homogeneous should participants in a stepfamily education course be? Research is emerging to help practitioners answer these questions.

Marital Status. In a study that specifically explored the experiences of married and unmarried participants, Higginbotham and Skogrand (2010) found as long as participants were experiencing stepfamily-related issues—whether it was through cohabitation, marriage, or serious dating—participants benefited fairly equitably. The implications of this finding are multifaceted. First, programmatically, it does not appear necessary to target or screen out stepcouples by relationship status. In this study, there did not emerge any reason why married and unmarried committed stepcouples should be discouraged or disallowed from taking stepfamily RME classes jointly. Married participants may consider the educational opportunity as "remarriage enrichment," while unmarried participants may see it as "marriage preparation" or "relationship education." Whatever participants call it, if the curriculum focuses on relationship skills in the context of stepfamily life, the material can be relevant and helpful to a diverse group of stepcouples.

A second implication is that joint attendance of married and unmarried stepcouples can have an additive benefit. Reports from unmarried participants in the Higginbotham and Skogrand (2010) study suggest that the participants value the different perspectives of those who are married and more experienced. One man enjoyed the diversity in his class, which included cohabiting, engaged, and married stepcouples. He described a benefit of the group's composition: "We were in there with stepfamilies who had been stepfamilies for long periods of time . . . and it really helped because a lot of the problems that we were going through, they've already experienced, and they would share with us what worked for them and what didn't" (p. 145).

If fear of marriage, commitment, or relationship failure is a concern for unmarried stepcouples, they may benefit from the normalizing and social support that occurs through group discussions with other stepcouples from diverse backgrounds and arrangements. Some unmarried couples may understandably be reticent about remarriage because of the things they see in the media (see Leon & Angst, 2005). However, in a RME class that includes married participants, unmarried couples can get a nonsensationalized or stereotyped message about the remarriage experience. For example, one female participant shared, "Everyone kept telling me, 'But he has kids!' . . . I thought that I was the only case, but now I realize that there are many people who are in our situation. . . . After taking this class, my life changed. It doesn't bother me that he already had kids" (Higginbotham & Skogrand, 2010, p. 145).

A third implication deals with the timing of stepfamily education. Because of some negative findings regarding cohabitation outcomes (Smock, 2000; Xu, Hudspeth, & Bartkowski, 2006), practitioners may question efforts that appear to promote this family structure. However, the question practitioners should ask is if the period of cohabitation is the "teachable moment" for stepfamilies. Unmarried stepcouples—especially those who enroll in RME programs—likely consider cohabitation to be a type of remarriage preparation, and increasingly it appears cohabitation is to remarriage what engagement is for first marriage (Higginbotham, Miller, & Niehuis, 2009; Wineberg & McCarthy, 1998).

Sexual Orientation. Regardless of sexual orientation, couples experience similar transitions and stressors in the process of becoming part of a stepfamily (Johnson, Wright, Craig, Gilchrist, Lane, & Haigh, 2008). Same-sex couples in stepfamilies can encounter the same issues that heterosexual stepcouples experience, such as parenting nonbiological children, finances, and relationships with ex-spouses (Ganong & Coleman, 2004). However, there is little information on the experience or effectiveness of same-sex couples participating in stepfamily

RME. Drawing upon participants in a multiyear stepfamily education initiative, Skogrand, Mendez, and Higginbotham (2013) performed a detailed case study of two different lesbian stepfamilies. They found a group stepfamily RME format was beneficial for both lesbian stepfamilies. In fact, their experiences echoed findings from the heterosexual participants in the same initiative (cf. Higginbotham & Skogrand, 2010; Higginbotham, Skogrand, & Torres, 2010). Many of the challenges faced by the two lesbian couples were shared by heterosexual participants, thus building a sense of normalcy.

As was the case with nonmarried stepcouples attending RME with married stepcouples, the lesbian couples found stepfamily RE helpful despite the heterogeneity of their class members' relationships. They specifically mentioned how helpful it was to hear and learn from others who had experience living in stepfamilies. The fact that the other couples in the class, who were heterosexual, experienced many of the same challenges was reaffirming and empowering. The group format facilitated social support and participants enjoyed the opportunity to share their personal approaches and solutions with other stepfamilies (cf. Skogrand, Torres, & Higginbotham, 2010).

Stepfathers. Stepfathers may be particularly difficult to recruit for RME. Research with stepfather participants suggests some may have an initial resistance to attending the RME stepfamily course. Although women are more likely to be interested in remarriage preparation (Higginbotham, Miller, & Niehuis, 2009), one study found that stepfathers, after encouragement to attend by their significant other, will attend and can learn from the experience (Higginbotham, Davis, Smith, Dansie, Skogrand, & Reck, 2012). In this study only a handful of stepfathers were the impetus behind their family's attendance at RME; it was more common that they needed a push or pull. This hesitancy might be due to the moderating nature of the couple relationship on the stepfather–stepchild relationship. "Because stepfathers have no rights or obligations to stepchildren outside of their romantic relationship with the children's mother, mothers might exert even more control over stepfather–stepchild relationships than they do over relationships between biological fathers and children" (Adamsons, O'Brien, & Pasley, 2007, p. 142). It could also be due to the stigma or historical "brushing off" that men have received from social interventions (e.g., Daniel & Taylor, 1999; Parent, Saint-Jacques, Beaudry, & Robitaille, 2007). This combination of maternal gatekeeping, unclear expectations, stigma, and few social norms might lead to hesitancy on the part of the stepfather to participate in a family-oriented activity.

The ongoing level of involvement of the biological father of the children might also affect a stepfather's motivation to attend stepfamily education courses. The complexity of the stepfather situation was captured by Marsiglio and Hinojosa (2007), who said, "Stepfathers must learn to coordinate their involvement in a pre-existing family dance in which women have established relationships and a family culture with their children and, in most cases, the children's biological father(s)" (p. 845). Stepfather hesitancy might simply be due to a characteristic of males in general to avoid seeking formal relationship advice, or perhaps advertising of RME course might appeal more strongly to women in stepfamilies. Lack of attendance could also be due to an already busy work or family schedule. In any case, practitioners should keep in mind that stepfathers might not participate in a family intervention without being encouraged, invited, and welcomed. In some cases, recruitment may be more efficient if efforts are aimed toward mothers in stepfamilies who are then encouraged to bring their spouses along (cf. Higginbotham et al., 2009).

Children. Practitioners of RME for couples with step-relationships should consider the participants' children (Nicholson, Phillips, Whitton, Halford, & Sanders, 2007). The defining feature of stepfamilies is the presence of a child from a previous relationship (Ganong & Coleman, 2004). A child may become part of a stepfamily by being in a remarried couple family or a cohabiting couple family (Teachman & Tedrow, 2008). The model typically used to provide general RME involves small groups of couples who come together for face-to-face programs with a facilitator who provides educational information (Halford, Moore, Wilson, Farrugia, & Dyer, 2004). This has historically been the case for remarriage and stepfamily education offerings as well (e.g., Nadler, 1983; Nelson & Levant, 1991; Webber, Sharpley, & Rowley, 1988). Although some might argue that marriage education is only for adults, when it comes to strengthening couples in stepfamilies, the involvement of children is clearly implicated and should not be underestimated. Leading scholars and practitioners have repeatedly called attention to the pivotal role of children for stepfamily outcomes (Higginbotham, Skogrand, & Torres, 2010). For example, Hetherington and Kelly (2003) explained:

> In first marriages, a satisfying marital relationship is the cornerstone of happy family life, leading to more positive parent–child relationships and more congenial sibling relationships. In many stepfamilies, the sequence is reversed. Establishing some kind of workable relationship between stepparents and stepchildren may be the key to a happy second marriage and to successful functioning in stepfamilies. (p. 181)

Despite this link between stepparent–stepchild relationships and couple outcomes, very few stepfamily programs use systemic family interventions. In terms of stepfamily RME programs that do include education for adults and children, there appears to be benefits to both. Increased parental awareness of common stepfamily issues, structured family time, and skill development—particularly empathy—help adults to be more sensitive and engaged. Furthermore, by attending their own class, youth develop and refine their own set of skills. They learn to empathize and are perceived by their parents to emerge with enhanced communication and anger management skills. Finally, the social support offered by peers and nonparental adults helps to normalize the situation and provides encouragement to work through their struggles. Collectively, these benefits appear to lead to more supportive, understanding, and adaptive (step)parent/(step)child relationships.

The extant research points to a number of programmatic implications. Remarriage programs that serve couples with children should consider broadening their interventions to include children. While the adults are working on knowledge and skill development, children can be working through their own issues and can be developing their own skills. Parents report youth skill development in the areas of expression, empathy, and communication to be common and beneficial for their children (Higginbotham, Skogrand, & Torres, 2010). For a youth class to be effective, the recommendations of Adler-Baeder and Higginbotham (2004) should be heeded. Specifically, if a curriculum allows for youth participation, "facilitators should be comfortable with the dynamics of the necessary learning environment for preadolescents and adolescents, and knowledgeable in child development and children's learning styles" (p. 455). Because the issues of emotional safety and facilitator support emerged as important themes, practitioners who are not accustomed to working with youth "may want to involve experienced youth development leaders as facilitators" (p. 455).

Although involving children in stepfamily education interventions appears to be beneficial, not all organizations have the space or staff to offer concurrent classes. Other formats likewise deserve future study and consideration. For example, Robertson and colleagues (2006) have recommended providing materials and exercises to parents so that they can go home and share them with their children. Through a variety of mediums, stepfamily RME appears to have the potential to help children better understand and successfully address the complex relationship issues and transitions that result from being part of a stepfamily.

Cultural Implications

Although research on RME with ethnically diverse stepfamilies is limited, there are several published best-practice recommendations for Latino stepfamily education (Skogrand, Barrios-Bell, & Higginbotham, 2009; Skogrand, Mendez, & Higginbotham, 2014; Reck, Higginbotham, Skogrand, & Davis, 2012). These recommendations include having facilitators that understand the cultural values of those they are teaching. Values such as familism can be incorporated to better facilitate stepfamily programs serving Latinos. For example, children are an important aspect of the Latino culture and Latino families and RME attendance will be enhanced if it includes the entire family. Facilitators should promote class discussion and sharing among participants. However, participants may express frustration with the lack of a universally recognized Spanish term for "stepfamily." Some Spanish speakers use the terms *familias reconstuidas* while others say *familias ensambladas*. Based on interviews with stepfamily RME participants and facilitators, Reck and colleagues (2012) recommended sensitivity to differing attitudes about family structures and regional idiomatic differences by using an array of terms that capture the linguistic and cultural diversity. Some possible terms include *Familias Combinadas* ("combined families") or *Familas Neuva* ("new families").

Cultivating trusting relationships between program staff organizations and participants is also important for initiating and maintaining relationships throughout the program. One way to do this is to use culturally appropriate pictures and videos when demonstrating points. That said, Latino participants may have strong family and religious values (i.e., the family is sacred) and videos and cartoons that 'poke fun' or highlight the complexities of stepfamilies can unintentionally be offensive.

Evidence-based Research and Evaluation

The research on the effectiveness of relationship and marriage education (RME) for stepfamilies is nuanced. According to a recent meta-analysis, the interventions tend to have *small effects overall, with slightly larger effects when examining specific outcomes* (Lucier-Greer & Adler-Baeder, 2012). There are published qualitative studies suggesting stepfamily RME can be beneficial to married, unmarried, and lesbian stepfamilies and their children (Higginbotham & Skogrand, 2010; Higginbotham, Skogrand, & Torres, 2010; Skogrand, Mendez, & Higginbotham, 2013).

Professional Preparation and Training Issues

The clinical and RME literature contains numerous assumptions about the qualities and characteristics of effective therapists, facilitators, and educators. The literature distinguishes between membership group similarities, which are defined as "biological or physical commonalities" between the professional and client (e.g. ethnicity, gender, and age) and experience similarities, which are "similar life experiences or styles" (Atkinson & Schein, 1986, p. 332). Examples of membership group variables include marital status, treatment history, education, and family history. In regards to RME, prominent scholars have advised facilitators "should be a male-female couple" and that programs "ideally should have facilitators or mentor couples who are members of the same race or culture" as their participants (Ooms & Wilson, 2004, p. 446). In the RME literature specific to stepfamilies, there has also been recommendations for facilitators who have stepfamily experience (Adler–Baeder & Higginbotham, 2004).

Implementers of stepfamily RME may wonder if and how to apply these assumptions and recommendations, particularly when their available staff may or may not have commonalities with the potential participants. To provide research-based guidance on this topic, Higginbotham and Myler (2010) used a large data set of stepfamily RME facilitators and participants to code membership group and experience similarities and to evaluate the relationship with participant ratings. They also measured and evaluated characteristics of the facilitation (e.g., facilitator's ability to get people to participate, explain the course material, manage time).

A number of trends emerged from their study. Contrary to popular RME assumptions, membership group variables (being of the same ethnicity, gender, and age) did not appear to influence women's ratings of the *overall quality of the facilitators' work*. Even when membership group attributes were the only variables in the analyses, they accounted for less than 1% of the variance in women's ratings. In contrast, for male participants, being the same ethnicity as the facilitators was consistently related to higher facilitator ratings. For both men and women, facilitators' stepfamily experience did influence ratings, however, the type of stepfamily experience had differential effects. Facilitators who grew up in a stepfamily were rated more poorly by the participants. If, however, the facilitators currently lived in a stepfamily, they were rated higher.

Similar trends occurred in the statistical models predicting *overall quality of the program*. Men responded more positively when the course was led by facilitators who shared their same ethnicity. Women did not appear to be influenced by ethnic similarity, but there was a significant association with gender similarity. Both male and female participants rated the program more positively when taught by women. The reason for this gender preference was not clear, although it is consistent with some of the clinical research which has suggested a cross-gender preference for female therapists (Atkinson & Schein, 1986). As was the case with prior analyses, facilitators' stepfamily experiences had differential effects for men's rating of overall program quality. Currently living in a stepfamily was positively associated, yet growing up in a stepfamily was negatively related.

Explaining these differential findings for stepfamily experience is difficult, particularly because it is not clear how much of the facilitators' backgrounds were openly shared with the participants. During the initial facilitator training, facilitators were encouraged to appropriately share their own experiences as a way to cultivate credibility (cf. Adler-Baeder & Higginbotham, 2004; Hawkins, Carroll, Doherty, & Willoughby, 2004), but the evaluation tool did not measure whether or when participants actually found out their facilitators were raised or currently living in a stepfamily.

Higginbotham and Myler's (2010) findings raise several questions about staffing RME classes for stepfamilies. Do facilitators who grew up in stepfamilies unintentionally convey negative "vibes" about stepfamily life? Are they more realistic about the difficulties and open about the challenges, particularly for children? When adult stepchildren facilitate a group do they see "challenges and deficits" more readily than "strengths and potential" (Ooms & Wilson, 2004, p. 446)? On the other hand, could facilitators who are currently in a stepfamily pass along the optimism and hope that they themselves are feeling in their personal life? Stepfamily experience does appear to be an important facilitator characteristic, but the type of experience, and most likely the quality of that experience, may have ramifications that still need to be explored.

Although the relatively minor explanatory power of group membership characteristics is congruent with the clinical literature, the fact that certain experience similarities were *not* significant is contrary to popular RME assumptions and merits attention. Treatment similarity is one of the more consistent predictors of therapeutic process and outcome (White, 2000), and the corollary for stepfamily RME is experience in a stepfamily (Adler-Baeder & Higginbotham, 2004). Higginbotham and Myler (2010) measured four related experiences; namely, being remarried, currently living in a stepfamily, growing up in a stepfamily, or taking a class on remarriage/stepfamilies. Only currently living in a stepfamily was consistently and positively related to the dependent variables.

It may be that shared treatment experiences become more important as the perceived stigma associated with the "condition" increases. Although there is certainly evidence of a societal stepfamily stigma (Ganong & Coleman, 2004), stepfamily membership may evoke less shame than does alcoholism or disordered eating, for example. Another explanation is that there are fundamental differences between RME and therapy that limit the applicability and generalizability of the two literatures toward the other. The stage at which the professional involvement occurs, for example, is a major difference between RME and therapy. Specifically, RME is very often conceptualized as a preventative measure, whereas therapy is more often viewed as an active intervention (Priester, Azen, Speight, & Vera, 2007). Lastly, the RME classroom is a very different environment than the therapist's office. Both the public context and educational nature of RME likely decrease the opportunity and perceived need for participant–facilitator bonding around personal experiences or characteristics.

Although more could be said about which membership group variables and experience similarities were or were not statistically significant, the more practically significant finding from the study was the relative contribution of *facilitation characteristics* in predicting participant ratings. When facilitation characteristics were added, the predictive ability of the models more than tripled. Both female and male participants responded more favorably when they perceived facilitators drawing upon personal experiences in helpful ways. Women also appeared to place particular importance on clear explanations, whereas men appreciated facilitators who managed the time well. Although only marginally significant, men's ratings of the facilitators also appeared to improve if facilitators effectively elicited group participation.

These findings suggest a reexamination of the emphasis some RME scholars have placed on specific demographic characteristics and life experiences of facilitators. Although ethnicity, gender, and even stepfamily experience did surface as statistically significant predictors, their relatively small predictive contribution to the overall ratings indicates that programmers would be prudent to spend more time worrying about the quality of facilitation than the physical traits and personal history of the facilitators. Without effective facilitation skills, programs will likely be a hollow presentation of information, regardless of the demographic characteristics of the facilitators.

The implications of this finding should be welcome news to counselors, family life educators, and organizations that provide RME. Recommendations in the RME literature often fail to acknowledge that most counseling and family service agencies are bound by federal and state hiring policies that forbid discrimination on the basis of race, gender, age, and marital status. In light of this reality, it is fortunate that participants can, and do, positively rate stepfamily RME even when the facilitators differ from them on demographic and life experiences. This is not to say that facilitator characteristics should be completely disregarded or discredited, as some variables were significant predictors of participant ratings. Agency directors may, however, do well to focus more on cultivating quality facilitation than matching participants with certain facilitators. When assigning or hiring new staff to teach RME, or when managing volunteers, agencies should apply the advice taught in many RME programs: Focus on those things that you can change and enhance.

There is nothing an agency director can legally do about a staff member's age, ethnicity, or family history. On the other hand, there are a variety of mechanisms to teach and improve facilitation skills. Stepfamily RME does appear to be enhanced by the quality of the facilitation, which implicates the need for multifaceted RME facilitator training (Hawkins et al., 2004). RME facilitator training should encompass more than just assuring familiarity with the curriculum. People skills, facilitation skills, and basic elements of humanism, classroom management, and so on are worthwhile training areas (cf. Halford et al., 2004).

Other Program Issues

Recruitment and Retention. Through qualitative interviews of both program participants and facilitators, scholars have identified several effective strategies for recruitment and retention of stepfamilies (Skogrand, Reck, Higginbotham, Adler-Baeder, & Dansie, 2010). These strategies include utilizing of community and partnering agencies, such as schools, counseling centers, and family service agencies, as important referral sources. Turning "in-house," or in other words, recruiting participants of other programs offered by the partnering organization can increase enrollment. Providing child care and dinner to minimize the costs and eliminate barriers is also very helpful. Another strategy is to cultivate a trusting facilitator/family relationship (thank-you cards, telephone calls, and friendly reminders), and to actively encourage former participants to invite friends and family to attend the course. Recruiting can also be increased by advertising the common stepfamily challenges and the promise of helpful tips and solutions. These advertisements should be in the language of the target population and in localized areas where the target population gathers for other familial functions. RME providers do not need large recruitment and retention resources in order to be successful at attracting and retaining participants. Incentives can be an additional strategy; the key is to make incentives meaningful to the adults and the children. This can be done by considering the interests and motivations of the targeted group by assisting the couple with their children, adding to their family time, and encouraging their family unity.

Provision of education. This chapter has focused on the provision of structured group RME for stepfamilies; however, it should be noted that this is one of the least frequent ways individuals prepare for remarriage. Although traditional face-to-face, group RME has its advantages, the research suggests individuals are much more likely to prepare by talking with trusted parties (e.g., parents, clergy, etc.) or read written material (Doss, Rhoades, Stanley, & Markman, 2009; Higginbotham, Miller, & Niehuis, 2009). Inasmuch as most individuals in stepfamilies do not sign up for formal RME, the field should be careful about the amount of emphasis and resources that go toward promoting formal classroom educational experiences. Rather, for stepfamily RME to have a broad reach, there should be a multifaceted approach that recognizes the value and positive potential of formal and informal, face-to-face and written, as well as professional and nonprofessional types of preparation. Mentor couples, books, and the web (i.e., chat rooms) are examples of nontraditional supports that hold promise and deserve exploration. Ironically, these informal modes of preparation are the most used but also the least researched (Higginbotham, Miller, & Niehuis, 2009).

The literatures on formal interventions continue to grow disproportionately to the number of people who actually go to a marriage counselor or attend a RME program. Although there is evidence of their efficacy, relatively few couples in stepfamilies, as is the case with first-marriage samples (Doss et al., 2009), pursue a formal route for their preparation. Rather, the most common forms of preparation are those that can occur in private—not public—settings. By one's self, with a partner, or with trusted friends, family, or religious leaders, remarrying couples can prepare at their own pace, receive free advice, and never leave their comfort zones. If this is the modern reality, and as a field the goal is to improve and enhance preparation, then much more attention needs to be directed to learning about—and infusing with research-based material—the counsel clergy give, the advice parents and friends share, and the information printed in the popular media.

Conclusion

Although the social climate regarding remarriage and stepfamilies has changed and more men are participating in preparation activities, there are still many women and men who see preparation as unnecessary. Social scientists have recognized the need for distinct content in remarriage preparation and have cautioned family practitioners that couples entering stepfamilies may not be adequately prepared if they only participate in educational experiences geared toward general couple relationship skills and issues (Adler-Baeder & Higginbotham, 2004; Halford et al., 2003). There is ample research to create and provide useful resources geared specifically to the needs of couples with step-relationships (see Ganong & Coleman, 2004, for a review of extant literature). Now the challenge for scholars and practitioners alike is to find ways to make quality, research-based resources widely accessible and attractive to these couples and the sources they look to for advice.

Key Points

- Stepfamilies face unique challenges compared to couples in first marriages without children.
- Same-sex couples in stepfamilies can encounter many of the same issues heterosexual stepcouples experience, such as parenting nonbiological children, dividing finances, and ongoing interactions with ex-partners.
- As long as participants are experiencing stepfamily-related issues—whether through cohabitation, marriage, or serious dating—participants benefit fairly equitably from stepfamily RME.
- When it comes to implementing RME for couples in stepfamilies, the involvement of children is clearly implicated and should not be underestimated.
- Effective facilitation skills are more important than the specific demographic characteristics of facilitators.
- For stepfamily RME to have broad reach, there should be a multifaceted approach that recognizes the potential of formal and informal, face-to-face and written, as well as professional and nonprofessional types of preparation.

Discussion Questions

1. In what ways might stepfamily RME differ from RME for couples without children?
2. How do facilitator attributes and facilitation characteristics contribute to participant ratings of stepfamily RME?
3. What are potential challenges and strategies to recruiting and retaining stepfamilies?

Additional Resources

National Stepfamily Resource Center: http://www.stepfamilies.info/
Utah State University Stepfamily Education Initiative: http://www.stepfamily.usu.edu

References and Further Readings

Portions of this chapter were reprinted with permission from articles marked with★.
Adamsons, K., O'Brien, M., & Pasley, K. (2007). An ecological approach to father involvement in biological and stepfather families. *Fathering, 5*, 129–147.

Adler-Baeder, F. (2007). *Smart steps: Embrace the journey*. Auburn, AL: National Stepfamily Resource Center.

Adler-Baeder, F., & Higginbotham, B. (2004). Implications of remarriage and stepfamily formation for marriage education. *Family Relations, 53*, 448–458.

Atkinson, D., & Schein, S. (1986). Similarity in counseling. *The Counseling Psychologist, 14*, 319–354.

Bosch, G., Gebeke, D., & Meske, C. (1992). *Stepping together*. Fargo: North Dakota State University Extension Service.

Currier, C. (1982). *Learning to step together: A course for stepfamily adults*. Palo Alto, CA: Stepfamily Association of America.

Daniel, B., & Taylor, J. (1999). The rhetoric versus the reality: A critical perspective on practice with fathers in child care and protection work. *Child and Family Social Work, 4*, 209–220.

Doss, B., Rhoades, G., Stanley, S., & Markman, H. (2009). Marital therapy, retreats, and books: The who, what, when, and why of relationship help-seeking. *Journal of Marital and Family Therapy, 35*, 18–29.

Ganong, L., & Coleman, M. (2004). *Stepfamily relationships: Development, dynamics, and interventions*. New York, NY: Springer.

Halford, K., Moore, E., Wilson, K.L., Farrugia, C., & Dyer, C. (2004). Benefits of flexible delivery relationship education: An evaluation of the couple CARE program. *Family Relations, 53*, 469–476.

Halford, W., Markman, H., Kline, G., & Stanley, S. (2003). Best practice in couple relationship education. *Journal of Marital and Family Therapy, 29*, 385–406.

Hawkins, A., Carroll, J., Doherty, W., & Willoughby, B. (2004). A comprehensive framework for marriage education. *Family Relations, 53*, 547–558.

Hetherington, E., & Kelly, J. (2003). *For better or for worse: Divorce reconsidered*. New York, NY: W.W. Norton & Company.

*Higginbotham, B., Davis, P., Smith, L., Dansie, L., Skogrand, L., & Reck, K. (2012). Stepfathers and stepfamily education. *Journal of Divorce and Remarriage, 53*, 76–90.

*Higginbotham, B., Miller, J., & Niehuis, S. (2009). Remarriage preparation: Usage, perceived helpfulness, and dyadic adjustment. *Family Relations, 58*, 316–329.

*Higginbotham, B., & Myler, C. (2010). The influence of facilitator and facilitation characteristics on participants' ratings of stepfamily education. *Family Relations, 59*, 74–86.

*Higginbotham, B., & Skogrand, L. (2010). Relationship education with both married and unmarried stepcouples: An exploratory study. *Journal of Couple and Relationship Therapy, 9*, 133–148.

*Higginbotham, B., Skogrand, L., & Torres, E. (2010). Stepfamily education: Perceived benefits for children. *Journal of Divorce and Remarriage, 51*, 36–49.

Johnson, A., Wright, K., Craig, E., Gilchrist, E., Lane, L., & Haigh, M. (2008). A model for predicting stress levels and marital satisfaction for stepmothers utilizing a stress and coping approach. *Journal of Social and Personal Relationships, 25*, 119–142.

Lawton, J., & Sanders, M. (1994). Designing effective behavioral family interventions for stepfamilies. *Clinical Psychology Review, 14*, 463–496.

Lengua, L., Roosa, M., Schupak-Neuberg, E., Michaels, M., Berg, C., & Weschler, L. (1992). Using focus groups to guide the development of a parenting program for difficult-to-reach, high-risk families. *Family Relations, 41*, 163–168.

Leon, K., & Angst, E. (2005). Portrayals of stepfamilies in film: Using media images in remarriage education. *Family Relations, 54*, 3–23.

Levant, R., & Nelson, W. (1984). *Skills training for stepparents. A personal developmental approach* [Leader's guide]. Unpublished manuscript. Boston University.

Lucier-Greer, M., & Adler-Baeder, F. (2012). Does couple and relationship education work for individuals in stepfamilies? A meta-analytic study. *Family Relations, 61,* 756–769.

Lucier-Greer, M., Adler-Baeder, F., Ketring, S.A., Harcourt, K.T., & Smith, T. (2012). Comparing the experiences of couples in first marriages and remarriages in couple and relationship education. *Journal of Divorce and Remarriage, 53,* 55–75.

Marsiglio, W., & Hinojosa, R. (2007). Managing the multifather family: Stepfathers as father allies. *Journal of Marriage and Family, 69,* 845–862.

Nadler, J.H. (1983). Effecting change in stepfamilies: A psychodynamic/behavioral group approach. *American Journal of Psychotherapy, 37,* 100–112.

Nelson, W.P., & Levant, R.F. (1991). An evaluation of a skills training program for parents in stepfamilies. *Family Relations, 40,* 291–296.

Nichols, M.P., & Schwartz, R.C. (2001). *The essentials of family therapy.* Boston, MA: Allyn and Bacon.

Nicholson, J.M., Phillips, M., Whitton, S.W., Halford, W.K., & Sanders, M.R. (2007). Promoting healthy stepfamilies: Couples' reasons for seeking help and perceived benefits from intervention. *Family Matters, 77,* 48–56.

Ooms, T., & Wilson, P. (2004). The challenges of offering relationship and marriage education to low-income populations. *Family Relations, 53,* 440–447.

Parent, C., Saint-Jacques, M., Beaudry, M., & Robitaille, C. (2007). Stepfather involvement in social interventions made by youth protection services in stepfamilies. *Child and Family Social Work, 12,* 229–238.

Priester, P.E., Azen, R., Speight, S., & Vera, E.M. (2007). The impact of counselor recovery status similarity on perceptions of attractiveness with members of Alcoholics Anonymous: An exception to the repulsion hypothesis. *Rehabilitation Counseling Bulletin, 51,* 14–20.

Pryor, J. (2008). *The international handbook of stepfamilies: Policy and practice in legal, research, and clinical environments.* Hoboken, NJ: John Wiley & Sons

Reck, K., Higginbotham, B., Skogrand, L., & Davis, P. (2012). Facilitating stepfamily education for Latinos. *Marriage and Family Review, 48,* 170–187.

Robertson, A., Adler-Baeder, F., Collins, A., DeMarco, D., Fein, D., & Schramm, D. (2006). *Meeting the needs of married, low-income stepfamily couples in marriage education services.* Final Report Prepared for Office of Planning, Research and Evaluation, Administration for Children and Families. Washington, DC: Abt Associates Inc.

Schoen, R., & Canudas-Romo, V. (2006). Timing effects on divorce: 20th century experience in the United States. *Journal of Marriage and Family, 68,* 749–758.

Skogrand, L., Barrios-Bell, A., & Higginbotham, B. (2009). Stepfamily education for Latino families: Implications for practice. *Journal of Couple and Relationship Therapy, 8,* 113–128.

Skogrand, L., Mendez, E., & Higginbotham, B. (2013). Stepfamily education: A case study of two lesbian couples. *Marriage and Family Review, 49,* 504–519.

Skogrand, L., Mendez, E., & Higginbotham, B. (2014). Latina women's experiences in a stepfamily education course. *The Family Journal, 22,* 49–55.

Skogrand, L., Reck, K.H., Higginbotham, B., Adler-Baeder, F., & Dansie, L. (2010). Recruitment and retention for stepfamily education. *Journal of Couple and Relationship Therapy, 9,* 48–65.

Skogrand, L., Torres, E., & Higginbotham, B.J. (2010). Stepfamily education: Benefits of a group-formatted intervention. *Family Journal, 18,* 234–240.

Smock, P.J. (2000). Cohabitation in the United States: An appraisal of research themes, findings, and implications. *Annual Review of Sociology*, 1–20.

Sweeney, M.M. (2010). Remarriage and stepfamilies: Strategic sites for family scholarship in the 21st century. *Journal of Marriage and Family, 72*, 667–684.

Teachman, J., & Tedrow, L. (2008). The demography of stepfamilies in the United States. In J. Pryor (Ed.), *International handbook of stepfamilies: Policy and practice in legal, research and clinical spheres* (pp. 3–29). Hoboken, NJ: Wiley.

Visher, E., & Visher, J. (1996). *Therapy with stepfamilies*. New York, NY: Routledge. ISBN 9780876307991

Webber, R.P., Sharpley, C.F., & Rowley, G.L. (1988). Living in a stepfamily. *Australian Journal of Sex, Marriage, and Family, 9*, 21–29.

White, W.L. (2000). The history of recovered people as wounded healers: II. The era of professionalization and specialization. *Alcoholism Treatment Quarterly, 18*(2), 1–25.

Whitton, S., Nicholson, J., & Markman, H. (2008). Research on interventions for stepfamily couples: The state of the field. In J. Pryor (Ed.), *The international handbook of stepfamilies: Policy and practice in legal, research and clinical spheres* (pp. 455–484). Hoboken, NJ: Wiley & Sons, Inc.

Wineberg, H., & McCarthy, J. (1998). Living arrangements after divorce: Cohabitation versus remarriage. *Journal of Divorce and Remarriage, 29*, 131–146.

Xu, X., Hudspeth, C.D., & Bartkowski, J.P. (2006). The role of cohabitation in remarriage. *Journal of Marriage and Family, 68*, 261–274.

PART VI

Future Directions and Conclusion

20

USE OF WEB-BASED RELATIONSHIP AND MARRIAGE EDUCATION

Emily J. Georgia, Larisa N. Cicila, and Brian D. Doss

LEARNING GOALS

- Learn how web-based treatments can increase the reach of evidence-based treatments to typically underserved populations.
- Identify the four different types of existing web-based RME programs, including how they are similar and different.
- Become familiar with the extent and quality of empirical evidence supporting certain web-based RME programs.
- List the relative advantages and disadvantages of the four types of existing web-based RME programs.
- Identify which types of web-based RME programs are likely to be most appropriate for certain types of couples.
- Know which web-based RME programs are currently available and how people can gain access to them.

Introduction

Romantic relationship distress and divorce has numerous far-reaching negative consequences on mental health (Whisman, 2007), physical well-being (Robles, Slatcher, Trombello, & McGinn, 2014), and child functioning (Ablow, Measelle, Cowan, & Cowan, 2009). Fortunately, efforts to improve relationship satisfaction are largely quite successful (e.g., Shadish & Baldwin, 2005). However, many couples fail to seek these **empirically supported** traditional forms of relationship improvement. Only 31% of couples participate in premarital relationship education (Stanley, Amato, Johnson, & Markman, 2006). Furthermore, fewer than 19% of intact couples have sought couple therapy and only 37% of divorced couples sought professional assistance prior to separating (Johnson, Stanley, Glenn, Amato, Nock, Markman, & Dion, 2002).

Further, the couples who *are* reached by traditional in-person forms of RME tend to be a homogenous population of well-educated, middle-class, Caucasian partners (e.g., Stanley, Amato, Johnson, & Markman, 2006; Sullivan & Bradbury, 1997)—who also tend to be at lower risk of relationship distress and divorce (Bramlett & Mosher, 2002; Broman, 2005; Copen, Daniels, Vespa, & Mosher, 2012). Unfortunately, this means that RME is not reaching the couples who have the potential to most benefit from it. Additionally, the lack of educational, income, and racial diversity within research trials of RME programs limits the understanding of whether these programs are efficacious for a wide range of couples.

Two important recent efforts, supported by the Administration for Children and Families, have sought to improve the availability of RME for a diverse population of underserved couples—*Building Strong Families* (BSF; Wood, Moore, Clarkwest, Killewald, & Monahan, 2012) and *Supporting Healthy Marriage* (SHM; Lundquist, Hsueh, Lowenstein, Faucetta, Gubits, Michalopoulos, & Knox, 2014). Both BSF and SHM were successful in reaching an ethnically/racially diverse sample of couples, many of whom were low-income (Wood et al., 2012) or below the federal poverty line (Lundquist et al., 2014). Despite their enhanced ability to reach underserved populations, these programs were generally unsuccessful in improving couples' relationships. The BSF program struggled to retain couples; only 55% of couples attended a single group session and only 17% received the recommended dosage of at least 80% of sessions. Additionally, the program was not able to demonstrate improvements in relationship quality or stability even amongst the 29% of couples who did attend more than half of the sessions (Wood et al., 2012). The SHM program was more successful in retaining couples; 60% of couples accessed provided services. Further this program was able to demonstrate positive improvement in relationship functioning, but the size of the effects was quite small (Lundquist et al., 2014). Finally, these programs were quite costly to deliver; estimates suggest that BSF and SHM cost approximately $9,000–$11,000 per couple (Lundquist et al., 2014; Wood et al., 2012).

Web-based RME

Within the broader field of psychoeducational interventions, **web-based interventions** have shown great promise in improving individual functioning. A recent meta-analysis of web-based interventions targeting depressive symptoms found that those based in cognitive-behavioral theory are efficacious (Andersson & Cuijpers, 2009). Factors found to improve treatment efficacy were contact and support from program staff and tailoring content to the individual's specific needs (Johansson & Andersson, 2012). Web-based interventions targeting anxiety have also demonstrated positive results. A meta-analysis of anxiety-focused online programs showed that they were highly effective in reducing symptoms across multiple anxiety disorders (Andrews, Cuijpers, Craske, McEvoy, & Titov, 2010).

Consequently, the efficacy of web-based interventions for a wide range of individual problems suggests that relationship-focused Internet programs might have a similar notable impact.

Fortunately, RME scholars have started to utilize the Internet as a new method to **disseminate** empirically supported treatments to increase the **reach** of RME to more, and more diverse, couples. The Internet provides a useful platform to deliver RME content due to its reach; over 70% of U.S. households report having broadband / cable Internet access (File, 2013). Web-based RME may also serve to reach those who have, up to this point, been underrepresented in many couple interventions. Among racial and ethnic minority groups, recent studies demonstrate that as many of 93–98% of African-Americans (Smith, 2014) and 80–89% of Hispanics (Lopez, Gonzalez-Barrera, & Patten, 2013) have access to broadband Internet access via a smartphone or home computer. Low-income households also have access to the web; 67% of families with a household income less than $30,000 and 79% of those with $30–49,000 report access to the Internet (Zickuhr & Smith, 2013). Adding to their potential reach, web-based RME programs are seen as an important way to improve relationship functioning. In a survey of individuals in romantic relationships, Internet relationship-focused resources were the most popular intervention strategy chosen; traditional in-person couple therapy was the second most popular chosen strategy (Georgia & Doss, 2013). Therefore, web-based RME programs clearly present a viable alternative that may circumvent many barriers to treatment (e.g., financial burden, logistical concerns, transportation; Hoge et al., 2004).

Web-based RME programs are accessible to individuals every day of the week, 24 hours a day. Additionally, they can be completed confidentiality or even anonymously, reducing perceived stigma, which is another commonly reported barrier to treatment (Hoge et al., 2004). Auspiciously, many web-based RME programs have been developed, with several in various stages of empirical testing. Existing programs are reviewed below and distinguished across four categories: Education/Advice, Assessment/Feedback, Enrichment, and Intervention (see Table 20.1). These four categories are presented in approximate order of the time and effort that couples would need to invest in each resource.

Education/Advice. One way to assist couples online in a very brief and accessible manner is by providing couples information that they can use in their daily lives. Armed with this information, couples can improve their relationship in a number of ways. First, for couples who are doing well, information can help them avoid future difficulties. For example, for couples about to have their first child (a period that poses risks to couples—even very happy ones; e.g., Doss, Rhoades, Stanley, & Markman, 2009), web-based RME can provide them tips and strategies to keep their relationship strong. Second, for couples in the early stages of relationship problems, it may be helpful for them to understand some possible origins of those problems, which when combined with some general communication tips, might allow the couple to solve them on their own. Third, simple education/advice can sometimes be extremely helpful for couples with severe problems like

TABLE 20.1 Web-based Relationship and Marriage Education

	Time	Contact	Tailored	Availability
		Education/Advice		
Twoofus.org	Variable	None	No	Free
Thecoupleconnection.net	1–2 hrs. per course	Counselor moderated forum	No	Free
Talkaboutmarriage.com	Variable	None	No	Free
		Assessment/Feedback		
RELATE www.relate-institute. org	35 min.	Optional Facilitator Interpretation	Yes	$40/couple
FOCCUS www.foccusinc.com	Not specified	Mandatory Trained Facilitator	Yes	$15/couple
PREPARE/ENRICH www. prepare-enrich.com	4–8 hrs.	Trained Facilitator	Yes	$35/couple
		Enrichment		
ePREP	1 hr.	None	No	$25
Power of Two poweroftwomarriage.com	Variable	Email with Coach	Yes	$18/month
Relationship Excitement	4 wks.	None	No	Not available
Forever Families www. foreverfamilies.net	12 hrs.	None	No	Free
		Intervention		
Schover et al., 2012	12 wks.	Email, Phone with Therapist	Yes	Not available
OurRelationship.com	5–7 hrs.	Email, Phone with Coach	Yes	Free

intimate partner violence. Although it is unlikely to solve the problem, information can help them clearly label the problem as dysfunctional and find appropriate sources of help.

Existing educational web-based RME programs usually provide information and advice on common topics such as intimacy, communication, and parenting through articles and videos. For example, TwoOfUs.org is a relationship advice website run by the National Health Marriage Resource Center and was funded by the U.S. Department of Health and Human Services. This site provides videos by psychologists and other experts giving advice on many topics as well as links to empirical research articles on relationship constructs. A similar site, TheCouple-Connection.org, based in the United Kingdom, provides quizzes, exercises, and a forum moderated by counselors in additional to articles on relationship topics. Finally, TalkAboutMarriage.com—the most visited educational website having received over 700,000 unique visits from June 2013–June 2014—allows couples to anonymously respond to each other regarding problems and solutions via an unmonitored forum. Despite their widespread use, these websites lack empirical testing and thus have not demonstrated whether they can improve important relationship outcomes.

Assessment/Feedback. If couples are willing to invest additional time and effort into web-based RME, tailored **assessment/feedback** programs can provide assistance for their relationship. In these programs, upon completion of numerous questionnaires across multiple domains of relationship functioning (e.g., conflict resolution, intimacy, commitment), couples receive tailored feedback on the state of their relationship. Feedback may cover strengths in the couple's relationship as well as areas of difficulty. Based on these strengths and difficulties, assessment/feedback RME can provide tailored feedback to a couple's relationship. Web-based assessment/feedback RME has the ability of helping couples throughout a variety of stages. For couples experiencing mild relationship unhappiness, assessment/feedback can help determine whether the degree of difficulty is typical of couples similar to them. Alternatively, couples often are aware of relationship distress, but are unsure of the cause. Assessment/feedback programs can help isolate the source of distress and identify factors that may be contributing to or causing the problem. Finally, once feedback on relationship difficulties and areas of strength is provided, tailored advice, tips, and/or recommendations can help the couple solve the problem. Additionally, if the problem is severe enough that the couple will likely need assistance to remedy it, appropriate, tailored resources can be provided.

One type of web-based assessment/feedback RME is the RELATE questionnaire, discussed in detail in chapter 10. This assessment tool consists of 276 items measuring personality traits, familial background, values, in addition to relationship variables (Busby, Holman, & Taniguchi, 2001). Following completion, a 12-page report is provided which summarizes similarities and differences across the partners' personalities and attitudes, and identifies strengths and weaknesses within the relationship. The report ends with tailored tips and resources for relationship improvement. In a single small **randomized controlled trial (RCT)**, results demonstrated that use of the RELATE questionnaires in combination with a 2-hour session of therapist interpretation was associated with larger improvements in relationship satisfaction and commitment compared to couples within a no-intervention control condition (Larson, Vatter, Galbraith, Holman, & Stahmann, 2007). Couples without a therapist interpretation intervention initially demonstrated no improvements in relationship outcomes; however, they showed fewer declines by 2-month follow-up compared to the no-intervention control group.

The Facilitating Open Couple Communication Understanding and Study, discussed in greater detail in chapter 9 (FOCCUS; Markey, Micheletto, & Becker, 1997), has also been translated into web-based assessment/feedback. A third web-based assessment and feedback program is PREPARE/ENRICH, discussed in chapter 8 (Olson & Olson, 1999). Both FOCCUS and PREPARE/ENRICH administer extensive questionnaires of over 150 items and provide tailored feedback. However, neither program has empirically tested the ability of the online translation to improving relationship outcomes.

Enrichment. Enrichment RME programs seek to prevent problems rather than alleviate relationship distress, typically targeting premarital, newlywed, and couples generally satisfied in their relationship. The content of enrichment RME programs varies from program to program, but typically involves a focus on teaching communication skills, enhancing existing relationship positives, and providing couples a more comprehensive understanding of personality or other differences that could create later friction between them. Compared to assessment/feedback programs, these programs are often more comprehensive and time-intensive because they contain the additional goal of strengthening the relationship, not just detailing the current strengths and problems in the relationship. As such, enrichment programs often include online or printable exercises that couples can do together or on their own to improve different aspects of their relationship. Enrichment programs have the potential to prevent problems and/or relationship distress. Further, by preventing the development of problems, couples may have the ability to begin focusing on not only reducing negatives but also increasing positives (e.g., intimacy). Additionally, although initially designed for satisfied couples, enrichment programs can also be helpful for couples with existing mild to moderate relationship problems; indeed, some studies suggest that higher-risk (e.g., Halford, Sanders, & Behrens, 2001) or couples with more relationship distress (e.g., BSF, Wood et al., 2012; SHM, Lundquist et al., 2014) benefit more from in-person versions of enrichment programs.

One notable web-based enrichment program is ePREP (Braithwaite & Fincham, 2007), a translation of the well-known Prevention and Relationship Education Program (PREP; Markman, Stanley, & Blumberg, 2001) described in chapter 12. The computer program ePREP provides skills to recognize and respond to risk factors such as conflict patterns, communication problems, and commitment issues. RCTs investigating ePREP have demonstrated its ability to improve constructive communication, symptoms of depression and anxiety, and decrease the occurrence of physical and psychological aggression (Braithwaite & Fincham, 2007; 2009; 2011). The effects of ePREP on relationship satisfaction, however, are equivocal—while some investigations have shown significant improvements (Braithwaite & Fincham, 2007; 2011) other have not (Braithwaite & Fincham, 2009). Further, the samples of couples studied in the ePREP trials have largely been undergraduate psychology students, which limits the generalizability of the findings. However, a recent investigation with community couples (Braithwaite & Fincham, 2014) found that ePREP created decreases in physical and psychological aggression that were maintained through 1-year follow-up; however, there were no effects on communication or relationship satisfaction. The web-based version of ePREP is available at https://lovetakeslearning/store/home.php.

Two additional online enrichment programs—**Power of Two** (poweroftwo marriage.com) and **Forever Families** (foreverfamilies.net)—have also been empirically tested. Power of Two is a relationship skills education program targeting communication, emotion regulation, decision making, positivity, and intimacy (Kalinka, Fincham, & Hirsch, 2012). In an empirical test of heterosexual community couples pregnant with their first child, couples were provided access to the Power of Two plus bibliotherapy and were assessed 1 and 2 months following access to the materials. Couples receiving Power of Two reported higher marital satisfaction and improved conflict management compared to couples who did not receive either (Kalinka et al., 2012). The Forever Families program (Duncan, Steed, & Needham, 2009) offers couples scholarly articles on how to enhance positives (e.g., fondness) and reduce negatives (e.g., conflict). In a three-group RCT, couples completing the material online experienced significantly greater gains in self-reported communication and relationship satisfaction compared to a control group of couples. Moreover, the magnitude of these gains were similar to couples who received identical material through an in-person workshop.

Intervention. Intervention programs target couples who are experiencing moderate or severe distress in their romantic relationships. Due to the distressed nature of the couples targeted, intervention programs may require more time to complete. To date, there is only one published RCT of an online intervention program for couples. Schover and colleagues (2012) compared the effects of a 12-week online sex counseling program to in-person sex counseling for couples in which the male partner was receiving treatment for prostate cancer. The programs both intervened with couples by seeking to enhance sexual communication, increase comfort with sexual activity by reengaging with one another sexually, and reduce performance anxiety. Couples in the web-based program completed homework exercises on topics such as how to increase the expression of affection, how to improve sexual communication, and others. Therapists provided couples feedback on homework exercises via email. Study results demonstrated that the online program was equally efficacious as the in-person treatment in erectile functioning improvement and decreased sexual distress for women. Unfortunately, the program is not currently available on the Internet.

A new program—**OurRelationship.com**—has recently completed a RCT of 300 distressed couples across the United States. The study, funded by the National Institutes of Health, tested the translation of **Integrative Behavioral Couple Therapy (IBCT)** into a web-based format (Doss, Benson, Georgia, & Christensen, 2013). IBCT has demonstrated efficacy with moderately to severely distressed couples in the largest and longest RCT of couple therapy to date (Christensen, Atkins, Berns, Wheeler, Baucom, & Simpson, 2004; Christensen, Atkins, Baucom, & Yi, 2010; Christensen, Atkins, Yi, Baucom, & George, 2006).

The OurRelationship.com program translated the in-person treatment to a web-based platform by providing three phases through which partners primarily work through separately from one another. At the end of each phase, the partners come together to share with each other what each has learned and experienced. The first phase, Observe, provides feedback on relationship functioning (e.g., satisfaction, communication, positives, negatives) based on an initial questionnaire completed by each partner. This feedback is used to help partners decide on a core issue to focus on throughout the program. The couple comes together at the end of the Observe phase to share with one another the core issues they have each chosen. In the Understand phase, partners are guided through the development of a tailored, objective analysis of the chosen core issue and come together to share with each other this new analysis or understanding at the end of the phase. Finally, in the Respond phase, partners consider acceptance and change strategies tailored to the core issue and share with one another their solutions at the end of the phase. The program requires approximately 6 hours of work, and couples are provided a "coach" to assist them in completing the program in 4 weeks. Each couple has four, 15-minute Skype appointments with their coach, once at the start of the program, and one following each of the three phases of the program. In each appointment, coaches address barriers to completing the program, and provide feedback on couples' progress throughout the program.

Although the results of this trial have not yet been published, preliminary results indicate that the program results in medium- to large-effect sizes on relationship functioning compared to pre-intervention functioning as well as a wait-list control group. Additionally, for individuals who began the program with significant symptoms of depression or anxiety, the program also creates significant improvements in those symptoms (Doss, Georgia, Cicila, Benson, & Christensen, 2014).

Conclusion

The next steps for researchers in the arena of web-based RME are to continue translating existing RME programs into web-based formats. Next, it is necessary for empirical tests to be conducted on the efficacy of the web-based programs. Empirical tests will also be required in understanding how these web-based RME programs can be integrated into larger treatment systems. For example, a web-based program could be delivered to couples prior to engaging in traditional in-person couple therapy or treatment providers could deliver the online programs throughout the active treatment process. Whether either types of integration improve the efficacy of treatment remains an empirical question.

In conclusion, web-based RME programs offer a viable method for increasing the dissemination of empirically supported couple treatments to serve a diverse range of couples across multiple levels of need. After upfront costs of website development, web-based RME programs can be maintained at a relatively low cost while serving a much larger proportion of couples than traditional in-person RME. Further, the review of existing web-based RME programs demonstrates that effectiveness is not lost in translating in-person RME to web-based platforms. Indeed, the existing evidence suggests that numerous types of web-based RME can be useful for couples—whether they want to invest just 10 minutes in reading information online or engage in an intensive intervention project. Therefore, when one considers its reach and efficacy, web-based RME has the potential to create meaningful improvements in relationship functioning at the population level.

Key Points

- Web-based treatments have the potential to increase the reach of evidence-based couples interventions to more couples by bypassing traditional obstacles to seeking treatment (e.g. transportation, finances, scheduling, stigma).
- Web-based treatments have been found to be efficacious in reducing relationship difficulties and individual psychopathology.
- Education/Advice web-based programs provide information and advice on common topics (e.g., intimacy, communication, parenting) through articles, videos, and forums, but these resources haven't been empirically tested.
- Assessment/Feedback web-based programs provide couples with information on areas of strength and weaknesses in their relationship based on their answers on comprehensive questionnaires.
- Enrichment RME web-based programs tend to be more time-intensive and focus on teaching communication skills, more effective problem-solving strategies, and enhancing existing relationship positives. Several of these programs have empirical support.
- Intervention web-based programs are more time-intensive programs that target the most distressed couples. One program, OurRelationship.com, is currently being tested as part of a large randomized control trial.
- Future directions include translating more in-person treatments to web-based programs, empirically testing those web-based programs, and integrating web-based programs into in-person interventions.

Discussion Questions

1. What challenges could arise in the delivery and maintenance of web-based RME?
2. What negative outcomes might come from participating in web-based RME?

References and Further Readings

Ablow, J., Measelle, J., Cowan, P., & Cowan, C. (2009). Linking marital conflict and children's adjustment: The role of young children's perceptions. *Journal of Family Psychology, 23*, 485–499.

Andersson, G., & Cuijpers, P. (2009). Internet-based and other computerized psychological treatments for adult depression: A meta-analysis. *Cognitive Behaviour Therapy, 38*, 196–205.

Andrews, G., Cuijpers, P., Craske, M., McEvoy, P., & Titov, N. (2010). Computer therapy for the anxiety and depressive disorders is effective, acceptable and practical health care: A meta-analysis. *Plos ONE, 5*(10). e13196. doi:10.1371/journal.pone.0013196

Braithwaite, S., & Fincham, F. (2007). ePREP: Computer based prevention of relationship dysfunction, depression and anxiety. *Journal of Social and Clinical Psychology, 26,* 609–622. doi:10.1521/jscp.2007.26.5.609

Braithwaite, S., & Fincham, F. (2009). A randomized clinical trial of a computer based preventive intervention: Replication and extension of ePREP. *Journal of Family Psychology, 23,* 32–38. doi:10.1037/a0014061

Braithwaite, S., & Fincham, F. (2011). Computer-based dissemination: A randomized clinical trial of ePREP using the actor partner interdependence model. *Behaviour Research and Therapy, 49,* 126–131. doi:10.1016/j.brat.2010.11.002

Braithwaite, S., & Fincham, F. (2014). Computer-based prevention of intimate partner violence in marriage. *Behaviour Research and Therapy, 54,* 12–21. doi:10.1016/j.brat.2013.12.006

Bramlett, M., & Mosher, W. (2002). Cohabitation, marriage, divorce, and remarriage in the United States. National Center for Health Statistics. *Vital and Health Statistics, 23*(22). Hyattsville, MD: Department of Health and Human Services.

Broman, C. (2005). Marital quality in black and white marriages. *Journal of Family Issues, 26,* 431–441.

Busby, D., Holman, T., & Taniguchi, N. (2001). RELATE: Relationship evaluation of the individual, family, cultural, and couple contexts. *Family Relations, 50,* 308–316.

Christensen, A., Atkins, D., Baucom, B., & Yi, J. (2010). Marital status and satisfaction five years following a randomized clinical trial comparing traditional versus integrative behavioral couple therapy. *Journal of Consulting and Clinical Psychology, 78,* 225–235. doi:10.1037/a0018132

Christensen, A., Atkins, D., Berns, S., Wheeler, J., Baucom, D., & Simpson, L. (2004). Traditional versus integrative behavioral couple therapy for significantly and chronically distressed married couples. *Journal of Consulting and Clinical Psychology, 72,* 176–191. doi:10.1037/0022–006X.72.2.176

Christensen, A., Atkins, D., Yi, J., Baucom, D., & George, W. (2006). Couple and individual adjustment for 2 years following a randomized clinical trial comparing traditional versus integrative behavioral couple therapy. *Journal of Consulting and Clinical Psychology, 74,* 1180–1191. doi:10.1037/0022–006X.74.6.1180

Copen, C., Daniels, K., Vespa, J., & Mosher, W. (2012). First marriages in the United States: Data from the 2006–2010 National Survey of Family Growth. *National Health Statistics Reports, 49,* 1–21.

Cuijpers, P., Donker, T., van Straten, A., Li, J., & Andersson, G. (2010). Is guided self-help as effective as face-to-face psychotherapy for depression and anxiety disorders? A systematic review and meta-analysis of comparative outcome studies. *Psychological Medicine, 40,* 1943–1957. doi:10.1017/S0033291710000772

Doss, B., Benson, L., Georgia, E., & Christensen, A. (2013). Translation of integrative behavioral couple therapy to a web-based intervention. *Family Process, 52,* 139–153.

Doss, B., Georgia, E., Cicila, L., Benson, L., & Christensen, A. (2014, November). *Effects of OurRelationship.com, a brief web-based intervention, on relationship functioning.* Paper presented at the Association for Behavioral and Cognitive Therapies, Philadelphia, PA.

Doss, B., Rhoades, G., Stanley, S., & Markman, H. (2009). The effect of the transition to parenthood on relationship quality: An eight-year prospective study. *Journal of Personality and Social Psychology, 96,* 601–619.

Duncan, S., Steed, A., & Needham, C. (2009). A comparison evaluation study of web-based and traditional marriage and relationship education. *Journal of Couple and Relationship Therapy, 8*, 162–180. doi:10.1080/15332690902813836

File, T. (2013). *Computer and internet use in the United States.* Current Population Survey Reports, P20–568. Washington, DC: U.S. Census Bureau.

Georgia, E., & Doss, B. (2013). Web-based couple interventions: Do they have a future? *Journal of Couple and Relationship Therapy, 12*, 168–185.

Halford, W., Sanders, M., & Behrens, B. (2001). Can skills training prevent relationship problems in at-risk couples? Four-year effects of a behavioral relationship education program. *Journal of Family Psychology, 15*, 750–768.

Hoge, C., Castro, C., Messer, S., McGurk, D., Cotting, D., & Koffman, R. (2004). Combat duty in Iraq and Afghanistan, mental health problems, and barriers to care. *New England Journal of Medicine, 351*, 13–22.

Johansson, R., & Andersson, G. (2012). Internet-based psychological treatments for depression. *Expert Review of Neurotherapeutics, 12*, 861–870.

Johnson, C., Stanley, S., Glenn, N., Amato, P., Nock, S., Markman, H., & Dion, M. (2002). *Marriage in Oklahoma: 2001 baseline statewide survey on marriage and divorce* (S02096 OKDHS). Oklahoma City, OK: Oklahoma Department of Human Services.

Kalinka, C., Fincham, F., & Hirsch, A. (2012). A randomized clinical trial of online-biblio relationship education for expectant couples. *Journal of Family Psychology, 26*, 159–164. doi:10.1037/a0026398

Larson, J., Vatter, R., Galbraith, R., Holman, T., & Stahmann, R. (2007). The RELA-Tionship Evaluation (RELATE) with therapist-assisted interpretation: Short-term effects on premarital relationships. *Journal of Marital and Family Therapy, 33*, 364–374. doi:10.1111/j.1752-0606.2007.00036.x

Lopez, M.H., Gonzalez-Barrera, A., & Patten, E. (Eds.). (2013). *Closing the digital divide: Latinos and technology adoption.* Washington, DC: Pew Research Center.

Lundquist, E., Hsueh, J., Lowenstein, A., Faucetta, K., Gubits, D., Michalopoulos, C., & Knox, V. (2014). *A family-strengthening program for low-income families: Final impacts from the Supporting Healthy Marriage Evaluation.* OPRE Report 2014–09A. Washington, DC: Office of Planning, Research and Evaluation, Administration for Children and Families, U.S. Department of Health and Human Services.

Markey, B., Micheletto, M., & Becker, A. (1997). Facilitating open couple communication, understanding, and study (FOCCUS). Omaha, NE: Family Life Office, Archdiocese of Omaha.

Markman, H., Stanley, S., & Blumberg, S. (2001). *Fighting for Your Marriage* (Revised and updated edition). San Francisco, CA: Jossey-Bass.

Olson, D., & Olson, A. (1999). PREPARE/ENRICH program: Version 2000. In M.T. Hannah (Ed.), *Preventive approaches in couples therapy* (pp. 196–216). Philadelphia, PA: Brunner/Mazel.

Robles, T., Slatcher, R., Trombello, J., & McGinn, M. (2014). Marital quality and health: A meta-analytic review. *Psychological Bulletin, 140*, 140–187.

Schover, L., Canada, A., Yuan, Y., Sui, D., Neese, L., Jenkins, R., & Rhodes, M. (2012). A randomized trial of Internet-based versus traditional sexual counseling for couples after localized prostate cancer treatment. *Cancer, 118*, 500–509. doi:10.1002/cncr.26308

Shadish, W., & Baldwin, S. (2005). Effects of behavioral marital therapy: A meta-analysis of randomized controlled trials. *Journal of Consulting and Clinical Psychology, 73*, 6–14.

Smith, A. (2014). *African Americans and technology use: A demographic portrait.* Washington, DC: Pew Research Center.

Stanley, S., Amato, P., Johnson, C., & Markman, H. (2006). Premarital education, marital quality, and marital stability: Findings from a large, random, household survey. *Journal of Family Psychology, 20*, 117–126.

Sullivan, K., & Bradbury, T. (1997). Are premarital prevention programs reaching couples at risk for marital dysfunction? *Journal of Consulting and Clinical Psychology, 65*, 24–30.

Whisman, M. (2007). Marital distress and *DSM-IV* psychiatric disorders in a population-based national survey. *Journal of Abnormal Psychology, 116*, 638–643.

Wood, R., Moore, Q., Clarkwest, A., Killewald, A., & Monahan, S. (2012). *The long-term effects of Building Strong Families: A relationship skills education program for unmarried parents, Executive Summary.* OPRE Report #2012–28B. Washington, DC: Office of Planning, Research and Evaluation, Administration for Children and Families, U.S. Department of Health and Human Services.

Zickuhr, K., & Smith, A. (2013). *Home Broadband 2013.* Washington, DC: Pew Research Center, Internet & American Life Project. Retrieved from http://www.pewinternet.org/2013/08/26/home-broadband-2013/

21

EVIDENCE-BASED RELATIONSHIP AND MARRIAGE EDUCATION AND BEYOND

James J. Ponzetti, Jr.

LEARNING GOALS

- Understand the fundamentals of relationship and marriage education (e.g., best practices, theory).
- Be able to utilize a logic model in program development.
- Describe conceptual and theoretical frameworks for RME.
- Differentiate inventory-based from skills-based programs.
- Comprehend the utility of RME with various distinct groups and the unique needs of each.

Introduction

The future of RME efforts rest with the expansion of **evidence-based practices**. The authors of the chapters in this book have offered astute insight into the conceptual and methodological issues raised in assessing and implementing such practices. In addition, descriptions of many of the best evidence-based RME programs available are also presented. The most significant challenge for the future is to expand approaches that are both more efficient and accessible.

In the first part of this book, the fundamentals of RME are reviewed. Duncan, in chapter 2, described best practices in RME which coincide with quality programming. Seven best practices were presented: (1) programs must be founded on theory and research; (2) programs are evidence-based; (3) fit program development and implementation to the audience; (4) encompass a broad range of couples; (5) recommend programs at change points; (6) encourage early presentation of relationship problems, and (7) expand accessibility.

Futris and colleagues in chapter 3 employed a logic model framework to outline the process involved in RME program development and implementation. This process requires ascertaining program relevance, recognizing critical resources to implement and sustain the program as well as activities and target audience, and identifying intended program impact. The community and potential participants are considered vital resources to design and implementation. In addition, educators must clarify the assumptions driving the program and the factors that could impact desired outcomes.

In chapter 4, Hawkins summarized evaluation research on diverse RME programs, including relationship literacy education, relationship development education, marriage preparation education, and marriage maintenance education programs; the research is encouraging.

Part II considers conceptual and theoretical frameworks for RME. Wiley and Bowers describe the connection between the multiple dimensions of health (including physical, mental, social, and spiritual) and relationship well-being in chapter 5. They draw on relevant theory and research to propose a model of health for relationship and marriage education.

The application of Gottman's extensive research on patterns and dynamic processes in couple interactions to RME is evident in the Sound Relationship House (SRH) model. In chapter 6, Robert Navarra, John Gottman, and Julie Schwartz Gottman explain how the SRH model can be used to help couples achieve the relationships they seek. The SRH model provides seven building blocks or levels from which couples can learn to develop or strengthen their relationship. These levels of the Sound Relationship House are (1) build love maps, (2) share fondness and admiration, (3) turn toward instead of away, (4) keep the positive perspective, (5) manage conflict, (6) make life dreams come true, and (7) create shared meaning. Trust and commitment were added to the SRH model, supporting the seven levels, or building blocks, needed for an optimal relationship.

In chapter 7, Goddard and Schramm addressed the importance of creating a model for RME program development through efforts and lessons of the U.S. Cooperative Extension Service. They noted that it is not easy to reduce a body of research to a simple, practical model. However, a comprehensive model is essential to related curricular efforts. The NERMEM model is presented in terms of seven components: care for self, choose, connect, know, care, manage, and share.

The evidence-based practices in inventory-based programs are discussed in Part III. The three most widely used relationship inventories are described in detail. Olson and Olson in chapter 8 describe PREPARE/ENRICH and the program based on the couple feedback from these inventories. The program has two components—the couple assessment and couple exercises designed to teach relationship skills (i.e., communication, conflict resolution, stress management).

In chapter 9, Williams describes FOCCUS. FOCCUS provides couples with feedback on their relationship in a number of areas that are important to building a successful marriage. With the help of a facilitator, FOCCUS encourages couples to explore and discuss their relationship in each of these areas. Finally, Loyer-Carlson describes RELATE in chapter 10. RELATE is developed specifically to be a sound and flexible instrument. It has the ability to serve the assessment needs of lay couples in relationships, professionals working in behavioral health and family life education, and all types of researchers, from those evaluating programs to those involved in statistically complex relationship modeling. All three inventories are available online as well as in a traditional structured format with trained facilitators.

Part IV considers evidence-based practices in skills-based programs. RME programs that merit particular attention are presented in subsequent chapters because of their prevalence and evidence base. In chapter 11, Scuka directs the ongoing training and research efforts for the Relationship Enhancement Program designed by Bernard Guerney. This program stands as one of the earliest psychoeducational approaches to helping couples have better relationships. The Relationship Enhancement Program is supported by an extensive and compelling empirical research base. The hallmark of RE skills-training is its emphasis on deep empathy in the context of a structured dialogue process designed to enhance emotional connection and foster constructive solutions to disagreements. The Mastering the Mysteries of Love version of the RE Program, as well as four additional adaptations for specific populations, are also available.

The Prevention and Relationship Education Program (PREP) is presented in chapter 12 by Tonelli, Pregulman, and Markman. PREP is a well-researched cognitive-behavioral RME program that offers some of the strongest evidence in support of its efficacy. By equipping participants with principles fundamental to good relationships and with practical communication techniques that allow them to constructively manage conflict in their relationships, PREP provides tools for couples to successfully navigate conflict. An abundance of research suggests the curriculum is highly effective in helping individuals maintain more stable relationships and aiding them in improving their relationship communication and satisfaction.

Job, Thurmaier, Engl, and Hahlweg review a number of RME programs from Germany in chapter 13. They provide an overview of the efficacy and dissemination of *A Couples' Learning Program EPL*, which is the most empirically supported couples training in Europe. Three additional programs targeting specific audiences—the EPL adaptations *KEK* for long-related couples, *KOMKOM* for dissatisfied couples, and *TTT* for adolescents—are introduced.

Bodenmann developed the Couples Coping Enhancement Training (CCET), an evidence-based RME program described in chapter 14. The program includes five units addressing issues such as the impact of extra-dyadic stress on couples' functioning, the enhancement of dyadic coping, communication and problem solving as well as equity in close relationships. CCET is skill-oriented and couples are trained in supervised exercises by providers. A main focus of CCET is the improvement of stress-related self-disclosure and the match of the other's supportive dyadic coping according to the needs of the stressed partner.

The Relationship Attachment Model (RAM), a visual picture of five major constructs that promote feelings of closeness within relationships created by Van Epp and Van Epp Cutlip, is described in chapter 15. Two RME programs were developed based on the RAM. These programs, Premarital Interpersonal Choices and Knowledge (PICK), and Lasting Intimacy through Nurturing, Knowledge and Skills (LINKS), are described and reviewed. The PICK program outlines five key areas to explore about a potential partner that foreshadow what that partner will be like in a committed or marriage relationship. LINKS focuses on the ongoing maintenance of a committed relationship. The guiding principle for successful relationship maintenance in the LINKS program is for couples to regularly assess their relationship with the RAM and to set practical goals to strengthen and balance the deficits in each of the five dynamic bonds represented by the RAM.

Chapter 16 focuses on RME aimed at youth and young adults. Pearson and Reed have had an integral role in the development of programs for this age group. Two comprehensive RME programs, *Relationship Smarts PLUS* (for 13–18 years of age), and *Love Notes: Making Relationships Work*, an adaptation for older teen and young adults (16–24 years), are reviewed. A brief history of the context in which these programs emerged is presented along with a discussion of the gaps and unmet needs of youth they were designed to address. These programs break new ground in prevention and offer a positive and proactive assets-building approach.

Part V presents evidence-based RME with varied groups. Whitton in chapter 17 considers RME for same-sex couples. With increasing societal acceptance and legal recognition of same-sex relationships, greater numbers of same-sex couples are likely to seek relationship education. This chapter presents the case for developing relationship education programs designed specifically for same-sex couples, along with qualitative research conducted to inform the adaptation of existing RME curriculum. The Strengthening Same-Sex Relationship Programs (Male and Female Versions) are described. Erickson and Hawkins in chapter 18 articulate the unique needs of low-income couples. Higginbotham and Goodey highlight extant research and outline potential implications for RME content and implementation in stepfamilies in chapter 19. Despite common experiences within stepfamilies, there is great diversity between stepfamilies that stem from their marital status, children, sexual orientation, culture, and other demographic and familial characteristics. Consequently, the research on the effectiveness of relationship and marriage education for stepfamilies is nuanced.

Finally, in looking toward future expansion of RME, Georgia, Cicila, and Doss discuss the use of web-based programs in chapter 20. Although programs to enhance relationships and ameliorate relationship problems are available to couples, the vast majority of couples do not seek out these programs. To increase the reach of RME, several recent developments in web-based RME offer exciting opportunities. Web-based RME programs circumvent many of the barriers to traditional RME reported by couples and subsequently are likely to increase the proportion of couples accessing them. In this chapter, the purpose, content, and evidence for existing web-based RME programs are described.

Conclusion

RME has experienced significant growth over the past five decades and such expansion is likely to continue. The time has come for RME to join other professions in using an evidence-based approach in the design, implementation, and evaluation of RME practice (Adler-Baeder, Higginbotham, & Lamke, 2004; Cowan, Cowan, & Knox, 2010). Using principles of effectiveness to enhance RME is critical to evidence-based practices (Small, Cooney, & O'Connor, 2009).

RME programs exist for many groups, including individuals (e.g., youth, fathers, mothers), couples (e.g., premarital, married), and families (Hawkins, Carroll, Doherty, & Willoughby, 2004). RME can assist couples to minimize problematic interaction patterns and achieve greater relationship satisfaction (Gottman & Silver, 1999; Stanley, Amato, Johnson, & Markman, 2006; Stanley, Markman, & Jenkins, 2002). These beneficial effects appear to last up to five years after the program (Hawkins, Blanchard, Baldwin, & Fawcett, 2008).

Cowan and Cowan (2014) articulately reviewed the equivocal nature of information on relationship and marriage education presently. Future endeavors must attend to the furtherance of evidence-based programs grounded in rigorous research designs such as random control trials. In addition, research must attend to the benefits of RME for children of couples who avail themselves of these programs. Greater consideration must be given to the preventive nature of RME because effective deterrence of relationship distress and dysfunction involves a thoughtful grasp of how relationships develop and change over time (Bradbury & Lavner, 2012). Yet, the investigation of how RME programs work and for whom has yet to be determined. Further inquiry is necessary to understand whether the changes made while participating in RME programs actually result from the processes and skills taught (Rauer, Adler-Baeder, Lucier-Greer, Skuban, Ketring, & Smith, 2014; Wadsworth & Markman, 2012). These efforts inform and promote insight into robust evidence-based relationship and marriage education activities that further enhance best practices in the field.

Key Points

- Best practices in RME coincide with quality programming.
- A logic model framework offers a useful process in RME program development and implementation.

- Evaluation research on diverse RME programs, including relationship literacy education, relationship development education, marriage preparation education, and marriage maintenance education, is encouraging.
- The connection between the multiple dimensions of health (including physical, mental, social, and spiritual) and RME merits ongoing attention.
- The three most widely used relationship inventories are PREPARE/ENRICH, FOCCUS, and RELATE.
- Skills-based programs such as Relationship Enhancement, PREP, EPL, CCET, PICK, LINKS, Relationship Smarts PLUS, and Love Notes: Making Relationships Work have proven to be effective.
- Varied groups such as same-sex couples, low-income couples, and remarried couples and stepfamilies are seeking RME.
- The use of web-based programs is evident in future expansion of RME.

Discussion Questions

1. Why is evidence-based RME necessary?
2. What frameworks or models are useful to program development?
3. How can program evaluation be increased?
4. How can inventory-based programs be integrated with skills-based programs?
5. Does cultural adaptation of RME compromise program fidelity?

References and Further Readings

Adler-Baeder, F., Higginbotham, B., & Lamke, L. (2004). Putting empirical knowledge to work: Linking research and programming focused on marital quality. *Family Relations, 53,* 537–546.

Bradbury, T., & Lavner, J. (2012). How can we improve preventive and educational interventions for intimate relationships? *Behavior Therapy, 43,* 113–122.

Cowan, P., & Cowan, C. (2014). Controversies in couple relationship education (CRE): Overlooked evidence and implications for research and policy. *Psychology, Public Policy, and Law.* Advance online publication. http://dx.doi.org/10.1037/law0000025

Cowan, P., Cowan, C., & Knox, V. (2010). Marriage and fatherhood programs. *Future of Children, 20*(2), 205–230.

Gottman, J., & Silver, N. (1999). *The seven principles for making marriage work.* New York, NY: Three Rivers Press.

Hawkins, A., Blanchard, V., Baldwin, S., & Fawcett, E. (2008). Does marriage and relationship education work? A meta-analytic study. *Journal of Consulting and Clinical Psychology, 76,* 723–734.

Hawkins, A., Carroll, J., Doherty, W., & Willoughby, B. (2004). A comprehensive framework for marriage education. *Family Relations, 53,* 547–558. doi:10.1111/j.0197–6664.2004.00064.x

Rauer, A., Adler-Baeder, F., Lucier-Greer, M., Skuban, E., Ketring, S., & Smith, T. (2014). Exploring processes of change in couple relationship education: Predictors of change in relationship quality. *Journal of Family Psychology, 28,* 65–76.

Small, S.A., Cooney, S., & O'Connor, C. (2009). Evidence-based program improvement: Using principles of effectiveness to enhance the quality and impact of family-based prevention programs. *Family Relations, 58*, 1–13.

Stanley, S. (2001). Making a case for premarital education. *Family Relations, 50*, 272–280. doi:10.1111/j.1741-3729.2001.00272.x

Stanley, S., Amato, P., Johnson, C., & Markman, H. (2006). Premarital education, marital quality, and marital stability: Findings from a large, random, household survey. *Journal of Family Psychology, 20*, 117–126.

Stanley, S., Markman, H., & Jenkins, N. (2002). *Marriage education and government policy: Helping couples who choose marriage achieve success.* Retrieved from http://www.smart marriages.com/choose.marriage.html

Wadsworth, M., & Markman, H. (2012). Where's the action? Understanding what works and why in relationship education. *Behavior Therapy, 43*, 99–112.

INDEX

Note: Italic page numbers indicate pages with figures and tables.